Never Alone

by Iris Fisher Smith

Remember, as long as we
have each other, we are
'Never Alone'

Iris Fisher
Smith

DORRANCE
PUBLISHING CO
EST. 1920
PITTSBURGH, PENNSYLVANIA 15238

Dorrance Publishing Co
585 Alpha Drive
Pittsburgh, PA 15238
Visit our website at *www.dorrancebookstore.com*

ISBN: 978-1-6461-0635-6
eISBN: 978-1-6461-0103-0

Contents

"9, two are better than one, because they have a good return for their work: 10, if one falls down, his friend can help him up. But pity the man who falls and has no one to help him up! 11, Also, if two lie down together, they will keep warm. But how can one keep warm alone? Ecclesiastes 4:9-11 (NIV)

"The most terrible poverty is loneliness, and the feeling of being unloved."

Mother Teresa

A Note from the Editor

As Editor of Iris's book, I have the privilege of endorsing her work. This is an Inspirational story of overcoming seemingly insurmountable obstacles. You will laugh with her, and you will cry, but you will also find hope in her theme of Faith, Family and friends. - Heidi M. Thomas

About the Editor

Heidi M. Thomas is an award-winning author and freelance manuscript editor in North Central Arizona. She grew up on a working ranch in Eastern Montana, with a grandmother who rode bucking stock in rodeos. She has a number of exciting books she's written. For more information, Heidi can be contacted at her website www.heidimthomas.com

Dedication

This book is affectionately dedicated to several people. To begin, I'd like to thank my husband Cy, for his patience and understanding of the many ups and downs and challenges I faced during this writing process. The hours he spent helping me with cooking, helping me organize this, and taking the load off in so many ways has been such a blessing. I could not have done this without his help and encouragement. To my son and daughter-in law for their love and compassion and encouragement. To the many, many friends who have loved me and been there throughout my life, I wouldn't be who I am without you. And for those not mentioned, you know who you are, I love you dearly. To my brothers, the two of you have always been there to inspire and encourage me, especially with this book, thanks for all your help and for cheering me on. To my Aunt Elaine, who has always been there behind the scenes since my birth. You have cheered me on and comforted me in those hard times I faced. I will always cherish our times together, our long talks, you have been an inspiration and always there, Thanks you so much. And most of all, to my mom and dad, for your untiring love for us, your children. The sacrifices you made and the love you gave, made us who we are. This book is a memoir to my whole life with you and a glimpse of who you were to the next generation, our children and grandchildren, nieces and nephews. I miss you both every day. I know you're praying for us up there.

My mother left us with this philosophy, "You should never put yourself above anyone else, put others first, and when you have a friend, you should be their friend for life. Loyalty is vital in any relationship, Love and you will be loved" You'll always be in my heart, Mom!

Foreword

Gunilla.

How do you do justice to describing a friendship of 25 years? When my dear friend Iris asked me to write an introduction to her book, I wondered how to begin. My mother-in-law's favorite poem came to mind.

What made us friends in the long ago
When we first met?
Well, I think I know.
The best in me and the best in you
Hailed each other because they knew
That always and ever since time began
Our being friends was part of God's plan.

George Webster Douglas

Some friendships have a sense of permanence and inevitability; ours is like that. Iris and I have each been enriched by our friendship. We have learned so much from each other. We share a faith in God, an optimistic spirit, compassion for others, and a similar sense of humor. Faith in God, prayer, and gratitude have carried Iris through lifelong life and health challenges. From her I have learned to persevere when things get tough. She has taught me about celiac disease and other autoimmune diseases and the many health and life challenges which can accompany those conditions. This acquired knowledge has been useful in my counseling work with individuals and families. Between us there is a spirit of playful interaction, which has been enjoyable for both of us. "A merry heart doeth good like a medicine" (KJV Proverbs 17:22). We have discovered that there is humor in even the most challenging situations. We laugh a lot! She is my funniest friend. We enjoy our time together, whether during a special adventure like a Joni and Friends Retreat or at Iris's son Paul's wedding or just during everyday conversation at the dinner table or over the telephone. The interaction just flows. Such a friendship is one of life's precious blessings.

Over the years, I have come to appreciate so many things about Iris. She is a committed Christian, which continues to carry her through many health and life challenges. I became acquainted with the painting titled "Christ by the Sickbed" when it hung on the living room wall in one of Iris's homes. It depicts an ill child in her bed, Christ seated beside her. Mom, Dad, and a nurse stand beside her bed. This portrays Iris's young life when the health issues began, and which continue to this day. No wonder she was attracted to that painting.

Iris has a positive, optimistic spirit. She has a child-like faith and trust that no matter what happens, everything will turn out all right. She definitely has a "glass half full" philosophy of life. A great sense of compassion combined with a sense of fun draws people to Iris. Not only is family very important to her, but she has also extended her concept of family to embrace many friends and acquaintances into her "extended family."

Sharing her faith, her family's history and life lessons is the impetus for Iris writing this book. Walking with God through the many challenges, with her husband Cy as her life partner, Iris envisions herself as a link in a chain of family members who came before her. Around her is a circle of faithful friends enriching her life as she enriches theirs. *Never Alone* is truly a fitting title for Iris' book.

Gunilla Kuniholm

Introduction

My story centers on what made me so spiritually aware, and the importance of being with family and friends with God at the center. It all begins with our weekly Sunday trips to my grandmother's home as a youngster to play and help with cooking Italian food and soaking up the Italian culture as she shared with me.

My grandmothers were my first mentors I could turn to for guidance and wisdom. Through my Italian grandmother, Leah Miller, and my other Russian/Yiddish grandmother Rose, I have learned throughout my life that the way to get through tough times is by sticking together and never being alone. There is strength in numbers.

I learned how to bond and be loyal, so I was not out there trying to figure it all out alone. If you don't have a large family, one can be created with friends. I have been blessed to have had both, but I had to reach out and work at it. It didn't just come to me, and I want to share this with you. We were never intended to do it alone. I love to recall the scripture found in Ecclesiastes, and it is certainly one my family modeled well for us while we were growing up.

It states, "Two are better than one because they have a good return for their work: if one falls, his friend can help him up. But pity the man who falls and has no one to help him up! Also, if two lie down together, they will keep warm. But how can one keep warm alone? Though one may be overpowered, two can defend themselves. A chord of three strands cannot be broken!" Ecclesiastes 4: 9-12 (NIV)

It is a reminder to me that we were never intended to be isolated and self-reliant. As I share my family's story, I look at the importance of my European culture and the special bonding that took place within. There isn't a day that goes by that I don't miss my mother, my father, my grandparents on both sides, and their uniqueness of culture they brought to pass on to us.

While learning to bond and connect so well was a blessing, later losing most of my family, some from old age and some geographically from where I reside now, has caused me to feel culturally out of sync. And orphan-like in different seasons of my life. After the passing of my parents and so many other family members, my son and several aunts convinced me that it was time to move on to the next generation and be near my son. So, my husband and I moved from New

England to Seattle to be near him. While we are very happy to be near him, and I've made so many wonderful friends, moving out of the culture I was raised in has been difficult. It seems no matter how many people I have around me, there is still that sense of loss and an isolation and loneliness only God can fill.

My son and my husband try very hard to fill that void, but still I feel I am in a foreign land. A place where people are so different. A land where people don't always seem to understand the meaning of bonding with family and friends; they seem to relish independence rather than bonding, isolating rather than being together. A place where I see people searching and rejecting God only to find their search for love and affirmation leads them to a place of isolation, not connecting, and addictions like I've never seen in my lifetime. Now, don't get me wrong, not everyone is like that. I have observed though, it is more prevalent than I would like to see.

When I reminisce about my growing up years, I think I didn't choose the road of isolation because my affirmation came from trusting in God and having family to talk to. I was benefitting from the time I had with people, face to face. Pouring out my heart to good friends gave me a new outlook with goals and dreams I hadn't thought of, all because I sat and listened. During my darkest hours, I always had someone there to hold me and tell me it would be all right. While circumstances were hard, my emotional and spiritual needs were still met. But what if things were different, what if I hadn't had those special, loving, caring individuals in my life? Would I be a different person? Would I have been focused on reaching out to others at all? Perhaps! But thanks be to God that I experienced such things, so I would understand other people going through similar struggles, and so I would have compassion for them.

2 Corinthians 1:4 states, "...who comforts us in all our troubles, so that we can comfort those in any trouble with the comfort we ourselves receive from God" (NIV). I fear this is something that is so terribly missing in our culture today. The voids cannot be filled with self-indulgence, drugs, alcohol, or any other addiction.

My story contains several chapters of historical events based on the lives of real people. I am creating this book as a memoir for my large family of many, many cousins, nieces, nephews, etc., and my close friends to encourage them in their places of struggle and to understand where my family came from! I know many of my cousins miss the large family gatherings we grew up with, just as I do. But many of them are back east. I am in the west beginning a new life in my elder years. I now have the privilege of focusing on the next generation coming up: my son, my daughter-in law, my nieces, grandson, and nephews, some starting families of their own. I want to inspire them in the challenges of life and to learn from what I've experienced. It's important for the older ones to teach the younger ones. I have been there, made mistakes, and hope to help them learn from mine, so they will be spared unnecessary valley experiences. Hey, there's enough valley to go through as it is; I want to see them reach the mountain top quicker than I was able to and still have integrity.

To continue, this is about two families that came to America from other places with their own stories. Together, they sought a better life, finding strength in sharing the challenges they faced, the struggles they endured, and the good that came from them. With every hardship, I believe there is goodness around the corner. We experienced joy in my family, despite struggles, because we had each other. It is a story of what I learned from them and can pass on to others! We had each other to listen, hug, and hold during some of the happiest times but also some of the most turbulent as well. We held tightly to one another and still do. I learned so much from them that I not only gained wisdom and strength, but I also learned to use my difficulties to reach out to others. I see this next generation as needing more comfort than ever! The day we are living in is so uncertain I feel it's dangerous to isolate.

My family is made up of such a diverse group of people, so many characters! Their difficulties and setbacks led them to find strength, comfort, and the will to survive through faith, humor, and by clinging to each other. Their fears and anxieties led them to an ability to navigate through those hard places. The example they set made me the strong, determined woman I am today. My story is about me but it's also where I came from. It's why I think the way I do and what has led me to have such deep spiritual roots, leaning on a faith that is truly immovable and unshakable during some very difficult times in my own journey.

This story may not be unique, as our country is made up of immigrants. Our wonderful country has been referred to as a melting pot. Everyone has a story to tell, and every voice deserves to be heard. Many have faced prejudice and opposition coming here from every walk of life. But the lesson I have learned through those role models I will speak of is that if we can stick together, help each other, and love each other, there is nothing that can defeat us when faced with faith and determination. We can successfully move forward. Success happens when we don't give up.

I believe those hard places in our lives, when faced together and with God's help, cannot ultimately destroy us. In fact, if we follow God's lead, they can somehow always work for our good, making us stronger and more determined. The word of God says so! We can accomplish amazing things we never imagined, not even in our wildest dreams. All things are possible with God. During the course of my life, when it became so difficult, it was from my family's example that I found direction and a grounding and security I cannot explain. I learned what looking at the glass half full really meant. The lessons learned from those who went before me have served me well. I would like the opportunity to speak to a generation that does not understand who God is and why I believe he exists. I have experienced the proof in the challenges of life and in his faithfulness! I believe faith doesn't come from our minds, it comes from our hearts and spirits.

It was my family's dignity and hope that caused me to be a survivor and a blessing to others in the process. God's love and the support of family does indeed conquer all things!

As my mother with her Russian background would have said, "Good, bad, or indifferent, it is who we are, this is all we have. We need to be there for each other always, it's not good to be alone. There is strength in love and loyalty for each other." She would refer to the Great Depression, "Back in the 1930s, the way they made it was they stuck together. They had each other. They had the fear of God. A place of direction and protection. When we throw God out of our lives, the man upstairs ain't happy." This coming from a Russian/Jewish woman.

I would listen and then giggle at her poor English. Oh, she spoke English but with a funny twangy Yiddish accent, like Fran the nanny on that sitcom from the 1990s. She started out so serious and then often ended with something kind of off the wall and funny. I didn't always know how to take her, but I respected her. And I smile as I think of her.

As I grew older, her message to me became quite clear. She would say, "Without God and family, we are nothing. We are left to the vulnerability of the world and its circumstances; it's a lonely place to be by yourself. A key is to think of others."

I knew she was right! And I see it more clearly now than ever. I want to encourage today's culture with its separatist mentality to grow away from it. It saddens me to see that people are so busy and so self-focused, justifying it as independence, as success. I've observed individuals wrapped so tightly in the computer and texting world that they can't see their fellow man is drowning in hurt and pain. They became so mesmerized and distracted with the technology, they couldn't hear me talk. They didn't seem to hear me, and it made me feel isolated and alone. If they have what they need, what does it matter! I am hearing this from others, too, and I see this more than ever, and it's not pleasing to our creator and it's not good for us as individuals or as a culture. I love people, and because I'm relationally oriented, I hate to see anyone alone and isolated.

I love to quote Mother Teresa, known in the Roman Catholic church as Saint Teresa of Calcutta, who said, *"Loneliness and the feeling of being unwanted is the most terrible poverty."* Isn't this true? She was a wise woman who loved God, and I am blessed to be a recipient of her teachings.

This generation, unlike the one I grew up in, just appears to be too busy to recognize the loneliness in others. While my generation and the generations before me saw their neighbor in need as a blessing, of bonding and being together, I have observed that today's culture may, at times, see their neighbor in need as a bad thing, sucking up their time. Is this true or is just my observation? If so, where did this mentality come from and how did it get so out of control? Has life become so busy that it sweeps people away from spending time with each other? Why don't people take time for one another the way they used to? I know this is not always the case, of course, but still too common. However, these are some of the questions I'd like to explore within this book, along with the world's history that surrounds my family's story and impacted me while growing up. I love learning from history, it's a great teacher!

Will we ever see as common again, people visiting with each other face to face, to feel that warmth and embrace that brings comfort and assurance? How vital it is to be able to look each other in the eye and see the facial expression of affirmation, knowing we are never alone. With a phone or computer between us, we can't wipe away each other's tears. The human touch, which is so healing, cannot happen through Facebook, the computer, or a smart phone. I understand it has its place but not for bonding. It cannot hold your hand or bring you a bowl of soup when you're sick. There's nothing like the human touch, nothing! This is the way God created us.

The lack of human touch has, in my opinion, encouraged more anxiety, more depression, more suicides, and more feelings of isolation than in other generations before us. Why? Because when people are hurting and afraid, they need a place of security to run to, a place of safety with family and friends where they know they are loved. A hand to hold onto, someone to say it will be all right! A shelter in the times of storms. Without this assurance, I'm afraid we are just like a ship sailing through a storm-tossed sea alone and isolated, sinking from the hardships of life alone. If there is no other ship or crewmembers to come to our aid, to rescue us, we will drown in that sea of isolation and loneliness.

It is my hope that through my story you, too, can discover the integrity, peace, and security that only God and relationship can bring during those lonely and difficult places you find yourself in. It is my prayer for you that through my story, you can discover how good and powerful our creator is. That he truly is a God of the miraculous! I believe he will do things for you, too, just for the asking, and he will never leave you alone. Hebrews 13:5 says, "Never will I leave you; never will I forsake you" (NIV). When it seems God is distant, guess who moved?

Holiness does not consist in doing extraordinary things. It consists in accepting, with a smile, whatever Jesus sends us. It consists in accepting and following the will of God. - Mother Teresa of Calcutta

My story speaks of this, no matter where my family came from, who they were, the challenges they faced, or the mistakes they made. This was my family! This was who they were, this was all we had. And I love them because they loved me. They were always there, "Good, bad, or indifferent." They taught me the love of God and loyalty to others no matter what. I have learned if you set your mind to something and work hard at it, you can reach goals, goals beyond your wildest dreams. And I have! Let me show you how I have! Here is my family's journey!

Chapter 1

From Europe to the Land of Opportunity

Andrea and Me with our siblings in our backyard,
Revere MA. 1963.

One particular Sunday afternoon in the 1960s, we were on our way to visit my Italian grandmother Leah Jean in her home with my parents. My brother Alan, sister Judi and I were giggling and laughing in the back seat. We couldn't wait to see our extended family members – our grandparents and cousins, several aunts and uncles. I can still feel the excitement and anticipation of who we would see, the games we would play, and the delicious food we would eat. While there were many such Sundays, this one stands out in my mind so vividly.

Back then, society and families seemed to be closer knit due to geographical proximity. This is something I believe has been somewhat lost today, and yet is very much longed for. Of course, not every family followed this way of living, but it was more common than today. So, we headed out in the car for the half hour ride from one side of Boston to the other, with my father at the wheel. As we traveled, I listened to my parents' conversations. My mother was all about teaching us how to live and think. She was constantly pointing out right from wrong. "Without the fear of God in our lives and the support of family and friends, our nation cannot stand because a nation divided against itself cannot stand." She would go on to say, "There has to be unity."

My mom in Canada in her early 20's on a family trip.

As I remember, she may have been recalling in part Abraham Lincoln's house divided against itself speech. From the back seat of the car, I heard her saying things like this to teach us, especially if we were being ornery and not listening. But I was like a sponge, always wanting to learn.

No wonder I'm so darn accountable today.

As many mothers did back then, mine lit up a cigarette and began to share how we should behave. I don't think she was aware of the second-hand smoke consequences to health and the oxymoron with life's lessons and lighting up a cigarette. Oh, well, she meant well. She wasn't thinking it would bother anyone in the car, not even her children. No one did back then.

It was warm that day, so we were in luck, she rolled down the window. I could now breathe. Alan and I were coughing a lot but didn't relate it to the smoke, we were too young to understand. Our car didn't have air conditioning back then, as many didn't, so we relished the breeze we felt. But then my mother, realizing the wind was going to mess up her hair, then rolled the window back up. As we arrived at our destination, we opened the doors and a literal cloud of smoke emerged from the car as we got out. We stepped out of the car, waiving our arms in the air to get rid of the smoke screen following us.

Now out of the car and smoke cloud, as we walked to our grandmother's door, which was just about a quarter of a mile from where we parked, we talked about what it might be like when we saw her. We asked questions, laughed, and enjoyed the time together on our way. But before too long, the unity between my siblings and I quickly escalated into arguing. Typical for kids. "I want to do this," "You can't do that," "Cousin so and so is my friend, not yours." My parents were quick to interject and tell us to knock it off, or no one plays when we get there. We got quiet because we didn't want to be in trouble or lose privileges. There was a sense of respect for our parents; it was clear they were in charge, not us. My parents were not abusive, but they did discipline us, sometimes with a strap, and it taught us to respect and honor them. In retrospect, they were teaching us how to get along with others.

As we approached our grandmother's home, we could hear others in the neighborhood cheering for the Red Sox, Boston's baseball team, as radios were blaring. Everything seemed so surreal and exciting! We were unaware of the world's difficulties around us and all the goings on. We were able to focus on what we were supposed to focus on as kids, just being kids and growing up. Things seemed simpler back then, or is it because I was younger and sheltered from life's hardships?

When we arrived at the house, other members of the family greeted us enthusiastically at the door. We entered with anticipation of visitation, play time, meal sharing, and the ball game heard on the radio in the background. My grandmother had five children and 16 or more grandchildren. Her home was the central point of family gatherings when we were young. Nonna was better with her grandchildren than her own children. Probably because she didn't see us all the time. It was special, and she loved it. She loved her daughters-in law and sisters visiting, too, and I have some very vivid and warm memories of those times spent with aunts and uncles. If there were family differences, I wasn't always aware of them.

Nonna was of European descent with Jewish-Italian mix. Where she came from was not always clear, as she told others and me many stories about her youth. I know she had many Italian friends, she was very good with Italian cooking, and even spoke the language, at least to me. I know her first love, my grandfather, was from Italy. I know she did a lot of work for the Catholic church with then-Cardinal Cushing, a prominent Cardinal in the church in Boston during the 1940s and '50s. My father and his siblings were around the church a lot because of her work making afghans to raise money for the needy. I have been told that she even received honors from the Cardinal for her work.

My father pictured in front turning to look at us, and his family gathering for a big meal together early 1950's.

Upon entering Nonna's home that day, I was one of the first to run and greet her. She embraced me with a big hug and lots of kisses. I looked forward to this every visit; it made me feel special. Visiting my grandmother's house was a big event I will always treasure, and it brought me a foundation of security, knowing I was not alone.

Within minutes of arrival, she would always ask, "Who wants to help?" She always had food cooking on the stove or starting to cook when we arrived. Since she was chronically ill and had disabilities, she looked to delegate where she could and teach the next generation a trade. Not every one of us liked to help, but a few of us did. And those of us who did help learned something we incorporated as adults. Several of my cousins ended up opening their own restaurants, delicatessens, or ice cream bars. Many of us, including me, became good cooks just for our families to enjoy. It was clear to me even then she was mentoring us to be others-oriented and able to serve!

Many times, there was a crowd of 20, and sometimes when we would meet at my dad's Aunt Ann's home, there would be up to 50 of us. I miss the large gatherings. It's where my brother Alan and I learned to bond over the joy of cooking and eating. Alan claims our grandmother is responsible for his chronic heartburn today. He swears he was the only eight-year-old with heartburn from all the spices and large portions he consumed. I laugh when he says that!

She was a great cook, especially with Italian food, and so creative, she rarely went by a recipe. She just seemed to know what ingredients to throw together and they blended beautifully in the right balance, bringing incredible aroma and flavors.

Nonna my grandma seated with daughters Gerry on the left and Barbara on the right.

When I asked her how she made it, she would reply to me, "With a lot of love." She made the best unusually flavorful lasagnas, chicken soups, chili, antipasto salads with fresh salami, olives, and cheese. She made a delicious Pasta Fazool, which had pancetta (like an Italian bacon), red onion, salt, pepper, lots of garlic, oregano, crushed red pepper, white wine, chicken broth from real, fresh-cooked chicken from the local butcher, never canned. She used chopped fresh tomatoes (also not canned), and cannellini beans. and When it was done, she ladled the soup into bowls, topped it with shredded Parmigiano-Reggiano cheese, fresh from the local Italian deli, and fresh basil, and served it with toasted bread. As I watched her carefully craft together this recipe, it taught me not only to love the taste of food, but also how to make it an art to behold the eyes. So, I could literally taste it with my eyes as well as with the aromas. She had a knack for making a beautiful display for the family to observe how it was carefully crafted together. How the cheese just had the right amount of crustiness set over the soup, to make it melt in your mouth even before you ate it.

I find myself having a knack for that as I cook for my family and friends, and, feeling that same sense of love and craft for them while I'm doing it. Is it memories of what I learned, or is it really a loving experience cooking for your family?

While there wasn't much attention on food sensitivities back then, I was able to enjoy eating, so the emphasis was more on enjoying food, not the symptoms I had after. I'm glad, in a way, I didn't know I had celiac disease. While it created health issues for me later, I was able to enjoy the moment. Watching her cook and loving her recipes, I was a young connoisseur in the making! When Alan and others visit and I cook for him or other family members, he's quick to tell me it's just like Grandma's. It makes me smile. I picked up on her mentorship, and I think she would have been proud.

Another one of my favorite recipes my grandmother was making that day was her chicken cacciatore recipe. She had so many Italian dishes she cooked so well. It was made up of her own mix of chicken thighs, chicken breasts with the skin and bones to enhance the flavor. She used salt, freshly ground pepper, flour, olive oil, peppers, onions, and fresh garlic cloves. She added white wine, diced tomatoes, chicken broth, capers, fresh dried oregano, and fresh basil. All her ingredients were fresh and not processed. I watched as she sautéed the ingredients together, the smell of garlic and onions and peppers cooking together in olive oil, were heavenly. This was the real Italian way of making it. I learned from the best. I still make her recipe today, and my friends and family love it.

Photo of me in first grade age 6, 1964-65.

That day I was in for another treat as the cacciatore simmered. My grandmother, while delegating help from family members, told me stories of her growing-up years as we cooked. I was her captive audience soaking up family history, and now I'm glad I was.

One of the stories she shared with me was her fascination with Bonnie and Clyde during her youth. I didn't quite understand the connection. Why was she interested at all in two famous bank robbers from the 1930s? As she shared her story with me, it caused me to reflect on my teens, wondering if maybe I was more like her than I realized.

Bonnie and Clyde together.

I thought of this because, during my youth in the '70s, I was following after a role model I considered intriguing for a time, Pinky Tuscadero (played by actress Roz Kelly), an Italian female hood from the show *Happy Days*. Her name on the show was taken from the real-life town of Atascadero in California. She played the older sister of Leather Tuscadero, who in real life was singer Suzi

Quatro, best known for her song, "Stumblin' In." It's strange for me to mention, but I was drawn to her tough persona for a brief period. Was I a little like my grandmother? My mother had a lot to say about the image I was following, and needless to say, my brief period of modeling after Pinky was just that, brief. She was tough, and without direction or real goals, similar to Bonnie and Clyde but not as extreme or violent. I don't think I would have been drawn to her if she was violent since it was not me at all. Since my mother knew of my grandmother's youth, she wondered about her influence on me and thought we should stick to cooking, but my mother listened in the background as Grandma began to share her story, making sure she wasn't saying something inappropriate.

My mother was one who demanded respect and integrity. She was all about making right choices, something that has served me well in my life and led me to the direction I took. It was often the look my mother gave me, shaking her finger, and the threats she made keeping me accountable and in line. She did this with all her children.

But back to the story at hand, I was helping my grandmother prepare a nice Italian meal for the family. I was blessed to be with her on many occasions, as often as we could. She loved to be with me and often referred to me as "my Iris." I felt loved and special. I enjoyed simply being with her and absorbing not only the incredible aromas of her cooking but also learning about where I came from and the history that made her the loving, compassionate woman that made me light up with each encounter. I didn't know her as a person, just as a grandmother, and in my eyes, she was special. I didn't see the tough side of her, she was Grandma. Through her example, I was learning to bond, to love, to share, to care, and to receive God's best through the people around me who loved me. I was incredibly blessed to have grown up in such a large, connecting European culture. It was as if I had grown up in Europe. The people around me spoke mostly Italian and Russian/Yiddish. The very first language I learned was Italian from time spent with my grandmother and her Italian friends. From age eight on, much of my time was spent recovering from a long illness, so I was a captive audience.

While remembering my time with family, I am reminded that I was truly set apart, protected, and sheltered from the influences of the world for quite a while. But not without incredible love and provision in the process. And this provision and love was repeated throughout my life, so I never felt alone.

My siblings and I with Mom in the car, I am in front wearing a dress, 1962.

As a friend once said to me, "You have more provision than most, and your prayers are answered so quickly." And she wondered why. Today, I don't wonder because I have learned that, not only is my God faithful, but where He guides, He provides. It has to do with walking very closely with Him. Listening to His voice and following the direction He set before me, you will see what I mean as I continue to share my story.

My Illness

I was eight when I suffered a burst appendix that left me for dead because it went undiagnosed so long. My pediatrician thought it was a virus and kept insisting

10

so. The wisdom of a pharmacist literally saved my life in the nick of time. He came to the door to deliver my penicillin on several occasions when he finally said to my mother, "This is not a virus. You need to take her to the hospital emergency right away." He knew it was a burst appendix. Unfortunately, it was let go too long and I became septic. It was almost too late, and I was pronounced dead for a few moments. This was very traumatic for such a young person. But I will elaborate later as the book progresses; it's a long story that effected my health for the rest of my life. It left me recovering in a coma for close to what I was told a month.

Having been so ill and needing to recover for at least two years, I spent a lot of time with both grandmothers, learning to cook and about life.

Saturdays were often spent with my grandmother Rose (whom we referred to as Bobe, Yiddish for grandmother) on my mother's side. My time with her was often spent cooking and listening to her stories about the old days. Hearing it directly from the family members that experienced it, while looking over old photos or cooking together, brought a bonding experience I'll never forget. It brought a closeness that the texting of today could never provide. In addition to being with family, it gave me an opportunity to feel a part of things and learn a skill. I believe now there was a reason I was set apart and surrounded by love. In my later years in life, I would be given ample opportunities to pass this on to others who didn't have such blessing in their life. It's a calling I have enjoyed throughout my adulthood. A calling that was inspired by another role model in my life, Mother Theresa.

Back to Grandma's Kitchen

Now, back to cooking with Nonna. I remember working with her and listening intently to her own story. As I assisted her in cooking the chicken cacciatore for the family, I heard the laughter and conversations of my other cousins and siblings as they played ball together outside. Laughing, running, and enjoying just being together. While I couldn't be a part of that for a time, I enjoyed doing various things in the kitchen with other family members. Outside the second-floor tenement apartment where she lived in North Boston, with the kitchen window open, I could hear conversations in Italian and some in English. Many of them were immigrants that came here from Europe. They were talking, laughing, sharing, and enjoying one another. On occasion I heard a little arguing. Not uncommon in these cultures, as that was often how they related to one another.

I peeked out the window and caught a glimpse of them sitting on their steel fire escape porches in beach chairs. It was summer, and it was a rather warm day but still pleasant. The men had those plaid shorts and white t-shirts on, the ones you used to see in the '60s. Some of the women who came out to join them had curlers in their hair and wore house coats with sleeveless tank tops underneath and aprons on the outside. Goodness, they certainly didn't dress to the nines for each other. With their hair pulled up in buns, taking a break from preparing meals for their families, they were conversing, some with laughter, some with the frustrations of an unfulfilled life. The conversations were in the language I came to know and love so dearly, the voices of Grandma's Italian neighbors. Unbeknownst to me at the time, it was a scene much like you would see in Europe where my family came from. The immigrants who came here to Boston and New York created homes, businesses, and marketplaces just like they had back home in Italy, Ireland, Russia, Germany, Poland, and other parts of Europe. Many cultures that immigrated here all through history did much of the same. It was familiar to them and they found comfort in sticking together and creating an environment of familiar surroundings.

My grandmother's apartment was nothing fancy, but it was a fun, warm place to be. Her apartment was decorated with Italian cultural paintings about the culture and villages, displaying *Frutti e vino*, Italian for fruit and wine. Homemade afghans she had crocheted with her friends from Italy covered every sitting surface. There were candy dishes out for the children to enjoy and bowls of fruit, which most kids avoided. One of her favorite candies were those jelly-like fruit candies in the shape of watermelons coated with sugar of many different fruit flavors with lots of sugar from the local penny candy store. Yikes! Something I'd never tolerate today. They were OK, not my favorite, but I ate them anyway because I didn't want to hurt her feelings. I was like that; even as a child, I was aware of people's feelings, and I wanted to make them happy. My mother was the same; she loved people and I learned that from her.

My grandmother's floors were spackled linoleum decorated with the old fashioned, multi-colored area braided rugs. Her furniture, couch and chairs, were covered with colorful stretch cloth slip covers to prevent damage from spills from her many grandchildren and to preserve the furniture to make it last. Many Europeans were frugal because they came from humble beginnings and continued to live in modest conditions. She had her special rocking chair, an old colonial-style with a pad on it for cushion, and her crocheted blankets on the top to wrap in when she got cold.

My Grandmother Leah Jean.

In this rocking chair, she took time to rock each one of us, usually the youngest grandchild to sleep or to wipe away a tear or two.

The gatherings were so much fun. I could have felt left out from the social aspect of child play while I recovered, but my family was good about re-directing any of us who couldn't participate for whatever reason. Mine was debilitating due to the burst appendix episode; tubes in my stomach to drain the poison caused me to be so limited in activity for quite a while. The peritonitis was so far reaching it never resolved completely. I wore a bandage across my lower abdomen to protect the drains, unfortunately it only could do so much, and It was upsetting to me. However, having had a lot of support, took the pressure off feeling so isolated and wounded. The comfort of family and friends also helped alleviate some of the underlying sadness I was dealing with.

I began to feel a hope that it was God in the midst, that was performing so many miracles on my behalf, taking special care of me all those years. My grandmother Leah Jean felt the same way, as her polio incident left her in a similar condition feeling much the same way. I learned from her that leaning on God (for her it was the Catholic faith) and focusing on others would divert me from the illness and becoming so self-focused and inward. Being others-oriented and reaching out would be one of the greatest blessings in my life.

Eventually, I could play some, but because I was still limited, both grandmothers took a special interest in me and taught me to shift my focus from victim to victor. Aunt Ruthie, my mother's sister on the Russian side, had developmental disabilities due to extreme epilepsy. Still I learned a lot from her. It was her example and simple-mindedness, along with her joviality, that provided an example and spoke most to me. Despite her challenges, she thought of others and was as helpful as she was able to be. It was her heart and the love she expressed that I saw as an asset to get through my own struggles and impairments.

I had another cousin on my father's side who was born with multiple problems that my grandmother also took a special interest in. It was my aunt Barbara's daughter, Pam, and she and I shared together and played at our grandmothers' home. We had limitations in common, but it didn't seem to faze us. In our minds, we weren't "different." We enjoyed our playtime together just the same. We had each other, so we were never alone. This is a constant theme in our family you will hear me repeat throughout this book. But that's how we did it, we stuck together. It brought us comfort and security in good times and hard times. It never occurred to us that we were too busy or the timing of helping someone else might be inconvenient. We just dropped what we were doing, helped where we could, and found in the midst of helping someone else, our own needs were met.

That's what God says, "Put others first, and the things you desire most will happen anyway." Not a direct quote, but it's the message I heard growing up and into my adulthood. When we become too self-focused, it only leads to loneliness, feelings of an unfulfilled life and depression. A very lonely place to be, would you agree? No greater joy is found, except by putting your brother before yourself. My mother, brothers Alan and Lance, and other family members have modeled this well, and I'm very proud of them.

Storytelling was common in my family, especially with Grandma. We had a lot of family members that were famous for storytelling, but I could only listen to so much without wondering if some of them were fabricated. I later learned some of them were. But as I grew older, I realized the difference and focused on the joy of cooking and personal time together.

My Recovery Underway

While I recovered from the appendix episode, I became interested in writing and began to write short stories and even songs to keep my mind pre-occupied. I started to write what I was hearing about, stories of the old country, memories I was making along the way, etc. I learned to imagine the things I wanted to do but couldn't do. For example, if I wanted to water ski or dance but couldn't because I was too debilitated, I would sit back and visualize myself doing it while listening to music. It was so real to me; it was almost as satisfying as doing it. It was such an exhilarating release of endorphins. And it turned my focus from inability to ability, thinking about what I could do. And don't you know, I eventually did do some of those things, all because I believed I could. This is something I kept doing even until the present. I loved it then, and I love it now. I found it was a way to use my imagination and dream a little. I often dreamt about being strong and healthy, doing things I couldn't do at the time. I imagined myself waterskiing so often, eventually I was able to do it and do quite well at it.

My mother would often say, "You can do anything you put your mind to." I understood what she meant and took that literally. I pursued the things I wanted most as best I could. And if I failed, she would remind me with a smile, "At least you tried! Better to have tried and failed, than not to have tried at all." The things she said to me didn't always sink in right away, but they eventually did. I was a slow processor but would finally say, "Ah, that sounds like a good idea."

My husband and I told my son Paul, who is an aerospace engineer, some of same things. As a result, he was able to accomplish incredible things we are so proud of. We taught him to work hard and that he could accomplish anything he set his mind to. The mind is a powerful thing, it can cripple us or drive us to do the impossible. And soon my son will have children of his own, and I expect he will pass on the same message of hope and a future. He's that type of man, and he has a good wife at his side with the same mind set.

I laugh sometimes as I share stories from my childhood with him because I know he's not always as engaged as I am. My life stories, while at times interesting to him, don't hold the same meaning as they do for me. How could they? He wasn't there to experience them as I had. He endures my family stories most of the time, just because he loves me and wants to share in them with me as best he can. I love that about him, he's very compassionate.

There isn't a day that goes by that he misses telling me, "I love you, Mom." I couldn't ask for more than to be loved and honored by your child. But he is a guy and doesn't often get too deep. I understand he didn't live what I lived, so it doesn't hold the same fond memories for him as they do for me.

But he humors me and lets me share, nevertheless, and even on occasion acts interested. And sometimes as busy as he is, I think he is interested. He's a great guy, very loving and caring and I'm quite blessed to have him. He was a miracle, no less considering what I had been through, as they thought I would never have any children due to all the scarring abdominally from the episode.

Back to Grandma's Kitchen

Back at Grandma's kitchen, in spite of being limited by illness, I continue to recall fond memories of preparing the food with my Nonna Leah Jean. I remember so much good that it makes me wonder if I chose to do that or if it was my way of coping with trauma. But I remember that day as clear as if it was yesterday. I can still see my mother coming in to see how I was doing and what I was up to.

With cigarette in hand and a smoke screen to follow her, she walked toward me. "How are things going in here? What are you doing?"

"I'm helping Grandma cook, and she's telling me her stories," I answered.

"Alright but make sure you're helping and not distracting her, it's getting late and everybody's getting hungry," she said.

"Sure," I answered. What else could I have said? While I was cooking with Nonna, I was listening; she had a captive audience in me, and she knew it.

With that, Nonna said, "She's doing fine, Charlotte, leave her alone, she's a good kid, she's being very helpful, she's my Iris."

While I smiled at her comment, which made me feel good, I also sensed a little tension between them as my mother gave Grandma a literal dirty look. My mother was good at that when she didn't like someone's comment. But we resumed when my mother escaped to the dining room table to converse with my two other aunts. Everyone had a cigarette in their hands, the smoke was heavy, but their conversation was light and humorous as they shared family stories with each other and the latest movies that were out and who saw what, etc. In the sixties, the conversations were long but light most of the time it seemed. But I could tell they enjoyed talking and sharing and taking a break from childcare while the children played together.

Both aunts, Elaine and Diane, later became my mentors as I grew older. They were a tremendous support to me the older I got. This was true especially when my mother passed away, which was the hardest thing I would face. They were married to my fathers' younger brothers, were both tall and thin, and could have been models; they were that pretty and glamourous. They had those tall sixties hairdo's and quite a bit of makeup. I really admired them and wanted to be like them, minus the cigarettes. I hated the smoke. So, I was half listening to them and half to my grandmother while resuming cooking. I was mesmerized by their stories of the latest fashions and movies and styles, all that they were talking about.

My Aunt and mentor Diane in her youth in the 1940's.

Nonna's Story

At the same time, Nonna was sharing her stories, some about living in England where she was born, some in Italy, and some from North Boston. She began by telling me the story of what it was like when she was born. "It was a cool March day in 1914, London, England. The sky was overcast but dry. It was 54 degrees that day." She loved to tell detailed stories; it was like listening to an Audible book.

She continued, "The leaves were still multicolored; the smell of spring was in the air. I've been told that during that time, folks were hopeful that spring was just around the corner."

I looked up at her, my brow wrinkled. "How do you know that, Grandma?"

She chuckled as she continued to chop the onions for the chicken cacciatore. "My mama told me so."

Even so, I was amazed she was able to recall the weather the way she did, but it was just as she said; her mother shared those details with her quite accurately when she was young.

I was able to confirm this. As I began to write this book, I looked up what the weather was like on that day on the internet. It was so close to what she said, it was remarkable. And while the day was nice to hear about, I was reminded while listening to some of her story that the day she was born was the day she loved to recall to me most. I saw the look in her eyes, it was a look of awe and wonder.

At that moment, Aunt Barbara (my father's younger sister) came in to lend a hand. She rolled her eyes a bit but smiled at me, indicating she had heard this story more times than she could count. Aunt Barbara was a great help to my grandmother, as she was aware that her mother was quite limited by her disabilities from polio she had contracted as a child. Hence, it is probably why she had so much compassion for me and my cousin Pam and was able to extend so much care for us.

I was anxious to get past the weather report and hear more history. Observing my impatience and restlessness, Nonna began to share more of the story, and it began to take a more serious turn. Thank God, while it was an overcast day in England, picturing it was making me fall asleep. "Things were tough back then," she went on to say.

Now she had my attention! "Go on." I listened while the chicken cacciatore was now cooking on the stove. We were enjoying those incredible aromas of spices, tomatoes, garlic, and chicken simmering in her aluminum pot, and I was getting hungry. Stirring the cacciatore with her wooden spoon and trying to go on, she kept getting interrupted again and again by children coming in with various needs or complaints. A scraped knee or two or just telling on each other. The blessing of a large family. I could see she was getting frustrated because she couldn't finish her story. My thoughts now turned toward. "Will I ever hear if it rained that day or the sun came out?" I wanted to eat already.

"Things were rough back then," she said again.

My mother, feeling like throwing her two cents in, interrupted from the dining room table, waiving a hand in the air, grumbled, "Have you ever known a time in history when things weren't rough?"

I took a frustrated breath. *She'll never finish the damn story.* It was to the point where I wanted to change the channel, but I couldn't because it was real life. My mother was famous for saying whatever was on her mind and interrupting at random. Today, they would call that ADD (attention deficit disorder). Naw, she was just rude at times. But my mother knew first-hand about the challenges of her family coming from Russia.

My grandmother used to answer her with this common phrase, and I think it's true, "Every generation has trouble of its own." Nonna would just smirk at her, raise her eyebrow, and give her a funny look for interrupting. This, of course, didn't bother my mother. She did it anyway! She was rarely intimidated by people. She was a great help to her family and friends but was also known for not having any trouble putting them in their place if they got out of line.

While there was tension between my mother and grandmother, Mom would find herself echoing my grandmother's words as she faced her own difficult times. So, we went on to listen, and I could tell my mother was listening, too, even if she tried to hide it!

The day of my grandmother's birth was the beginning of her time to face life's challenges, and she was anxious to share and finish her story. For her, as with many people, the challenges started early, and I think sharing her life helped her put things in perspective.

So, she continued, as she lifted the lid and tasted the sauce, "Umm! Perfect" she said. "Things were rough because this was a turbulent time in history where we were on the brink of World War I."

At the age of ten, of course, as I listened, I believed every word she said, as in my eyes, she was my loving grandmother who could do no wrong. Years later, I would find she was not Mother Goose in her early years, but more like Ma Barker. History tells me Ma Barker was a tough outlaw of a woman from the 1930s.

"When are we going to eat already?" my mother asked again. At that moment, both Aunt Barbara and my mother came in to help to move things along.

Grandma tried once again to continue. I think she wanted to enjoy the time with me as we cooked, and so did I. I just shook my head and wondered if the poor woman could ever finish her story. There was so much commotion in her house that day, but there were about 20 of us. No wonder!

I remember her saying, "It's amazing I can finish telling a story. For God's sake."

And my mother answered, "Yes, for God's sake, but there's a lot to do here, we need to eat today, don't we?"

She glared at my mother and Aunt Barbara. "Can I finish a story already?

And then Aunt Barbara said, "We are, we're trying to get food on the table." So as my grandmother continued her story, my aunt prepared the antipasto salad and my mother prepared the Italian bread, bought hot and fresh from the local Italian bakery. She did so by cutting the bread into small pieces and putting it in baskets on the table with dishes of butter on the side. Aunts Elaine and Diane prepared the table to be set. There was a lot of preparation for such a large number. A lot of work it seemed, but we all enjoyed it just the same.

"Thank God, Iris is listening," my grandmother said, apparently feeling a little slighted in her story. I am told I was always a good listener because I learned early on it was easier to listen than argue.

"As I was saying for the fourth time," she went on to say, "World War I broke out, as I was told, on July 28th of that year. My parents faced so much uncertainty with a young family in Europe. History, if you read it, Iris, tells us, 'The war started in Europe, lasted four years, and ended on November 11th, 1918.' Britain, France, Ireland, and Russia were all a part of an alliance known as the Triple Entente. At that time, Germany aligned itself with Austria-Hungary, then known as the Central Powers. The assassination of Archduke Franz Ferdinand in Sarajevo on the 28th of June 1914 triggered a chain of events that started World War I. Sounds scary, doesn't it?" Nona, peering over the top of her glasses looking up from the pot on the stove.

Several of us nodded and answered yes.

"Well, it was! Seems there's nothing new under the sun, these stories all have a familiar ring, in other words, it happened before and it will happen again, like history repeating itself." Now she had several people's attention in the room, more ears were perking up. This was getting interesting. "Each generation does have trouble of its own," she went on. "I want you to know this, you can learn from history because it does tend to repeat." I knew she was right.

She wiped her hands on her apron. "In fact, if we can learn from history and our forefathers from things they faced, understanding the wisdom they gained, what worked and what didn't, how they dealt with things, what got them through, it would help encourage us through those rough times we face as life's challenges come our way. It can save us from a lifetime of struggle and frustration if we choose to learn from it. History is a great teacher."

I have learned from previous generations how to avoid unnecessary problems with lasting consequences that cause great pain and hardship. But I had to have a listening ear and be teachable. She wasn't always perfect at it herself, but she learned enough to warn us. Today I realize she was getting some of this from the Bible.

I didn't always know what she meant by being teachable, but I was going to look into it. I guess by doing that, I was beginning to learn.

"I learned from their strengths, their mistakes, and what made them victorious, and you can, too. What made them happy, healthy, worse or better. We are not born just knowing these things, they are learned through the process of life."

So much of what she was saying was getting me thinking.

"Wisdom, true wisdom," she said, "comes from the word of God and the generations that have come before us. If you want to be successful, there is no room for being a smart Alec, a know it all!" She continued, "When faced with insurmountable pain, isn't it better to know we are not alone? Family and history is a great teacher."

Although I didn't quite understand her words of wisdom at the time, I still listened and find that today I recall her words echoing in my mind and heart when I feel trapped by circumstances and don't know what to do. I sometimes talk to her in my mind, wishing she could hear me, and I say to her or my mother or my other grandmother, "This is happening to me, and I don't know what to do, I wish you were here to tell me what to do." I find my cries for help are just that, and of course I don't hear anything from them anymore because they are gone. All I have now are the echoes and memories of what was once said to me, and I lean on that.

Memories of what they used to say to comfort me.

But with the passing of everyone, which has been incredibly painful, it's now God's voice I hear echoing in my mind and He tells me what to do. And if I listen closely, I will find His voice and answers are more assured and complete than any man could ever provide for me. He is the one who now tells me it's going to be OK and why. He speaks to me words of comfort and assurance through the Bible, and in dreams and visions. And I find I have a peace that I can't explain, and the parental role model I now speak to is him. He is there always, he never leaves us, and he never will die. People will always disappoint us, not because they want to, but because life isn't forever here. People move, people die, etc. But God never changes, he is eternal, we can always count on him.

I miss Grandma and her stories of the old days. I miss hearing how she did it, when she was afraid, or hungry, or worried about money, or whatever she faced. Hearing her stories gave me strength and hope.

She taught me that in each generation, there are wars and rumors of wars. Different faces but familiar challenges! For my ancestors, it was family and family increase and faith in God that gave them the security they needed. A place to go for shelter in the times of storms. Grandma's story at this point seemed more like a lecture. But I continued to listen out of obedience and respect and wanting to learn something. I guess it was a little history and a little lecturing at the same time. Whatever she had intended, I was her audience, a very hungry audience.

So, trying again, she went on.

The Story is Told

"On that cool March day…" (I will never forget that piece of information.) "…a new generation was being birthed." *Not the weather report again! Yikes!*

"A special time and a special day. It was for them, and it is for me," she declared. "March 24th, 1914. On that day, a baby was born to Polly and Charles Miller. This baby was one of six children and that baby girl was me."

How exciting, I thought, *but was it raining or cloudy?* Now I was getting cynical but still moderately interested, rolling my eyes at this point. She had to grab my attention back.

Grandma stabbed the air with her index finger. "Polly and Charles, my parents had recently immigrated from Lithuania, then Italy, where they were born and raised. They decided to come to England for a better life, but due to unrest in England at that time, their thoughts turned toward Italy again, but for whatever reason, they chose the United States. It was probably because it was commonly known all over Europe back then that America was a land of promise, freedom, and bright futures. Where hard work could pay off with prosperity and a better life for your family. While in Italy, between the years of 1914 to 1918, it was the scene of unrest, periodic waves of protesting the war. A lot of detail, history that I want you to understand, Iris." She looked at me. "Are you listening?"

"Yes," I said, but I was about to take a spoonful of cacciatore, I was so hungry, and things were close to being done.

Leaning against the counter, she went on to say, "Opposition to military intervention became the common feature. Also, they had trouble uniting politically. There was enough happening there, and I'm sure they felt it was safer to bring the family to the United States.

I often wondered though, how people got around from country to country back then. It could not have been easy. Most travel was by boat. Not like the ease of travel from country to country today."

I nodded and glanced at the simmering pot. She then waived her hand at me and said, "Iris hand me the oregano please"

"So, with a baby daughter to care for and so much going on, my parents, my family, found themselves at a loss for a name for me. But there was lot of name changing back then. I always thought the name Leah was too plain! Although my parents thought it was nice. I guess I'll keep it," she said. "But the documents to relocate required a name, and they certainly would have needed it if they were thinking of traveling and relocating to another country. Not to mention, I needed an identity. So, it was my father who finally came up with a name—Leah Miller and my mother agreed. Daddy just liked the name. Seemed fitting to him! I don't know what they called me before the name: 'Hey, kid' maybe?"

She laughed. "What often happened back then as people immigrated to this land is quite a few underwent name changes. If the last name was too long for instance, or children, even in their teens, if they didn't have family when they came over, might be adopted if they were lucky and underwent a complete name change. Leah Miller not being such a common name back then, especially in Europe, made it easy to remember with six children and so much going on, I'm sure."

"Polly and Charles, my Mumma and daddy, headed for America. With six children in tow, they were successful in immigrating to the land of the free. They, like so many other immigrants came to Ellis Island by boat from Europe during very tumultuous times. There at Ellis Island, they were carefully screened for disease. They also had to have a trade and a sponsor. In other words, someone from their family already living in America had to sponsor them to come here. There were a lot of U.S. requirements and restrictions back then. Also, some could stay, even if they didn't have relatives to sponsor them, but it was rare or overlooked somehow. I'm sure they dealt with their share of stowaways coming in illegally even back then, much like today. Some things never change, you know. Are you still listening, Iris?" She caught me peeking out the window, wondering what the neighbors were up to. I was also focusing on the games my brother Alan and cousins were playing while taking in the incredible aromas from the food still cooking. Needless to say, I was noticeably distracted.

My own recollection of those times came from what I was told by not only my grandmother but also other relatives. I felt what they shared with me was accurate. As accurate as memory would allow, as they were much older when they told me their stories.

And it's been pondered before, "Does time really rewrite the lines of our lives of what really happened?" I believe to a degree it does. But we remember the gist of the important events, both happy and painful. Even so, my family shared with me to teach me, and I knew this. And as a child, at times I was like a sponge soaking up all I was told, often mesmerized by every word of their experience they shared with me. As Grandma told me this story, it reminded me of myself. I had similar convictions. I wanted to know all about them and how they lived, too. My grandmother said it gave her strength and hope to hear how her family before her overcame their challenges, knowing if they could make it, so could she. As I listened, I was relating. It dawned on me, as she was speaking, that she loved me and it showed. I went on after that to be her captive audience for quite a while due to my childhood illness, and while it was hard to listen sometimes, I'm glad I did.

Her story continued after we all finished dinner together. She was determined to finish it that day and I was determined to have her finish. I wanted to hear a happy ending, if there was one, at the very least.

As we all leaned back, full and happy, she sat up straight. "My mother and father told me the restrictions coming to this country were good and necessary. They were put in place for reasons, like preventing diseases from being spread. They had to have a trade, as it was believed it would help the economy. People were told they had to work to eat, a biblical concept for sure. Then the Great Depression hit later, so I'm not sure how successful they felt they were with things happening as they did. Even so, because they had to be able to work to come into the U.S. II Thessalonians 3:10 (NIV) says, 'If a man will not work, he shall not eat.' I believe this applies mainly to people who can work and contribute to society but choose not to. It is referred to as freeloading."

When she said that, I frowned. *But surely it doesn't apply to the sick, elderly, mentally ill, veterans, the disabled, etc. I fit into that category already.* I asked her about this and as she shook her white curls said, "No, I believe this applies to healthy able-bodied people who could work."

Nothing wrong with that! I'm not even sure where our country stands on that politically today. It's such a divided subject. There are differing opinions on how to meet everyone's needs. This is not a subject I'm wanting to spend too much time on, I have my own convictions. Let me just say this, we need to extend that hand of mercy to those who cannot help themselves.

She went on to say to me, "Throughout the decades, we did have to be concerned for those who could not help themselves." She had disabilities from polio but still found work through her crocheting; on many occasions, I heard her friend call it "Uncinetto," Italian for crocheting. She helped her friend Teresa Polcari from Italy establish a restaurant in downtown Boston. The restaurant, called Polcari's Italiana, still exists today. I wouldn't be surprised if some of my grandmother's recipes are still made there. Like Nonna in the midst of a disabling condition, I learned to do what I could. In addition, I was learning to work hard at staying well and keeping myself mobile. Something not everyone is able to do. Some need advocating for their needs.

After all, my grandmother would say, "What would Jesus do?" She would answer her own question, "He would help and step up for those in need. So, we need to also."

Today, I can see it's on people's minds more than ever, as it should be. I'm grateful it is!

I feel it can be done in many ways, not just the government. There are churches, synagogues, special groups, families helping families, neighbor helping neighbor, etc. So that no one is alone! Could it be that there was more accountability back when my grandparents were experiencing their generation of issues? Perhaps! But I think every generation looks back and thinks that. Or so I've heard! It was what they experienced and their view of it. I am sharing what they saw and what they did and their reaction to the times around them. I'm hoping we can all learn something from the previous generation. Something like how to navigate with confidence and assurance through the difficulties we are experiencing now, in addition to helping one another.

Presently, we are in very difficult times. As we meet the needs of others, I believe the needs we have will be met anyway.

My Grandmother Not Fitting In

My grandmother continued to share with me that when her family came over during the 1914 era from a foreign land, there was this feeling of not fitting in anywhere. So, they stuck together culturally, to feel supported and secure, making their own community like the one that was familiar back in Europe. She said to me, "Iris, they truly cared for one another, at least in my family they did and our neighbors, too."

My grandmothers Family photo from 1940's, she is seated 5ᵗʰ from the left next to her mother Polly to her right, her sister Aunt Ann is next to her mother Polly.

I saw the longing in her eyes for the way things used to be. She was feeling the changes taking place in society back then, just as I'm feeling them today. And I find my thoughts gravitating toward "where are my people?" as I'm aging. I'm not sure my relatives of long ago always got along, but they were loyal, and they were always there. Integrity and loyalty really meant something. In Italian Catholic and Russian Jewish families, it seemed they were loyal to each other. On the other hand, someone once told me that when they argued, it was how they related to each other, a sign of kinship. I guess my family knew when they were close to someone, a good verbal argument was the seal of bond in the relationship. It was strange to others but familiar to us.

And I have to say that in my walk with God, I have found other much more mellow and sustaining ways to close a bond with my friends. Instead of a good argument, I found praying together to be much more effective and less stressful. Growing up with my family wasn't *Leave it to Beaver*, but I loved them and respected them just the same, and I knew they loved me.

So, at my grandma's home, the food was amazing, as it always was. And it was finally time to relax and share.

She Resumes her Story

Soon it was time to clean up, not something we all looked forward to. But doing it together made it less arduous, and as we did, Nonna resumed her story.

"So, my family immigrated here, and something that I thought was sad in the process was while they were traveling to the land of the free, they endured so much. Obstacles and challenges, we could never imagine, it brings tears to my eyes to think of what they went through." I could see the passion in her face as she talked. "No wonder they were so melancholy at times." She blinked back a tear, as she wiped her brow with a towel.

My mother, moving in on the conversation began by saying, "A lot of people would come here with such high hopes, traveling a long way to get here, expecting a much better life. Some immigrating from Russia, Italy, Romania, Lithuania, like my family."

"Really, Mom?" I remember thinking how neat it was that my family was so interesting. I didn't know our family had such a rich history.

"Yeah, really, Iris, it's true. What, would I lie to you?" Mom spoke with sarcasm in her tone, and with a funny look of "are you kidding?" I wondered if she thought I was questioning her integrity. But instead I quickly realized it was her way of saying, "Look, I'm loyal, I would never lead you astray, learn from what I'm saying." In my own way, I grew to understand my mother and read between the lines and appreciate her opinions.

She continued to speak to me, "Really, it was like this, upon arrival and being carefully screened, they had to carry their weight and be healthy enough to work."

"That's right." My grandmother nodded.

"You know," my mother continued, "Coming over on a dirty, disease-ridden boat and trying to stay healthy was a great challenge for them. Without proper nutrition and not enough water at times, it was no wonder some died along the way. Their sponsors had to be in place, or they were sent back... Right back on that dirty, disease-ridden boat. It was heart-breaking. Families were separated, sick, and without places and families to go to. Sometimes the children stayed with a relative, if one was already in place, while the parents were sent back or vice versa due to illness or lack of money or sponsorship. This process took up to six weeks at Ellis Island." Her voice held a note of intensity. "My mother was held there for six long weeks being screened. What she went through! It was no cruise ship vacation, that's for sure; they went through a lot." We listened with amazement and our thoughts I could tell went to counting our blessings that we didn't have to endure that. Disabilities seemed like small potatoes at that point.

"Charlotte, let me finish now," my grandmother said with a look like, *stop horning in on my story.* "So, my parents were held there with us children for the six-week process during the screening period. It was very arduous, and the screening process could be demeaning. There was a language barrier, and names were shortened if they were too long or too hard to pronounce. They were asked to undress in front of others to have physicals, they had to sleep on cots alongside strangers. I have a hard time remembering anything because I was so young. It wasn't home, it was an unknown place with strangers. People dressed differently, they spoke differently, laughed at different things, they weren't always friendly. People were judgmental and cruel at times. A whole host of things to acclimate to. They didn't read or speak much English either, only some. But they did it, and they had each other to get through it. They stuck together, held each other, and prayed for one another. They found strength and hope for a better future. A better future for their children and grandchildren. They were a determined people who wanted a better life for the next generation. Over time they did find a better life but had to work hard in the process. There was no free lunch."

Now there was a statement my mother and grandmother could agree on. I could tell, because as my grandmother said this, I looked over at my mother and caught a glimpse of her nodding with a vague smile.

"I admired my parents," my grandmother said. "So did I." My mother's eyes misted. Everyone else in the room was mostly just listening, some puffing on cigarettes as they did so. I have home movies of this. It's really neat to look back on.

As I thought about what Nona was sharing with us, it was amazing what my ancestors went through for my generation and me. I'm not sure I will truly understand just how hard it was. But their stories gave me hope and strength to face what I consider tough times today. I'm grateful I have always had their lives as examples. Their faith and determination inspired me as I faced my own battles.

With that, my father and uncles came in from playing catch outside, and I heard my father say, "It's getting late, let's get going, I have to work tomorrow." So, we all got up and prepared to go our separate ways till we met again for another family gathering.

I do miss those times of sharing together, but I am passing the stories on to the next generation of family, hoping they will embrace the bonding and the security it brought, finding the same sense of not being alone during turbulent times they will face.

Another Visit with Nonna

On another visit to my grandmother's, she shared again. She loved to do that. No wonder I'm such a communicator. Look what I learned! I think it brought her comfort to have a listening ear about the old days and where she came from. It brought back the old days to her. So, she shared with me, seeming like she remembered where she left off. It was uncanny that she could do that.

Sipping her coffee, she said "I remember telling you that soon after my family passed the screening process, they were released. With a voice of compassion, she said, "What a sigh of relief that must have been. My family had other relatives they were sent to and settled into New York for a while. Then about two years later, they moved to the Boston area where my father Charles found work as a tailor. This was a common trade back then, as many were trained in Europe as seamstresses and tailoring and furs. For my father, things became stable enough where they could finally settle in and raise their children. But not without a lot of sweat and hard work."

I remember her telling me it wasn't very long after being in Massachusetts that little by little they all became U.S. citizens. For some of the children, it took decades. For instance, my grandmother shared with me that she didn't become a U.S. citizen until December of 1942, around the age of 38, and I have the records to verify this. She was back and forth to Europe from time to time, during her childhood and some in her adult years, too. The details are a bit sketchy, and Grandma wasn't always clear. I think some of it was hard for her to recall, and perhaps some of the memories were too painful to recall.

Over time and many visits with her, she continued to share her stories with me. With each visit, she shared a little of each chapter of her life. Was all of it accurate? I may never know for sure, but what I do know and believe is that she would never purposefully make up stories, she just may have forgotten details, clouded by time and space.

She said she grew up in a good neighborhood in Boston and had a good upbringing. However, while they were still in New York, when my grandmother was a toddler, there was the polio epidemic of 1914-1916. My grandmother was only four at the time, and the only child amongst her siblings that contracted the disease. This left her crippled in one leg and in need of a leg brace to help her walk. And she walked with a limp for the remainder of her life because of it. The disease also left her with lifelong health problems.

The polio epidemic hit hard in 1916 in New York City while my grandmother and her family lived there. I read that it was the city's first large epidemic, with over 9,000 cases and 2,343 deaths. The 1916 nationwide toll was 27,000 cases and 6,000 deaths. Polio, also known as infantile paralysis, was most often associated with children. The epidemic happened during the summer months, which had become common in this era and would lead to the closing of public pools, amusement parks, and other places where children gathered. Polio also did effect teens and adults, too, just not as commonly. The ones who didn't die were left paralyzed. Franklin D. Roosevelt, our former President who served his presidency from March 4th, 1933 until April 12th, 1945 was one of the ones also stricken with the disease in 1916. It took its toll and left its victims quite disabled. It wasn't until the 1950s that Dr. Jonas Salk finally developed a vaccine. I know people were praying and his vaccine was an answer.

I also read that on January 3rd, 1938, Roosevelt founded the National Foundation for Infantile Paralysis, now known as the March of Dimes. And because he founded the organization, a dime was chosen to honor him after his death. The Roosevelt dime was issued on January 30th, 1946.

My sweet grandmother, unlike Roosevelt, who was honored for having polio, would be less than honored for it and instead known as a cripple for the remainder of her life. I'm not sure she ever felt any good came from it, as she may have felt it was just a lot of suffering. However, throughout her life, mainly as an adult, she reached out to help others in need with crippling conditions and those less fortunate, and that brought her satisfaction and purpose. It taught her to be less self-focused and more confident. That's another thing I learned from her. I understood it made her more compassionate from the story's family members told me. I did observe her reaching out to a lot of handicapped individuals, as it was known then.

Her disabilities did affect her self-esteem, because growing up, she was teased a lot. She didn't always handle it well either. After all, things were different back then. She didn't always have the resources needed to cope with her handicaps, although her family tried very hard with her. They did stick together, but as a youngster, Leah rebelled and did not take advantage of family security that carried into her teen years. She began to drift away from family, which is common for teens. She looked for her security outside the home, which led to some bad choices that affected generations to come. My mother and father and various aunts would later, as I got older, reiterate stories she had told me to confirm what they came to know.

On that day of her sharing, we again made chicken cacciatore together. Our cooking complete, the cousins, siblings, and adults came to eat and then my grandmother would close out her story for that day and resume another time when we visited. I got to eat and play indoors, which I loved. I loved all my cousins, being with them each Sunday, and the memories of our times together bring me great joy. All of us thank God that we have those childhood memories that will stay with us forever. As we age, those memories will continue to comfort us, and give us strength and hope as we move on to the next generation. I feel every generation needs the comfort and wisdom of the generation that went before them. I wonder how we would learn otherwise. We gain knowledge when we allow others to teach us what they lived. By listening and being mentored by the older ones, we can avoid a lot of pain and unnecessary frustrations by just listening. A concept I have found helpful is, without accountability, I believe we drift into places of wrong choices or choices that could have brought more positive outcomes. By learning from others, we could avoid unnecessary mistakes.

Nonna Leah Jean Earns a Nickname

My grandmother Leah would later earn a nickname and come to be known as Leah Jean Miller. Aunt Barbara, along with several other aunts, told me the story. It surprised me, as this was another aspect of my grandmother I couldn't have imagined. Jean was not an official middle name for her, as she was not given one. Although I can remember as a child thinking my grandmother's full name was Leah Jean. That's what the adults called her, at least around me. I was confused by this sometimes, because some people called her Leah, some called her Jean. I, of course, called her Grandma or Nonna. Other cousins called her Nana. I never understood how in the world the woman could have answered when she was called. Since she was called everything but late for dinner, how did she know when someone was calling her?

One day while visiting her, I hollered, "Fee-fee" just to see what she would do. I was laughing my head off in the process.

I did it just to see if she would answer, but as I did, she gave me a dirty look and exclaimed, "Smart Alec, keep it up, and I'll give you a spanken." Spanken? Really? Wasn't the word pronounced spanking? Oh, well, her English wasn't the best. "Spanken" was a real Bostonian term, one of many. While growing up in Boston, I heard phrases like, "Geet." Which in Bostonian meant, "Did you eat?" Or "It's wicked pissa." Which meant, "It's really good." How about this, "Are we going to the packy?" which for us teens meant, "Are you going to the liquor store?"

Bostonians have a language of their own. And you had to live there to understand it. Otherwise, if you went other places, you were often misunderstood as being from a foreign land. Bostonians also did not pronounce their R's. So, if I was told to "get in the cah," what it really meant was, "Get in the car."

Later, in college while majoring in music, my vocal coach said this to me: "You have to first learn to talk before you can sing, you will never be able to sing pronouncing words that way, oh, my God." At first, I didn't know quite what she meant, but I learned to pronounce my R's so well, after a while, I almost completely lost my Italian Boston accent. I wasn't completely willing to give it up, as it was who I was and where I came from, and I was proud of it.

So, why did my grandmother have so many different names anyway? I found out later it was because she wanted her many grandchildren to call her whatever they felt comfortable with. It was confusing for us, but it seemed to work. Something else that struck me as a kid was she had a brace on one leg to help her walk, with lovely black patent leather orthopedic shoes, very stylish, not! When I went into a leg brace myself, thank God you could use regular shoes, the orthopedic ones were not what I was ready for. I didn't mind sometimes modeling after her but maybe not the outfits. I didn't want to dress like my grandmother. That's another story, but I think you get the picture.

I did finally learn the story of how she got her nickname. As I grew into my teens, my father and my mother told me her nickname or middle name, "Jean," was one earned over time by reputation during her teen years. "Mean Jean," they called her, after the boxer Gene Tunney. "You mean she wasn't called mean Leah, or mean Nana, or mean Nonna?" I said to my parents. Talk about an identity crisis. I was being smart with my parents, and they knew it, and they just looked at me funny.

They said something like this, "Oh, cut it out, Iris, we're trying to be serious." This coming from my father, "Chuckles the clown." He was always joking and rarely serious. But this time, he was being serious, something I rarely saw in him.

Reverting back to my grandmother's nickname and reputation, let me give you a picture of who Gene was. Who was she modeled after, and why? Well, he, and yes, I said he—I thought for years he was a female boxer. But I don't think they had female boxers back then. Anyway, he was a male boxer from 1915 to 1928.

My grandmother compared to a male boxer. It was hard to imagine. He was really something back in the day. Gene Tunney held the world heavyweight title from 1926 to 1928. His real name was James Joseph Tunney. I took the time to look him up and saw his photo and read his story. He was a great looking guy and very well-known back then, with strong features! According to history, he successfully defended his crown against the then-famous Jack Dempsey in 1927. Big deal for that time. So, for my grandmother to be compared with the likes of Gene Tunney and Jack Dempsey, she had to be one tough young lady. Like a pirate with a limp. Picture that! I guess all she needed was an eye patch and a parrot. Then we could give her yet another new name. Like she needed one!

Photo of Gene Tunney & Jack Dempsey, 1927.

And between you and me, she did have a pet parrot. I loved that parrot and how it would repeat certain words back to us. Grandma taught it to say my name. I thought that was the coolest thing. My family life was like growing up in a sit-com at times. It was fun and so humorous in the early years, for the most part.

Advertisement for a Boxing event from the era of 1927 with both Gene Tunney and Jack Dempsey.

So, my grandmother had this title name, but what did she do to earn that title as a young woman? I am picturing the eye patch and parrot as I'm writing this part of the book, was she pirate-like? Probably not, but from what I hear, she was just very tough. In every generation, there is teen rebellion, we can't escape it, it's a natural part of growing up. Testing the boundaries, as they say. "But with prayer guidance, they get over it," my mother once said.

In my grandmother's case, from what I understand, if anyone crossed Leah Jean, or got in her way, she had no trouble taking them down verbally, without boxing gloves. She was known as tough and strong willed. My brothers and I feel this explains our resilience as adults. But I still couldn't believe this was the same grandmother who had a crippling condition that left her using a cane and spending a lot of time in her rocking chair as she aged. She was compared to a male boxer and went by the title "Mean Jean" as a youth! What did that mean? It took me years to put it into perspective, as I really wanted to understand her, and because I loved her. My mother, on the other hand, thought she was full of it! Of course, my mother thought everyone was full of it. My Grandmother was to be admired for her drive and determination for sure.

My mother didn't understand her crippling condition, and she was misunderstood by many others, and this hurt her deeply.

My grandmother, the woman that showed me how to cook Italian meals and do rosary beads, rebelled as a teen. What did happen? I was told My Grandmother became known as a rough and tough teen often getting into fist fights in her youth. She was angry and frustrated and lashing out at those around her, sometimes causing physical harm to others who upset her.

But I came to understand that as she grew older and weaker because of the polio, she became humbled as a result. That's the woman I remember.

The name Gene (and again, she spelled it Jean, the female way) stuck with her for the rest of her life. I understand why! It's not easy to be different. Back then, signs of weakness were hidden so others wouldn't judge. It was common to wonder, "What will happen if they know my situation? What will they think? How will I ever fit in?" It was a shame to waste time worrying about what people thought when it was who she was and all she had. Who else could she have been? I wish she could have liked herself and accepted who she was; it would have made all the difference for her in her relationships with others. But she was clueless.

Today, I can't imagine going through life trying to measure up and be what others expect me to be. I came to understand it can't be done, no one person can provide all your happiness, only the Lord. I learned early on through my own challenges that this is who I am, this is all I have, and this is who God made me to be, and it's OK. As long as we are good to others, don't cause harm to anyone, and are a blessing to those around us, what else should we be? In my eyes, being kind and loyal is all that is expected.

So, why was my grandmother in survival mode? What happened? I'm not sure where Leah Jean took a hard turn and dealt with so much resentment and anger. I simply know this caused her to make some hard choices in her life with lasting consequences that affected her children and some of her grandchildren.

I was told while growing up her mother Polly, after the death of her first husband Charles, married two more times. First, to Isadore and then to Abe Naglin. She always remained close to all her children. She worked part-time as she was able at the laundry at Massachusetts General Hospital in Boston; she also worked as a midwife. Through one of my great-grandmother's marriages, she even acquired another child, Francis, who came into the family with Isadore, her father, at age 13. Isadore is who I was named after! I have been told he was a man to be admired, well-liked by many. I heard he helped many people who were down and out, and he was very kind, gentle, and sweet. It was nice to be named after such a person of integrity.

Polly made sure her kids were busy. Her son Tommy was a marathon runner, and the others were busy growing up and finding careers and marrying. Some traveled back and forth to Europe—some to Italy, some to England, and some to Germany. Europe was their familiar culture, so they visited often.

As my grandmother's siblings grew, most seem to have made good choices. There were a few bad choices amongst her siblings that caused some serious problems, but they kept a low profile to keep some of the consequences under the rug, so to speak. The boys in the family were very protective of the girls. The family was close. However, my grandmother's struggles were becoming more visible to neighbors and other relatives. My great-grandmother Polly tried to keep a tight rein on her, to protect her from bad choices. But her life was consumed with a large family and work and could only do so much. So, when my grandmother began acting out as a teen, my great-grandmother didn't quite know how to handle her.

Leah apparently was a rather wild child, reeling from the loss of her real father. She now had a stepfather and another reason in her mind to feel different, adding more confusion and insecurity to her life. Even though my grandmother made some bad choices out of frustration, I choose to believe that not all bad choices bring bad consequences. Sometimes they can work for good. I trust in her case it did.

In the word of God, it says just that: "All things work together for good." When times are tough, it's hard to remember that and see a very tough challenge bringing something good out of it. But my great-grandma Polly did see the glass half full. She was strong and positive and loved her family dearly. She was a good mother. She chose to see the good in her children.

However, my grandmother's story is a mix. She was given good leadership to help her along. But the choices she made didn't always have positive outcomes. Some eventually did, but it was a long road for her to get there.

Her mother would try to tell her, "Perspective is half the battle. Look at the glass half full. Right choices bring good consequences."

And Leah would answer her in a frustrated tone with something like, "You don't understand, my life is harder than most. Just look at me, I'm crippled, and I look weird, I'm made fun of."

My great-grandmother would just throw her hands in the air and say, "I don't know what to tell you then. You'll have to see what I mean."

My grandmother was not one to learn from being told. As is often the case, teens don't always listen while in the process of trying to find themselves; they are not always open to parental suggestions, guidance, and discipline. They see it as intrusive and nonsense, often having to learn the hard way. They express feelings like "What do they know? They don't understand." Because she refused to listen, she would get lost and make wrong decisions which had lasting impact that couldn't be undone, only made better by time and better choices. She learned as we all must, life is a process! And in that process, there is pain, and pain, as many of us know, has little mercy, sometimes bringing us to our knees in despair. But there is also joy that comes after. I believe that!

I loved my grandmother! What upset me in hearing of her struggles was that I never saw the side of my grandmother people spoke of. All I saw most of the time was a loving grandmother who had family gatherings and dinners bringing family together. When we visited, my grandmother welcomed us with the biggest hugs and kisses a kid could ask for, and that's what I have focused on, that's what I remember.

Later, as I got older, I found stories told by other relatives not only hard to believe but hurtful, as this wasn't the grandmother I knew and loved. After all, she was a hero in my eyes, and no one could be as great as she was. I looked at her through a child's eyes and felt warmth and security from her. It was evident to me that she loved her family, so how could it be that there was another side to her?

Chapter 2

Leah Jean's Journey

Grandmother Leah Jean holding Baby Uncle Martin, with her husband Isaac and her other son, with my father in the front acting silly. His joviality started young.

I always wanted to understand my grandmother because I loved her. As a youngster, I was sensitive to people's feelings, in tune with my family's thoughts, actions, and emotions. I still am today. I was a very observant child. As time went on my conclusion was, she was young and searching, very human, and perhaps even a little lost, trying to deal with things that were very hard for her, not always knowing how to respond but instead often acting out of her emotions and fears. How many of us have had this experience?

Back in the day, during my grandmother's teen years, there were all kinds of things happening. As with any generation, some exciting and some a little unsettling. After all, during her life, she saw some substantial events unfold— the polio epidemic of 1916, World War II, Bonnie and Clyde and gangsters, the Great Depression, and the dust bowl to name a few. She also lost her father at an early age. From what I understand, he died quite young of a heart attack.

Two husbands her mother married after Charles were good men but could never take the place of her real father. Missing out on being Daddy's little girl impacted her, and she didn't know what to do with her sadness and grief. All situations combined, it impacted her as a teen. After all, the teens are the years when young people are trying to find themselves. And with many added stresses combined, it can make things confusing for a young person. Divorce and death can really take its toll with fear and uncertainty, often leading to rebellion. I believe this was her story. She experienced a lot of pain both physically and mentally that made her a fighter, very angry but determined. No wonder she was compared to a famous fighter of the day. My grandmother, while frightened in a sense, was one tough cookie in another and a side of her I rarely saw as her granddaughter.

I recall seeing this only once when my father and brother Alan and I were visiting her on a Saturday. Alan and I were acting up, being kids, running around, yelling too much, etc. and her patience was slim that day as I remember. I was five years old, Alan six and a half. As we were misbehaving and wouldn't stop, she grabbed a hold of me and spanked me. That "spanken" she threatened me with before caught up with me, something she had never done before. I remember feeling shocked and scared, as this was out of character for her, at least as far as I was concerned. But now as an adult, putting myself in her place, I believe she may not have felt well and may have been quite overwhelmed.

Here I am at 2 with brother Alan on Dad's lap, he loved to be with his children.

I ran to my father who admonished me. "You should have stopped when she asked you to, that's what happens when you don't behave, don't do it again." He then hugged me and comforted me, and I felt safe. I felt affirmed by his attention to the matter. As I look back, I can see he made a good decision that taught me rather than humiliated me. He acknowledged both of us and didn't play one against the other. I'm not sure how he knew to do that as he was only 32 at the time, but I'm grateful as those were impressionable years for me. I respected him for it, and I always remembered the discipline and love that molded together, bringing me affirmation and security that gave me the confidence I needed later as I got older.

Reflecting on My Grandmother's Teens

Reflecting on my grandmother's teen years, I'm aware that each generation has trouble of its own. And, boy, does it! Her adolescence was the era of the 1920s, moving into the 1930s. The 1920s in the United States was termed "roaring" because of the exuberant, freewheeling popular culture of the decade. The twenties were a time when many people defied prohibition (illegal use of alcohol), indulged in new styles of dancing and dressing, and rejected many traditional moral standards. It almost sounds like today, doesn't it? I have heard that history repeats itself, and this certainly sounds familiar.

During her teens, Leah went to movies starring the latest Hollywood actors like Charlie Chaplin , considered to be one of the most pivotal stars of the early days, in *The Great Dictator*, and Rudolph Valentino, Hollywood's original Latin lover who was an actor famous for the silent movie, *The Sheik*. I recall her mentioning to my father, that John Barrymore, with Twentieth Century Fox, was one of her favorites. She liked Buster Keaton, a popular vaudevillian comedian-turned actor who starred in the movie *The General*. My grandmother also liked Lon Chaney, an actor who was famous for his creepy, scary role in horror movies, and Douglas Fairbanks from Denver, Colorado who played Robinhood. She loved going to the movies with family members, especially her mother. Silent films were popular and not expensive in the day.

The average cost was 25 cents for a double feature and a live show. Compared to today, where the average cost per ticket for one movie is $8.12. Quite a contrast, ha. During her time, instead of music on the screen because it was a silent film, they had a live organist playing while the film was being shown. I understand that at that time, 85 percent of the movies were made in Hollywood, I imagine because travel wasn't that easy and could be costly as well. The radio was a major source of entertainment.

My mother and grandmother talked about how much better radio was than television because more was left to the imagination. It encouraged learning and daydreaming. They said it was exciting and fun and kept the mind active, a time for the family to sit around the radio and share in dreams together. In the movies and on television now, we are shown too much, I'm afraid, leaving very little to imagination. Much of television, in my opinion has become too graphic, encouraging bad behavior and violence.

In the 1920s and '30s, bootlegging (illegal sales of alcohol) was also very prevalent. My family had its hand in that a bit, too. My grandmother and her Italian-Jewish family's history and life story read kind of like a gangster movie. Some were bookies, and in mob-related activity with liquor store ownership as a front, once the sale of alcohol became legal again around 1933.

Moving ahead a bit, I was told a story that was so sad. My grandmother's stepsister's first husband (Uncle George) was murdered by the mob back in the early 1950s. He was found in the back bay of the Italian north end of Boston, shot to death in the back of the head, assassin style because of a deal gone bad. Her stepsister was devastated for years. It left a terrible scar on her life and never quite got over it. She later married another man and had children and a better life but never forgot George. But as difficult as things were, she managed to move on, and she raised a good, well-adjusted family with children and many grandchildren, from what I was told. A happy ending to such a sad story. But not without a lot of pain in the process.

What made the difference in her recovery from such a tragic event? I've been told it was because she had family, with God and prayer at the center to support her during this very rough period. She was able to move on because she was not alone in her struggle. This gave her a faith and strength that is unknown to the natural mind. We will all go through tough times, it's inevitable! All of us have them. It's because we are in this world and subject to its problems, the Bible says. No one gets out of this life without something to challenge them. It's just that some have more than others.

This brings to mind a question. Have you ever wondered why some people go through more than others? I believe there are good reasons for this. It's my feeling that hard times are good for us. While painful in the moment, they build character and make us stronger, more others oriented, lest we become weak and self-focused. It causes us to look more to God and cling to him and others around us. If we never struggled, we would never learn the meaning of true emotional strength and maturity. We would never have the opportunity to grow. We would never learn how to help and care for others. And most important, we would never learn to lean upon God and admit our dependence on him.

I believe the more pain and hardship; the greater purpose God has for us in life and in the lives of others.

A wise woman once said to me when I was in the midst of so much pain myself, "God must have a mighty plan for you for Him to have chosen for you to go through so much at such a young age." She was right, my journey led me to a place of love and compassion for others, a ministry of outreach to the broken hearted. To help set the captives free. Isaiah 61:1 states, "The spirit of the Sovereign Lord is on me because the Lord has anointed me to proclaim good news to the poor. He has sent me to comfort the brokenhearted and to proclaim that captives will be released, and prisoner's will be freed" (NLT).

I could not have learned this any other way but in that valley. But with every valley, there is a mountain top experience awaiting us. We won't get to the mountain without trudging through the valley of hardship first. It's interesting that people feel when a bad thing happens, it's always a sad thing, wasted time, and it can make you feel awful. Feeling like nothing good can come from it. The things we think we will never live through, we do because of faith, perseverance, keeping perspective, and staying determined, keeping our eyes on the prize ahead. We only lose when we give up and stop trying. Success comes when we don't give up. Most successes don't come easy. In addition to hard work, we can conquer most anything with the love and support of family and friends and faith in God. Keeping perspective can make all the difference in how things turn out. If we have not love, and if we don't believe God has a plan in those hard places, it can seem a waste of time with a lot of unnecessary suffering.

We just won't understand what that suffering was all about. That's it! We can accomplish all things through Christ, beyond our wildest dreams, as we trust in him and follow his lead. Hard as it is, you got to get up, pull yourself up by the bootstraps, and keep going, heading toward the prize. Take advantage, if you can, of every opportunity before you, if there isn't one, make one and never look behind, only ahead. All my life, I have had friends that were like sisters to me, my grandmother did, too. Lifetime loyal sisters who were always there, helping and encouraging as I navigated this thing called life, which is not always easy for many.

My Grandmother's Story of Mistakes

My grandmother's story is one of making mistakes and trying to hide the truth at times. She didn't always make the most of opportunities. Sometimes she tried to use her challenges to reach out to others, which was more gratifying and fulfilling. Her history also speaks of friendliness and closeness of family and friends, and I learned through her example how to do this.

So, my grandmother was trying to find herself in all this during her youth. Before the Uncle George incident in the 1950s, during the late 1920s and early 1930s, she was going with the times. She was intrigued by Bonnie and Clyde who were well known for their killing sprees and robbing people all over the country during the Great Depression between 1931 to 1934. Their story was big news back then and created a lot of fear. As the story goes, eventually they were ambushed and shot to death.

The ambush of Bonnie and Clyde's car.

If only my grandmother had known the truth about the choices she was making and who she was idolizing. Choices she made affected not only herself but also the lives of those around her. But she was young, impressionable, and perhaps feeling a little lost, maybe even frustrated and feeling left out. Her contraction of polio in her childhood left her with feelings of low self-esteem and were worsened with each challenge that came along. Her feelings of insecurity grew, causing her to act out. With one leg with crippling pain and weakness, causing a noticeable limp, her frustration of wanting to fit in worsened. She wanted desperately to hide her disabilities and to be seen as attractive and normal but to no avail. How could she ever fit in? I can't say what she was feeling for sure, I can only imagine as I try to put myself in her place. All I can think of is how lost she was, and like many of us, found herself in a dark place. She had family support but didn't choose to take it, and I often wondered why! Her life choices left me with many questions!

First, I wondered if at one time in her life she was in such a dark place that she just couldn't accept the help that loved ones could bring her? Maybe because she felt she wasn't deserving of it. A lot of people feel this way. She unknowingly isolated herself and rejected the comfort and truth of others that could have set her free. My father once told me she lacked confidence and didn't feel worthy! But I wondered if she just didn't understand that maybe her family could be the ones to help guide her into making right choices and move into a place of security and hope. Grandma once told me herself that she felt hopeless, helpless, and like she didn't quite measure up. She told me this when she was trying to comfort me during the course of my illness when I was feeling inept.

She said, "It was like I was different and I, too, often, didn't feel accepted." But she also learned later on, that much of this was in her mind and not in reality. But because of this lie she believed, she found her comfort in being around the less fortunate and not the well-doers. If she could have only understood the truth of who she was and that it was okay, I wonder how different her life could have been!

Back then everything was kept in secret, and most things that were considered embarrassing were kept hidden and swept under the rug, not to be viewed for fear of judgment. Talk about being misunderstood and what pressure and anxiety it caused for people. I know it did for her! How many of us have felt like that for different reasons? I'd like to look for a moment at how we are taught and how it has affected who we are today. I know things I was taught, good or bad, helped to mold me and shape me into the woman I am today. Because I learned accountability and to think of others, that's how I think as an adult. But what if I had never learned that stealing was bad? I might have been tempted to do it, right? I would not have fully understood the consequences of taking from others what was not mine in the first place. So, there's no sense of right or wrong there, it's about me and only me. So, how are we taught? Some are never taught at all, so what happens to them?

Well, that's where God and his word comes in. His word is how he speaks to us since he is a spirit, and we don't see him, we worship him in spirit and in truth. Our spirit connects with his. His spirit speaks to ours. You see with your heart and hear with your soul, guided by a hand you cannot hold. You trust in a way that you cannot see. It's faith, and that's what it must be. It's why we don't see him. So, for someone who was never taught by man or treated justly, it's His word that can teach us, and so much in there that can show us how to live. Not because of rules and so God can dominate us, but to help us, so we can be happy and stay out of danger. The Bible is like a compass to guide us into the truth of knowing right from wrong and how He expects us to live in general, not so He can control us but so we can live good prosperous lives. He wants the best for us!

So, no matter what you were or were not taught by your family, you can still learn the truth of right and wrong from God himself. You are never alone. I've come to understand that God doesn't want to limit us, but he loves us so much and wants to bless us. He created us for fellowship, first with him and then with each other, so we are never alone. Are you getting the picture of who God is yet? I pray so, during the course of this book, that you can come to the understanding of who God is by experiencing with me His goodness through the example of my journey and how he has always provided for me, knowing he will for you, too. But you have to seek Him and listen and learn and then apply it. You, too, can be renewed by God himself. I have some to know He's real and very much there for you.

Some don't realize God has a plan and purpose for all of us. Sometimes out of frustration, we lash out at the people around us, at God himself, denying His existence because of the stresses of our experiences. We don't see, so we don't believe. But the Bible says the opposite, "He who believes without seeing is blessed." In John 20:29, "Then Jesus told him, because you have seen me, you have believed; blessed are those who have not seen and yet have believed." (NIV). If we embrace God and his word, the conviction would cause us to make right choices no matter how we are raised. That's the benefit of knowing God.

In my grandmother's case, she was raised with integrity but made wrong choices that affected her and those she encountered. The generations that came after her were impacted as well, some for good, some for not so good.

Some of her choices caused a lot of pain and hardship, especially for her children. My father for one. I'll explain more as I share his story.

The consequences for wrongdoing can and usually are greater than we realize. Life and natural consequences are a great teacher of what to do or not do.

Reflecting Back

So, I continue to reflect back, why didn't my grandmother turn to family? Was she even aware of God back then? I know she was taught about him. What was going on in her mind at that time? Was she jealous of her siblings' good health, feeling like a black sheep? As I share my story, you'll be able to see how much I inherited from her genetically and the commonalities in her story and mine. What we inherit from our ancestors that we cannot control; we relinquish to the Lord and trust Him to work for good. What we can control is the choices we make from what we might have inherited that we don't like so much. And those choices can impact others around us, for good or bad. It's a choice! We can't choose always the challenges in life that come our way that cause us to want to crumble in fear, but we can choose what we do with them.

I'm reminded of another Bible scripture that I love to cling to, "There is now therefore, no condemnation for those who are in Christ Jesus." It means God loves you and forgives you and wants you to come to him just as you are, no one else. Not as someone you think you should be, better, more complete, just simply just as you are. Who else could you be? During her times of so much uncertainty in her young life, I wish my grandmother could have known this. It would have brought her so much more confidence, contentment, and peace and better direction with greater choices. I believe I learned from her story. I learned from her mistakes, I learned from her triumphs, and it has led me to a better place by watching and learning from the choices, good or bad, she made.

The Choices She Made in her Teens

So, it seemed my grandmother was on a roll as a teen for a while making the wrong choices. As I said, she was quite tough; behind the scenes, she was smoking and acting out in other ways, even stealing some.

Recently, my husband and I were watching the old movie channel and came across *Bonnie and Clyde*, starring Faye Dunaway and Warren Beatty. Based on the lives of Bonnie Parker and Clyde Barrow, it was originally released on August 13th, 1967, and their story is a big part of history. It made me think of my grandmother and what might have been so appealing about them to her. I guess they seemed exciting to young people back then. So, during the height of all their drama, when she was 17, she made a choice that would affect the rest of her life. And my dad's life of too. At 17, it was the perfect age for trying to find oneself, and she went down a road she didn't quite understand and the consequences that would follow.

But first, if you think back in history, some of you may remember that Bonnie and Clyde were the Farmer's Bank Robbers from the 1930s. Right in the middle of my grandmother's youth. To her, at age 17, the likes of Bonnie and Clyde were very exciting! She was unaware and vulnerable.

History tells us that Bonnie and Clyde met in January 1930, and for approximately four years, carried out their crime spree together that ended in their violent deaths. They went down in history as blood-thirsty killers. It was such a sad story, and many had wished they had made better choices.

So, how did they start out life anyway? This made me curious. So, just to put myself in my grandmother's shoes for a moment. I wanted to become, as she did, familiar with their story. As legend has it, Bonnie was an honor roll student in high school where she excelled in creative writing. Can you believe it? Talk about lost potential. Her father was a bricklayer and an interim pastor at a local church. I was surprised to read she was raised this way. Clyde's life started out entirely different. He was born in Texas just south of Dallas to a poor farming family. His first arrest in 1926 was when he was just in his teens. He cracked safes, robbed stores, stole cars, and then went on to bigger things, like robbing banks. Makes you wonder what he was taught.

Of course, I'm sure my grandmother didn't see this side of the story, she only saw what she perceived as the glamour of it all. She was caught up in all the excitement and notoriety they were receiving. Crazy how teens think when they want to be noticed. I can only imagine what she was thinking as she read their stories in the newspapers and heard of their crime spree on the radio. Was she caught up in imagination of their notoriety? Was she intrigued by where they were headed next? Was it exciting to hear of their next move and what bank would be held up in the next county? Would they land near where she lived, and did that frighten her? While I may never know what she was imagining, I trust it wasn't to join them.

But what my grandmother didn't realize, I'm sure, was that Clyde's goal in life was not to gain fame and fortune from bank robberies. Rather, he hungered for revenge against the Texas prison system for the abuses he suffered while serving time for earlier crimes. We don't know for sure if Clyde was offered any other choices or mentorship. Could it have been that he was just plain rebellious with a bad attitude? Perhaps. Some people are like that. But what if he had been offered other choices? What if he really intended to do good and didn't have anyone, he was accountable to, to teach him right from wrong? Maybe he just didn't know any better. Maybe he had a chemical imbalance. Who knows? Either way, his behavior was so extreme, it's hard to justify why he did what he did and the very destructive road he chose.

I wondered once if God held him accountable for his actions when he died? Or did He speak to him directly, on the other side, offering repentance and forgiveness?

As I read the Bible for guidance, here are some scriptures I have come across that speak to this a bit. *"For rulers hold no terror for those who do right, but for those who do wrong. Do you want to be free from fear of the one in authority? Then do what is right, and he will commend you. For he is God's servant to do you good. But if you do wrong, be afraid, for he does not bear the sword for nothing. He is God's servant, an agent of wrath to bring punishment on the wrongdoer." (Romans 13:3-4, NIV)*

Oh! In one sense, it sounds like God is harsh, doesn't it? And in the other, he says to do right and he will commend you. Well, the God I know is kind and compassionate with no condemnation. He just wants his children to do good, follow him, and make right choices. It's good for us, and I believe God knows that. I also believe God could have forgiven both of them, if they asked. If you ask for forgiveness, I believe God is quick to forgive and commend you. The God I have come to know loves and forgives, it's up to us to ask for it.

On the other hand, Bonnie, I believe, should have known better. She was raised with the truth, according to history books. She came from a decent family. But was she like my grandmother, drawn to bad situations that seemed exciting? It has been said she heard the word of God from the Bible. She was taught right from wrong and had the proper guidance.

History tells us that, but why then was she such a rebel? She was drawn to crime for a reason. Maybe she was deceived and thought it would be exciting. Maybe she was in defiance of her parents, spiting them in some way out of resentment for being too strict and then rebelling against their authority.

When she met Clyde, who really didn't know any different, she could have shared the Gospel with him or tried to guide him a little in a good direction. Instead she was attracted to all the excitement, and she chose to follow Clyde down a dark, destructive, dead-end road to destruction. She believed a lie, that all this was exciting, and did not realize the devastating effects of bad choices. What greater consequences can someone suffer for doing wrong than to be gunned down the way they were (they were shot more than 50 times) in an ambush in such a brutal way.

Are there lessons to be learned from history? I think so! That's why I enjoy reading the subject. It teaches us life's lessons and provides guidance on how to live if we learn from the mistakes others have made, the victories they achieved, and how they achieved them. We can learn from the stories, from the choices made, good or bad.

God has ways of speaking to us, and I believe history is one of those ways. We have those choices to do right, to do wrong, to put others first, or just remain self-centered. These choices can lead us eventually to a very dark and lonely existence, or one of joy, prosperity, and blessing. We can choose to follow the wrong voice (and believe me there is a wrong voice that lies to you every time) and can end your life in tragedy and terrible mistakes. Maybe not like Bonnie and Clyde, but tragedy for some can mean not knowing the truth and spending all your life with regret and grief over things that could have been prevented. All from choosing the wrong path.

I think of my grandmother and how young and impressionable she was during this time. With gangsters being glamorized all over the radio, in the movies, in the newspapers, they became my grandmother's role models, along with the Italian mob. Role models like Bonnie and Clyde, James Cagney in the movies, and Humphrey Bogart glamourizing gang related activities were exciting to them back then. Even then movies were sending compromising messages to our youth. On the radio, you had some wild shows back then, too. But those examples are in every generation to tempt our kids in directions we might not have chosen for them. They call it entertainment, some of us call it influence. I call it role modeling. As children are trying to find themselves, they look to older people to be like. Can we be good role models for the younger generation today? I hope so. Because of the technology, bad examples with bad behavior are more accessible than ever, and yes, so are the good ones, it's true.

This generation needs more security and comfort and hope than ever. Many don't even understand who God is or if he even exists. Do you?

My mother used to say, "Every generation has trouble of its own, this is ours. We can do it just like they did. But sticking together is key." I never understood the true meaning of what my mother meant until I grew older. But she sure said it a lot. Maturity brings wisdom, understanding, and a feeling of being settled. Living does that, too. Life has a way of teaching us if our parents didn't, good or bad! We can choose to grow and become stronger, or we can become bitter and lose the destiny that might have been in store for us. No matter how you were raised or what you experienced, you still have choices and you can make the right ones. True freedom is making right choices.

My Grandmother's Hard Breaks

I found myself wondering, did my grandmother's hard breaks contribute to her lack of confidence in herself? Did it affect her ability to make clear choices? For one, I have thought her crippling condition might have made her feel like being tough, to somehow compensate for her disability, and give her a false sense of confidence.

A very hard break for her came in 1930 (the height of the gangster depression era), while she was working in Cambridge, Massachusetts at one of the Boston Hospitals as a laundry attendant.

The story she told me goes like this: "I hooked up during that time briefly with an older man who also worked there. He was 27 years old, and I was 17. Just at the height of my teen years." She later shared that he came from Italy with four other brothers. They had a brief courtship, dated for just a few months. Then she broke it off with him and claims she never saw him again after that. However, her sisters knew him, so I imagine he was close to her for a while.

It was through that encounter she became pregnant with my father. And back then, that was not acceptable! It was kept under wraps for fear of judgment. To hide it, she was sent away to a reform school or unwed mothers' home to have the baby. It felt like a punishment for bad behavior to her. So, for all those months, she was made to feel ugly and dirty, of not belonging, and it was such a hard time for her. Not the fun and maturing years a 17-year-old should be having. My great-grandmother Polly did her best to hide this.

*My great grandma Polly peering out a window greeting my
grandmother Leah Jean who was coming to visit her.*

After my grandmother came out of the unwed mothers' home, my
father was given the name Thomas Miller. I was told his original name was
Tommaso, Italian for Thomas. His father's name at that time was kept under
wraps. Only my great-grandmother and her sisters knew the man's identity.
After a lot of agonizing, my great-grandmother Polly gave my father to her
other daughter, Ann, to raise until he was around eight years old or so. This
was because she was already married and established. This gave my great-
grandmother time to set my grandmother on the right track and find her a
husband. She did find someone for her, and he later adopted my father and
renamed him Leonard Fisher.

My father struggled all his life wondering who his real father was. His
mother would never tell him. I always thought that was selfish of her and hard
to understand why she would do such a thing. Was this my loving grandmother
making such a selfish choice, not considering how this would affect her son, it
made me hurt for him. I have also been told that the man from Italy knew she
was pregnant and offered to marry her, but she refused for reasons I will never
know. This man never had a chance to even think of being there for my father.
The shame my grandmother must have felt may have been one of the reasons
that caused her not to tell my father who his real dad was. But still she wasn't

thinking of him, and this bothered me. This was my father, and it hurt me to see him agonize over this. And long-term.

My Italian grandfather, Leonard Miceli on the beach with his family in Boston I believe circa 1930's.

So, it was a choice and not a good one. Her choice affected another life with lasting consequences. I guess she was too ashamed and frightened to reveal who he was. I have a lot of thoughts as to why she did this, but most I have come up with seem very selfish at best. This was one of the choices my loving grandmother made that made me realize she wasn't the perfect grandmother I thought she was, but still, I loved her. That would never change. I cannot account for any excuses why she wouldn't tell my father. It was said to protect his identity. 1932 were the Al Capone years and wild times with boot legging and prohibition and all. Need I say more? My family has such a unique history, I never knew until I was almost 40. Was my father's identity changed because of the Italian mob connection? Some say yes. Some say no. Through ancestry.com, the truth was later revealed to me.

My Father While Growing Up

Growing up, my dad never felt like he quite fit in at times, much like his mother did. While he was grateful Isaac was there and had adopted him, he always wondered about his real father. Who was he? What was he like? He imagined them spending time together. He longed for him, all his life. While Isaac loved my grandmother and my dad and tried his best to hide the truth, over time the truth became known. While he was raising my father, he became very busy and found it difficult to give him the individual attention he needed, so others stepped in. This made my father long to know who his real father was even more.

Grandma Leah Jean and her husband Isaac.

My father at age 8 circa 1939.

He and Isaac never did connect the way Isaac expected and it was unfortunate, but there was another relative my father had always admired. His aunt Ann, the one who assumed custody of him during the first eight years of his life. She was like a second mother to him as she was his foster mother for that duration. But my grandmother loved him dearly and couldn't wait to a have him as her own again, so, when my father turned eight, the custody shifted back to her. He was special and a lifetime reminder of that brief encounter with her Italian love. This man lived in her memories, and I think she may have wondered what life would have been like if she had married him. But she was only 17, and I later learned her mother stepped in with the attitude of, "What will people think?" And as hard as it was, for the first time, my grandmother complied with her mother's wishes for fear of unknown consequences.

Polly Great grandma and Grandma Leah Jean together with my cousin Baby Steven circa 1963.

This is a photo of Grandma Leah Jean and her mother, whom we called Grandma Polly. I remember visiting Grandma Polly's house and the big spreads of food we shared. I was very little but can still remember my father holding my hand on the way to Grandma Polly's house. The baby is my cousin Steven who was Aunt Barbara's son born in 1963. I later learned from my father's cousin Myron, with whom my father was close, that he was brought into this world by Grandma Polly, who was a mid-wife for quite a while. Myron, now 87, recalls the closeness he had with my father while growing up together in Boston during the 1930s and '40s. He, like many others, spoke very highly of my father's character, his joviality, and care for others, particularly family members. Myron was my grandmother's stepsister Ida's son.

Secrets Hidden

So much of what people went through was hiding in their closets with so much shame and resentment. There was always this fear of what would people think. I understand accountability, and it has its place for sure, but why did people have to suffer in silence like that? Was it necessary to hide if what you have seems different from the norm? I believe as we share our lives, others can gain strength and confidence from our story and find the courage to go on. Sharing and knowing that we're not alone is a gift. And we will never reach our true potential unless we understand the freedom of being whom God created us to be. Only then can we be free to live out the destiny He's called us to. I only wish my grandmother could have understood this concept and had the courage to be who she really was and the freedom to make things right for my father.

As I'm recalling what I was told, my grandmother was married to a man she didn't necessarily love, at least at first. She was fixed up in a marriage for convenience, so my father could be given a proper name and a good role model. Her son was illegitimate, and this bothered her, but she didn't know how to handle it. And like we all do, when we don't know how to handle things, we do what we can and hope for good results.

But this was also a turning point in her life where she began to learn more about God and lean on him. During this time of transition and uncertainty, she turned to the Catholic faith while acquiring more Italian Catholic friends. At the same time, she was wondering what life would have been like if things could have been different.

She didn't know herself much of the time. Then marrying a man out of obligation and for convenience added to her confusion and unhappiness. I have often wondered if she ever learned to love Isaac over time. According to many relatives, they felt she had; he was a good man and I believe she came to realize that. But other times, as many of us had observed, she seemed annoyed by him. Most of us knew him as a nice, sweet man, always there for her, and it was hard for him to understand her ups and downs. But he loved her, even while she kept him at a distance emotionally on occasion. It's my guess she may have resented the fact that she couldn't marry her Italian love from 1930. Much of her feelings were held inside, and counselors were scarce back then, so a lot went unsaid, causing frustration and lack of perspective.

On the flip side of things, Isaac was a good man, and from what I understand, loved my grandmother and wanted to provide a home for her and my father. He was loyal and dedicated, had a lot of integrity, and I remember him as a sweet man. I do wish my grandmother could have embraced him as a gift rather than someone to fill the gap. But she was in the midst of so much transition that I think it was hard for her to see things clearly, and people didn't have the freedom of choice back then as they do today, and I'm sure this frustrated her. The confusion caused her to turn a corner, one of making better choices for her situation. My grandmother finally did listen to her mother. She began to realize the wisdom in her council and feared how things would be if she didn't take her advice.

Like a lot of people did back then, my grandmother moved on as best she could, and leaning on the Lord was more prevalent in her mind than ever. She longed for peace and stability, which she began to realize could bring her to the place where she could live the life God intended for her. Come what may, with God in her life, she realized she could thrive instead of just survive. She thought about her unhappiness and her longing for things to be different, she prayed for direction, and as she did, things began to unfold. She wanted more children, a stable life, and siblings for my father, so he wouldn't be alone. And her attitude would affect her future and the other children she and Isaac would later have together. My father was close with them, and there was never any mention of him being illegitimate or a half sibling. They were siblings of an older brother and that was all that mattered. They did look up to him, he cared about all of them, and they all remained close knit, being there for one another while growing up.

While she and Isaac were raising her family, her health issues regressed. He worked hard and long hours as a street sweeper while my grandmother, with her limitations, began to struggle. As a result, she leaned more on her oldest daughter, my aunt Barbara, to help with the family.

The more I heard about her health issues, the more her problems reminded me of my own. She had a lot of symptoms of what we now know as celiac disease, which was not recognized back then. It's the disease I suffer from, and even in my generation, it took a long time to diagnose. I have heard it tends to run in Italian and Irish families. So that fit us, with our Italian background. Aunt Barbara told me my grandmother had to have several abdominal operations where she lost half her stomach and was very sickly as a result. In addition to polio, there was clearly something else going on. She had arthritis, as well as other ailments they couldn't account for.

It made it hard for her to be the mother her five children needed. She became so sickly that her own brothers and sisters stepped in where they could, especially her sister Ann. Over time, and as the children got older, as children of sickly parents often do, they tried to help but couldn't always understand why she needed so much rest. My father's younger brother, her son Murray, was born with health problems due to dislocated hips at birth, causing lifelong chronic pain and disability for him. So, she also had a child with challenges. This was an inherited, debilitating condition similar to one her sister Ann was born with and suffered most of her life as a result.

To add to her struggles, her son Martin had learning disabilities that were not recognized back then, so he needed extra attention. But they made it because they had family, and they stuck together. And she did her best to keep them God-centered by taking them often to Catholic services and exposing them to volunteering for the needy. She tried to give them the sense of thinking of others, but for a few of them, it didn't seem to catch on. At least not in their young adult life. However, church and family did give them a sense of security in the midst of a lot of pain and struggle, and I think my grandmother knew this.

Later, my grandmother's greatest disappointment came when, little by little, three out of her five children ended up in divorce, dividing the family. One of them was my father. Divorce is such a hard thing, and my grandmother wondered if she had failed in some way, if it was because she couldn't be the strong, healthy mother they needed. She agonized over why they had trouble maintaining relationships, in good times as well as bad. As people often do, she blamed herself for their decisions. But she later received the assurance that as a mother she did the best she could, given her circumstances. As adults, her children did have choices, and no matter how they were raised, they were responsible.

Two of her children were dedicated, as their father Isaac was, and remained married till death parted them. The other three didn't quite grasp the meaning of others and loyalty, and it came out in some of their relationships. But one of my uncle's sons learned from his father's mistake, and my cousin went on to be a good father. He was very family oriented and a loyal, dedicated father and husband, from what I understand.

Aunt Diane, his mother and one of my mentors, was quite proud of her son and she told me so often. She has since passed but was always there when I needed her. She left a legacy of loyalty and sincerity. During the course of her life's most challenging moments, she made it by clinging to family, friends, her Jewish roots, and God. And while life was often painful for her, she was never alone. It brought great comfort to her knowing that, and she in turn brought great comfort to others. In her wildest dreams, she could never have imagined the good that could come from such painful moments with disappointments. Watching her family excel brought her great joy. The closeness she had with my other dear mentor, my aunt Elaine, brought her great joy, too. What helped my aunt's son, my cousin, that she was so proud of, make good choices in life? It was that while he had an absentee father, due to the divorce of his parents, he had an amazing and loyal example in his grandfather. Isaac filled in as dad role for him. My cousin followed him and his example as a dedicated father and grandfather, and family has been and continues to be priority in his life.

I had several cousins that carried on the tradition of family, and I was in awe at what good, caring people they had become. One of my favorites was my cousin Shelley. She worked hard with family and career and became a successful lawyer. As my dad's aunt Ann's granddaughter, she followed in her grandmother's footsteps by looking at the glass half full. The joviality and positive attitude that brought her so much joy led her to a bright future. While she sought a career, like her mother and grandmother before her, family was most important in her life. We had the privilege of spending a lot of time together as children until we both went our separate ways. She had parents I really respected, and I learned a lot from them.

Our aunt Ann, like Shelley's father was for me, was instrumental in my father's joviality and love for fun and wanting a family of his own. After all, she fostered him for eight years. I know it doesn't always work out for good, but in this case, it did, and I wanted it, too.

My cousin Shelley's father, who recently passed away from a long bout with Parkinson's disease, was someone I really admired. He modeled for me an example of what a husband should be like; he didn't tell me, he showed me. When I was young, I admired him so much I wanted to marry someone just like him, and I feel I did. My husband is as her father was, kind, loyal, family oriented, and a great father. He was not only my role model but also my friend. He was so kind and great with kids in general. Do I think children need role models and the fear of God? My answer is yes! Children do learn what they live. They do seek out people to model after. You can see it in the results of the choices they make and how they live their lives. And I believe it does get passed on to the next generation, good or bad. It truly does!

Family, friends, and role models are vital to our peace and happiness and our overall growth as human beings. Had I known my grandmother's struggles as a child, it could have been a much different experience for me! I may have modeled some of her behavior of when she was young and searching for herself. It may have given me a sense of confusion and rebelliousness rather than a sense of security as I looked up to her. I felt my parents did a good job of sheltering us from the goings on in the background, and today, I'm thankful for it. It was better they didn't share with me her struggles until I was much older. They just let me experience her as she was, my grandma. Another very important tool I learned in parenting, to shield your children from bad influence as best you can and encourage the good. The rest will be their choice, hopefully good ones. Unfortunately, it doesn't always turn out that way, but it often does.

So, there is more to share about my grandmother's life. I could write a book on just her. But I want the focus to be on my whole family history and what made me the woman I am today, along with some of the role models that helped to shape my future and choices I made.

My greatest memories of Nonna were as the kind, loving grandmother that taught me about God and Rosary beads and Catholicism and how to cook good Italian food and how to embrace a good hug. That is what I choose to remember about her. Her past was her past. Her mistakes were her mistakes. It does not negate my love for her and the good things she taught me as a child. I loved my time with her, cooking, sharing, and watching her lean on the Lord in good times and tough times was all I needed to know. While she was not perfect, she loved me and my family, and that was enough to give me the grounding I needed to navigate through the future I would endure.

Her Legacy to Me

In summary, my grandmother's legacy to me was the many things I admired about her. I only saw the good in her; only who she was resonated with me. I recall one of her friends from Italy, Teresa Polcari, along with Grandma, opened an Italian restaurant in Boston called Polcari's Italian restaurant. This was sometime back in the 1950s. And if you were to go into the restaurant today, I wouldn't be surprised if some of my grandmother's recipes were still on the menu.

Her legacy has also left me some wonderful memories at her tenement apartment each weekend. Grandpa Isaac listening to the Red Sox game on his radio in his bedroom while family visited with each other there. There are good times and bad times, but what we choose to focus on makes all the difference. Family! Good, bad, or indifferent, a place of security we call home. While home is not always a secure place for some, most of us can recall enough good to override the bad and disfunction we endured growing up. And we all have it, just some more than others. To me the glass will always be half full, as this is what I learned.

A Special Memory

My grandmother had a favorite recipe, chicken cacciatore, she would make for us while we visited on Sundays back in the 1960s. I began her story with us making it together. I can still remember the aroma of it cooking, the amazing, warming smell in her kitchen, just like an Italian restaurant. I can still taste the flavors of her recipe and still hear her voice as she shared with me some of her story. Her cacciatore recipe was modified as her own version of it made from leftovers. She rarely cooked from recipes but from just plain old throwing things together. That's how a lot of Europeans cooked. I still cook that way today.

As I'm taken back to her home once more, on that day we cooked together for the family, I have one more fond common memory to share that was prevalent each time we visited.

Where I Learned to Love Baseball and Family, a Special Memory

I can still hear the voices and conversations that took place in her home as she cooked. The memories of that day bring back to me my mother and aunts conversing at the table before dinner. My cousins who were like siblings played outside and in the background, I could hear the Red Sox baseball game from Fenway Park in Boston on the radio. We all loved baseball! And these memories will remain for me as long as I am here to share them.

Voices of the Past

I can still hear in my mind the voice of the announcer, Ken Coleman, calling the plays as the crowd cheered in the stands. As my grandfather was usually listening to the game in the background as we entered the house, I remember hearing my grandmother say to him, "Isaac, turn that radio down!" He was hard of hearing, so the volume was quite loud. Gosh, you could hear it coming up the hallway to my grandmother's apartment (?). I will never forget the tenement home in the west end of Boston with neighbors close by. All seemed to be Red Sox fans, too. My father and his brothers loved their time together in Grandma and Grandpa's home, as Red Sox fans. Who wasn't if you lived in New England? This was the 1960s when Carl Yastrzemski and Rico Petrocelli were popular. Later, we had Tony Conigliaro. I'll never forget one year when Tony was seriously hurt during a game, which, as I remember, ended his career. I can still see the newspaper headlines in the Boston Globe with his picture and his eye injury. As a young person, I remember thinking how horrible it looked. I felt badly for him because I remember thinking he was kind of cute. Yes, I started noticing boys early.

This is what I remember and focus on, the memorable times for us as a family. But unfortunately, it didn't stay that way though, for most, it often doesn't. As the book progresses, you will see what I mean. Life, while it can be so good one day, can change in the twinkling of an eye and challenge us in ways unimaginable the next. What a difference a day can make. It began with my grandmother, and then my father, and one by one, my family's example impacted me, some for good, some for not so good. But thanks be to God, I knew enough to follow the good and the good Lord.

Chapter 3

My Father's Identity Crisis

Tommaso Miceli, Thomas Miller, Leonard Fisher, Who am I?

My dad at approximately age 6 on his pony,
where he is was not clear to me. Circa 1937.

The next role model in my life was my father. Dad was someone who I would describe as resilient, funny, jovial, amazing, and a little all over the place at times. Described by today's standards, perhaps he had ADD (attention deficit disorder). Back then it was thought of as just someone with a short attention span, as he had a hard time focusing. As a child, I never thought about why he was the way he was, I just thought he was fun. His joviality carried us through some rough waters.

His life choices reflected those qualities I've mentioned. He was our father, and we loved him. And we are certain he loved us. He grew up without knowing the identity of his real father. He was only told he came from Italy, so he knew he had Italian roots. The rest was kept from him for reasons not known to us. Although we have heard many accounts from people who were there, we may never know the real story. My father didn't even know, so, how could we? Or could we?

Growing up, I heard him speculate about his biological father and who he might be. He would ask his aunt Ann, his mother, uncles, cousins, anyone who could give him information. But it was to no avail. He heard vague accounts of who his father was or where he might be. Some were sworn to secrecy, and others just didn't know who he was. Most seem to know he was from a family from Italy and immigrated here. We were told he might have been an electrician. And maybe still living in the Boston area. The stories weren't always clear. My father was born either in Italy where my grandmother may have gone to have him, or according to his first birth certificate, he was born Tommaso Miller, given his mother's maiden name, in Tewksbury, Ma. But this was his second birth certificate; again, vagueness. While we are not sure what the original one said, what was consistent was that both certificates showed the father as unknown. The first birth certificate may have had his father and him listed with Italian names. So many unanswered speculations. We still don't know the whole truth as to why my grandmother kept his father's identity such a secret! There is much speculation.

I have asked these questions: was he such a bad influence that she didn't want my father exposed to his ways? Or did she just not want the father to know she was having his child? Maybe out of embarrassment to her family? Perhaps he was engaged to someone else at the same time. The answers often came back to me as vague and unclear as the questions I asked. During that era, it was a big deal to have a child out of wedlock. Things were often kept secret, for fear of rejection and judgment. Another thought I had was maybe she didn't want him to know because their relationship was rather brief. Or perhaps she didn't want to strap a new child on him, being an unwed mother unsure of where she stood with him. Question after question went unanswered, and this was perplexing and upsetting to my father and later to me. The truth wasn't always told to us, and he and I had that in common—we wanted to know the truth.

Today, along with my son Paul, I've been researching through ancestry.com, and 23andMe, along with some cousins on the Italian side of the family. This is something my father could not have done due to limitations in technology back then. His only resources were paper files and records and family accounts. Neither gave him the complete story. Unfortunately, he was haunted by this most of his life. It was difficult to observe, and it broke my heart as a child to hear him talk about it to my mother and his close friends. He asked my grandmother about this numerous times during the course of his life while she was still with us. But she never gave in, not even on her death bed. I know he had people searching for information on his real father, but to no avail, without a name or any records or information at all; back then it was nearly impossible. There just wasn't enough information to go on. His name, place of birth, and any other information was kept hidden.

My grandmother and her mother were determined for whatever reason to keep this from my father and others. And they did a darn good job, not realizing the lifelong impact it would have on my father. Crazy as it sounds, I believe they meant well, but I wish they had thought things through and did the math. His generation, and even mine, didn't have the computers and ancestry.com and 23andMe available like today. All he could do was imagine who his father might have been.

He said he often daydreamed about him being someone famous. He even wondered at times if he might have been from English royalty because his mother was born in England. But that didn't fit; he was Italian. That was a far-reaching dream for my dad, but one can dream, can't one, and I believe his imagination was what kept him inspired, hopeful, and jovial, rather than sinking into despair and missing out on what he had and the future he could have. While this bothered him, he chose to enjoy his life and appreciate the people around him, his aunt Ann especially. Deep down, he knew it wasn't realistic and was counterproductive to agonize over something he had no control over. Although over the years, he did ponder all the Italian connections and thought that would lead him to answers, but it never did. He knew his mother had a lot of Italian in her and that several of her best friends immigrated from Italy, as my real grandfather did. But no matter how hard he tried to fit this complicated puzzle together, unfortunately, he was to never know. My grandmother may have made a bad choice, but I believe God had reasons as well.

After all, to know and trust that God has everything under control and that even the very hard things we face work together for the good, can sometimes be hard to do, but it sure can be freeing to understand that everything has a purpose. We had to trust, knowing that God knew my father and there were no mistakes. But even so, life is life, and it can bring challenges that can be difficult to endure. Even with the greatest amount of faith it can bring heartache and sadness and grief and shake us to the core. We are human beings with human needs. And knowing where we come from and who we are as a people, I feel, are basic human needs. It gives us a grounding and a place to call home, a sense of belonging. Knowing that with God all things are possible, is where my grandmother, my father, and I have found strength and the will to believe and go on. And to believe whatever challenges we may face, facing them together can be a great comfort. And you never know, your circumstances may bring comfort and hope to someone else in the process.

From what I understand from documents I've seen, my grandmother was sent away to have my father, possibly to a reform school. Again, I'm not sure if it was in this country or in Italy. Either way, it was a hard time and her young age and lack of maturity hindered her in decision making. I have been told that at times she was treated quite poorly while there. Other times she was treated better. Conditions were not the greatest, and the doctors and nurses were not always kind back then. Sometimes they treated these young women as they were viewed back then, like tramps or being less than. It was sad because often they were victims. Of course, not all unwed mothers' homes were like that, but unfortunately where my grandmother was, it had its moments, as I was told. There was a lot of underlying, hidden abuse, not always obvious to the families.

But the girls were sent away to hide the shame of a premarital situation they got themselves into, as it was viewed back then. Their illegitimate children were called bastards, and it was very demeaning, to say the least, a joyful time in life turned into a nightmare. This took its toll on Leah, and left her hurt, bitter, and feeling somewhat abandoned. While her other siblings were enjoying normal lives with the normal everyday challenges of life, moving toward their futures and raising families, she was stuck as an outcast once again, feeling little support. It was there, she just didn't always see it and then take it, because she had a stubbornness that limited her ability to move forward.

Here she was, with disabilities, probably not even understanding what had happened, with nothing but shame to further encourage insecurities, anger, and bitterness. Her mother, who had been a mid-wife herself, did her best for the family's name and reputation's sake. And for my grandmother, the consequences were great. Her struggles were evident. How would she get through this? Over time, however, she would see that this illegitimate son would bring her a lot of joy with his easy going, fun-loving spirit.

My Grandmother's Struggle

I can imagine my grandmother questioning how her family could have allowed her to be sent away, feeling abandoned, to spend several months basically feeling like she was sentenced to reform school. Her days were spent with other young mothers cooking and cleaning the home they were in, being monitored with the health of the pregnancy. Sometimes there was recreation, but it still seemed like a sentence until she held my father, her first born, for the first time. And that changed everything. She fell in love with him. However, after the birth, due to her age, and the fact that she was unwed, custody of my father was handed over to her sister Ann, who was married and considered to have a stable life.

Ann raised him as her own and loved him dearly. She took care of him until my grandmother was able to marry and have some stability in her life. He remained with his aunt Ann until he was eight. Until now, she was all he knew as a mother figure. He was first known as Tommaso (Italian for Thomas), or in English, Thomas Miller and later underwent a number of name changes. In a conversation with one of my cousins (Aunt Ann's daughter) I learned that the Italian fellow did know she was pregnant and offered to marry her, but she refused for reasons that were never clear. So, after being raised by Aunt Ann, Dad's name was changed again, so his father could never find him.

When I heard this story as an adult, it saddened me that she made a choice like this, to never reveal his identity to my father. Knowing my grandmother as I did, I found it hard to understand how she could handle it this way, but as I look back, I don't think she had a choice. Her understanding of all of this must have been limiting and confusing to someone so young. And I questioned why her sisters were sworn to secrecy. While I tried to understand the disfunction, it caused me to see my grandmother in a very different light. My mother found it hard to understand and also felt sorry for my father, as she loved him and hated to see him agonize over this. He had moments where he would move on, but it always came back to haunt him.

The man my great-grandmother Polly found for my grandmother to marry, Isaac Fisher, was 20 years older, was a Russian Jew whose family had immigrated here from Russia. My grandmother wanted custody of my father so badly that she agreed to marry him. After Isaac and my grandmother married around 1939, my father was legally adopted by him and then became Leonard Fisher. He had a total identity change. My heart sank when I heard this. How incredibly confusing this must have been for him. The situation must have caused him a lot of identity confusion and took him a long time to figure out who he was. I'm referring to who he was as a person and who his people were. Identity confusion can mean a lot of things, as many of you know.

I believe he did struggle with this most of his adult life. While he remained jovial, still it effected choices he made and the way he thought. One person's decision affect another for a lifetime. Could God change things for him? I believe so, and in fact, over time due to his faith, he came to a place of peace with this, but unfortunately it wasn't until his elder years.

On the flip side, he also learned some positive things from his mother. No situation is ever all bad. There were good things, as there often are. He learned to laugh, have fun, be social, and he had his aunts and uncles to encourage him along the way. His family was large and close knit. While struggling with his real father's identity, he was far from alone in the world, he just didn't always recognize it. He was well loved and thought of but couldn't always see it. Because of his charismatic, magnetic personality, people were drawn to him. It's no wonder he later chose to be a salesman for some significant firms as a career.

Like my grandmother, he had close friends and learned through his aunt Ann to stay close to family, and she was always there for him all of his life. The toughness he learned from his mother came in handy during his challenging times in life, but her resiliency stuck for sure. He was more outgoing than my grandmother, however, and I often wondered if he inherited that trait from his real Italian father. And perhaps his aunt Ann, as she was quite grounded, stable, and jovial. I remember her as always smiling and friendly. She was a great choice to care for him. I believe this accounted for the stability and some of the good decision making he experienced, too. I believe God knew what my father needed and gave him Aunt Ann. As child, I remember her well, although at the time, I never understood why she called him "her Leonard." I now understand their close connection and unshakable bond. When Ann later had two children of her own (Michael and Elaine), he was very close with them, too. Michael was like a brother to him, and Elaine, of course, like a sister.

During the course of this book, you may hear me refer to the phrase "good, bad, or indifferent" from time to time. It was a catchy phrase my mother quoted quite a bit. My mother was the funniest woman I knew. I loved my parents and their unique personalities. They were fun to grow up with as I'll continue to explain. But she would often quote that phrase, referring to my father's story and how hard it was for him. She would say, "Right, wrong, or indifferent, those choices were made, and he needed to move on to better things. He now has his own family, and he should be thankful and not look back." She had more colorful terms, but I'll leave that to history. Let's just say it frustrated her that my father couldn't do that. She was trying to encourage him in her own way to let go, and move on, so he wouldn't be a prisoner of "what could have been" for the rest of his life. He was missing the opportunity to know who he was by just living in the now and what is. Unfortunately, it was easier said than done. And I believe he kept striving for it because he believed that one day, he would figure it out.

My Father's Story Continues

So, as my father's story continues, my grandmother was struggling with her life after marrying Isaac. Her health was challenging, declining with age, and her early in life bad choices began to take its toll on her emotionally, causing her to live in guilt and condemnation. However, she still found the energy to be there as much as she was able for my father. But it wasn't long after she and Isaac were married that the four other children came along.

So, how did my father do it as such a young child with the challenges he faced? The new siblings coming along and knowing their real father was one challenge. As they realized they had a different father, it was tough for him, and at times, I'm sure he felt a little resentful. He shared with me there were times he never felt he belonged, but he still had them as his family, and he embraced them that way. And that became his focus. At times he felt torn between Ann's family and his mother's. It must have been tough. He had his aunts and uncles who stepped in and supported him, but still he never felt like he belonged. His thoughts, as he told me, were hard to understand. He had so much support and love, why couldn't he focus on that?

In my early twenties, I once said to him, "Hey, Dad, some people didn't even have one family. At least people wanted you, why couldn't you see that?" He didn't really have an answer for me. He just smiled and changed the subject, as he often did. For reasons I may never know, he didn't always see the true picture. He was a complicated man, my father. What he didn't understand, he would often laugh off.

He struggled as my grandmother aged and her health became more challenging. He wasn't sure what to do with that. So, when she was too overwhelmed or too sick, once again her younger sister, Ann, was there to help. He turned to her and found great comfort and security in her. Her comfort brought him a place of solace to go to. She was always there for him. He had her to come alongside and guide him, especially when he felt lost and out of sync. She was his security when he felt lost or afraid. As much as he had his insecurities, he had a grounding and a place of security in loyal family members. It helped to fill the gap for him. As he began to discover what he liked, he found his place with close friends and various activities, such as horseback riding, boating, and swimming, and this seemed to redirect him.

One thing that was clear to him was that he loved to have fun! It was his escape. He became surprisingly positive and his charisma was contagious. I think it was a choice he made; he didn't like always being uncomfortable and unhappy. While he may have inherited these traits from his real father, as Italians are known for being charismatic and jovial, they are also things I believe he learned from his aunt. She was a positive matriarch of the family. Like her, Dad was one of the most playful, fun-loving people I knew. But in the background, there was his striving to fill that void of not knowing his real father, which caused him to want to search for love most of his life. Sometimes in the wrong places. Laughter and fun became a coping mechanism for him, people were drawn to him for that reason, and he was never alone. He was handsome, and yet he struggled a little with self-image. It's like the old saying, "Ten people can tell you how beautiful you are, but if one comes along and tells you you're not, you tend to focus on the one negative, and then you believe you're unattractive." I never could understand why this is, but it's true with a lot of people. I find myself doing that at times, too. It keeps us humble, I guess!

As I grew older, I came to understand my father's struggles. I believe he may have struggled with abandonment issues. He mentioned it from time to time, and there was always an underlying sadness in him I couldn't always understand, even in the midst of his laughter. But he was later also a prisoner of war, which may also have attributed to this sadness behind the joviality and laughter. I'm just speculating, but it has helped me to understand him better.

Keeping his thoughts and choices in perspective would be his greatest challenge as he navigated through his life—a challenge and void that he would learn over time could only be filled by a relationship with God. Knowing God as his real father would be his greatest freedom. Knowing his creator would reveal to him who he was, and would later make all the difference in his feeling whole.

"It's a God thing," he would say to me when I was young.

"If we have not love, we have nothing, remember, He never leaves us alone!" And he would always laugh. His laugh was contagious. And one I'll never forget. As he grew older and experienced more of life's challenges, he struggled to keep all of this in balance. For example, one of the first frustrations he experienced is that he loved his mother but didn't always understand her. He was trying to be a kid while living with a mother who unfortunately spent much of her time just trying to survive.

I understand that illness can make you feel overwhelmed and put you in survival mode, with not knowing what to expect next. Trying to function in a body that doesn't serve you well is frustrating at best. How do you live in a body that doesn't serve you well and you can't count on? It's one day at a time. You add the judgement of others to the mix, and it's a recipe for low self-worth. This was my grandmother's greatest challenge.

"What would people think," was how a lot of people dealt with things back then. How sad, that this was what swayed them in decision making. She was left with some hard memories to try to sort out on her own, being worry-driven instead of faith-driven. And it had its impact on her kids, who were trying to find their own way. They had a busy father and a sickly mother, so it left them fending for themselves at times. My father managed better than his other siblings because he had his uncles and his aunt Ann. This became apparent when they all became adults. There was my father, his next younger brother, then another brother Martin, then a sister Barbara, and the youngest was my aunt Gerry.

My father, Aunt Gerry, and Uncle Martin did pretty well in terms of life choices and the way they raised their children. But his next-to-youngest brother however, struggled with staying on track, sometimes leaving his family hurt and confused. He had a lot of health challenges of his own, he was born with dislocated hips, and I think this made it hard for him. But his decisions, right or wrong, eventually led him back to seeking the Lord and the Catholic faith, which helped him.

I was around Aunt Gerry but not as much as I would have liked to have been, mainly because of the distance geographically. I hadn't seen her in years and when I finally did, I met her kids, my cousins, and I could see what a good mother she had become. Her two children were very sweet and seemed happy. She raised them with lots of love and the fear of God. Even after the death of her husband, she still managed to remain focused on the Lord, and she enjoys her family, including grandchildren. She and I talk from time to time, and I can see we have a lot in common. She's an aunt that I enjoyed being compared to. It was her faith that drew me to her.

I was also close with Aunt Barbara. My grandmother put a lot of responsibility on her at an early age, resulting in some resentment. Grandma's health issues required my aunt as the older daughter to care for her brothers and younger sister.

My mother, in Barbara's defense, once said, "Your aunt was given too much responsibility too soon, and right, wrong, or indifferent, it was too much pressure for such a young girl. She should have been allowed to be a kid."

That caused me to feel compassion for my aunt, and I enjoyed getting to know her better. We were close while I was growing up and into my adult years, eventually going our separate ways. When we do connect, that bond is still evident as if we had talked yesterday. Aunt Barbara loved me dearly, and I knew it; she understood the importance of bonding and sharing. She was there for me to talk to if I needed it and that brought a sense of security to me. This, even as she struggled herself. I was more blessed than most with aunts and other family members, just like my dad, and I loved it. It seemed to get passed down to me, but I was willing to receive it, and I'm glad I did, otherwise I would have missed out on some special relationships.

I also looked up to Uncle Martin and Aunt Elaine. Despite her challenges with losing her parents at an early age, she was the solid, grounded one everyone seemed to go to for comfort and wisdom, advice, or just to talk. She was the Auntie Ann in my life. She was, and still is, loyal and there if I need her.

She was a mentor to me, and after my mother died, she picked up the ball and said to me, "Iris, I know how hard this is, but you know, as you have known before, I'll be there for you." She and Uncle Martin became the patriarchs of the family, and we felt secure in their mentorship and desire to help when we needed it.

Our parents' siblings can play such an important role in our lives and can make such a difference. I can't say enough about the role my aunts played in my life. Each one brought individuality, direction, a sense of security, and family bonding that I'm not sure I would have learned any other way. It taught me the importance of extended family. I thank God every day that we had them. Love and closeness of family with God at the center. Once again, it echoed its message to me: I wasn't alone!

As hard as losing my mother was for me, having the warmth and security from both aunts, Elaine and Diane, brought me comfort and security during a very devastating time. I have always admired both of them. Today, in the wake of Aunt Diane's passing, my dear aunt Elaine and I still talk and share, and I love having an auntie still to talk to. There will always be this childlike part of me that needs that older mentor to bring comfort when life seems frightening and overwhelming. We are never too old to need an auntie. And yet I am now one, even a great aunt several times, and I enjoy them and being there for them, too. I learned from the best.

I also loved my dad's brothers and spending family time with them and their children. I thought my dad's middle brother was handsome when I was little. He was tough but on occasion had a soft side, as he held me a lot when I was little. He was also a complicated man that I'm not sure a lot of people could understand back then. To others I think he appeared tough and resilient and even distant and hard at times. I didn't see him that way, I saw him as my cool uncle.

His ex-wife, Aunt Diane, was another sweet mentor in my life. She loved me dearly and spent a lot of time with me. If I called her, she always made herself available to me and others. She and Aunt Elaine were very close, like sisters, and even after her divorce from my uncle, they remained close till Auntie Diane passed away just a few years ago. I have tears in my eyes as I write this because I miss her dearly. She was an amazingly strong woman and so elegant and pretty. She and Aunt Elaine both could have been models. It was interesting, when they and my mother were all married during the 1960s to my dad and uncles, they were real head turners.

As I think back and watch home movies of them, I can't help but see a resemblance to the Kennedy women of the '60s during the Camelot era—the hair styles, clothing styles, mannerisms, cigarettes and all. I miss those days and the family get-togethers with them. As I view those old home movies with my husband, my son, and my brothers on occasion, we smile and reminisce about the things we did, the people we loved, and what we remember as the "good old days." But were those days really as good as we remember? Or is this just the way we choose to remember times past?

It brings to mind that song Barbara Streisand sang from the movie *The Way We Were* from October 1973. I saw it with my young friend Stacy. We were 14 at the time, way too young to even fathom any time of the way we were. The way we were was the way we was. (Pardon my English.) To us, it was simply a love story with a handsome actor, then-heart throb Robert Redford. I can still recall the lyrics that asked if it was really all so simple back then, or has "time re-written every line?" That's the line that struck me most. That song had a significant meaning, didn't it? It got me to think about how I remember things. Is it true, no matter what has happened in life, it is the laughter we choose to remember and what was too painful to remember, perhaps we do choose to forget? But in remembering my family and how close they were, supporting each other, I do choose to remember the good times of the way we were. My mother taught me to acknowledge the pain but move on quickly, so I wouldn't stay stuck.

And the Bible talks about "thinking about the good, fine lovely things." Philippians 4:8: "Finally, brothers and sisters, whatever is true, whatever is noble, whatever is right, whatever is pure, whatever is lovely, whatever is admirable, if anything is excellent or praise-worthy think about such things (NIV)." And I have chosen that. In doing so, I have discovered that it brings a peace and level-headedness that frees you up to move on. I've come to realize that hanging on to pain can paralyze you emotionally. Of course, everyone is different, but that's what I learned, so that's what I do.

Dad's Growing Up Revisited

Growing up, my dad was always striving to do the right thing, too, his focus much of the time was on joy and laughter, even in the midst of pain. To him the glass was often half full. Maybe sometimes too much, according to my mother. But it was the laughter he chose to remember and passed that on to me. My grandmother did her best to make life fun for her children in their growing up years. When she felt well and had more energy, she would rent cottages on Revere Beach in Massachusetts and in Kennebunk Port, Maine, always enjoying summers by the water. She felt the ocean was very healing, not only for her polio issues but also for her children's well-being. I often heard her say this to me while I was growing up. She thought this would be good for me, too, while I was healing from a childhood illness. She always encouraged me to be by the ocean as often as I could. As I remember breathing in the ocean air, I can still smell the saltiness of the breeze. Because of her influence, wherever I have lived in my adult life, most of the time there was an ocean nearby. I love the sea, Atlantic or Pacific, it's amazing.

Back to my father and his relationship with his mother. To help out, he took on small jobs where he could and did chores at home when he could, to give his sister a break. It was a pressure and responsibility he took on without really understanding who he was in the process of growing up. He tried to stay out of the way a lot and not add to Grandma's issues by making wrong choices and instead tried hard to be responsible. It was hard for him though, as he was a bit of a clown. It was his joviality, I believe, that kept him on a more positive road, able to cope with hard situations much of his life. I have been told he was always laughing and making jokes, he was quite the prankster. He was also very handsome and that's probably the reason people were very drawn to him.

My son, now an adult in his thirties, looks and acts much like him. He even has that Italian nose. I have told my son, if you ever get plastic surgery, don't you dare touch the nose, it's all we have left of Grandpa.

He laughs like my father would have, and says, "Ok, Mom, will do. No touching Grandpa's nose."

A Choice My Father Made

My dad in his late20's circa 1959 around the time I was born.

A good choice my father made, I thought, while he was growing up was when he chose the Catholic faith and began to seek God. As a result, he found comfort, strength, and peace in prayer. Later, so did several of his siblings. His example came when he used to watch my grandmother and her Italian Catholic friends do their rosary beads together while attending Mass. This intrigued him. He observed the comfort, peace, and joy it brought them. The sense of unity and supporting each other spoke volumes to him. In Italy the basically religion is Catholic. My grandmother modeled after this. She enjoyed not only attending Mass but being with close friends brought her a lot of joy and gratification.

So, my father was emulating what he saw. But to bring a monkey wrench into the situation and a bit of confusion, his stepfather was Jewish and from Russia. This gave him a little exposure to the Jewish faith; his aunt Ann was also a practicing Jew and married a Jewish man. My grandmother and Aunt Ann, if you remember, had different fathers. But my father's exposure to Judaism was limited because if Isaac attended synagogue, my father didn't go with him; he favored going with his mother. It was Uncle Martin who went with Isaac to synagogue on a regular basis, from what I've been told. So, religion was a big interest for my father and getting past the religious differences would be a challenge for him. It was the socialization that spoke to him most, I've been told. It brought him a feeling of unity.

"There had to be something to it because each time she (his mother) went, she came back looking a bit more serene and joyful. It seemed to center her, and she seemed happier," my father once told me. A contentment he saw only when she attended church and prayed. It made him happy to see her that way, as he felt she was suffering much of the time and he was concerned for her happiness.

As he grew older into his teens, he identified more and more with the Italian Catholic church and the culture. He loved the people, the food, the wine, and the language.

Also, during the 1940s as a youth, he and his friends found ways to hang out and recreate. They used to swim the Charles River in Boston on those hot Boston summer nights. They would buy ice cream or peanuts or popcorn from the vendors that would pass by. My father's favorite ice cream flavor was always pistachio. I remember every time he took us for ice cream, he always ordered that. He and his friends would ride the trolley from one part of Boston to the other. He spent time at the movies and went to the soda shops. He was on the right track, making right choices for a time, all the while in the background trying to fill a void. The void of "Who was my father?" He seemed unphased by the poverty and challenges of the life he endured growing up in the projects in the west and north end of Boston. He took odd jobs as a shoeshine boy and also paper routes when he was young, whatever it took to earn some money for the outings with friends and time spent with his brothers.

Dad with friends in his youth, on Revere Beach in Massachusetts. Circa late 1940's.

One of his longtime close friends was the actor who played in *Star Trek* from the 1960s as Mr. Spock—Leonard Nimoy. They were close, did everything together, and were known back then as Len and Lenny. My dad spoke of when they used to hide behind the school together, learning to smoke cigarettes. We now know the results of that and the price Leonard Nimoy paid with getting COPD later on in life. At least that was what the TV documentary I saw reported. I hated to hear that about him. They remained close until they both graduated high school and went into different branches of the service. They vowed to stay in touch, but due to the difference in direction life took them, they drifted apart. Something my father later regretted, but life, as it often does, can divide friendships through different experiences.

Leonard Nimoy with Dad's cousins, pictured from left to right my cousin Brenda, her father Benny, Leonard Nimoy, and Benny's nephew, my father's cousin Jerry.

He was close with his cousins and spent a lot of time on Revere Beach north of Boston, especially in his teen years, when checking out girls became the center of his thoughts. He spent time with his uncles as he got older, and from them learned some realities about his family. It's an example of one of his uncles revealing truths about the family by coming to his aid. Uncle Dick, as he was known, was particularly close to my father and came to my father's rescue often. Uncle Dick was my grandmother's sister's husband and another father figure my dad looked up to. I think his uncle took a liking to Dad because he understood that deep down my father missed having his real father. And so, Uncle Dick became like a second father to him. They were very close, and it showed. He treated my father as one of his own.

My father told me this story, and it was reiterated by his Aunt Ann later. So, I could tell it wasn't just a tale. Hearing it from more than one source has always given validity to stories as far as I'm concerned.

My Father's Uncle to the Rescue
Here is the story as I remember it.

In the 1940s, my father attended middle school in north Boston. The school had a mix of wealthy kids and some gangs, Italians, Jews, and some Irish. Much like today, I guess. My father was caught somewhere in the middle. One afternoon after school, a gang of tougher kids of Italian descent cornered my father and forced him up against the school's brick wall outside. They pushed him and made fun of him because somehow, they knew he was adopted.

They made fun of the fact that he didn't have much money and that he had a Jewish stepfather. Real prejudice in action. Heaven knows what else they came up with, but that was enough. Talk about a scapegoat! I don't think they could make up their minds on which account to give him a hard time. But it was quite humiliating and scary for my father. They called him Guinea (derogatory slang for Italian) and Kike (slang for Jewish). I could almost understand the Jewish reference, but what were they thinking as they were Italian, too? That part made no sense to me. But, whatever, I was hearing this years later.

So, my father being as sensitive as he was, had a difficult time understanding the hatred he was enduring. In addition to the name-calling, they roughed him up a bit, punching him in the face and in the stomach. While he put up a pretty good fight, he walked away with a black eye, bloody lip, and torn shirt. He was pretty upset and felt quite humiliated and alone in this. He wanted revenge. They just laughed it off, waving what looked like butter knives from their mothers' kitchens at him. They yelled threats that he'd get worse next time. Anyway, it was clear someone was praying for him because he got away with a just few bruises. Talk about West Side story! These things really took place. As he came home and entered the kitchen, my grandmother was horrified and angered in seeing my father's condition and hearing what happened. She immediately called her sister's husband Dick who became irate and acted quickly.

Isaac, Dad's stepfather, was not available, as he worked long hours. But, to his advantage, my father had those uncles who looked out for him, and he found comfort in the fact that he could go to them if he had trouble. He rarely felt alone with them in his corner. Some of his uncles, I understand (and it wasn't common knowledge back then) were connected to the Mob, so whatever he faced often was short-lived, if you know what I mean. This is an example of how they looked out for him.

After being roughed up at school, at Dick's request, my father went to see his uncle. He felt violated, singled out, and humiliated. But he was also concerned about how Uncle Dick would handle this. He walked into his uncle's house with a pit in his stomach. Knowing what his uncle's reaction might be concerned him. As my father entered the kitchen, his uncle was seated at the table eating dinner and drinking wine. I was never there and never saw it, and my father's description was very vague. All he said was, "It just looked very Italian, like something out of the *Godfather* movie. And the aromas in the kitchen were of Italian cooking from my aunt and it smelled amazing." He went on to say, "The smells made me forget the pit in my stomach and instead made me very hungry. With that kind of cooking going on every night, I could see why Uncle Dick was such a big guy."

When his uncle saw him, he reacted with a Marlon Brando Godfather-look of disdain, and in a very angry tone, said, "What happened?"

My father said, "Uncle Dick, I was beat up after school."

"Lenny, I want to know who the ringleader of this crap was?" Dick got up from the table, slamming his cloth napkin down.

"Take it easy, Dick," my father heard my aunt yell from the kitchen. So, Dad apprehensively told him, "It was Tommaso," knowing his uncle knew who he was. His uncle didn't like the family as it was, and my dad was afraid of the consequences.

But in spite of the tension between the families, Uncle Dick felt if he approached the gang leader, it would diffuse the situation. Well, no kidding! Since he was a very large man who looked like the Godfather, he could be a little intimidating to say the least. But his family knew he was more like a puppy, even though he resembled a bulldog, and I'm not kidding. He was very sweet with all of us kids, especially when we were little. I always thought he was a very nice uncle, we all did. None of us knew about the behind the scenes goings-on; we were never told as children. I had heard from other family members; however, you just shouldn't cross him, but I didn't always know what that meant. And there were others in my family like that as well.

So, my father went on to say, "It was Tommaso, they call him Tommy in English." Tommy's family was from southern Italy and it seemed he was having his own troubles adjusting to American life.

Uncle Dick found out where Tommy lived and went over there with my father at his side. Since Tommy lived in the north end of Boston, where most of the Italians who immigrated from Italy lived, and there were gang problems, he brought his gun. Oh-oh! It was known back then as "Little Italy," and I think it still is today. Most of the people, including my father, lived in tenement style homes. While culturally many people stuck together, it was the gangs that separated families at times, if you get the picture. I'm telling ya, *West Side Story*! My family lived it.

As they approached the building where Tommy lived, his uncle looked up, realizing it was four floors up and gulped at the thought of climbing all that way, knowing he was not in great shape. It was quite a climb for an older, heavier man, but he wasn't letting on how difficult it was and climbed the four levels, breathing harder with each level. It was amazing he didn't have a heart attack, and too bad the tenement homes back then didn't have elevators. I'll bet people didn't have such high cholesterol either because they were climbing stairs instead of sitting behind computers. When they arrived on the fourth-floor level, his uncle stopped for a moment to catch his breath, but as soon as his breathing settled, they approached the apartment. Uncle Dick knocked on the door, and they were surprised to see Tommy answer it right away. My father recalled how nervous he felt because he was afraid of this kid. Tommy was a slim, tall, teen with an angry expression most of the time.

Upon opening the door, Tommy's dark-complected face turned white, and he unsuccessfully tried to shut the door on Uncle Dick and my father.

"Sorry, Tommy." Uncle Dick stepped in the door, forcing it open. Now I don't know what was said after that, but whatever he did say to Tommy, according to Dad, he also pulled out his revolver and let him know he meant what he said. The long and short of it was few kids in the school bothered my father after that.

Though unsettling, it had an impact on my father. While he was grateful Uncle Dick protected him, he was always uneasy about how he did it. My father always tried to avoid conflict after that, he never wanted to solve things with violence, although he had his moments. But right, wrong, or indifferent, this was an example of family sticking together. My father, while degraded by the rough teens, was still never alone and always had his family. They loved him and he had some incredible bonding experiences—not the usual way sometimes—but he knew he was loved and protected, and this incident did teach him what not to do in dealing with people. He instinctively knew right from wrong in this situation and felt God's conviction. It was also not what his aunt Ann would have taught him. While he loved his uncle, he didn't agree with the way he handled this situation. It didn't fit with what he was learning from going to church, and the scripture he had read that says, "A gentle answer turns away wrath, but a harsh word stirs up anger" Proverbs 15:1 (NIV). I guess his uncle hadn't read that one, but it was a scripture my dad always remembered.

Chapter 4

Missing in Action During the Korean War

My father in the Air Force.

When I was growing up in the 1960s and 1970s, it was fun to see how my Dad loved watching his friend Leonard Nimoy on the show he loved so much, *Star Trek*. He shared with us how he regretted them losing touch as friends. They were buddies but then parted when they joined different branches of the service. At age 18, going on 19, they both needed direction for future careers and work, and my father felt the service could be a way to get that direction and opportunities he was searching for. Leonard Nimoy worked at odd jobs for a few years, then enlisted later toward the end of the war.

One of my father's favorite quotes from Nimoy, in addition to "Live long and prosper," was one that would stick with him the rest of his life: "The miracle is this: the more we share, the more we have; give and it will be given."

As they both grew up during hard times, they learned to make choices to better the future of their families and of those they came in contact with. Whatever they had; they gave. During this time, my dad gave what he had, his time and energy. Leonard Nimoy gave what he had in a different way. He gave his gifts in acting and singing to encourage the men in the service.

In Luke 6:38, it says, "Give, and it will be given to you. A good measure, pressed down, shaken together, and running over will be poured into your lap. For the measure you use, it will be measured to you" (NIV).

In other words, they understood that by putting others before themselves, their needs and happiness would be met anyway. While we don't do it with that intention, it's just how it works. Some call it Murphy's law, like karma, what you put out will come back to you, I call it "God's plan." His ways are perfect.

War broke out just after my dad's enlistment in the air force. So, he found himself caught up in a war, career choices were put on hold, and serving his country became a priority. He realized serving was an honor. His friend Leonard Nimoy decided to go into the army special services branch in 1953, where he put on shows which he wrote, narrated, and emceed.

We may wonder why things happen the way they do, but I have found there are reasons for everything, and I believe, as you will hear me say often, good things can come out of even the bad that happens to us. Thinking that way has helped me look at my own challenges with the glass half full rather than the victim mentality and "poor me" attitude, which I have found only leads to an attitude of inwardness and depression. My father thought the same way, and it was his example that taught me. "Thinking of others first is the key to true happiness." It was something he learned from the Catholic faith while growing up. Although like anyone else, he didn't always set an example that way. It's a tall order, who could? But he understood that it's rewarding to make a difference in someone's life and he, like many others, did his best. In this case, it was our country he was thinking of. Fighting for freedom and the cost that was involved was something he wasn't truly prepared for.

After the Korean War began, June 25th, 1950, Dad was sent on a mission right away. It was the first time U.S. jet aircraft entered battle, a ground-breaking experience I'm not sure many of us want to be in on. But my father's attitude was like many servicemen: "I wanted to serve and protect my country but had much apprehension." I always admired his attitude. While trying to figure out a career was important, serving his country was that much more important. He felt good about it, too, as it gave him confidence in his abilities.

Dad in the air force with two buddies. My Dad is on the far left. Circa 1950.

I have read in Wikipedia that Air Force F-86 Sabre jets took control of the skies, as American fighter pilots bested MiG-15 fighters and their pilots in combat against aircraft, and the Russian tactics of the Soviet 64th Fighter Aviation corps. They were World War II era prop-driven F-51D Mustangs that were pressed into the ground air support role. And large formations of B-29 super fortresses flew for the last time on these strategic bombardment missions. The Korean War my father found himself in the middle of also saw the first large-scale use of rotary-wing helicopters. During this time, my father flew one of these helicopters during a mission. It has been documented that the USAF suffered 1,841 battle casualties, of which 1,180 were killed in action. It lost 1,747 aircraft to all causes, including 1,466 to operational causes.

During one of my father's missions, his helicopter was shot down by Soviet pilots, but the rest of the story is unclear to me as my father had a hard time recalling the horror he experienced. It was painful for him to recall. He was rather short and vague in his story to me and others about his experience, but I can only imagine what took place. I have seen enough war movies.

He was shot down, taken into custody, and held as a prisoner of war. He was missing in action through December of 1950, almost six months. Our president at the time was Harry S. Truman, and he had the military looking for him and other service men missing in action.

Dad coming back from being a Pow, he looked terrible in this photo. You could see the struggle on his face. Circa 1950 during the Korean war.

Along with President Truman and the military, the main person who orchestrated the search for him was then-Senator John F. Kennedy. It was a grey, cold, fall afternoon when Kennedy came to my grandmother's door with some soldiers to inform her that her son was missing in action. As he broke the news to her, her heart sank. She received the news alone as her other children were in school and her husband at work. The news of her oldest son missing in action was more than she could bear. This was a very scary time for my grandmother. As she later broke the news to his other siblings, they feared he was gone forever. She began telling friends and family members, who held prayer vigils. My grandmother, clinging to her rosary beads, prayed with her friends daily, and felt comforted by all the support but was still afraid for her oldest son.

"What is he going through?" she would ask herself. "Is he alone, is he sick, is he afraid?" Her thoughts were running away with her. Months went by and still no word of Dad's whereabouts. She tried not to imagine what he was up against and what might be happening to him. But Senator Kennedy remained steadfast in his search for him and other servicemen missing at the time. And this is why; let me share a little of President Kennedy's story from my own perspective.

John F. Kennedy executed an astonishing act of heroism during World War II. Many of you have heard his story from history. But I'll give you a little refresher.

On August 1st, 1943 then-Lieutenant John F. Kennedy's PT 109 had an encounter with a Japanese destroyer. It was the most famous small-craft engagement in naval history. It was evening in Blackett Strait, south of Kilimanjaro in the Solomon Islands. The thick blackness that

night could have been disorienting even to the most experienced sailors. The PT 109 was one of 15 boats stationed at what was known as the Tokyo Express. The Tokyo Express was made up of three Japanese destroyers acting as transporters, with a fourth serving as an escort. In the blackness of night, the patrol boat encountered three destroyers, and as you can imagine the encounter did not go well at all. Thirty torpedoes were fired from U.S ships, not damaging the Japanese ships at all. And no U.S. ships suffered damage or casualties. Boats that had used up their torpedoes were ordered home. The few that still had torpedoes remained in the strait for another try. The PT 109 was one of those left behind.

Kennedy rendezvoused his boat with two others: PT 162 and PT 169. The three boats spread out to create a picket line across the strait. It was now about 2:30 a.m. when a shape loomed out of the darkness about 300 yards off PT 109's starboard side. First, Kennedy and his crew thought it was one of their PT boats. When they realized it wasn't, but was in fact a Japanese destroyer, it was too late. There was not enough time to react. So, the destroyer, later identified as the Amangiri, struck the PT109, and to make a long story short, sank it. Kennedy himself was knocked around the cockpit while other crew members were tossed in the water. There was only one man below deck who miraculously escaped, although he was very badly burned by exploding fuel. Kennedy feared the boat would go up in flames and ordered the rest of the men to abandon ship. In the water, Kennedy swam to help one of the injured men and towed him by a life vest strap. He had been on the swim team at Harvard University, and that worked in his favor. All the men were injured from impact in various ways and became exhausted from trying to swim to safety. Well, to continue to make a long story short, Kennedy and the remaining men that survived swam to safety.

The PT109 remained afloat for a while, but finally after taking on water, sank on the morning of August 2nd. John F. Kennedy was decorated as a war hero. And when he was asked how he became a hero; his answer was funny.

"It was involuntary, they sank my boat." He was quite a man. So, now he was trying to save my father. He became a personal hero to my family back then. It was as if he had taken my father by the life vest and pulled him to safety. What happened next was so incredible.

He sent my grandmother a personal letter in November 1950, which my father saved and later had framed, stating they were still searching for him but to no avail. Then finally, after months, he was found. It was noted that after being shot down, he was taken prisoner by the Russians, held captive and tortured for information. He was given some form of truth serum and other drugs. The impact it had on him was unknown in some ways and obvious in others. After many arduous months of captivity, he was finally rescued but had been given a medical discharge from the service because of all the damage he suffered both physically and mentally from his captivity.

Hearing this story broke my heart. The father I knew was so upbeat and he was there for us, at least most of the time. My father had a big heart and loved us dearly, especially while we were very young. At times though, he was limited in his outreach to us as children. While he had this joviality and playful spirit, there were times when he seemed distant and preoccupied and even a little sad. He also was easily overwhelmed by circumstances, which is probably why he liked to play and laugh so much. It likely brought him a level of peace, and a safe place to be in the wake of having what he later thought was post-traumatic stress disorder from his ordeal. But as children, we just thought he was a fun person, and we also had cues from my mother when to leave him time to be alone. My mother had a hard time keeping him focused, but it worked out for us as a family, at least for a while. She made sure we knew we were loved and that she cared about him.

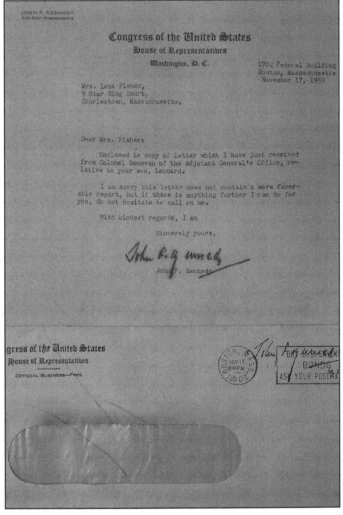

The letter from then Senator Kennedy, who later as you know became President in 1960, declaring they were looking for Dad, but to no avail.

When he was missing in action was such a sad time for my grandmother. When he returned, she had to care for him and nurse him back to health. She had to explain to the other children what had happened and assured them that in time their brother would be all right. Eventually, he did recover, but he was never quite the same. He suffered flashbacks from the horrific captivity he endured and suffered with an anxiety disorder that remained with him the rest of his life, which would account for why he felt easily overwhelmed.

The things our service men and women have had to endure in all the wars. They deserve a lot of honor and praise sacrificing their lives for our freedom. This is something we should never forget.

Chapter 5

Life Can be Challenging, but Respite is on the Horizon

So, my father recovered with the help of medical personnel and family after his captivity. With that support he began to, over time, feel safe again.

It was now May of 1952, and my father was on the mend and able to work again. The family was very grateful! (And by the way, after all that, my father became a staunch democrat.) He later voted for John F. Kennedy for president, as he was his hero; after all, he was instrumental in saving his life. It wasn't long before he went back to work for a lumber company called Plywood Ranch. Also, during that time, a close friend of his who was concerned for him thought it would be good for him to start dating again. The last real girlfriend he had was back in high school, a young girl named Irene.

Dad with his first love, Irene back in 1947. The car you see behind them was a 1947 mercury, her family's car at the time.

Of course, he thought she was the love of his life, but the war and circumstances drew them apart. So now at age 21 and back on his feet, he was ready to date. In those days, people married much younger; anyone in their early twenties was considered ready for marriage. So, his friend arranged a blind date. As they went out together, his friend, his girlfriend, and you guessed it, my mother all went out to dinner together and to a movie. I was told they had an amazing evening.

Mom and Dad on a date, this may have been an engagement photo. Circa 1952.

The movies were pretty exciting back in the early 1950s. Popular actors and actresses were Gary Cooper, Elizabeth Taylor, Jimmy Stewart, John Wayne, Bette Davis, Audrey Hepburn, Lucille Ball, Desi Arnaz, and James Dean, to name a few. My mother was particularly fond of Doris Day and Donna Reed. I'm not sure what movie they saw, but knowing my father, it probably was a comedy. Humor became a coping mechanism for him with the post-traumatic stress disorder he suffered from. However, my mother loved the Alfred Hitchcock movies, like *Vertigo, Dial M for Murder*, and that old musical with Gene Kelley called *Singing in the Rain*. Today, I watch American movie classics, and I love the old movies. My parents loving them made me love them, too. I have vivid memories of how they talked about the movies they saw back then and what they thought of them. To me, it keeps the memories of my parents alive. I was one of those children who was blessed to have had good parents. Not perfect but loving. My parents, while together, loved to be social and have a good time.

So, my father and mother's first meeting went well. I was told they were really drawn to each other and enjoyed their first date. They both told me it was love at first site. As time went on, they fulfilled a need in one another, a void that needed to be filled. It's weird for me to think of my parents as romantically involved; to me they were just my parents. As children, we don't think of our folks as human, but they were very human with human needs. It brings me joy to think of them being happy together, at least for that season of their life. I can't picture them any other way. However, even now I can't envision them as lovers. Eew!

My mother fell head over heels and never stopped loving him. His good looks, charm, and joviality were what she was drawn to. He was fun, and my mother needed that in her life at that point as her life was challenging. She was caring for a developmentally disabled sister and working to help her widowed mother. There's a lot to tell there, and I will as the book progresses.

The idea of marriage in her young mind may have been a way out of a hard life and into happiness and fulfillment. And it was for a while, but like most, she found life certainly had its ups and downs. My father was enthralled with her, too. What he saw in her was stability. She was very grounded, hardworking, loyal, helpful, family oriented, and she was fun-loving and social, too, given the opportunity. She kept things in motion and together. She was the most stable thing in all our lives. I had been told by someone that she would do anything for her family, and I was blessed to witness this repeatedly. The woman rarely thought of herself, and my father could see this, they had so much fun together while they were married. After that first blind date, they were together as much as possible. They dated just two weeks and then became engaged. Can you imagine? As I heard their story, I often wondered if they moved too quickly into marriage. But lots of young people did back then, it was common to move into family life very young.

My parents wedding photo, July 10, 1952.

They were married on July 10th, 1952. As I imagine what that year was like and what they might have been encountering in the world around them, I took a moment to look up some information to see what was happening at that time. History tells me that in 1952, the first Holiday Inn opened, and the *Today* program debuted on television's NBC station. Speaking of which, while there weren't televisions in all homes in 1952 yet, you'll be interested to know that the first electronic television was invented in 1927. Since one of my parents' best friends was a television repairman at the time, my dad said he often spoke of the history of television. They got inside information to the history of this common-place device we all have today. Allow me to elaborate on our common place entertainment box:

The first electronic television was invented by 21-year-old Philo Taylor Farnsworth. History tells me, he lived in a house without electricity until he was 14. We may never know if it could have boredom that drove him to invent the television. No matter the reason, I learned that as late as 1947, only a few Americans owned televisions. You have to wonder how this niche invention became a living room mainstay. And for a bit more history, prior to electric televisions, we had mechanical televisions as early as the 1800s. One of the first mechanical televisions used a rotating disk with holes .Two inventors worked independently to create this device—Scotsman, John Logie Baird and American, Charles Francis Jenkins. Both were invented in early 1920. By 1934, all TV's had been converted to the electronic system. All early systems were in black and white while the first color TV was theorized in 1904. The first television stations appeared in America in the late 1920s and early 1930s. It was Not until 1938 however, that American electronic televisions sets were produced and released commercially. In light of Its revolutionary history, it's hard to imagine today that American networks play thousands of different programs daily and every one of them owes its existence to America's first television. Television went from a niche technology to a critical form of communication found in living rooms across the nation, and around the world.

Other happenings in history in 1952 included the polio epidemic which became a frightening scare for parents (50,000 estimated cases), and my Mom and Dad worried about this effecting their future if they were to have children. The diary of Anne Frank was published for the first time, which was interesting news since it hadn't been long since the Holocaust ended. Nelson Mandela was arrested that year, and my role model Mother Teresa opened a home for the dying and destitute in Calcutta. Puerto Rico became a self-governing Commonwealth of the United States. Communist teachers were banned from teaching in public schools, and it was reported that the London smog killed 4,000 people. That was big news at the time. It caused a lot of fatal lung ailments. Terrible story!

Also, in 1952, despite the war in Korea, Americans considered themselves to be prospering with the average worker earning $3,400 per year, and a college teacher could expect to earn $5,100 per year. Three out of five families owned a car, two out of three families had a telephone, I'm certain my mother was one, and one in three homes now had a television, so TV was on the move as home entertainment, as I said, it came a long way. The average woman in

America would be married by 20 and looking forward to raising a family. Housewives (stay-at-home moms) were common, and the home was more secure and stable as a result. Fast food restaurants were growing in popularity, many more cars in America were now fitted with automatic gearboxes and gas cost $.25 per gallon. Twenty-five cents a gallon? Yikes, we'd all be very wealthy with that price compared to today. Then the world's first passenger jet, the Comet, was produced in the UK, signaling the start of faster and cheaper air travel in later years. And what about music during that year?

Popular songs back in 1952, which I particularly liked, were "Jailhouse Rock" by Elvis Presley, "Mack the Knife" by Bobby Darin, "Bye-bye Love" by the Everly Brothers, "Blue Suede Shoes" by Elvis Presley, "Goodness Gracious Great Balls of Fire" by Jerry Lee Lewis, to name a few. I know my parents liked those songs and so many others. My father, being of Italian background, loved Dean Martin and Mario Lanza, the famous Italian operatic singer.

This gives me a picture of how life was when they were first together as a couple. In their first year together, they were hard-working but very social, and loved their family and friends. As the years progressed, they spent a lot of time at community center events where they met many people, and they went to a lot of dinner parties. Every weekend was a social event. My father and mother were quite happy.

Dad and mom looking like Dick Van Dyke (Rob Petrie) and Mary Tyler Moore (Laura Petrie) a fictional couple on the T.V. show "Dick Van Dyke" from the early 60's. They remind me so much of them.

As I look back at photos and home movies, recalling memories of them, it was much like the old Dick Van Dyke show with Laura and Rob. My parents were quite like them. My father was just like growing up with Dick Van Dyke because he was so silly, goofy, and laughed a lot, which was amazing considering what he had endured during the war. As I said before, he loved to have fun and play! He even resembled the actor somewhat in his looks. My dad was tall and thin and attractive like Dick Van Dyke. I was told by many relatives that the room would light up when he walked into it, as he was very charismatic. He was fun and always laughing and smiling. I'm certain he had his moments of grieving from the war, or life in general at times, but this was the side of him we saw most. When he did get angry, and he did on occasion, it was short lived, and he would move on to something positive fairly quickly.

It wasn't long before their first child was expected, the first grandchild in the family on both sides. You would have thought a princess was being born. Princess Judith, my oldest sister, came along in May of 1953. Both sides of the family celebrated. She was a beautiful baby with perfect features. And for the first five years, she was an only child and quite doted over. And of course, my parents and grandparents loved every minute of it.

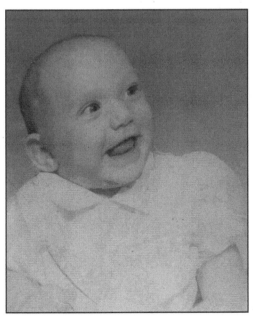

My Baby picture May 1959.

Then my brother Alan came along in August 1957, then me in May 1959, and then finally my brother Lance in February 1966. Life was good for our family for the most part. Like my father's family, we had a lot of family and friends around us, and we were very social. We were never alone it seemed. We, like our parents, became social butterflies and enjoyed each other as siblings. I guess you could say we inherited that charismatic, joviality from our dad. Dad, with the encouragement of my mother, excelled at a number of different jobs. He had my mother's support, and if he struggled, she encouraged him along, sometimes with an iron fist. She was a strong woman of Russian descent. What can I say?

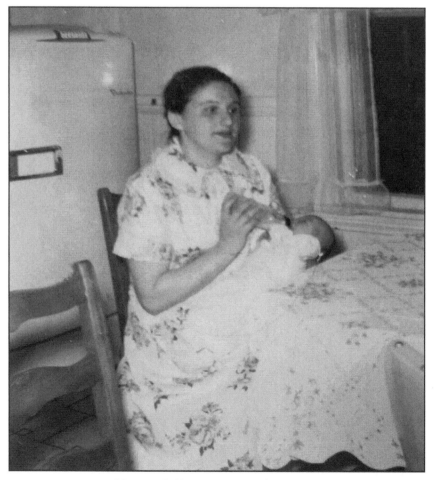

My mom holding me as an infant, 1959.

My mother was tough but could also be very funny and loving at the same time. She was a very determined woman with a lot of tenacity, and she loved her family. We got away with nothing, and yet, in contrast, occasionally with everything. She loved to give to us, but at the same time, demanded respect and loyalty. She was the glue that held us together. And I can honestly say she was always there. Try and blow her off! Forget it! She was staying with us.

"From the womb to the tomb," she used to say to us. OK! I'd think to myself and wondered what that meant. After that comment, I had this weird picture of her always living with me, even when I got married. I had to give this some thought. I loved my mother but didn't want to be smothered. And yet, that ship had sailed long ago. She wanted us for herself and made that abundantly clear.

But before I get into my life and events, I wanted to give you a little background on my mother's side of the family. Oy!

She was of Russian Yiddish descent, unlike my father of Italian descent—two very strong but different cultures to be raised in. My brother Lance has said on more than one occasion, "No wonder we are so resilient and determined, we had the Bolsheviks on one side and the Mafiosi on the other." While we got a chuckle out of that comment, we couldn't help but know it certainly had some truth to it.

My mother's family came from Zaslov, Russia and immigrated here during the Bolshevik revolution. You see what I mean by oy! What they went through!

It was a scene, like the movie *From Russia with Love*, a 1963 James Bond thriller/action movie from Ian Fleming's book by the same title. Sean Connery starred as agent 007. I was a Bond fan, as was most of my family. There was so much passed down from my Russian grandmother to us with love. She enjoyed making special Russian dishes for us and share the family stories from Russia that went with the meals she served to us. I loved to listen to her interesting stories about her family! Some were hard to listen to and imagine; others were quite pleasant and entertaining. They were about her life and growing up at the turn of the century during the Russian revolution. She and only two other siblings (out of 11) survived the revolution and came to the United States. If you've ever seen the movie *Fiddler on the Roof*, the story of her immigration from Russia was even more likened to that than the Bond movie I mentioned.

Pictured below from left to right: My grandmother at age 18 in the pink dress, her mother seated (Martha Kaplinovich), her sister Bessie, and her husband Avram and their three children, (Jenny, Hymey, and Esther). Her father is seated on the far right with the beard and hat. This photo was originally in black and white; my mother had it colorized for her home sometime around 1974. The photo is circa 1920. Just before the Bolshevik revolution broke out.

I would go over to her house when I was very young because we lived nearby. I loved to have breakfast with her. She lived in a grey house with a side porch that she called the piazza. She was a petite woman with an erect bearing that commanded respect. In English her name was Rose, and I always think of her when I see roses, even to this day. From Russian to English, the name Rose is translated to Rhazelle or Rosa. Then there's Yiddish, which was the European version of Hebrew then pronounced "Royz." In any language, she loved roses. You see, there were rose bushes on the slope beside the stairs that went to the piazza door. When it was springtime, I breathed in their fragrance as I waited for her to answer the door. Upon my arrival, I could see her peering through the kitchen window. She'd turn her head this way and that to make out whose face was behind the lace curtain. She always wore an expression of apprehension until she saw it was me. Then, I would hear multiple clicks of lock after lock as she unbarred the door that protected her from a decaying neighborhood, where she had been broken into once while she was home.

Bobe and Zadie in their home in Revere, Massachusetts Circa early 1960's.

While listening to her unlocking the multiple locks, I was thinking about the break-in that happened in the early 1970s. I cringed at the thought of this happening to her. The robbers tied her, my grandfather, and my aunt Ruthie up and stole what they could get. It was difficult to hear about this, but I was so grateful they were all okay. Thank God, the thieves didn't hurt them, although my brother Lance recalls our grandfather getting roughed up a bit and ending up with a lot of bruises about the face. After he related that to me, I then remembered it.

Auntie Ruthie in her elder years, circa 1989.

Then as the door opened, I remember her giving me the biggest smile and held out her arms for a hug, saying, "Iris'l, you're here." This was her Russian/Yiddish pet name for me (my other siblings had pet names from her, too). Then this tiny woman would hug me. She had a teased coif (hairdo) that looked like brown cotton candy, the style of the day. People back then said she resembled Rose Kennedy, then-President John F. Kennedy's mother. It was a major compliment to be told you look like the president's mother, as his mother was a very attractive woman. So, we called her our Bobe, which means grandmother in Russian/Yiddish. True spelling of that is "Bobe." She always dressed well. As I grew up, she always told me how nice and pretty I looked.

With a knitted brow and holding me at arm's length for a good look, she would say in a heavy Russian accent, "Iris'l, you look so pretty in your new outfit, but you are too skinny." (Something I'd give my right arm to hear today. But as we get older, our bodies do change.) "Lovely." But being too thin at the time had a lot to do with celiac disease that I didn't know I had at the time! I got diagnosed with celiac disease much later on in my thirties.

Bobe and Zadie together mid 1970's.

She invited me in. "Come sit on the piazza and I will get you a nosh! What would you like?" The choices were sponge cake, mandelbread, poppy seed cookies, and even Wheatena cereal, all made from scratch and no preservatives but all wheat products. I loved all of these but didn't like the digestive upset after, nor did I understand why I was getting that. I used to question why I never felt well around mealtimes. But I have to say, everything she made was delicious, and I knew it was made with a lot of love and healthy ingredients.

Bobe and I would sit and visit, and she shared some of her cooking thoughts with me. I would first answer her questions until the conversation turned to the past, as it did so often. These were the stories I loved to hear, those stories about relatives I never met and about the Russia she fled as a young girl. Then, I would ask a question of my own, such as, "What was the name of the village where you grew up, Bobe?" I always listened so carefully because I loved her and felt what she felt, even at a young age. Her spoken English was still very poor, and she couldn't read it either. She had newspapers delivered to her home that were in Russian or Yiddish. The Italians I knew also got newspapers from Italy or local news translated into Italian. As a youngster, I learned to read Italian that way, inspired by my father's mother. Back then there were so many immigrants from Russia, Italy, etc. that they made newspapers available to people who couldn't read English. Thinking back on this, it was a really neat thing to help them feel a part of the culture here, a little bit of familiarity went a long way.

Anyway, back to Bobe sharing with me.

"I grew up in the village of Zaslavl near the city of Minsk," she told me. "I was a beauty then, though you might not guess it now." Hey, was she kidding? She was a dead ringer for Rose Kennedy! She'd laugh when I would remind her of that.

She went on, "Anyway, I was just coming of age prior to the Russian revolution. I had a big family of 11 brothers and sisters but only three of us lived to grow old. I know it sounds hard, and it was. There were no antibiotics or shots for polio or measles. It was hard to get enough food for the whole family and to keep warm and dry in the bitter Russian winters. To look at me, I was just a little bit, but I was a healthy, strong girl. My cheeks were pink, and I had thick dark hair that hung down all the way to my waist. All my sisters were jealous of my hair. I used to wear it in two braids crisscrossed on the top of my head like a queen's crown. I had the family's dark eyes, and I used them to tease all the boys my age."

At my young age, it was hard to imagine my very prim and proper grandmother teasing boys. Hey, that was my job! While it was hard to picture my grandmother teasing boys, I continued to listen while smirking to myself. She said she only did it for fun because there was only one boy she really loved and wanted to marry. His name was Mache (*pronounced mayshee*), which translated in English was "Morris." She went on to tell me that they had known each other since childhood, and he was always her favorite. He even talked of marrying her when she was in her late teens. He didn't want to live without her. Through her I learned what to look for in real true love that would last! It's funny, but I married a man much like Morris and have been married now 38 years. I'll tell his story later. You see how you can learn from the generations before us. Especially about how to tease the opposite sex. I'm joking! I was teased about being a prude.

On a more serious note, Bobe shared that unfortunately while she and Mache were thinking of marrying, political tensions in Russia were mounting. Life for Russian Jews became increasingly difficult. There were "pogroms" in all the villages. Pogrom is a Yiddish term for an organized massacre of helpless people. It was terrifying for me to hear Bobe's account of this at times. The

Gentiles organized pogroms against all the Russian Jews. She described how they stampeded into her village on huge horses, like in the movie *Fiddler on the Roof*. The galloping of the horses sounded like a horrific thunder. The dust they kicked up looked like a tornado coming to destroy them. They looted the Jewish shops, burned Jewish homes, and raped the Jewish women. They took whatever they wanted and killed anyone who got in the way.

My great-grandmother had asthma, and she had a bad attack during one of the raids in her village. My great-grandfather Avram (Bobe's father), couldn't do anything for her during the chaos. There were no doctors around, and no one to help her, so she died. I have asthma myself and can't imagine this! I have woken in the middle of the night gasping for air, but I had an inhaler. It was awful to think that my great-grandmother died that way. When my grandmother told the story, I could see it still affected her.

After my great-grandmother's death, my great-grandfather decided it was time to leave Russia. He'd seen too many of his family members die. He wanted a better life for the remaining children, so he began making plans for escape. So, to not be noticed, my grandmother and her brothers and sisters were taken one by one to the Poland border by guides her father paid. They were smuggled across in a small band with other Jews who were also desperate to escape. My grandmother was one of the first in the family to make the trip. After crossing the border, she made her way to Warsaw, where she waited for the rest of her family. Warsaw was like heaven compared to where they had been. There were no soldiers. The streets near the train station were paved with beautiful tiles. There were great opera houses and fine museums. The streets were full of colorful markets filled with food and trinkets. There was music and theater. It was like a new city compared to the old village she had left behind. She waited 13 months in Warsaw for her family.

"It would have been a wonderful time," she told me, except that she was preoccupied worrying about her family. She wondered if she would ever see them again.

Finally, they came and were all together again. Her older sister, Bessie, had the hardest time of them all. She had been married by then with a home of her own. All the plans were in place, the guide was waiting, and the bags were packed. The night before her turn to leave, the Russian soldiers got wind of her plan and raided her home. They opened all her luggage and took everything they wanted: silver that had been in the family for generations, jewelry, candlesticks, and handmade linens covered with embroidery and lace that were the pride of her household. Then, the soldiers beat Bessie almost to death as her children watched.

My grandmother said, "She was lucky they didn't rape or kill her." She was in prison for two weeks and then released.

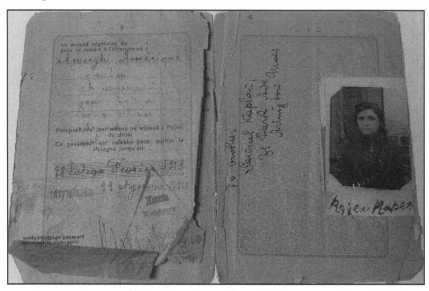

My Bobe's passport photo at age 18. She was then known as Rose Kaplinovich. Coming to this country they shortened her name to Rose Kaplan in English. My brother Lance often commented on how very much I looked like her. I still do. As I'm aging, I look in the mirror, and want to say Oy!

Her sister Bessie's passport coming from Russia.

Eventually, she and her children were able to join my grandmother in Warsaw. From Warsaw they traveled to Paris, and from Paris, went on to Holland where they boarded a ship sailing for Ellis Island with many other emigrants. The farther they got away from Russia, the safer they felt. But they weren't to America yet. The ship they sailed on was dirty and crowded. Many people were sick. Day after day, the waves of the sea tossed them to and fro. My grandmother said it was hard to sleep. There was food for them, but it was terrible. She said she liked to stand on deck and look for land because the hold of the ship smelled so bad. She couldn't wait to see the country where she and her family would be safe at last. My grandmother was only 18 years old when she experienced coming to America on such an arduous journey. No wonder she was so strong. She had to be. As I listened to her tell this story, it was hard to understand every word because her English was so poor. But I was both fascinated by the stories and chilled to realize these things really happened to people in my family. And I thought a burst appendix and celiac disease was bad! What was I complaining about?

In New York City at Ellis Island, they were detained for six weeks while they were screened for diseases, etc. They then traveled to Boston to start a new life. She found work as a seamstress in a garment factory. Then, she met my grandfather (Joseph Millman). They married and had two daughters (my mother and Aunt Ruthie). Even though she loved Joseph, she never forgot Morris. They were separated during the revolution and she had no idea if he survived.

This is a photo of my mother's father about a month before the fire in her home.

She never forgot the friends and neighbors and family members lost. My grandmother lived with Joseph until my mother was ten years old, in May 1942. That day was a sunny, beautiful afternoon. While my grandmother was at work, my grandfather headed up the street where they lived. On his way home, he would stop to pick up my mother who would usually be playing at a friend's house under the supervision of her mother, also an immigrant from Russia.

As he approached my mother and her friend, he motioned for her to come with him to head home, which about a block from what my mother described. She was just a little girl, so it may not have even been that far. As they began to walk, they heard the sound of fire engines. At that point, my mother's friend ran to my mother and grandfather to see what was going on. My grandfather gasped and grabbed my mother by the hand. As they approached their home, they realized that it was on fire. In all the excitement, my grandfather fell to the ground. He died instantly of a heart attack while holding my mother's hand. She kept trying to shake him to wake him up. But he never responded!

Mom at age 10 with Bobe, her mother in front of their home, this photo was taken just before the fire in their home.

My mother in a grade school Photo around age 10. Circa 1942.

The impact this had on my mother was lifelong. She never got over the feeling of abandonment after that. She loved her father, and it hurt her deeply that he died right in front of her. My mother became a strong woman as a result. Hardships in life can either make or break us. My mother and grandmother chose strength and moving on over crumbling in times of great trials. I am so grateful for these role models in my life, where giving in to weakness was never an option or even a thought! My mother was the apple of her father's eye, and she loved him so much. They were very close, and my mother would always miss the attention and love her father gave her. My mother never shared that story with me until she was quite elderly. When she did, it helped me to understand better her difficulty with abandonment issues. I loved my mother so much, it hurt me to hear this, but it certainly helped me to understand her tough exterior. And tough she was.

After the death of my grandfather, my grandmother went on to raise her two daughters. She worked hard as a seamstress in Boston, a trade she learned in Russia. My mother took odd jobs to help with the finances and often worked at local Jewish or Italian bakeries or delis. Life was challenging for my mother and grandmother. In addition to losing my grandfather, they had to care for my developmentally disabled Aunt Ruth. But they did Okay. They had each other, other family members, and always very close friends to lean on. In the midst of this, my mother managed to have quite the social life. She always recalled to me how close her classmates were and all the fun she had with friends in between having to work. She told me in ninth grade she was in the same class as Albert DeSalvo, who later was known for his antics as the Boston Strangler. Later in the 1960s when it was reported on the news that he was caught as the Boston strangler, she and some of her classmates couldn't believe what they were hearing. "We went to school with the Boston Strangler?" they would say.

Here is a copy of the Boston Globe reporting on the capture of the Boston Strangler. My mother and her classmates were horrified to think they were in homeroom with him in their schooldays. My mother said she sat next to him in one of her classes. She said, he was a little strange. No kidding!

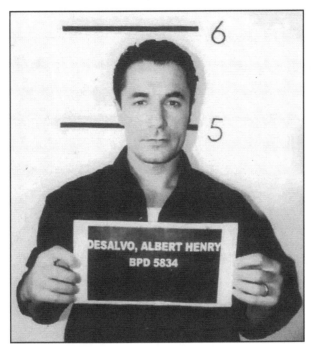

Boston Strangler upon his capture.

Speaking of school, my mother recalled a special gift my grandmother gave her for her 16th birthday—a typewriter. My mother was interested at the time in writing. I still have her typewriter as a memento. I guess my mother and I had something in common. I'd like to mention on another note that my grandmother was my first godly example. As a devout Russian Orthodox Jew, she prayed often and trusted God. All the time I was growing up, she would often light the candles on Friday night at Sabbath and pray, believing for God's provision and strength. She would also take me to shul (or temple), as it was referred to back then, just the two of us. It was special for me. Memories I will always hold dear.

Back to my mother's childhood, during her teen years, while trying to adjust to her father's death, she worked hard, helped my grandmother with her sister, graduated high school with her best friends, dated several Italian boys (I have the photos to prove it). And then she went on a blind date after high school and fell in love with my father, another Italian, although my mother assumed he had some Jewish roots, too. But I think that was more for grandmother's benefit, as she really wanted my mother to marry someone Jewish.

Aunt Ruthies High school graduation photo, she too, could have been a model. She was beautiful.

My mother remained in the Boston area and stayed close with her friends from high school. She had a close-knit class that met for reunions about every two years, it seemed. It was her life. She always enjoyed the closeness and security of having close friends and family. I guess I learned that, too. I really wish the culture of today could know the love and benefit of close relationships. We do need each other. As I have said already, when you go through those hard times, it's very difficult to do it alone. A lonely place to be. It can be very isolating and anxiety provoking.

Later on, after my mother had been married for a while, at age 27 and now with three children, another interesting thing occurred. One morning my grandmother was walking to work. As she approached the factory where she worked, and began to open the door, she glanced down the street. As she gazed into the sun, which was blinding her a bit, she noticed a man walking toward her who looked vaguely familiar. Because it was hard to see, she walked toward him, and as she got closer, he recognized her. Her heart sped in up in disbelief and she backed up for a moment. It couldn't be, but it was! It was Morris, her old love from Russia. She was dazed and even a little confused by the chance meeting, but it was him.

Well, they immediately realized (as the conversation progressed) that they were both widowed with children. They shared and embraced with absolute delight. They agreed to meet after she got off work to further catch up on their lives.

Was this a coincidence that he had been recently widowed also? I doubt it! These things don't just happen, it was an answer to her prayers. God is faithful, and his timing is always perfect. My grandmother was a praying, God-fearing woman. This was certainly God's answer to her prayers! You know, they fell back in love and soon married. They were in their 50s by then. Morris was well-to-do in a fur business he had worked hard for. Nothing was handed to either one of them. He took very good care of my grandmother for the remainder of her years, and my grandmother never had to work again. Finally, she reached a place of peace and rest provided by the man she never forgot and always wanted to marry. Fairy tales really can come true!

Bobe, like my other grandmother, loved to cook and went on to make many potato latkes (potato pancakes) as they called them, and so much other delicious food for us. We certainly didn't starve as kids. No wonder I like to cook and eat, I learned from the best.

My grandmother passed on to me many recipes from Russia with love and through several generations to mine. She was my 007 agent. She was amazing! So strong and relentless! But soft and loving at the same time. I'll always miss her. She was the light of my life. My role model, my best friend. When she passed away, a part of me went with her. A part of me I can never get back, only in my memories and special times spent with her. In photographs and home movies, I can still visit with her memories. There's nothing like a grandma to grow up with.

I only hope I'm as good a grandma as she was. Stay tuned! We'll see what God has in store for me. I pray so. I do have one grandchild on the way now. I do love children as much as she did. I was blessed to have two grandmothers who loved children and family as they did. I will always remember the example they set of people that not only loved God but showed it to others. An example I've tried to carry on to the next generation of children, whether they are my own or someone else's, if they're in my life, they will be loved. I miss you, Bobe, this memory was for you.

Chapter 6

My Mother and Father's Life Together with their Children

Me and Alan with our then dog Dukey, in the back of our home in Revere, Massachusetts circa 1963. I was 4 going on 5, Alan was 6.

As I said earlier, my parents were married after two weeks of knowing each other. And as moving quickly would have it, a year after they were married, they had their first child, my oldest sister Judith, in May of 1953. She was the only child for almost four years, then the next child, my brother Alan, came along in August of 1957. From what I was told, because my sister had been the only child and the center of attention for that amount of time, she had a hard time adjusting to another child coming along. Several of my aunts told me my parents had doted on her quite a bit. And understandably so, she was the first child and the first grandchild. They loved her unconditionally, as loving parents do. She was the very first grandchild in the family on both sides, so she was a big deal. She was also a gorgeous baby, and she grew into a beautiful woman. I spent a lot of my childhood looking up to her because of her beauty. She was also healthier than I was. My mother tried to soften this for me, but it was hard, as I had a lot of health challenges back then.

My brother Alan was born premature on August 4th, 1957. While he arrived a little early, he grew into a very healthy child, and went on to lead a very good life. During this time, there were other happenings in the world.

The U.S. president was Dwight D. Eisenhower and was a Republican. Leave it to Alan, a staunch Democrat today, to be born into a time of a Republican president. Famous people born on this day included John Wark, who is a Scottish former footballer who spent most of his playing time with Ipswitch town in the United Kingdom. He won a record four player of the year awards before becoming one of the four inaugural members of the club's hall of fame. Alan, being a football fan of every kind and having a daughter-in law from England, noted that to me.

Brooks D. Simpson, an American historian, was also born on that day. He specialized in studies of the American civil war. In that special week of August, people in our country were listening to "Let Me Be Your Teddy Bear" by Elvis Presley. In the UK at that time, people were listening to Presley's "All Shook Up" and enjoying his music in general.

On television, people were watching the Arlene Francis show, which my mother tuned into regularly. There was the Ed Sullivan Show, which was very popular, where Elvis Presley made his final appearance before moving on in his stardom. Howdy Doody was a popular children's show. There was *Candid Camera, George Burns and Gracie Allen Show*, a popular sitcom of its time, along with the *I love Lucy* show. *American Bandstand* featured popular music and its teen idols for teens at the time, hosted by Dick Clark, *The Adventures of Superman*, which starred George Reeves. *The Mickey Mouse Club* was a favorite of kids on Saturday mornings. *Captain Kangaroo, The Lawrence Welk Show*, and so much more. While television was limited to a few stations back then, there was plenty to view and it was really growing.

But so much more happened on that day back then 1957. That year was also an important year for film theater and television. Leonard Bernstein's West Side Story opened on Broadway. Of course, that movie reminded us a little of my father's story, a fun fact to note. In film, *Jailhouse Rock* was released, starring Elvis Presley. It was also the year that *The Bridge in the River Kwai* premiered in the United Kingdom. That film was to be featured at the 30th Academy Awards in 1958. My dad loved that movie.

In television that year, Rogers and Hammerstein's *Cinderella* was telecast live on CBS. I remember viewing the re-run of it in 1964, on a small black and white television set. I recall being in the kitchen cooking dinner together as a family and how much fun it was. 1957 was also the year Paul McCartney and John Lennon met for the first time in Liverpool, England, imagine that! No pun intended because of his later hit, "Imagine."

But in August 1957, our claim to fame was my brother Alan being born! Since everyone smoked back then, it's not surprising he came early, as pre-maturity is now said to be linked to smoking during pregnancy. And my mother was a big smoker! Had she been aware of this, I'm sure she would have stopped.

My Mother's Smoking Habit and the Cost

Winston Cigarettes was the brand my mother smoked for years. As I remember, she smoked four packs a day. Whew! It wasn't as expensive as today, and it was so common. No one knew of the health risks involved in smoking back then either. To give you an idea of how easy they were to access, in the 1960s, a pack of Winston Cigarettes was only 27 cents. Can you imagine? They were so inexpensive and easy to get. Today, the average pack of cigarettes is now $6.69 a pack, although it varies from state to state. It is so much harder to afford this habit now. It's certainly an incentive to avoid it though.

Winston Cigarettes were introduced in 1954 by the R.J. Reynolds Tobacco Company and became the top selling brand of the day. The top position was held until 1972 when Marlboro overtook the lead.

Winston was one of the original sponsors of *The Flintstones* cartoon (popular cartoon for children back then) up until 1962. If you Google it, you'll find that in the commercials from that time, characters Fred Flintstone and Barney Rubble were seen promoting Winston, and every episode ended with Fred lighting a Winston for his wife Wilma while singing the product's jingle. By the third season, however, the show's ad became more children-oriented, and Winston was replaced by Welch's Juice, which was much more appropriate for children watching cartoons. As a child, I just thought I was watching a fun cartoon. Because my mother smoked and so did several aunts and uncles and friends of my parents, I didn't think anything about it. When Alan was born, he was only about four and a half pounds. I still think him being premature had a lot to do with the smoking. I've heard studies that have proven that is one of the causes.

Anyway, back to baby Alan.

"He was very long and skinny, only weighing about four pounds," my mother commented once to me. She was amazed at the fact that a premature baby could grow up to be so tall and strong. As the years went on, you would have never known he was premature. As a teen, he was quite stocky and grew to just under six feet, with the healthy appetite to match. I always admired him as an older brother, he was compassionate and fun to grow up with. Of course, we had our sibling disputes here and there, but we always made up and stuck close, even to this day.

We were so close in age, people often thought we were twins. His personality was a lot like my mother's, he rarely thought of himself. No matter how he struggled, he always put others' needs before his own, even as a young child. I remember him being a very heavy sleeper, so if I needed him in the night, forget it, he was out like a light. Whatever it was, it had to wait till morning and then after breakfast. He was "Cuckoo-for cocoa- puffs" (for those of you older folks that remember the commercial), and we both really liked Lucky Charms cereal. It was because of the mini marshmallows in the cereal that rarely made it to the bowl, thanks to me. Alan got tired of always looking for a marshmallow in the box, and finally out of frustration, switched to a different cereal he knew I wouldn't like. I think it was Alpha Bits.

Andrea and Me with our siblings in our backyard, Revere MA. 1963.

Both my grandmothers from Europe used to cringe at our American diet. They couldn't believe how much sugar and fat my parents would allow us to eat on occasion, with the preservatives to match, and then add the smoke exposure. But back then, nobody knew of all the consequences of these choices, just our European relatives, who cooked all homemade real food and never smoked or drank. I stand corrected, they didn't drink heavily, but they did like their wine. I think our parents enjoyed going out to eat because it was new and different to them, not the way they were raised. Because we were so active outdoors, we could get away with eating a lot of calories. We had no trouble burning off what we ate. We weren't sitting behind computers and telephones because we didn't have that back then. We were always outdoors moving.

I have observed that the technology today seems to be keeping children more inactive, which is very unfortunate for their health. Our habits are quite different now, we are indoors more and sitting more, which isn't great for anyone at any age. As far as our menu goes, I've gone back to what my grandmothers taught us about healthy eating, and Alan is still working on it, so is brother Lance. We are all getting there. We are all a work in progress. I just want to keep them as long as I can. I don't want to face this life without them.

Our Birthing Order

Back to my parents having children and our birthing order. In the early years, we lived in the northern part of Boston, and a little less than two years after Alan was born, my mother had another child, a baby girl in May of 1959. Guess who that child was? You guessed it, me! And it wasn't a cool fall day as it was with my grandmother in England. It was a warm, bright May day, according to my mother. I was born at 3:50 am. When the sun came up, it was a nice day. I'll take it easy on the weather report. Alan and I were just shy of two years apart. This probably accounted for why he and I were close as siblings. Relationships amongst siblings are a blessing, and I was lucky to have him.

There is always something in history that strikes us and leaves a mark on our memories of what once was. In my mother's case, while still in the hospital recovering from giving birth, she heard something on the news that really bothered her, as at the time, it was rare to hear of stories like this.

Having young children of her own, it was this story that struck her as she held her new baby daughter in her arms. And I remember her recalling this story from the day I was born. I recall her saying, "It was frightening that a body was found in shallow waters of the slow wetland on the river near Camas, Washington." As I'm recalling her story, it's weird to me that I live in Washington today.

"It was the body of a ten-year-old whose name was Susan Martin. Susan was one of five members of a Portland, Oregon family that had gone missing on December 7th, 1958, almost five months before you were born," she said. "I saved the newspaper article if you want to see it. What reminded me of it is that shortly after you were born, it came on the news that they still couldn't find this family and the three young daughters they had. As I remember, they were so young. And it made me afraid for the safety of my own children." What a sad story that impacted my mother and her care for us during the time of my birth.

I listened to her, and it was another reminder to me of how much my mother loved us and wanted the best for her children, and how very sensitive she was to others. Since she often saved newspaper articles of major events back then, this was one of the stories from the Boston Globe from 1959in an old shoe box. I recall seeing it but has gotten lost in the many moves we've made over the years. She saved articles and recipes back then, too. I can remember her always cutting and pasting things in her scrap book, which I saved after her passing and still have. Today, on occasion, I take a moment to look through those old clippings, and it brings me back to observing her doing this when I was a young child. What was she was thinking? I wondered, as she carefully read and then cut and pasted the stories one by one.

After My Birth, Our Lives Together

While we lived in Boston in my early years, those were great years for us as a family. From my birth till age six, we lived on a street where our neighbors were quite close and looked out for one another. The adults used to sit on the porches (or veranda or piazza as my grandparents and parents referred to it) on hot summer nights and talked to each other. They talked about good things, hard things, old things, new things, whatever was on their minds. There was a sense of trust between neighbors back then. They really looked out for one another as many of them shared a commonality. They were immigrants starting a new life with family and children. And their children all played together while the adults visited.

Many of them spoke broken English, some very little English at all. Some spoke in Italian, and some spoke in Yiddish (the European version of Hebrew). Since I had both in my family, I heard a mix. But I picked up the Italian language quite well. It was easier and closer to the English language. While the Yiddish was harder for me to grasp, I did pick up some of the language but never learned to read it or speak it fluently as I did the Italian. With the Yiddish, I picked up mostly slang terms, like Shmootzic, which meant dirt or dirty. Then there was Gay Kaken, afen yam (not sure of the spelling, but that's how it sounds), which basically was a favorite in Russian/Yiddish for go take a shit in the ocean. Shmatah, which means a rag a cloth for cleaning or a sloppy outfit or not good quality. Then there was Fe', which meant not good, yucky. These were slang terms and funny and comical. There were more, but it's Okay, you get the point.

But I must ask the question, who says those things to people anymore? And why did they say that in the first place, sheesh! Not very uplifting to say the least. My European family, while they could be loving and supportive in one sense, could be so crude and not classy when they felt threatened. And that was the side of them I didn't want to emulate. My thoughts on why they could be defensive at times was their experiences of persecution and the pain and prejudice they endured. In my grandmother's case, it was the Russian revolution and losing so many family members and all she had to endure, I guess. While I understand her pain, either way, I can't imagine going up and saying that to someone, no matter how much they might have hurt me. Talk about a harsh word stirring up strife.

The Bible says, "A gentle answer turns away wrath, but a harsh word stirs up anger" Proverbs 15:1 (NIV). I would rather encourage gentleness, wouldn't you? Rather, tell them to take a nice swim in the ocean, not to relieve themselves there. Besides, it would add to the pollution!

So, the Italian language was smoother to me and appropriate. While I did hear an occasional Italian swear word, it wasn't quite as abrupt as the Russian/Yiddish. I loved the Italian language and culture while growing up; I still do today.

I admired my Russian/Yiddish grandmother very much but could always sense an underlying defensiveness that I couldn't always explain, but I knew she loved me. I had a harder time understanding that culture since it had so many negative overtones due to the stories I heard of the Russian revolution and Jewish persecution. My grandmother and her family went through so much. It made me apprehensive to grasp that culture for fear of what would happen to me. Then the Holocaust stories literally frightened me, and I wondered if it was safe to be Jewish. To think my grandmother's family went through so much horror just because of who they were and how they believed. It didn't seem fair. And it hurt me to think the grandmother I loved had to flee for her life.

It was a special time growing up with them, I remember though. In many ways, I can recall feeling so secure like nothing could touch us. As we sat on the porch together on those hot summer nights, I also recall we had an ice cream man who used to come down our street. Back then they made home-made real hot fudge sundaes for us, and what a treat that was. The man who drove the truck, we knew personally through our upstairs neighbor Carolyn, it was her brother Roger that served on it. My Russian grandmother would often walk from her home to ours, which was just a few blocks, with my aunt Ruthie, to buy us the ice cream and sit with us. There was a feeling of security and bonding in one sense, until I listened to some of the stories of Russia. It then became frightening to hear and made me fearful.

Here I was, living in a neighborhood where we could walk up and down the streets as kids or ride our bikes without fear of harm and my grandmother grew up so different and, of course, wanted different for us, and I think she was pleased to see just how happy and free we were. And yes, there were some things to watch out for, as there always is, but nothing like Russia. Because everyone knew each other and looked out for each other, it was a little safer in general. And yet society is different in this country today. It's harder now because people are more separatist and don't easily trust each other, there seems to be more disconnect and even more violence with less support. There isn't as much commonality, as I have spoken of. A feeling of culture and community seems to have diminished in some ways. You see it some today, but it's not as common, I'm afraid. Today, people must really work at communing, and many do, I do see that, too, and I thank God for it.

When I was growing up during the 60s, there was plenty going on in our country and around the world. I was quite little then, sheltered from most of it though. But I remember two scary events that impacted our nice, peaceful neighborhood and family security. One being the Cuban missile crisis, also known as the October crisis.

The missile scares dated from October 16th, 1962 to October 28th, 1962 when John F. Kennedy was president. I was only three years old. Alan was four and a half. My older sister was 11. I still have a vague memory of how frightening it was. The Cuban Missile crisis was where the leaders of the U.S. and Soviet Union engaged in a tense 13-day political and military standoff. It was over the installation of nuclear armed soviet missiles on Cuba. This was just 90 miles from U.S. shores. In a television address to the nation (my parents watched on their black and white television with just three channels), President Kennedy notified Americans about the presence of the missiles. History says he explained his decision to enact a naval blockade around Cuba, and he made it clear to the U.S. that he was prepared to use military force if necessary, to neutralize this perceived threat to our nation. In hearing this news, panic spread because the American public believed (and understandably so) that we were on the brink of nuclear war. Even as a youngster, I remember my parents talking about this with family and friends. But my parents tried to assure us children that things would be all right and that President Kennedy and the Lord wouldn't let anything happen to us.

Disaster was avoided when the U.S. agreed to Soviet leader Nikita Khrushchev's offer to remove the Cuban missiles in exchange for the U.S. promising not to invade Cuba. Sounds to me a little like what's going on today. With Korea wanting to launch missiles, we must believe by faith that our current President Donald Trump and his cabinet will make right decisions and keep our country safe. Nothing new under the sun as they say. But regardless of who the president is, I believe God is in control, and as we pray, God in his loving sovereignty will help us and give us grace.

I just remember during this time feeling very secure because of the comfort of family around me, that no matter what, I would be held and comforted and feel safe.

The other major event was, as most of us remember, was the assassination of our beloved President Kennedy. I was four years old when that all took place. What a time of uncertainty it was for our country. But again, I recall my mother and my father encouraging us that everything would be all right and that we weren't alone, we had each other, and of course, there was a lot of mention about prayer and trusting in God.

On the day this happened, it was on a Friday, November 22nd, 1963 to be exact. Many of you know the story. But from a more personal note, as four- and five-year-old's, my brother Alan and I were at home with Mom. We had a neighbor, Carolyn Pivnick, we rented our second floor to in our two-family home my parents owned.

Upstairs Neighbor Carolyn Pivnick with daughter Kim circa 1963.

She reminded me in one of our recent conversations of where she was that day upon hearing the news. "I was pushing my third child Kim in a carriage down the main street of Revere, Massachusetts, on Shirley Avenue, when I heard people screaming. I saw them coming out of stores and shouting, 'Did you hear the news?'" She said it was startling and frightening. And when she heard what had happened, an overwhelming sense of helplessness and fear overcame her. At the same time, a sense of sadness as her thoughts turned toward her children and what would the future hold for them. What was happening and why, she wondered. She felt disoriented but quickly realized she needed to get home to her other two young children, Andrea and Michael. As she headed back, observing chaos everywhere in the streets, it was frightening, and she couldn't get there fast enough.

Andrea, and Michael as small children, pictured on their porch right above us. Circa 1963.

When she got back to the house, my mother was there waiting, and they comforted one another. At the same time, in another town next to Revere, a parallel event was taking place. Aunt Elaine was also pushing a baby carriage with my cousin Elise in it, and she, too, said, "There was so much chaos, people were running around screaming, the news was coming over the radio everywhere. I remember one woman crying and saying she was headed to church to pray with others." But my aunt, being an optimist, thought to herself that everything will be all right, until she heard over the radio "The Star-Spangled Banner," which meant he was gone. At that point, her heart sank with so much sadness and she wondered what was to be?

This brought her back to the memory of another president's death, Franklin Delano Roosevelt. That day was April 12th, 1945 when she and others were dismissed from school for the same reason. She lived on Warren Street in Lynn, Massachusetts at the time, a big brick apartment with 21 families on three floors. Our families lived this way back then; it was fun, and people really connected and supported one another. She recalls she was in second grade; she was maybe seven or eight and not really understanding what was going on because she was so young. The teachers, upon dismissing the students, wouldn't let them talk because there was supposed to be silence out of respect for his passing. So, my aunt and a close little friend just walked together holding hands, looking at each other, respecting the silence until they reached their big building where they both lived. They had each other, but they were not alone in the fear of what was to come. So, this brought back memories for her. Two losses of presidents in one lifetime. Astounding!

Meanwhile, back to the day Kennedy was assassinated, our oldest sister was at school, just like my aunt back in 1945. My sister was 11 then and a sixth grader, I believe, just a little older than my aunt was during Roosevelt's passing. I can still see the tears on my mother's face, and I can still hear her conversations with Carolyn and different neighbors and family who were calling on the phone. It was clear by now; everyone had heard the news. I remember my sister being dismissed and walking home from school. They had early release all over the country because of the assassination. All the kids on the street, along with my sister, were crying as they headed home. There was a lot of fear, no one knew what was happening, but they had each other to cling to and family to come home to. They were blessed to have come home to find solace and comfort with their families. It was a pretty dark day. And it must have been so frightening for the adults and children to experience this.

Being only four, I can remember a little of this, and I can still see the newspaper with my mind's eye: the photos of President Kennedy, and Lee Harvey Oswald, the alleged assassin, being arrested. And then another newspaper showing Oswald being assassinated by Jack Ruby, but during this, I still found solace and protection in the arms of my mother, my grandmother, my father. I had my brother Alan and sister to cling to, and that was all I needed. I remember people praying during that time. The whole country was in an uproar. People were asking what would happen next? There was a lot of fear for quite a while, but we all had to go on as families after that terrible day. I'll always remember how we all stuck together and found hope and a future with God and family. It was prayer and faith and God's grace that gave us the ability and assurance not to panic. Knowing that we did have hope and a future despite such a tumultuous time brought us to a place of acceptance. And it was particularly hard because back then, as Carolyn told me, "Our presidents were trusted by the people, not like today, and his death was devastating because of it."

She went on to say, "This was a new experience for our country, and when the vice president, Lyndon Johnson, took over, people just accepted it. There wasn't all this protest, like there would be today. Politics were much quieter, a candidate got in, and people just accepted it." Wouldn't that be nice today? Right!

Andrea with Carolyn Today, Beautiful.

Carolyn, now 80, whom I have always respected, also said to me, "We didn't have Facebook back then, there were no cell phones. We didn't have the arguing amongst people that didn't even know each other. Today, there's just too much division amongst the media." As I listened, it was so nice to hear such words of wisdom and level headedness from the generation that experienced all this. People I know personally and respected. This was a woman I looked up to at such an early age and still do.

So, during this time of people searching for hope, I also remember someone quoting that scripture from Jeremiah 29:11, "For I know the plans I have for you, declares the Lord, plans to prosper you and not to harm you, plans to give you hope and a future." And God's promise was real, and it came into fruition during that time. After a while, we did see hope and certainly a future. Never in my wildest dreams did I imagine feeling so supported during such a turbulent time, it gave a grounded level-headed feeling, even while so young.

So, while the country was recovering from such a traumatic time at the loss of our president, we remained in the Boston area for another three years. There we spent time picking up the pieces, remaining positive with family and friends. We began to refocus on weekends and enjoying our local community center and times together. While it was important to grieve a loss, it was also vital to move on together with God's help.

Chapter 7

My Life Away from Family Begins

Nursery school photo with Andrea and Stacy. Early 1960's. I'm the one in the center furthest to the right in the front with the black shirt. Andrea is standing behind me. Stacy is seated just 6th from the left, just two away from me to my left.

Two years after the Kennedy tragedy, I was now six and ready to begin nursery school, or so we thought. Many of the people I was around as a youngster spoke either Italian or Yiddish and my grandmothers' English was limited. So, when it was time for me to start nursery school, I had a hard time. In fact, the first day, I felt so out of place with all the American English-speaking children, I hid in a corner and refused to participate, all I could think of is "I want my mommy and Grammys."

While I did have two close friends at the time and very American (Andrea and Stacy), still, I wanted the culture and home environment I was used to. Both girls would fill the gap, however, and helped me ease into nursery school because they were children my age and daughters of my mother's close friends, Andrea, who was Carolyn's daughter, along with her father and brother Michael felt like family to us because they basically lived in the same house with us living upstairs. While we had separate families and separate lives, we were together a lot and shared much.

Me, Michael, and Andrea enjoying an afternoon together, in front of the home we shared in Revere.

Andrea and I became quite close as children. It was like having another sister right upstairs. I loved Andrea, and while we don't see each other as much anymore, we still stay in contact, and on occasion, reminisce how nice things were back then, at least in our little world. You never forget those early special friendships; I believe they have a lifelong impact on us. Because of her, I was not alone in nursery school. We did quite a bit together, and our families socialized often. Andrea was one of my first best friends as a youngster. My older sister even babysat her and her younger siblings, Michael and Kim, on occasion.

Carolyn also said to me in our conversation, "What a good babysitter your sister was at just 12 years old." From my own memory, I remember she was good with us, too. If my mother or Carolyn went shopping, either my sister would watch us or one of them would take us so the other could go do errands. It was a time when people stuck together and helped one another. No one ever said they were too busy; if someone was in need, they just met it.

Andrea and I would play on the swings out in our backyard together, and often we would have lunch together. Little girl lunch dates, I call it. I recently spoke with Andrea about this, and she remembers us loving peanut butter and fluff sandwiches, a popular sandwich for lunch back then but full of sugar and not much nutrition. We would get it all over our faces. It was fun to be messy and not worry about it. We just enjoyed it and didn't think of the negative consequences of diet; we were little girls, what did we care. We had little picnics with those sandwiches while playing on the swing set my dad set up for us in the backyard we shared. I didn't quite remember it like Andrea did, but I can picture it. And it's funny what one person remembers, another person doesn't and vice versa. Having each other to fill in on those memories makes it all the more special.

Revere Beach, in Massachusetts, around the time we would have frequented there. Circa early 1960's.

We share in the cherished memories of going to Revere Beach together with our families, playing in the sand and building sandcastles. There were a lot of amusement park rides on the beach, and we remember riding the bumper cars and the Ferris wheel and other fun amusements. We remember the excitement of bands playing on Saturday nights underneath the pavilion on the beach with lots of families gathering to listen to the music together. Seeing people, we knew and bonding. Having ice creams together on the hot summer nights, even going to the drive-in movies with our families, we had so much fun.

On hot summer weekend nights, Andrea and her family would be in one car, our family packed us in another, and on occasion, Stacy's family would load them in yet another car, heading to the drive-in movies in our pajamas. Going on a family outing with my two little best friends was extra special when our parents would let the three of us ride in the back of one car together with the windows rolled down. We sat on a blanket while we played a favorite children's game called Jax. There was nothing like it. Our parents put our pajamas on, so that when we got home and it was late, we were all ready for bed, it was less for them to do.

On occasion when we got home, I would pretend to be asleep in the back seat, just so my father would carry me in and tuck me in bed. Sometimes he could tell I was faking but carried me anyway. He would say something like, "Charlotte, I think she's pretending to be asleep, I saw her eyes open," and I would giggle a little, and my mother would say something like, "It's Okay, she's probably really tired, put her to bed, it's been a long night." I loved it when he carried me, that way it was a feeling of security and warmth I can still feel as I describe this.

I was stuck on my family and I remember wanting to be with them forever. Our friends, too. It was a magical time for us, and to this day, I wish it could have never ended. But as life goes, so do those magical moments. It seemed everyone we knew was socially an activity oriented, I don't remember a lot of stressed out people. There were no computers to distract the interaction that we were having and needed. We were there, front and center, and there for each other. It seemed everyone knew how to recreate back then and take time out and be together. We felt rarely alone. It wasn't like the disconnect you see today that I see. And Carolyn, Foomie, and my mother were all good-looking women, and I remember wanting to dress just like them, speak like them, etc. because I was around them. I didn't see them in a picture on Facebook. I stood right next to them, side by side with a mirror, imagining myself looking and dressing like them. Especially Carolyn, she was beautiful, she could have been a model, too.

Of course, as time went on, I learned to be myself and a little more independent, and I discovered I was more of a tomboy. Being close to my father and having a close older brother encouraged that. But that's who I was, and it was just fine. Andrea was more feminine; she liked to wear dresses and nail polish, whereas Stacy and I liked to dress more relaxed and painting our nails seemed like too much work. We stuck them in the dirt instead. My mother spent a lot of time washing my hands, to say the least. When I see pictures of Andrea today, I can see how she still loves to dress so nice and she turned out like her mother, beautiful and elegant. I, however, still ride ATV's with my husband and brother Alan while camping in the woods. I am definitely as I've been described as easy going, not easy rider, but easy going and relaxed. Today, it would be referred to as a type B personality or very laid back. I call it content, so does my husband.

While I hear from Andrea from time to time still today, I lost touch with Stacy in my early 20s. After college, I got married and she went off to college; we went our separate ways. But the memories of our childhood still bring warmth to me as a past first best friendship that meant so much. And it was special also because knowing our mothers were friends since nursery school made it all the richer. We were emulating good role models who taught us the meaning of being a good friend at an early age. As with Andrea's family, our family was close with Stacy's family, too, because my mother and her mother were friends since nursery school. Their friendships lasted a lifetime until death parted them.

Back to Starting Nursery School

When my parents tried to start me in nursery school, I remember, my teacher (Miss Bertha) spoke to my mother, and they both wondered if I was ready for school yet. I was very attached to being at home with parents, European-speaking grandparents, and Stacy and Andrea. My older siblings seemed to do Okay. But I hated the idea, even as a little person, being away from home. Maybe it was because I was a middle child. I am not sure. So, the next day proved I wasn't ready yet. Get a load of this! I was sneaky from an early age. Grandmother Leah Jean's personality was showing a bit.

So, it was the first day of nursery school at the local community center in Revere, Massachusetts. My mother brought me into the class, and I asked if I could go to the little girl's room. Stacy and Andrea were in my class and waiting for me. Here's where my independence and my own ideas were beginning to show. They were a little bit more compliant than I was.

Well, anyway, I went, and my mother left, trusting I would do Okay.

And I went without resistance at first. But the little stinker in me had a plan. *I'll show them. I'll hide, so they can't find me.* Plotting as a little girl! What did that foretell what I would be like in the future? I had a thought: *Then I won't have to go to school.* So, instead of going to the girls' room, I hid myself behind a door to the front entrance. I decided I would do it for a little while and then come out. This out of the scheming mind of a nursery school age child. So, just when I decided to try to come out (which seemed like hours), I saw through the corner of the door Miss Bertha and the principal in a panic because they couldn't find me. *Oh-oh! Now what do I do? I'll get spanked, I know it!* Facing my mother at that point seemed gigantic.

So, no way was I coming out now. I think by this time I had been hiding behind the door for about an hour or more, but it sure seemed much longer. I was getting in deeper by the minute. Then I saw the fireman go by; now I was scared. Then I saw the janitor, Roger, comforting Miss Bertha who thought she lost me or I was kidnapped. Then before I knew it, my mother went by with Carolyn for support, then Stacy's mother came. And, oh, boy, now I was never coming out! Because now I was really in trouble, but I had to pee! Now what do I do? Before I knew it, Roger the janitor decided to look behind the door, as they were looking everywhere for me. For crying out loud, I even saw my whole class go by and Andrea and Stacy wondering what happened to me. I could almost hear them talking and I could almost make out what they were saying. So, as Roger the janitor peered behind the door, he got a glimpse of me smiled, as not to startle me, and said, "I found you."

I said, "Please don't tell." Roger said he had to, and he gently took me by the hand and led me to Miss Bertha and my mother who breathed sighs of relief like I've never seen. Mom did scold me later, but because she was so relieved, decided not to punish me. Needless to say, it was clear I wasn't ready for nursery school yet. My parents kept me home and sent me a year later; I remember Mom talking with her friend Foomie on the phone and then in the hallway with neighbor Carolyn. Foomie was living up the street from us at the time. She told both women she was so relieved they found me but that I wasn't quite ready for school yet. My first experience with manipulation, but I do remember feeling embarrassed and a little ashamed. Oh, good, I had a conscience. I was off to a good start. My father, being the jovial one, thought it was funny. I didn't need any encouragement from him.

My Childhood Antics

Later, while still in Revere, I remember another incident where I thought I wanted to be a hair stylist at age six. I decided, as I woke up the middle of one night, to cut my own hair. It was patch work at best.

The next morning, my mother saw all the hair in the bathroom sink, gasped, and then yelled, "All right, which one of you kids cut their hair?"

I hid again, this time in the closet. *She'll never find me here*, I thought. I was such a little stinker. But eventually I came out because Alan found me and told on me. Needless to say, my mother had to take me to a hair stylist to fix it. Let's just say, I had a crew cut for a while. My brother Alan and I looked like twin boys, and that was embarrassing, but not for him. That cured me of ever doing that again. I was trying to look like my sister and ended up looking like my brother. Not what I expected. What can I say, I was testing my independence! So, I was a little sneaky. So, what! Isn't every kid? No, Alan wasn't, we could count on him. And again, my father laughed! My mother had her hands full. He was a real support during times of discipline if you didn't mind being disciplined by Chuckles the clown. He often made hard things seem fun. And people wonder why I laugh so easily today.

Dad, around the time he worked for Grossman's.

So, in 1965, when I was still six, getting ready to turn seven, my father was transferred in his job from Plywood Ranch Lumber Yard to a newer and upcoming expanding company known as Grossmans Inc. My father was climbing the ladder of success by being promoted to a management position. (Or because it was a lumber company, was he just climbing ladders? Ha-ha!) Well, anyway, he was being promoted to a manager of the store, but it was in New York on Long Island. We moved and left behind the people and family members we were so close with. This was hard. I was moving away from family and my two best friends. But still, we weren't alone, we had each other, and the thought of moving to a new state began to seem adventurous to us children, so that helped.

And remember the little girl my mother was playing with—her best friend Foomie (Florence)—when her home caught fire and she lost her father? They were parting for the first time in their friendship and that was very hard on them, too. I observed and experienced more bonding than most. As we left, we left behind a lot of history and emotion, and some sad faces. History from Russia and Italy all the way to Long Island, N.Y., along with some lovely memories. Memories of bonding so tightly with Stacy and Andrea, my first best friends who taught me the importance and specialness of friendship. After that move at such a young age, I would always look for friends like them wherever I lived. And while it was time for a new beginning, I had learned to bond in a way I would never forget and would have many opportunities to pass on to others throughout my life.

Our New Start in New York

We transferred to New York in May or June of 1965.ndrea's and Stacy's families visited us several times while we were there, and this was a relief because we really missed them. My mother, during this major move, also discovered she was pregnant again. Not planned, but she and my father and we all were very excited. My mother at 34, with her fourth child on the way, was both excited and overwhelmed at the same time. But in the midst of this, she and my grandmother were missing each other; especially in light of the news with the new baby coming, they found it hard to be away from each other. She was also missing her close friends from high school and the familiarity of the Boston area where she had spent most of her life. Her high school class was very close, and they stuck together, in fact most remained in the Boston area and did reunions every few years. She was concerned she'd miss some of this. But she was making a change in a new state with her husband and children and tried to make the best of it.

The move to New York was a particularly hard adjustment for my older sister as well. She was quite a bit older than the rest of us, and she was missing her close friends and had to make a new start. She, too, had learned to bond socially following my parents' example. You see, at 13, the adolescent years were just beginning for her. Adolescence is probably the toughest time to pick up and move away from your friends. That's the time you need them most, and to add another change to her adjustment, she was now anticipating the arrival of another sibling, probably making her feel a little left out. Even less attention was going to be on her and perhaps more responsibility required with her being the oldest. I am not sure why, but she required a lot of attention. My sister was the type of girl that people respected and looked up to. She was different than the rest of us. I remember her being quite popular and was always with the tough, cool kids at school.

I used to envy that about her. As I was shyer but confident, I didn't feel the need to gravitate toward the cool kids. I was more independent and assured. I occasionally hung out with the tough kids but certainly not the popular cool ones. I was more of a floater socially in school, even at a young age. I had a lot of friends but not in one group. I tended to look for deep, loyal relationships instead of being concerned about popularity. I was social but desired to be behind the scenes, not so noticed. I was content with family and a few friends. Probably why I hid behind the door in nursery school. I liked to be behind those scenes but maybe not behind a door. But my sister liked being the center of attention. I guess everyone is different. She was very attractive and had a lot of boys noticing that. The downside of that was that other girls she knew were jealous. I remember an example of this.

While we were still living in the Boston area, I remember my sister and two girlfriends walking to Revere Beach from our house. We had to walk a couple of miles, and we had to go through several neighborhoods to get there. We also had to go through downtown on Shirley Avenue, where we would eventually reach Revere Beach.

That area brings back memories of different songs that I can remember were being played on the transistor radio my sister carried with her. She would hold it to her ear as we walked, but I could still hear it. Ah, the memories of a transistor radio, and what did I hear? Songs like, "Beyond the Sea," by Bobby Darin, a beautiful song by the righteous Brothers called, "Unchained Melody," Leslie Gore songs, like "You Don't Own Me," and "Sunshine, Lollipops and Rainbows Everything." I loved that song because it was a happy upbeat tune, and I was a happy upbeat kid. I remember hearing songs by the Beach boys, and the Beatles were just coming on the scene. The Rolling Stones were new and just coming on. The Kinks, Ricky Nelson, Buddy Holly music was still played on stations, even though he was killed in a plane crash in 1959. I remember hearing the song, "Love that Dirty Water," sung by the Standells. The lyrics spoke of Boston being their home, like us, and of course, Boston at that time was my home.

As we walked the beach that day, we observed teenagers hanging out with transistor radios blaring with some of the songs I mentioned playing as we walked by. The beach was beautiful back then. It was the early '60s and there were all kinds of amusement park rides to go on. I had the privilege of going with my big sister, and I was quite proud. I thought she was the prettiest girl in the world. I was about five years old and thought it was so neat to go with my sister and her friends, Anita and Roberta, who also lived on our street. As I remember, we went on several rides, and my sister and her friends talked to some boys. Now there was a surprise!

After a few hours, it was time to head home, as she did promise my mother, we would get in before dark; while the streets were safer back then, we had to still be careful. So, we headed home. We were almost to our street and were passing the home where Foomie and her family lived. A little further down was my grandmother Bobe's, house. See, we all lived in the same vicinity. As we turned a corner, just passing Bobe's house, a gang of kids waited to pounce on my sister. They were mostly girls but a few boys. They surrounded my sister and me, and her friends ran off. Nice friends, ha! But I later found out they went to get my mother. OK, I'll give them credit. This was sort of reminiscent of when my father was surrounded in his youth at school. Was history repeating itself? Anyway, they had squirt guns. Now there was a threat on a hot afternoon. We were hot, and it could have been refreshing. However, they were threatening to beat my sister up with squirt guns?

Even as a five-year-old, I was thinking to myself, *you've got to be kidding*.

Suddenly, I stepped out in front of my sister and declared," Leave her alone!"

One of the girls said, "No, leave them alone, we don't want to hurt the cute little girl." I couldn't believe it, but they let us go. And called me cute. Boy, did I feel special. I felt like Bat Girl on *Batman*. I felt strong and brave.

The whole way home, my sister kept saying, "Iris, it's because of you I didn't get beat up. You saved me!" That made me feel proud, as my sister's approval was so important to me. I loved the adoration; it was all good. There were lots of other sweet things that happened between me and my sister when I was young, but as time went on, and I grew older, sadly more distance grew between us. My sister still recalls that story today. She recalls how brave I was at such a young age and how strong I was and still am. I attribute some of that to my strong roots of family, like my grandmother and my mother; they were strong women. But a lot of it has to do with my faith in God and trust in Him. And I trusted him at a very early age.

In light of that, I want to recall one more story that I remember about my sister and how special she was. This was around the same time period. I can remember walking up the street by myself, feeling quite big at the time. We had a local grocer in a small garage just one block up the street from where we lived. It was a tiny penny candy store called Joe Snow's, owned by a man named Joe Snow. He and his wife Etta, an elderly couple, worked together in the store. Gosh! As I think about it now, they were probably the age I am now, yikes. A little eye-opening!

Well, anyway, my mother decided that I was big enough to go up the street to the store to get a small amount of groceries, as it wasn't more than a block. She wanted to teach me to shop and to show she could trust me. I can remember my sister wanted to go with me. But my mother encouraged her to give me a chance to go by myself but encouraged my sister to watch from a living room window. Of course, back then it was much safer to do so. Today, there is no way you could do that today with a five-year-old child, it just wouldn't be safe. It goes to show you how times have changed so much.

So, I confidently and bravely walked up to Joe Snow's, walked in, and said hi. He and his wife were looking out for me, too, as they seemed to know I was by myself. I have often wondered if my mother had called to alert them, I was coming.

"All by yourself today, ha, Iris? You're big enough, ha," Joe said.

I smiled, purchased a few small items, and began to head back to my house with a paper bag in my hand of groceries. Just as I reached the house, it began to rain and rain hard. The bag got wet and fell apart and the groceries scattered all over the ground, just outside the house. I didn't know what to do, so I started to cry.

But I can still see my older sister in the window watching for me, and when she saw that I was struggling, she quickly ran out to help me, brought me in, and dried me off. She said, "It will be okay, you still did a good job, you are a big girl." I remember how warm that made me feel and how comforted I was by my sister from just that one incident. For a 12-year-old, she sure was mature and attentive, and it was clear she loved me.

But unfortunately, a distance grew between our family and my sister over time. She began at 13 to drift from the family toward friends and outside influences. I'm not sure if it was because there was such a huge age difference and she had a hard time relating, or what. But she went her own way, had her own ideas of independence, ways of doing things, and made her own choices away from the family. I always wanted to understand but couldn't. She went from being so close and compassionate to me to drifting away. I often wondered if it was because of me. And it hurt! But I don't think it was me or us, I think she was just curious and loved being with her friends. It was her choice. And as an adult, I miss her. We are now 3,000 miles away geographically and it's been hard to connect. But even though we don't see each other much, as long as she is happy, that is all I cared about. Some of the choices she made and things she did, drew concern from my parents, so they encouraged her as best they could.

But as siblings go, Alan and I remained close. By the time our last sibling came along on February 13th of 1966, we were once again elated with a new family member, our baby brother, Lance Paul. He was like our little doll we played with. There was a spread in age of 13 years between my oldest sister and the youngest. It was quite a gap. We loved our new little brother. He was the baby of the family, and even today, we remind of him of that. My parents taught us to stick together. And now that they're gone, I can't tell you how much it means that my brothers have remained so close to me. Perhaps one day my sister will be again. I pray so! I thank my parents and God for them. As we travel our circles, my brothers and I remain true to each other and bonded.

Like my mother said, "Good, bad, or indifferent, if we have each other, if we can cling to each other, we'll always feel secure, and we'll make it. We have each other to lean on! What could be bad?" She always encouraged us to stick together like glue. She always said, "We love you kids all the same, no one is left out, no one is favored. You are all special. We love you all the same. No favoritism." She was amazing!

I must tell you that much of the time growing up, it was like living in a sitcom in some ways; humor was our greatest strength in both the good and the bad times. It would lighten things. My parents, while they were together, made life fun in between life's challenges, it was a gift that we all benefitted from. They worked so hard at this, there were times I almost felt sheltered from the storms of life, literally set apart, and I wonder if it prevented me from understanding and being prepared for the real world. In fact, in some ways, I felt it didn't prepare us for the real-life situations we would face as adults, the hard times that would come. Mom and Dad came out of the war era, where they didn't have much, and life was hard for them. They all had to work so hard and help the family, even as children. It sure taught them integrity and being others-oriented, the opposite of entitlement. I remember my parents saying their generation didn't want their children to go without like they did during the depression and that time period. So, their generation of parents spoiled the dickens out of their kids, giving them whatever they wanted. They wanted them to be happy, not realizing the consequences of making things too accessible. I did feel my parents had a balance, probably more than most, though. They taught us work ethics and how to recreate in between. There were rules and regulations before we could have fun.

But that generation thought material things and less hard work would make their children happy. What a deception! You tell me, look at our society today and all the entitlement. Did it work to our benefit? I don't think so; we now live in one of the most selfish, indulgent generations known on record with everything at our fingertips. Just my opinion. Never in my wildest dreams did I ever imagine our society being so separatist after all the bonding we experienced back then; it seems to have faded. Struggle and hard work, as I've been told and have experienced, makes you stronger, not weaker. What people thought would make them happy appears to have made them more arrogant, and less compassionate toward others, more demanding, and certainly more entitled. It didn't happen right away but accumulated over time. Today, we have so many hurting and needy people in need of friendships and support and bonding. And it's happening in a time when people are more separate than they've been in many, many decades. It's a scary contrast, and it's sad!

It says in the book of Ecclesiastes, "Two are better than one, for when one falls, the other one picks the other one up. But pity the man who is alone." And you better believe it. We need each other more than ever. I pray this nation wakes up to this. The lack of communication combined with all the busyness, seems to have made people lonelier than ever. This should not be.

I remember my brother Alan saying how lucky we were to grow up when we did, in the '60s and '70s with the parents we had. He would say, "What were the odds that we should be so lucky to be born when we were?" I always remembered that. Alan was kind of quiet in some ways, but when he had something to say, it was profound. He and I just remember feeling so secure with our parents.

I imagine my brother Lance, being the baby at the time, felt secure, too. At least he should have! We used to kowtow, as it were, to his every command. I remember when he would want a glass of orange juice when he was a toddler and still in a highchair. He would bang the empty plastic cup and yell, "Juice, juice!" One of us would come running to meet his need. I guess we couldn't stand to hear him yell. And if we didn't answer him, I guess we thought we were depriving him in some way. Boy, as a baby, he had us wrapped around his little finger. His teeny little finger! I think we gave in also to help our mom, and he was cute. Talk about spoiling someone. Yes, he was a bit spoiled, but he was the youngest. He loved it and so did we. And even so, he grew up to be one who comes alongside the rest of us. That bonding and caring mentality rubbed off on him. He's become quite giving, caring, resilient, and strong. I guess we didn't do too bad with Lance. We can count on him, too.

So, this was 1966, and I remember my brother Alan and I watching TV at night sometimes with my father. The favorite shows we used to watch that year were a lot of action adventure shows such as *The Green Hornet*, *The Time Tunnel*, *Star Trek*, of course which starred my father's childhood friend, Leonard Nimoy. *Batman and Robin* was a favorite of mine and Alan's. I loved the show *Bewitched*, starring Elizabeth Montgomery. I really liked her; we had some good role models back then to follow after. *F Troop* was a favorite of Alan's. *Get Smart*, *Gilligan's Island*, *Green Acres*, *I Dream of Jeanie* to name a few. My father, Alan, and I would watch *The Three Stooges* reruns, as if we needed them as role models. The way we act today, you can tell we watched way too many *Three Stooges* episodes. Alan and I blame it on brain injuries,

146

but I think the Stooges had something to do with it. But it was a fun thing to do together.

And my parents watched *The Twilight Zone* together. That was a creepy but exciting show for them, but I wasn't allowed to watch it when I was young like that. They felt it was too scary a show and that it would keep me up at night. We watched so much television at night, sitting together laughing at the sitcoms so much, it's no wonder when Alan and I get together today, we watch and recall sitcoms together and laugh. We did do lots of other things together, too, but nighttime before bed, if we did our homework, our mother let us watch out favorite shows. Till this day, I love reruns of *My Three Sons* and *Andy Griffith*. Good, clean entertainment. No swearing, no drama, no crap. Just plain good humor with healthy messages, messages we could learn from and model after. Role models that we could really learn life's lessons from.

In 1966, Lyndon B. Johnson was president, and his wife Lady Bird Johnson was in the news quite a bit. Her given name was Claudia Alta. The first lady and American socialite, she was notably well-educated for a woman in her era. She proved a capable manager and shrewd investor. She married Lyndon B. Johnson in 1934 when he was a political hopeful in Austin, Texas. As first lady, she broke new ground by interacting directly with Congress, employing her own press secretary, and making a solo electioneering tour. She was also known as an advocate for beautifying the nation's cities and highways with flowers. As they would bloom, she declared, "So does hope." This was known as the highway beautification act. These were some of the ways she impacted our country during her husband's presidency. Hope, something we could use today!

That fall while we were in Patchogue, N.Y., my mother got us tickets to a Halloween dress up party at the local movie theatre to see the movie *Old Yeller*. Oh, boy, what a mistake that was for a little girl of six who loved animals. The party and the costume contests were fun. However, by the end of the movie when they had to shoot the dog because he had rabies, I ran out of the movie theatre crying.

My brother Alan was right behind me, chasing me, saying, "Iris, it's Okay, it wasn't real, they didn't really kill the dog, it's just a movie." I still couldn't stop crying, and as we came out of the movie theatre, my mother was waiting for us, with a look of horror on her face. She thought I was crying because someone had beat me up. I ran into her arms, and she comforted me. Then, when Alan told her what happened, she gave a sigh of relief but had a very hard time convincing me that it wasn't real. To this day, I can't watch that movie. I'm too much of an animal lover. I'm still crying as I write this. I'll call Alan, he'll know what to do! Today, he always warns me when there is a movie with animals dying. He tells me to leave the room, or as he says, "You'll lose your mind again." We stick to shows like *The Three Stooges*! They were safe to watch. Right! Especially if you were insane! NYuck, nyuck, nyuck! I learned that language from Curly. And sure, hitting each other was really a good role model for us to see. And no wonder my grammar is so bad. Hours and hours of *The Three Stooges* will do it.

Also, that year in Patchogue in November, just a few months before my brother Lance was born, three other incidents took place. One was when we were planning a trip back to Boston to visit family. The night before, we were getting ready to leave, and had all our things packed and ready, so we could get an early start. We headed to bed for a good night's rest. And rest we did! The next morning, my father started out to the car with hangers of clothes in his arms to pack the car. As he stepped outside and onto the driveway, he stood there (I can still see him, as I was watching him), and he stood there, and to his amazement, there was no car in the driveway.

He yelled to my mother, "Ah, Charlotte, can you come here?"

This is a likeness to the 64-country squire station wagon our dad had that was stolen on Long Island in New York, Circa 1966.

I could hear her yell back, "What do you need, I'm getting the kids ready."

He then said, "I don't think we can go," still standing there with the clothes hanging on hangers in his arms.

148

She came to the door with my brother Alan. "Lenny, where's the car?"

"I have no idea." They both stood there in shock, pondering what to do next. There was only one conclusion. "I think the car has been stolen, Charlotte, I don't know what else could have happened."

Then my mother answered him with such a frightened and disappointed look on her face. "How awful, are you sure we're not behind on the car payments?"

My father, still standing there with clothes in hand, answered, "No, I'm sure I made the payment." At that point, I can remember him walking back up the narrow driveway in the front close to the front door. He stood next to my mother. "Well, let's go in and call the police and see if they can help find out what happened to it."

My mother agreed with him, followed him back in the house, and did the next thing next. I could see she was comforted by him and his support of how to handle it. They always did support each other back then and talk things out. Unfortunately, that would not always be the case, as you will read about later.

As I think back to the 1960s, the cars were so different. They were much easier to break into. Back then the cars could be hot-wired and started up easily for someone who knew how. Thieves both young and old knew how to do that back then. It was easy to open a locked car also with something as simple as a coat hanger. My father was locked out of the car on more than one occasion, and I would watch him as he would take a wire coat hanger and stretch it out with a little hook on the end to be able to reach the button that locked the door. Usually with a little patience and maneuvering, the hook would catch the button and my dad would pull up on it, and Walah! The door would un-lock. It was easy for thieves to do this. Today, the cars are much more secure, it's not so easy to do this. Too many security devices and electronics to make it that easy. We know that cars can still be stolen but not with that much ease as it was in the old days.

Well, reluctantly and very disappointed, my mother proceeded to unpack with the help of my older sister. Bewildered and with no car, my father reported the incident to the police. I remember my parents feeling violated by the incident. It was clear someone or several someone's took our property during the night. However, I remember them speaking of being thankful they didn't break into the house.

So, my father called the police and reported it stolen. As I said, it was kind of obvious what had happened. To further confirm that it was stolen, the car was found days later floating in the Long Island Sound. Just to give you a picture, the sound is a tidal estuary of the Atlantic Ocean, lying between the eastern shores of Bronx county, New York, New York City, southwest Chester county, and Connecticut to the north, and the north shore of Long Island where we were living at the time. How it stayed afloat that long is beyond me. They say strange things do happen, and this was a strange incident.

Unfortunately, the trip to Boston was cancelled. My grandmother was so disappointed that she decided to come to us by train. Here begins another story. Does anyone remember the famous blackout of 1965 in Niagara Falls? My poor grandmother was stuck in a train coming to visit us during the famous blackout. This incident left the whole eastern seaboard without power. Let me explain.

The Northeast Blackout of Tuesday, November 9, 1965 was basically a major disruption in the supply of electricity. It effected parts of Ontario, Canada and Connecticut, Massachusetts, New Hampshire, New Jersey, New York, Rhode Island, Pennsylvania, and Vermont in the U.S. It left over 30 million people and 80,000 square miles without electricity for up to 13 hours. I remember it well!

The cause of the failure was due to a safety relay that failed near Niagara Falls. It had to do with it being a very cold November night and unusual high demands for power. To sum it up, the transmission lines were heavily overloaded. It happened at 5:16 pm, eastern standard time. I can still remember because in November in New England, it got dark around 5:00 pm or so. At the time the blackout occurred, I was up in the attic playing with my dolls (as I was only six) and my brother Alan was nearby playing with his army men. It was how we entertained ourselves back then. No video games, no computers, only our imaginations and each other. And we loved it.

Anyway, as I was playing, suddenly, the lights went out and here's Alan and I in the attic, not being able to see how to get down. I called for my mother, who was in the kitchen preparing for my grandmother's visit. She called for my father, who was scrambling to try to find a flashlight and some candles. He hollered to us to stay put until he could bring us some light. Fortunately, the attic had stairs, instead of a hole in the ceiling. So, we waited, which was only about five minutes, but it seemed much longer. I remember being scared, but Alan was nearby, and he kept telling me things like, "Daddy will be here soon, don't worry." Alan was a very attentive and protective older brother, so I felt a little more secure. Of course, when my father arrived, I felt even better as he picked me up and carried me to my mother. Talk about feeling secure. My parents were amazing back then. They loved their kids, and it showed.

When my dad, Alan, and I arrived downstairs where my mother and my sister were, Mom grabbed us and held us close, I think she was scared, too. I remember her talking to my father about how worried she was about her mother traveling during all of this. Of course, at this point, no one had any idea how widespread this outage was. My father fished around to find a transistor radio, and we were able to hear what had happened.

With that news, my mother panicked. "How can we reach my mother on the train?"

My father got a hold of one of the neighbors, who let him borrow a car. He then went to the train station, where one of the conductors explained that because of the outage, the train was stopped and couldn't be started again to continue its route until the electricity was restored. My father's jaw literally dropped. He wondered how he could go back and tell my mom that her mother was lost in the blackout. I know he must have prayed because by this time, the outage was in its fifth hour. He did go back to the house, and I remember my mother being beside herself. He was upset as well.

Dad continued to listen to the radio, and by the eighth hour of the blackout, decided to go back to the station to see what was going on and if there was any news on the train's arrival. During the blackout, because it had happened during the height of rush hour, millions of commuters were delayed. It trapped 800,000 people in New York subways and stranded thousands more in office buildings, elevators, and trains. Ten thousand National guardsmen and 5,000 off-duty police officers were called into service to prevent looting. And here was my grandmother, trapped in the middle of all this.

But five hours later, my grandmother's train arrived, the lights were back on, and my father arrived with Bobe, who was quite upset and shaken to say the least. I remember her hugging all of us and saying a lot in Russian/Yiddish concerning her ordeal. We were all so grateful she was safe, the blackout was over, but many people were upset for quite a while, I remember.

My grandmother begged my father to look for a job back in the Boston area, so we weren't so far away, and within a year, he did. My father was a kind man and wanted his family happy. I think he also missed his family, too, as they lived in the northern part of Boston.

But it was a year before we would move back, and a lot occurred in that time. We saw the birth of my brother Lance on February 13th, and my sister decided to play a dirty trick on me by pretending she was the tooth fairy. I lost a tooth and put it under my pillow one night. As she pretended to be the tooth fairy, she didn't pretend to be a nice tooth fairy, and she whispered in my ear that she was going to kill me. She was 13 and I was six.

My mother had tucked me in for the night with the tooth under my pillow, and my parents went to bed. Alan was fast asleep on a trundle bed with me, and I was facing him. I had my back turned toward the bedroom door, which was closed. I heard the door creak open, and I then felt a hand go under my pillow. I was thinking to myself, *Gee, I hope she doesn't know I'm awake.* I then heard a female voice whisper, "Iris, I'm going to kill you." My heart sank. What kind of a tooth fairy was this? Where are my parents? I was trying to quietly blow at Alan, so he'd wake up and rescue me, but to no avail! Nothing woke him up. I laid there frozen with fright for what seemed like an hour.

When I finally couldn't take it anymore and jumped up and screamed, I turned to see my sister laughing. My parents rushed in to see why I was screaming; my father picked me up and held me. He put me in their bed for the night, and I woke up to a nice big silver dollar under my pillow the next morning. My sister was majorly grounded for that incident, and Alan slept through the whole thing. Crazy! I never really was able to get close to my sister after that, no kidding! Not sure why she did that, but it was a bit extreme, and over time, she became more distant from the family. We did everything to include her, but she was different and had her own way of doing things. I was glad when she had children of her own that she never pretended to be the tooth fairy. I guess she outgrew it. Thank God.

The next incident within that year, was the *Old Yeller* movie incident. But another even more challenging incident, which was quite traumatic for me and my family, was when my brother Alan was hit by a car while riding his bike in our neighborhood. I can still see with my mind's eye what happened. I loved my brother and looked up to him, so it was particularly hard for me. Not that it was easy on my parents.

It was a summer evening back in 1965, still in Patchogue N.Y. We were just finishing dinner, and Alan and I decided to go out and play with the neighbor kids as we often did back then. My parents were Okay with this as it was still light out and playing in the neighborhood back then was much safer than today.

Alan took off on his bike and agreed to meet me at a neighbor's house around the corner. As he rode off, I walked with a child my age and her father. So, together we turned the corner to one of the neighbor homes, expecting to just hang out and play. Suddenly, we heard the screeching of tires and a crash. My friend's father took us by the hands, and we rushed up the street together to see what was going on. As we approached the scene, we saw Alan lying in a pool of blood. He had been hit by a car while riding his bike. I was horrified!

My friend's father said to me, "Run home and get your parents, but he will be all right." I remember how scared I was, running home to tell my parents what had happened. I ran as fast as I could, crying all the way. As I arrived at our house, I remember shouting in front of our house that Alan had been hit by a car.

My mother yelled, "Lenny, help." And my father flew out of the house, ran up the street in his t-shirt and flip flops. He told me to stay behind. I felt compelled though to go behind him and watch. I wanted to know Alan was okay. I remember the teenage boy who was 16, still on a driver's permit, standing there looking very frightened. He stopped when he hit Alan and stayed at the scene till the police arrived and willingly spoke to them. He did the right thing. But I remember how horrified he looked. He and I watched as my father came to Alan's aid. My father held his son in his arms until the ambulance came. Alan was taken away unconscious. Dad went home to get the car, went to the hospital, and stayed with Alan the whole time. He took off time at work, wanting to be with his son. I remember how much my father loved Alan.

There were consequences for the teenager for the accident and driving without a license and without a Chaperone. But I don't remember all that happened to him. Although, we later ran into him at a restaurant during Alan's recovery. I remember looking up at him and feeling sorry for him, as he was very uncomfortable seeing us. He seemed nervous, and you could tell he felt bad. He was with some friends, which seemed to give him some comfort. I often wondered if he was involved in a church youth group, as he and his friends seemed like nice, well-behaved teens, as my mother mentioned.

So, over the next few days after the accident, I stayed with the neighbors while Alan recovered, with my parents at his side. And I was updated regularly that he would be all right. Alan suffered a severe concussion, some bumps and bruises, and needed to rest. I remember my parents speaking of how miraculous it was considering how far he was thrown after being hit and bouncing off the windshield. Alan doesn't remember most of it, which is just as well, but I'll bet that teenager who hit him remembered it for a long time.

Eventually, Alan came home and recovered. I've always been close to him, and I'm recalling it was a very scary time for me. I remember thinking as Alan was lying on the pavement in the pool of blood that he was dead. I really thought that. And it horrified me. I can still see it. That was one of my first experiences of hearing about prayer and God. It caused me to think of God as kind and faithful. We prayed, others prayed, and it turned out Okay. What a spiritual light bulb moment for a six-year-old to experience. Tragedy turned to triumph because we asked God. And we were able to move on after that. As a family, we continued to stick together and that always got us through. I remembered feeling so good that Alan was alright. And I was often aware of God's presence in our lives because of this experience. My mother, being Jewish, prayed. My father was more Catholic-oriented, with his family praying. I learned how much I loved my brother and our family. It was a hard but magical time.

Today, when Alan even gets a cold, it worries me. I want him to be well. My parents made sure his recovery was complete. Otherwise, my mother would have never had an opportunity to chase him with the telephone and boomerang in the process. There was much more both laughter and challenges to come but thank God we had Alan with us to go through those times.

Later, we truly did move on. One of the things I learned while growing up was to acknowledge pain but move on quickly from it. My mother always emphasized to me that if I stay in that pain, it will cripple me from moving forward and being successful. She was right, and her advice has served me well. I had good parents. I didn't always know it then, but I know it now. They did a good job of preparing us for the challenges we would face much later in life. They taught us not to fear what was ahead. That God would always help us. And in my journey, I have found this to be true.

The Phone Chord Incident

When we were in our early teens in the 1970s, our mother spent a lot of time on the telephone visiting with her friends and family. One day she caught Alan not doing what she asked him to do. A chore of some sort neither one of us remembers for sure.

Needless to say, she told her friend to hold on, "while I deal with Alan for not listening. He's not doing what I asked him to do, he's goofing off, and I don't like it."

What was funny is the phones back then. They were attached to the wall, and we had choices in how long a phone cord we could have. My mother chose the longest cord possible to allow her to be on the phone and still be able to get things done. She acted like she was chained to it. While on the phone conversation, she wouldn't let go of that cord for all the tea in China. I guess it never occurred to her that she could put the phone down. She needed a cell phone, but they weren't invented yet. I think she was the first person to be stuck to a phone. It may have been that they invented cell phones for someone just like my mother. She seemed to really enjoy all the connections, laughing, crying, and feeling bonded with her friends and family members. Giving advice, taking advice, sharing the latest episode of a soap opera, etc. She modeled how to really connect and gave multitasking its first name. This explains why I'm so social!

Anyway, she began to chase Alan with the phone and the extra-long cord in her hand, not remembering the cord would only go so far, however. She chased him from the kitchen, phone in hand, to the garage, threatening him with the phone. That was one long cord. Till he ran far enough that my mother came to the end of the cord (or the end of her rope as they say). Alan breathed a sigh of relief when, with the phone still in her hand, she flung back like a boomerang, preventing her from catching him. Still not realizing she could have let go of the phone at any time, she was yelling at him to come to her. You might have thought she was glued to it.

This phone cord was wavy and curly, designed to fold up like an accordion and be placed neatly by the phone when you weren't on it. But my mother stretched the boundary of the cord so often, it straightened. She was the only one I knew, of all my friends, who had a stretched-out cord. Stretch the call to the limit; she had the cord to prove it. And I thought my mother was a smart woman! Meanwhile, I was observing all of this. I suggested she put the phone down, but she didn't; she wasn't going to let go of that person on the other end. She was loyal to the end of the cord!

Alan, realizing what was going on, stood far away, laughing his head off; she couldn't reach him, and I think he knew she wasn't letting go of that phone. Of course, later we heard of Alan's punishment. And I don't think he ever ran away from the phone again after that. He realized how hard it was for my mother to keep stretching that phone cord and having to replace it over and over again. Today, Alan has a cell phone; he's glad there's no cord.

Alan was basically a good kid, but as kids do, he always looked for opportunities to get out of chores and test the boundaries. His most common incentive to behave for my mother was her threatening him with having to pay for the new phone cord. He didn't want to part with his allowance. And it worked; it kept him in line, no pun intended, of course. The phone thing didn't make sense to me, but I didn't want to experience the wrath that may have followed it. I was determined to learn through Alan's mistakes. A shake of her finger and a dirty look was enough for me to stay in line, no pun intended again. I didn't want to see what might come next.

As I share this story of my own, I'm remembering what a fun time it was growing up in our house. My mother in the midst of her disciplining was so funny to look back on. She unintentionally was very humorous, and everyone was in agreement on that. The nice thing about growing up in my household was that we could laugh at most things. If not at that moment, certainly as we reminisced. Later, when we would point out my mother's actions in the moment, she couldn't help but laugh, too. With this one, she laughed hard when she realized what had happened.

Several of my aunts recall that she was so funny because half the time she didn't realize it. She was great, and I miss her. My mother, while demanding at times, was a constant in all our lives; with a shake of her finger, we knew to respect what she said. However, there was never any doubt in mind that she loved us, we all felt that way. And she was always there, we were never alone. This memory is for you, Mom! I miss calling you every day, and the long phone cord, and your long conversations.

Chapter 8

Our Move Back to the Boston Area

Me and my siblings in Canton MA. Circa 1967.

After we all recovered from Alan's accident and celebrated the birth of our youngest brother, Lance Paul, in February of 1966, my parents felt it was time to move back to the Boston area. Back? Back to what? I didn't understand why we were being uprooted again. But between the Niagara Falls Northeast power outage and Alan being so seriously hurt, my parents missed family and the support during rough situations. Italians and Jews, as well as many other cultures, tend to stick together and help each other in both good times and bad. It brings a sense of security, so you are not alone. I didn't understand at the time; my young mind couldn't comprehend the reasons why my parents did what they did, but still, I trusted their decisions because I felt secure with them.

So, I asked, "Mommy, why are we moving again? I thought you liked it here?"

Once again, my attentive mother explained. "We are moving back near family and close friends. We need to be near our family and friends. I miss my mother and my friends, Daddy does, too. Life is too empty without them. We need them and they need us, true friends are your friends for life. Ever since Alan's accident and the Northeast outage, and what I saw your grandmother go through coming here to visit, it was too much on her. I want to be near her, we are too far away, and you kids need to see your grandmother."

I could understand her heart, even at my young age, and as I moved throughout my adult life, I would find I had the same feelings. I guess my mother's ability to bond had already begun to rub off on me. And I am so grateful! I learned to love and receive love. I also learned, along with my other siblings, adaptability. So back we went to where we felt bonded and secure. Back to where we could have the support for those challenging times we would face in the future. Even then I felt it was a good choice and great discernment on her part, and you will, too, as you read about what comes next.

So, my father put in for a transfer to Grossmans Lumber Company from New York to Canton, Massachusetts. It was a year later, after another move, he transferred over to sales. I remember my mother encouraging him to do something different to climb the ladder of success and to better himself. She thought he lacked confidence in his abilities, so she felt she had to push him a bit. The problem was he wasn't always ready emotionally for the push. So, it would sometimes not turn out so well, and my mother often misunderstood this as laziness in him. Unfortunately, she kept pushing and sometimes too much.

I know she had good intentions and wanted the best for him and for us. But I have also come to understand, as I have grown into adulthood, that my father was limited emotionally due to the heavy drugs and torture treatments he endured during his captivity in the service, during the Korean war. He suffered from an anxiety disorder that no one recognized back then. He had a very hard time coping with stress, which led him to often retreat to other places than home at times for peace. This was something about him my mother never understood, and it would later lead to problems in their relationship.

Since he didn't have a college education and barely finished high school, how could he do well in sales? I know my mother saw strengths in him that she felt he could use in the workplace, but was he ready for those positions she was encouraging him to pursue? So, at times she was very supportive with him, other times she was rather frustrated. He had a natural flare for salesmanship, as he was very charismatic and good with people but lacked confidence, and stick-to-it-iveness. He went on to excel in automatic data processing and began to earn pretty good money for the family. It seemed his confidence was building. Things were really beginning to improve for our family.

By now we were in Canton, Massachusetts, and our family was once again about to undergo some curveballs that would change the course of events for us. During these times, while visiting with my grandparents, mainly my grandmothers, I often observed both of them praying in their own way to the Lord for protection for our family and that God would surround us with his angels. And I believe it was their prayers that helped us through what I'm about to describe.

I've shared with you some background on my family, what they were like.

Now let me share my story and why I entitled this book, *Never Alone*. I chose that title because so much of my life that was met with challenges, mostly health challenges. But you understand that challenges come in many ways, and we certainly got a variety. However, I can say with certainty that all the things we have faced ended up with miraculous outcomes due to prayer with blessed outcomes. And, of course, you know the miraculous didn't always come right away. Hard times have no sense of time. But knowing the love of family and my heavenly father made all the difference. Walking with a hand I can't see or hold but knowing he was there. With each step I took, I found him not only there but quite faithful as well. He always provided a way of escape for me before I got into trouble. He has literally kept me set apart my whole life. Because of God, I was truly "Never Alone."

I hope you will experience not only my story but the remainder of the story of my family as well. They were such a big part of my life, and I loved them; they were bonded in my life till they died and will always live in my heart. As I share my story, it brings back both bitter and sweet memories of my life with them. I am blessed because of them. While they were not perfect and made mistakes, there was never any doubt in my mind that we were loved.

So, it was the summer of 1967, we had just moved to Canton, Massachusetts. I was seven years old at the time, Alan, nine, and youngest brother Lance, still a baby. Our oldest sister was 14 by this time. It's funny, my father took home movies of us back then hanging out in our living room the first week we moved in. It shows all three of us just being together, holding up our baby brother Lance to show him off for the camera.

During that summer of 1967—half a century ago—things headlining in the news were protests that erupted around the world against the Vietnam War. A famous photo taken in 1967 shows U.S. Navy Lieut. Cmdr. John McCain being examined by a Vietnamese doctor. And if you remember the story, John McCain was captured in 1967 in a lake in Hanoi after his Navy warplane was downed by the north Vietnamese Army. McCain said that upon capture, he was beaten by an angry mob and bayoneted in the groin. If his name sounds familiar to you, it's because in recent years he was in politics. But, unfortunately, he became very sick and died in 2018 from brain cancer. I have always looked at John McCain as such a war hero. He went through so much on behalf of this country. I have always admired him for that.

Another memory of 1967 was the Montréal-hosted Expo 67, race riots in the U.S. that destroyed parts of Detroit and other northern cities, Elvis Presley married Priscilla in Las Vegas, and O.J. Simpson who was considered a hero back then and highly looked up to, was a running back for the University of Southern California. Israel was fighting the Six-Day War against Egypt, Jordan, and Syria. The 20th century limited passenger train made its final run from New York City to Chicago and so much more going on. Just before the summer started on May 17th, 1967, a large group of an estimated 5,000 listened intently to Dr. Martin Luther King speak at Sproul Hall University of California administration building in Berkeley, California. At that time, Dr. King was reiterating his stand for nonviolence and urged the young people to support a peace block that would influence in 1968 elections. And if you remember, Robert Kennedy was active in politics at that time and later announced his candidacy for presidency.

A prominent singer back then was Sammy Davis Junior. I personally loved his song "The Candy Man" as a kid. It was such a happy upbeat song, as that's how I was. The song "R-E-S-P-E-C-T" was on the charts, "The Beat Goes On," by Sonny and Cher, "All You Need is Love," by the Beatles, The Monkeys also were pretty big in 1967. I had posters on my bedroom wall of them and my favorite song by them was "I'm a Believer." Diana Ross and the Supremes, "Love is Here and Now You're Gone" topped the charts in 1967. Janis Joplin was starting to gain her fame, along with Jimi Hendrix. There were so many artists back then I remember really liking. Some of the teenage idols, like Michael Jackson and his "Rockin' Robin" song. I'm not sure exactly when this song came out, but I just remember really liking it and dancing to it in our basement with my brother Lance when he was little older.

I recall that summer as we watched TV, my brother Alan and I liked to watch *Batman*, starring Adam West and Burt Ward. I loved the show *Family Affair* with Brian Keith and Sebastian Cabot. We were big TV fans. Some of the shows listed at that time were *The Lucy Show, Gomer Pyle, Gunsmoke, Bonanza*, and who doesn't remember *The Red Skelton* show? My parents enjoyed watching Jackie Gleason and *The Dean Martin Show*. And NBC back then featured Saturday night at the movies. Others included *The Ed Sullivan Show*, which featured prominent singers of the day, *Greenacres*, and the *Smothers Brothers comedy hour*. And all my grandparents adored Lawrence Welk, who I thought was so boring back then. And now I love that show and would give my eyeteeth to be able to sit and watch it again with my grandparents. I have such sweet memories of being with my family and sharing all this time together.

Back in Canton

One afternoon before school started, I noticed a little girl playing outside her home directly across from ours.

I asked my mother, "Is it Okay to introduce myself to the little girl across the street? I'd like to see if she'll play with me." She looked about my age, and I was eager to make a new friend.

I think Alan was getting sick of me clinging to him, and my older sister was usually off doing something else. I could only dress Lance up so many times in different outfits before he was sick of it and began to cry. I had to realize he was a baby, not my new doll. I thought he was neat; he was a baby and my brother. And after all, it was time for me to spread my wings and get out there and explore a new friendship. It was something my mother always encouraged.

My mother was a little hesitant at first, but said, "Okay we'll see." Her famous words that really meant, "Give me a minute, and I'll do it." My mother rarely said no to doing something constructive and positive. She not only loved to see us productive, she also loved to see us moving forward toward right choices and good goals. She was concerned about me going over there alone because we lived on a main road with a lot of traffic, and she also didn't know who they were yet. Since she was a stay at home mom, she had the time to explore all this.

I remember our address was 1671 Washington Street There was a lot of traffic that day, and I felt a little intimidated because I wasn't used to crossing such a busy street myself. I was afraid of getting hit by a car; unfortunately, Alan's accident left an unpleasant memory for me and caused me to be very cautious with traffic. Caution is never a bad thing.

My mother, being who she was, reassured me I would be Okay if I held on to her hand. I loved how secure that made me feel back then, I was all right as long as she was with me. She then got ready to take me. It was a beautiful sunny day, so all she had to do was get her sandals on, fix her hair a little, freshen her makeup, and we were good to go. Even back then, I knew very few women who would go out without makeup. And my mother was no different.

"Okay, Iris, let's go. I'd like to see if her mother is home, I'd like to meet her, too. Can you comb your hair a little? I want you to look nice for the new neighbors."

I did what she said, wondering how else I could make a short pixy look any neater, as it was a very plain, easy style for a seven-year-old as it was. It tended to just fall into place. But whatever, I did what she asked. When I came out, she looked me over for approval, and said, *"Andiamo,"* which in Italian means, here we go! My mother knew a few Italian words from my grandmother. So, my mother carefully walked me across safely to the neighbor's home. As we approached the little girl, we said hello and my mother asked this young lady her name, her age, and if she could meet her mother.

She was a delightfully friendly, young Italian girl, small and skinny with long dark hair. Of course, aren't all little Italian girls like that? I can name at least six I knew! To move on, as they say in Italian, *andare avanti*. Her name was Angela Forte. And I was right, she was seven years old as well and headed for the same grade in school, second grade. We noticed a sign in front of her home that indicated her mother did real estate for a living: "Forte Real Estate." Angela's home was a small ranch-style home with a large finished basement. It was positioned right next to a small cemetery, which my mother thought was different. "Lively at best," she would later joke. I'm mentioning specifics about the cemetery and where Angela lived, as significant to what happens later in the book, so stay tuned! Don't touch that dial! Or in this case, that page!

To make a long story short, my mother went inside to meet Mrs. Forte, Angela's mom. Her mother was friendly and hospitable, but I can't recall much of what she looked like.

She offered Mom coffee and me some chocolate chip cookies. I remember they had coffee together and got to know each other as neighbors while Angela and I played. When Angela pulled out her Barbie doll collection, I was in heaven. She had a Barbie dream house with a Ken doll to boot. Ken had convertible car and fun clothes and accessories, and he was a cute little doll. This was such a relief from playing army all the time with Alan. His toys weren't as cute; they were little and green and plastic. He wasn't budging on playing dolls with me, whatever we did together, it was usually more masculine. Don't get me wrong, I loved playing with Alan but desired to do girly things with friends occasionally.

At last a girl to play with. I was elated. We became instant best friends and really bonded together. My mother stayed with me for about an hour and a half while chatting with Mrs. Forte, then we said our goodbyes, thanked them for their hospitality, and headed across the street back home to where my father and two brothers were playing together in the yard. My older sister was off with a new friend she had met.

Angela and I spent the rest of the summer playing together. We played with her doll house, we played house, on occasion we would play a board game, which was popular with little girls called "Mystery Date," jump rope, swing set, you name it. Our mothers would take us on occasion to the movies or out to lunch for pizza. We had so much fun and used our imagination together. Angela's family was quite religious and some of her little Bibles caught my attention, and sometimes she would read me little children's Bible stories. I began to be drawn more to Christianity due to her example.

Before we knew it, it was time to be thinking about getting ready for the new school year. I recall my mother taking me shopping for new shoes and buying me what was known as fish net stockings back then. And they were just that. Fish nets with holes in the stockings, no insulation, and really bright '60s colors, like orange and red. I didn't know what to make of the fish nets, as far as liking them, but they were in style and my mother thought they looked good on me, so what the heck, go with the fish nets. But she'd never get me to wear them today. We had to have stockings to wear because back then there was a dress code and the girls were required to wear dresses, no pants were allowed in schools. Oh, my, we had accountability!

We were disciplined well, and it taught us respect. I'll say it again, it taught us respect for authority. Back then we respected and learned from our elders.

I see today respect for authority is really lacking. Perhaps it's the example our generation set. I don't think it's the same example our parents set. Hopefully the next generation can do better. I pray so! Maybe bringing back the fishnet stockings would help, it certainly made me fall in line.

So here I was, September in New England and a little chilly waiting for the bus with those fish net stockings. As we waited, Alan and the boys were dressed warmly in long pants, and here was Angela and I with the fish net stockings, freezing to death but sucking it up because we were in style. We were going to fit in no matter what it took. Anyway, we arrived at school and were assigned classes. Angela and I were disappointed because we thought we'd be in the same class together. We assumed that because both our last names began with F. We just missed it! Oh, well, we rose above that quickly, realizing we couldn't be together every moment. But we could always share our fishnet stockings. Sorry I couldn't let that one go; I'm sitting here laughing as I'm writing this. I guess simple things amuse simple minds. But we remedied that by playing together after school, and on the weekends, as best we could. She had other friends, and I soon met other little friends, too. We had to branch out, it was too early to be co-dependent. But that came later, as all my life I had many good friends to share my life with. While Angela and I were together, we watched over each other like sisters and it was another real bonding experience with a friend.

My mother taught me that when you have a friend, they're a friend for life. Today, I have quite a list and you can only imagine how hard it has been on me throughout my life to have a best friend wherever I have lived to try to let them go. I had no trouble letting go of the fishnet stockings, however. (I'm still laughing!) But seriously, each one was special in their own way. Most I never did learn to let go of. I loved and cherished every one of them, and they loved me. I always found a way to keep in touch with each one. That's what real friendship is. Nothing weird, just plain, old, ordinary, sisterly love. My own sister was so much older than I was, we were very different, and she was into her own routine by then, so we never really had a chance to get close. As they say, things happen. It saddened me, but my mother would later explain it as it being our age difference. And perhaps she was right. I just know that after that, I did look at my friends as sisters. I just couldn't have too many. I was one of the lucky ones.

Early Friendships

Andrea and I were best friends back then, and it was so special, as first friendships often are. Andrea's parents, Joel and Carolyn, along with her younger brother Michael and little sister kim, were also close to us. Because we all lived in the same home, we became very close, like family. It was hard to move away from that old neighborhood of Jewish/Italian mix with my grandmother's nearby and other relatives. The place where we had established such close relationships with people we could count on, would now be in the past. But we must move on. I still hear from Andrea today, and will always miss her childhood friendship of playing in the backyard swings, riding tricycles, playing barbie dolls, going to the beach together as families, barbecues, etc. She was a sweet child and easy to get along with. She grew into a beautiful woman inside and out. You never forget first friends.

Back in Canton, I had a party for my eighth birthday on Saturday, May 4th, 1968. My actual birthday is May 3rd, but because the third fell on a Friday, we had the party the next afternoon. All my cousins, along with some new and some old friends were there, including Andrea. We have that on home movies, too. I was opening my new gifts, playing pin the tail on the donkey, dancing to records on the record player, we were probably listening to one of the teen idol's singing a popular song, possibly Bobby Sherman. I also remember playing a record, which was a 45 rpm back then, by Michael Jackson, "Rockin' Robin." It was a cute, upbeat song. When I hear it now, it brings me back to that birthday party. We were all having such a fun afternoon with cake and ice cream to top off the day. My mother went to great lengths to bless my day and make me feel special. She did that for all of us. She loved to see her children happy. Everyone was dressed up in party outfits and dresses.

We did that back then, got dressed up just to go to someone's home. We would look at *Tiger Beat* magazines, to emulate the latest styles of clothing. The magazine featured the latest teen idols, like The Cowsills, (a family of singers with a television special each week), The Monkeys (portraying four male singers with a television show), The Osmond Family" (a family of singers, featuring Donnie and Marie Osmond), and I can't forget the Partridge Family, which also portrayed a family singing together and traveling on the road. I also loved Michael Jackson's song, "Ben." All had variety shows., Television was innocent and fun back then. As young girls, these were our role models, and I felt they were good ones, as they were portraying family values. I remember being mesmerized by Ricky Nelson who was a popular rock n' roll singer back then. I became obsessed with him, a real crush from such a young girl.

I envisioned my life like the Ozzie and Harriet of the show from the 1950s and '60s, being a housewife and living happily ever after. It remained a goal of mine that I would pursue until it was time for me to think about marriage. What seemed at the time like silly little girl imaginations I felt was actually the destiny that God called me to and I would learn that as time went on. Sometimes we lose sight of the fact that as we have desires like this, it could be God leading us in the very direction that he intended for us. And if we didn't have a burning desire to do that. we wouldn't be willing to. As you read my story, you'll see just how I followed those wholesome role models I saw on television and how I followed much of my mother and grandmother's examples, too. They made their mistakes, but I learned from them as well. Part of learning as you grow up can be learning what not to do. I guess I was intuitive that way.

I also liked David Cassidy. I had posters of these guys on my wall as I got older. Oh, those little girl crushes. There were lots of other parties every year, but that one really stood out to me, as it was a turning point in my life.

Adjusting to a New Place

The party ended, everyone went home happy and fulfilled from such a nice time. The next day, I awoke, and as I lay in bed, I was contemplating the new area where we were living. I was thinking about Lance, our baby brother, wondering what he was doing. Was he up yet? Was my mother feeding him, was he in his play pen? I really adored him. I enjoyed helping to tend to his needs. He was a real living doll; he was so handsome as a baby. In fact, I used to call him Lance Paul, my doll! I was looking forward to hanging out with my parents as it was a Sunday. Well, I got up, went into the kitchen to find everyone eating breakfast at the kitchen table. Alan was eating his favorite Frosted Flakes cereal, with Tony the Tiger on the front of the box, my father eating bagels and cream cheese with orange juice. My mother was having coffee and a bagel with cream cheese. At the same time, she was feeding Lance baby food cinnamon and apples or peaches along with rice cereal. My sister was having toast with jelly and orange juice.

My mother greeted me. "Glad you got up, it's about time, what do you want for breakfast?"

"I guess I'll have what Alan and Daddy are having." So, I fixed myself the cereal and poured a glass of juice while my mother toasted a bagel for me. I was quite underweight back then, so as I poured myself a bowl of cereal, my mother thought it was a good idea to add the bagel. My mother, coming from a Jewish background, bagels and cream cheese in that culture is quite common, and we all loved it. I sat down with everyone, and we chatted about the day ahead. I tended to, most of the time, eat more like my Russian grandmother and would eat hot healthy cereals with fruit and milk or healthy whole grains. But this was a fast breakfast morning, so we ate easy prep food that day. Perhaps everyone was tired from yesterday's party. Other Sundays, my father would prepare us eggs, sausage, or pancakes to make it special and to fill us up for chores around the house that needed to be done.

When I finished, I went into my room, got dressed, brushed my teeth, combed my hair, etc. and quickly moved on to what do we do now. Sundays could be a mix of activities; we would do chores to help, then my father would play games with us. Mostly with me and Alan, as Lance was still a baby and my sister was much older, and often doing other things. Other Sundays, we would travel to see our grandparents, as we were geographically close enough again.

Being in Canton and with all the newness, my older sister was finding her niche and began to find friends. The commonality you find with teenagers was nothing unusual, and some of her friends were quite nice. By that time, she was more interested in her new friends and less interested in family gatherings. She was in her adolescent years and really looking forward to getting ready for high school, plus she was discovering boys. A typical teen drawing.

Alan, however, had a harder adjustment while in Canton. In school, he was bullied quite a bit. I remember feeling so bad for him. It hurt me to see him struggle so much. But my father reminded him that this could make him stronger if he let it. My father was concerned and spent time teaching Alan how to defend himself with boxing.

Alan age 8.

This gave Alan the confidence he needed in dealing with the stress of some hardcore kids. An older kid who lived next door cornered Alan one morning on the way to the bus stop and pounded on him just because he was new to the area. My parents went and spoke to his family. And it mostly stopped, with only one other incident. It was a tough year for Alan. He had trouble fitting in, and I'm not sure why, although he was a shyer, more sensitive middle child.

As I look back on it today as an adult, and a mother myself, I think that may have been why. I also think his head injury and trouble learning added to the conflict he was feeling. Feelings of being misunderstood and out of sync with others at times. But Alan was always a kind boy, and he grew into a very kind, others-oriented adult. I think his hardships worked for good. They seemed to make him a good, caring, compassionate, sensitive man that I see in him today. He turned out to be a great husband and father and now grandfather as well. We have all reaped the benefits of Alan in our life. The car accident he experienced was just a bump in the road, almost seeming to try to prevent the destiny that God had for him. And that was being there for his family and is no greater calling. What helped him was he had family to fall back on. We all mattered; we all help each other. We all had that place to go for shelter in that time of troubles. As hard as being bullied was, he was never felt alone. He had his family, and as a result, he loved to be home.

Shortly after my huge eight-year-old birthday bash, I think it was about a week later, I began to experience stomach pain on the lower right side of my abdomen. Because it would come and go and the symptoms seemed vague, my mother wasn't quite sure what to make of it. I had stomach aches, a lot back then, and some food sensitivities, and was unusually thin. But this seemed different! So, she took me to our family pediatrician, who happened to be one of my mother's old classmates, whom she liked and trusted. She brought me in several times within a two-week period. Each time he insisted it was a virus. Just to be safe though, he ordered penicillin. There was the key; till this day, I'm thankful for that penicillin. The last time she took me to see him, he insisted I was making more of it than it really was. I never understood why doctors didn't think you knew yourself, and why they thought you had to make up symptoms like you had nothing else to do. How ridiculous! Well, within a few days, I began throwing up green, couldn't eat anything, ran a very high fever (I'm getting symptoms as I'm writing this). Ugh! I was literally in and out of consciousness. I was deteriorating rapidly. I could no longer get up out of bed. My mother knew at that point that something was seriously wrong. Hello!

The doctor kept me on penicillin. We had a pharmacist who would deliver it to our home, and by the third time he came with more penicillin, he said to my mother, "This is not a virus, I think she has appendicitis. You need to take her to the E.R. right away."

My mother's face flushed, she began to tear up, and said to him, "Thank you, I know this is serious, I just didn't know what to do, as the doctor was certain it was a virus." She had put her trust in her friend the doctor more than her own instincts. And unfortunately, it almost cost me my life. But she assured the pharmacist she was going to act quickly. He patted her on the shoulder, trying to assure her it would be all right and then left. Well, in a flash, my mother called my father at work, and he rushed home and picked me up very carefully, driving me to the hospital himself with my mother along. My sister stayed with Lance and Alan. My dad rushed me to Norwood Hospital in the next town over from Canton. He ran several red lights in the process and was grateful he didn't get stopped. Everyone was worried. I can even remember Angela and her mother and several others from a prayer group coming to look in on us and comfort my mother while I was in bed at home. Calls to my grandparents and other relatives were happening, I was told.

With all this going on and being quite sick, I remember it made me afraid, but I was so sick, wasn't aware of a lot of it. Why was everyone so concerned? What was happening? Before my father took me to the hospital and I was declining in bed, Angela came to see me, held my hand, and said a little prayer at one point. I personally didn't remember that, it was something my mother later told me. Angela was amazing for an eight-year-old, no wonder she's in ministry today. After that things were foggy to me. I barely remember being brought to the hospital. It wasn't long after that I lapsed into a coma, and now again, I'm going by what my mother told me about what happened next.

My father pulled up to the emergency room, and told them I was very sick and needed to be carried in. They quickly appeared with a stretcher from the E.R. I was then wheeled into emergency where we met immediately with a Doctor Brown. I'll never forget him! He was the kindest pediatric surgeon one could ask for. Of course, I knew more about him during my recovery, but he examined me and began to put things in motion quickly for the operating room. I was already unconscious!

After telling her that my appendix had burst, probably days ago, he asked my mother, "What made you wait so long to bring her in? The peritonitis (gangrene, poison to the system) has now spread throughout her system. We will open her up and see what we can do, but I'm afraid it's just too late." He later told my parents that, "Ten years ago because of the medical technology being what it was, she would have certainly died."

Well, at that point, my mother tried to explain about what the pediatrician said, and with that, she became overwhelmed and fainted, taking on the guilt of waiting so long. As I look back, I felt terrible that she felt this way, as she was such a loving, good, attentive mother. I think she did what the doctor told her, she trusted him and his assessment of the situation. I'm sure it was agonizing for her. Well, my father caught her as she fainted and sat her down. They used smelling salts to revive her. All the while, I was headed for emergency surgery. I came to for a moment and remember being wheeled by nurses quickly down a long corridor to an elevator.

One of the nurses noticed I had come to and said, "It's going to be all right." She put a doll in my hands to comfort me; the next thing I knew, I was in the operating room, where I saw Dr. Brown washing his hands. I remember feeling so sick and so weak.

He turned to me and smiled. "We are going to take good care of you. You will be asleep in a minute, don't be afraid, we are going to help you."

That's all I remember when I woke up what seemed like just hours later, but it had been weeks, maybe even a month. I was in ICU and had been in a coma that long. The first thing I saw was my mother's face.

She stood over me, with a great big smile, and exclaimed, "There she is!" I couldn't understand why she was so excited to see me. And why did I have all these tubes in me? Down my nose, in my stomach, in my arms, and I was strapped to the bed with railings on the side. I was disabled, disoriented, and had a hard time communicating. I was so confused but very glad my mother was with me. It made me less afraid. It literally took months to get me rehabilitated to where I could go home. I had suffered a huge trauma to my body and brain. But there was a prayer group praying for me, along with other family members, and I believe even though it took so long to recover, it's why I made it. No one expected me to live, there was that much damage.

Now the doctor was telling my mother he didn't know what my life would be like. Would I have children? He didn't think so because of all the damage abdominally. The time I spent in the hospital rehabilitating was long and arduous! But people were kind. Eventually, when I was well enough, they moved me to a four-bedroom hospital room with other girls who were also sick. But two out of four of us could get out of bed. I remember a girl about my age, Annie, took a liking to me and loved helping me as she realized how sick I was. She was one of God's little angels that came to watch over me. Or at least that's how it seemed. When the nurses couldn't come right away, she would get my things I couldn't reach. I was bedridden for a long time. Annie became so attentive to me that the nurse had to remind her that she was sick, too, and should call her if I needed something.

I want to interject here as you continue to read my story that throughout my life, anytime I would struggle, God has always sent me that special person or persons to watch over me and come alongside me. A gift I have always cherished.

After leaving the hospital, I only saw Annie once in Dr. Brown's office when I went for a check-up. And it saddened me because I had become quite bonded to her within the time that I was there. I always wondered what became of her, as she was such a kind, gentle, compassionate child, much like Angela.

I was missing her, another friend I had bonded with but was to never see again. I never forgot her unusual kindness. When I did finally come home from the hospital, I had to be specially tutored because I now had severe learning disabilities. And I was never totally well after that.

I only saw Angela a few times and eventually we went our separate ways because of geographical distance, but I never forgot her either. I wonder what she ended up doing in life. It wouldn't surprise me at all if she became a missionary. So, was Annie and Angela a sisterly love provision from the Lord to watch over me when I couldn't do for myself? I was just beginning to understand God's ways. And although he allowed such a debilitating trauma to take place in my life, I learned that he would never ask me to go through something alone or without making provision for me in the process. As you read my story, you will see this pattern in my life. I was just beginning to learn the meaning of what a true friend was. It had such an impact on me; the role models, both young and old, taught me how to be a good and loyal friend, and I would never find myself alone.

My Recovery

It took a long time, and I could not go to school yet. Alan and Dad played games with me and my dad encouraged me to enjoy what I had and not to be discouraged. He and my mother had me watch funny shows on TV and laugh. As I got stronger, my mother took me out to be tutored just to get me out more. I remember being in one of the tutor's homes. I can still see her in her kitchen as I sat at her table while she prepared dinner for her family. She was kind and a good tutor. I was re-learning things and it was tough. I was experiencing learning disabilities that would plague me for the rest of my life. I still have a tough time learning but have found ways through therapy to get around this and to be able to use my gifts, like writing for example. They told me back then I was very intelligent, but I was also impaired. So, I had to learn ways around that, and it would not be easy.

While still living in Canton, I was able to go back to school for a day or two but didn't do well. So, I was kept out of school until I was strong enough to handle being with other kids. Playing, studying, and everything.

Another thing that comes to mind is I remember my mother and father and grandparents talking about the fact that they could have sued the pediatrician who misdiagnosed me. But they decided not to. They felt because he was a close friend of my mother's and he felt terrible, it was enough. They also were so grateful I had lived, they wanted to leave it alone and move on. They also recalled him visiting me in the hospital, and with tears in his eyes, he apologized to me for missing this. It was after I came out of the coma, and I do vaguely remember him doing this. What can I say, my parents had integrity, and to this day, I am very proud of their decision. I just wish my mother hadn't carried the guilt of what had happened to her grave. As she watched me struggle through life with health challenges, it was a constant reminder to her. I tried to soften the blow and so did others. But I was her child that was scarred for life and she felt she should have done more. She couldn't bear the thought of me struggling so much and how close she was to losing me.

Shortly after all of this—it must have been 1969, but the details are a bit sketchy to me still—my father was transferred again and moved to a more stable sales position with automatic data processing in the Boston area. This was during the time we saw Robert F. Kennedy assassinated the year before Richard M. Nixon was inaugurated as the 37th president of the U.S., and Senator Edward M. Kennedy pled guilty to leaving the scene of a fatal accident at Chappaquiddick, Massachusetts where Mary Jo Kopechne was drowned. We heard of Apollo 11 astronauts Neil Armstrong and Ed Aldrin Junior take the first walk on the moon. In 1969, the cost of a postage stamp was only six cents. Unemployment was at only a 3.6 percent. The New York Jets played in the Super Bowl defeating Baltimore that year, and in the World Series, the New York Mets defeated Baltimore also. I guess it was a bad year for Baltimore. In that year, a big, big event that was very intriguing to my older sister was that in August, more than half a million people gathered in a small upstate New York town of Bethel near Woodstock, New York. They gathered for four days of rain, sex, drugs, rock 'n roll, etc., with performers like Janis Joplin and

Jimi Hendrix, along with many others entertaining the event. It was an eventful year, and I remember a lot of adults being nervous about the times we were living in.

At that time, we moved to the next town over, Sharon, Massachusetts, very different from the north end of Boston and Canton. I never did have an opportunity to say goodbye to Angela or her family or the special prayer group that prayed for me. But I prayed that God would someday make it so I could thank them, because this was the first miracle in my life I had experienced where people prayed, and God answered. He must be real, I thought. Because

I should have died, in fact, I was told I did for a moment. As I look back on this experience, I believe it was the penicillin given to me that saved my life. I believe it was God's provision.

Moving to Sharon

So, we moved on to Sharon. The houses we were in before in Canton and in New York were rentals. In Sharon, my parents were able to buy a house. Can you imagine, a three-bedroom ranch-style home with a basement that could be finished, two and half acres of land, all bought for $23,000. Can you even buy a car for that today? Yikes! Maybe an electric wheelchair. When we moved in, it was such a nice neighborhood with decent neighbors for the most part. It was safe, too. We really liked it there. A great town to grow up in. We were quite blessed to be there. It was summer again, 1969. I was now nine years old. Later in the '80s, Brian Adams wrote a song about the summer. I really like that song.

But at nine, I was still not well, but well enough to scout out the neighborhood a little bit. The street we lived on had many homes with families, but everyone had land enough to have their own space. Not like today, where people are on top of one another in many communities. I thought of my best friend Angela and missed her. I thought of Annie and wondered how she was. I remember saying a little prayer under my breath as I walked up the street to see if any other kids were around. "Lord, will you send me another friend!"

Two houses down, I came upon a little girl with long blond hair pulled up into a ponytail. She was playing in her sand box under a maple tree in front of her house.

As I came closer, she turned to look at me and said, "Hi, my name is Karen, what's your name?" Like Angela, she was so friendly and welcoming. I answered her, and she invited me to shovel sand with her. So, I did. I felt I was a bit old for this type of play activity, but I remember thinking it was something to do. After all, I was still only nine, so boredom didn't take long to set in. And as I was learning to think of others, I thought maybe it would somehow be fun for her. This was my first experience of meeting others where they were at. Karen was younger than me by three years, so she must have been six. I was aware of the age difference and it made me a little uncomfortable, but it was kind of like having a new little sister. She was so bubbly and fun. And as time went on, that would be what our relationship would become like. Just like Angela and Annie had been.

174

In fact, I had so many little friends by this time, it's difficult to mention each one. But they are all special to me, even to this day. So, was Karen another answer to prayer? She was, and she remained that way for many years to come. She and I still talk today. We have shared many ups and downs of our lives together and prayed each other through, then she is one that remained a long-time close friend and the memories of growing up together will always have a very special place in my heart.

Upon my first meeting with Karen while we played in the sand box, her mother came out and inquired who I was and where I lived. As a good attentive mother should! I told her I had just moved in. Soon she met my mother, and before I knew it, Karen and I were together a lot in spite of the age difference. Not too long after, before school started again, the rest of the kids from the neighborhood came out to play together, playing tag and ball and all sorts of things. There were a lot of kids in this neighborhood. I quickly made friends with two other girls my age from the street, Marsha and Lisa. But Karen was different and remained like a little sister to me throughout my school years.

I got close with her family and discovered they were very involved with the local Baptist church. I even remember the pastor's name—Pastor Robert Butler. I remember him as being kind and gentle, really caring for his congregation. He was a great Christian example, and of what a human being should be like. He made himself available to whomever needed him, even though he had his own family. Karen's family, with my mother's permission, would take me with them to church events and family outings. They became like a second family. They knew I had physical challenges, and while they didn't always understand them, looked out for me along with my own family.

It seemed every place I went, kind, special, caring people mentored me, encouraged me, and helped me grow into being the best I could be. I can see now it was God's provision for me. Because I was chosen, called by name, I was His. And he was proving his love for me along the way. In Isaiah 43:1, "But now this is what the Lord says, he who created you, O Jacob, he who formed you, O Israel. Fear not, for I have redeemed you; I have summoned you by name; you are mine" (NIV).

Today, looking back, I know God knew I lacked self-confidence and had trouble with self-image due to the scars on my belly and the difficulty learning. Plus, I walked with a limp. Sounds a bit like my grandmother, doesn't it? I always found it interesting that we had that in common. As I thought about it,

I often wondered if some of this special provision was from the Lord and if it could have been a result of that group's prayers back in Canton.

Did God allow me to live and receive so much love and provision, so I could be later used in a special way? Stay tuned, more to come, as this is often the case. And I was called by Him for His purposes, and I would see this in my journey with Him. My life was to be used for his purposes to be there for others. It was why I was created—my destiny in the making as it were. It unfortunately would be rather long and arduous at times. But not without His hand on my life and all the help I needed in the process. I had to learn to follow His voice and remain faithful to him. I have learned that we are either for God or against him, there is no in between.

There is a scripture that promises this. Deuteronomy 28 :1-6, "And all these blessings will come upon you and overtake you, as you harken unto the voice of the Lord thy God." Blessed you will be in the country, and blessed you will be in the city, blessed will be the fruit of your basket and kneading bowl, blessed you will be when you come in, blessed you will be when you go out, and everything that you set your hand to will be blessed."

Now at nine years old, I was just beginning to discover who God was, not realizing that later I would experience numerous miraculous events in my life. Events that would bring me not only closer to Him but also to discover the destiny that was about to unfold for me. Great and mighty things that the Bible states, I have never known. Jeremiah 33:3 says, "call to me and I will answer you and tell you great and unsearchable things you do not know" (NIV). Events would remind me that things would take place I could not have imagined. Not even in my wildest dreams. Times spent with large family dinners and gatherings at Auntie Anne's home, etc.

As children, we learn what we live. And I was blessed to have learned about love, serving others, determination, and the Lord himself at such an early age. Not always from my parents and immediate family but from other role models that the Lord placed in my life through many avenues. Living in Sharon, just south of Boston in the suburbs, was so nice. Being in a good neighborhood and having a good school system was a blessing. The Lord was at work in me and my family. But because I had physical challenges with learning disabilities, my parents wanted me to do more and live. Literally live. My mother began pushing me a bit, she was concerned that babying me too much would cripple me emotionally. And she wanted me to be strong. It was difficult though because I rarely felt well like other children my age. I felt different and had trouble communicating at times, not that people would notice; I just felt socially awkward and lacked the confidence I needed. Who the heck wouldn't after all I had been through?

Tubes had been left in each side of my abdomen to drain the poison continually for almost two years. Eventually, the bandages came off, and the doctors decided they could take the tubes out for good and that I could resume normal activity but with care. The peritonitis would remain dormant in my lymph nodes, however; it was so far reaching, they were never able to fully resolve it. My activity would never be what normal children would be. I always had close friends and loved being with them. I was a happy child, both my brothers and I got along well and played together daily. We looked out for one another. Lance, my youngest brother, was still only three at this time, but he was close to me and Alan. We were happy to play games together with him, both inside when the weather was cold or snowy during the winter months in New England and in the spring and summer months outdoors as well.

This photo depicts the closeness me and younger brother Lance shared. I loved being an older sister, it gave me a chance to practice motherhood at an early age, it was fun, and Lance made it easy. Circa 1971 or 72. Those were the groovy days!

Chapter 9

A Place Called Wampatuck

(My Treasured Memories and Destiny is Established)

Camp Wampatuck

It was still the summer of 1969. Included in more events I recall in that year was the Beatles singing group's last public performance on the roof of Apple records. I also remember the first Concorde test flight was conducted in France, and the Boeing 747 made its first debut. I never imagined that years later, my own son would be working there as an aerospace engineer. Funny how things happen! Also, that year, the Pontiac Firebird Trans Am, the epitome of the American muscle car was introduced. A disturbing thing in the news was Charles Manson and his cult headlined as having murdered five people. I remember my family talking about how awful it was. One of the victims was actress Sharon Tate. That was very sad, and I remember my family talking also about how scary things were. If I remember correctly, I think I remember Frank Sinatra and some of the other famous actors tried to take precautions because they thought they would be the next victims of Charles Manson. But if you recall history, eventually he and his cult were caught and put in prison for life, so those fears with other actors finally died down.

PBS was established in 1969, and the first man walked on the moon during the Apollo 11 mission. I remember all of this as both an exciting and turbulent time in history. Lyndon B. Johnson was finishing up his last term as President, and Richard Millhouse Nixon came behind him. With all this going on, I still felt very secure and sheltered from all these events. Again, it was because of the closeness I had with family.

Some of my family's favorite shows on TV were *The Doris Day Show*, *Bewitched*, *The Beverly Hillbillies*, *Hee-haw*, and *My Three Sons*. I thought Don Grady on *My Three Sons* was so cute back then. One of my many crushes. My parents and grandparents continued to watch *The Lawrence Welk Show*, *Dean Martin's Show*, *The Ed Sullivan Show*. We spent so much time with television, it was amazing we did anything else. Alan and I joke that if there was ever a game show about television trivia, we would enter it and certainly win. My parents were aware, however, that we needed to do other activities besides watch TV. I loved laughing and sharing that with Alan, Lance, and our parents; it was a great bonding experience, one I don't think we ever got over.

But I was willing to do other things, and I began getting daytime babysitting jobs, which I enjoyed since I had maternal instincts at such a young age. I started out by babysitting younger brother Lance once in a while but usually with Alan around or someone older to supervise. Caring for other people is a process when you're young like that, you start out with small windows of time and someone older around to monitor things as you learn what to do. Also, it was summertime and my mother began looking into summer camps for me and Alan because she knew I loved the outdoors. My mother wanted to keep us busy, so we weren't bored, so I did a little babysitting until where and when the camp was decided. While my parents were deciding on camps, Alan was letting them know he didn't like that idea. He was very bonded to our family and wasn't crazy about overnight camp and being away from family, particularly my mother at the time. But it was soon to be discovered as they pursued the process.

Alan recently described to me just how attached to our mother he was, saying to me, "Iris, it was like I was like gum to a shoe, you couldn't get me off." I laughed at his comment, as I laugh at a lot of his comments, and was grateful he felt that way about our family.

In her pursuit of camps, my mother, along with some close friends, found an overnight camp called Camp Wampatuck in Hanson, Massachusetts. This was a great girls camp for me. A lot of my childhood friends were going there, and my mother thought I would like it. It had two-week sessions at a time, all summer long. Alan was to go to an overnight boy's camp. My parents took the leap to enroll me for the first time at Wampatuck at the age of nine for two straight weeks. I was without my family and familiar surroundings and it was a bit of a test, or so it seemed to my child-like mind. But I was tougher and more independent than Alan, as most of my family recalls, so I was willing. I think some of it had to do with being laid up for so long and desiring independence. At first, I remember it was fun. I was meeting new friends and finding my place in the activities, all seemed well. Because of my physical challenges, I had to check in at the nurse to be sure the places where the drain tubes used to be in my stomach were not getting infected. And to be sure I was taking a long-term penicillin to keep the peritonitis at bay. We did wonder if the peritonitis would ever be resolved. But that would remain to be seen. Despite the health issues, I still was a little firecracker and wanted to participate with the other kids as much as I could without feeling like I was standing out. I had issues with stamina and a little trouble walking, I had damage to the shin bone in my leg from the whole episode with the appendix.

Today, as I think back, the bone problems and long-term damage may have been from having undiagnosed celiac disease and the malabsorption I was experiencing, which wasn't diagnosed until much later. No one could understand why I was so thin and yet could eat so much. It was as if I had a hollow leg. And the camp's food, which was primarily homemade, was very good. I'm not certain what caused the bone damage, but either way, it left me with a lot of challenges with mobility. But I was lucky it wasn't that noticeable to others. I guess people could see something was wrong but weren't quite sure what to make of it, and I didn't like talking about it, as I just wanted to fit in. At Wampatuck, I had a lot of support from counselors and the directors, so it was easy to feel secure and be able to fit in. So, I tried to move on and begin the journey of enjoying my camp experience and learning about the activities.

There were activity sign ups at the beginning, and one of the things I signed up for was horseback riding. I remember getting on the horse for the first time at age nine that summer. It was a hot summer day, and I went to the riding ring for the first session taught by a young woman nicknamed Mazz._

She may have been in her early 20s, but she was a senior counselor and a great riding instructor. As she began to work with me, I think she didn't quite know what to do. She wasn't sure why I was so apprehensive and rather uncoordinated.

It seemed people didn't know much about disabilities back then or perhaps they just know more today, I'm not sure. But I was really struggling with trying to get on the horse and then remaining on the horse due to my leg problems.

My parents, upon signing me up, didn't mention much about my challenges, except to the camp nurse, and only the health issues that needed to be monitored. They wanted me to do whatever I could, not to stand out as different, they were with me on that. My grandmother Leah Jean was instrumental in encouraging that, as she had a similar background and didn't want me to go through what she went through, she wanted better for her granddaughter. It was Okay for some activities but set me up to feel inadequate with others.

So, under Mazz's instruction, I climbed on the horse and got settled in the saddle. Then I realized how high I was. My bad leg was stiff and hurting in the stirrup, and it was no longer straight but crooked. I was struggling and began to cry. I wanted to do this but suddenly found it overwhelming. It was also hard to be up on this huge horse in the ring with the sun beating on me. I was downright scared but determined. Mazz at first was patient, but then as I continued to insist on getting off, she then came to me and did a good thing I'll never forget.

After ten minutes of me carrying on, she simply got very stern with me. "Why you are carrying on like this, I thought you wanted learn to ride?" She wasn't giving in to my fears. She then softened somewhat. "Come on, I know you can do this, I know you want to; once you do it, you'll never want to stop. It will be great, show me how brave you can be."

I kept saying, "I can't, I'm scared." But I eventually built up the courage to keep trying, and I finally was able to ride the horse at a walk around the ring. That was it, I was hooked. And being an animal lover, I enjoyed being with the horse and petting him. This was better than being known as a big baby to the other campers. Young peer pressure, you know! Mazz's encouragement was working; she was compassionate but didn't give in easily, which was good, and it helped me for sure. I could see her smile as I rode past her, and she had such a look of approval, I felt I was doing okay. She was an encourager. That last word from her gave me the confidence to press ahead, and I grew through the process. It was one of those situations you were afraid to pursue but were glad later you did it, and I overcame a fear.

"You can do it, but you got to try, don't give up, or you'll never do it," were her words and all I needed. It gave me the confidence I needed, and she knew it. I remember her as having a lot of guts and a lot of wisdom for such a young woman. I wonder if she still rides today. I will always remember Mazz and other campers fondly.

Her insistence that I get a hold of myself inspired me in other areas of my life just to push through. So, I let go of my fears, and little by little with her help and a few years of being at camp, I became an advanced rider. I couldn't walk far but became an excellent young rider, and much later, I was even put in charge of taking care of the horses. I also had advanced to the privilege of being able to go on what they referred to as night rides. These were evening horseback rides outside the campgrounds around the town and through the cranberry bogs to the candy store. Now that was fun! I was hooked and loved every moment of horseback riding after that. Today, I still ride periodically as I am able, and thanks to Mazz, I was able to overcome my fears and go on to enjoy this equestrian sport for many years to come.

I rode mainly western saddle, for reasons I had explained. I did try English riding once but with my feet turned in and having to post, I found it difficult for my leg. The way you hold your feet in the stirrups caused too much pain for me. I had broken my shin bone, which further compromised my ability to ride an English saddle. The western saddle allowed my feet to rest in an outward position with no posting, a much more relaxed position, and not awkward for my leg. To further explain, posting while riding in an English style saddle is where you performed an up and down motion while holding the reins. You pumped up and down with your feet in a turned-in angle in the stirrups as if you were doing push-ups with your legs, this is how I would describe it. It was easier for me to maintain the western style of riding because there was no up and down motion, it was quite a bit more relaxed. I loved it for many seasons to come.

Mazz's persistency enabled me to move away from fear and move into a place where I felt confident enough to press on to a place of enjoyment that I would have missed had I allowed fear to paralyze me. This was a Wampatuck counselor, and she was all about integrity and strength. They were all like that, that's why the camp had such a good reputation. They hired people like Mazz. A few years later, while I was still at Camp Wampatuck, a new counselor that taught horseback riding came on the scene. Her name was Pat Clark, and she was just as inspiring and fun to be with as Mazz was. This was the Wampatuck experience and many of my fellow campers in their adult years would agree it was a fabulous place that all of us were very blessed to have experienced. Thanks to all the wonderful counselors that mentored us and built our confidence! I couldn't be more grateful!

This is one of my favorite memories of me and my Dad, it was visiting day at the Camp. Alan took this photo of my dad greeting me with Lance at his side. Miss you Dad. Circa 1972.

The Wampatuck Experience

The rest of my years at camp were great. As I attended Camp Wampatuck, I enjoyed many fun activities that allowed me to learn new skills. Skills like swimming where eventually I became a lifeguard at a YMCA camp as a teen. Being a lifeguard was hard for me because I lacked stamina due to my earlier illness, but with a lot of determination, I was still able to excel. I always tried and learned to never give up. I heard this from many camp counselors as I went on to attend each season. I learned to be strong, not just emotionally and physically at camp, but also, I learned much about spirituality while I was there. It was a great camp. I can't say enough good things about it. It was so well-liked; we even have a Facebook page where we can share memories together in addition to the website. Some even have reunions as they are able geographically.

In addition to the activities I enjoyed while I was there each summer, and because I had a religious background, I also enjoyed the church activities we were required to attend. No matter what religion you were, the camp's policy was that we were required to attend a church service of our choice every single Sunday. As campers we got to choose between Catholic and Protestant. I chose Catholic most of the time because my grandmother on my father's side and my father were more Catholic-oriented, as I've mentioned. My mother, being Jewish and wanting me to be Jewish, wasn't crazy about this. But because we were required to go, I learned a lot about Christianity from this camp and some of the staff. We were also required every Wednesday evening to attend Vespers. Basically, this is a service of evening prayer inspired by the divine office of the Western Christian church.

We learned about prayer and connecting with our heavenly father. Through this accountability, we learned respect. We learned to respect the staff members, our older adult role models, connecting with each other, and we learned about God. The Jewish campers that attended, which was sort of me, were still required to go but kept their own religious beliefs, which the camp also respected at the wishes of their parents. At Vespers we sang old hymns of praise and I remember how peaceful that made me feel and how it connected me more to God and the Catholic faith than expected. Especially for a child.

I attended Camp Wampatuck several years in a row, I believe I was 10, 11, and 12 years old, possibly up until I was about 14. But while many campers did not connect spiritually and went there for a summer camp experience and activities, I and a few others benefited from the spiritual aspects of the experience. By the close of the two-week sessions we attended, we always had a closing ceremony.

This was a photo of one of the closing ceremonies at Wampatuck. It was special because our parents would come, and watch us receive awards for achievements, we earned during our camp time.

We had practice for the ceremony, were required to wear all white, and our families were invited to attend this closing ceremony with us, which always took place in the evening. I believe it was always on a Friday evening. They had a beautiful campfire that was set for a beautiful evening ceremony, where our families gathered together in bleachers in a circle around the campfire.

We campers stood at the top of the hill in a line, prepared to march down to where we would be seated by the campfire to begin the closing ceremony, which was led by our camp director Prof. Longley. Who, by the way, was a nice, compassionate man. We all have fond memories of him and his wife. They were the directors of the camp each summer back then and some of their family members worked at the camp. But one of the things that really bothered my mother, coming from the Jewish faith, was that we were required to march down behind a cross, and to sing the song "Onward, Christian Soldiers" with the girl at the front of the line holding up the big cross. I remember my father describing my mother's mouth dropping. She could see the Christian influence in my life coming to fruition. While my father thought this was fantastic and moving, my mother was upset by this because she could see that I was being more influenced in the Christian faith than the Jewish. My father realized how religious the camp was, and he was quite touched by it and enjoyed the ceremonies and how I was growing spiritually. In contrast, my mother hadn't realized how religious it was and was nervous about the impact it was having on me.

Later in life, when I was much older, about a year before she passed away, I asked, "Mom, if you were trying to influence me in the Jewish faith and didn't want me to be practicing Catholicism, then why did you send me to a religious camp with such Christian influence?"

She shrugged her shoulders and said, "I didn't realize they would require you to go to church. I had heard about the camp from other mothers, and it had such a good reputation and was affordable. In addition to that, a lot of your friends from school were going there and they seem to really like it. I never heard any complaints. I also felt good about the fact that some of your cousins were going there and that you would have some friends and family with you. I wanted you to feel secure away from home. The directors of the camp had a great reputation, as they were very nice people that could be trusted."

And then I said to her, "You must have realized what an impact it would have on a child that was religiously oriented and searching for God, and what about Grandma Leah and Dad's influence?" I said that to her because she was disappointed that I would be drawn to the Catholic faith and not Judaism. I had the influence of Camp Wampatuck and the influence of my grandmother, who worked for the Catholic church and Cardinal Cushing back in Boston, our neighbor Carol Huerth and her daughter Karen and attending church with them. My destiny, as I said, was unfolding, and it seemed she couldn't stop it. What did she expect? There were many other Christian influences in my life as a child, and I'm afraid I never really understood and related to the Jewish religion. My grandmother and many other people portrayed Christianity as uplifting, rewarding, and due to Christmas, fun.

When Judaism was presented to me as a child, mostly what I heard from my grandmother on my mother's side were stories of the Holocaust and the Bolshevik Revolution and how the Jews were being persecuted and even killed, and how there is still anti-Semitism in the world today. When my mother would take me to Temple, I even met some Holocaust survivors and saw the numbers on their arms, and it frightened me. It left me feeling if I were to be Jewish, I would be hated. So, of course, it left an impression on me that it was safer to be a Christian. Although today, many cultures and religions are under attack, back then, my young mind couldn't comprehend the realism of both religions. But I know now that God allowed this to take place in my life, so I would be drawn to where I was supposed to be and that was a relationship with him as a Christian.

Now that is my story, and my heart, because I can tell you my grandmother on my mother's side and my mother loved God dearly as Jewish women. And after all, they were still wonderful role models of women that loved God. They were the very reason I was searching in the first place, because I knew they were sincere in their love for God and each other. They were both very dedicated to Judaism, and I loved and respected them very much. But my calling and my heart was different, and I had to follow that calling. Because of this experience, I have always felt that a person cannot make somebody believe a certain way. It must be in their heart as Judaism was in my mother and grandmother's heart, so was Christianity in my heart.

Catholicism was in my other grandmother's heart as was with my father. So, I felt a little torn at times. My mother spent many years being hurt by this with me, but I'm not sure what she expected from me since my father's heart was also with Christianity. He was my father and an example to me as well, and he and his mother shared spirituality with me, too. His sisters and one brother and his mother also followed Christianity. I watched their lives unfold as a result. But in my own walk with Christianity today, I do not expect anyone else to be like me. Realistically, I don't want to try to make anybody else believe the way that I do, it's not right to try to make people do things. I don't feel it's appropriate; everyone has the freedom to choose. And while I believe that God gives us the freedom of choice and wouldn't force himself on anyone, that's a rule I follow, too. It's counterproductive to assume otherwise.

My own son has said to me, "You can't make people believe things they don't believe. You lead people by example and the rest is up to them." He's very wise, and I believe I've taught him well, as I once said those words to him during his nurturing years. It's nice to hear him speak them back and consider others. I believe it's the Holy Spirit's job to draw each person to where they're supposed to be. While I believe the way to heaven is through Jesus Christ, and I believe it's the only way, I also believe in not forcing those views onto others, it has to be their choice. I have learned that Christ never ever imposed or forced himself on anyone, he came to them in love, offering them a better way. I want to have the same attitude. It's not my job to do that, just love someone; that always works.

It's always angered me and upset me when I've seen other Christian people pushing people and trying to force through guilt and condemnation to believe, only forcing them farther away. It's just wrong, it doesn't work! If you want to reach somebody and tell them about God, the best way is by example and extend the hand of help in love. And if they will ask you what makes you different, then you can tell them. And if they are drawn in that direction and they want to be believers, they will make that choice, not to you and not me. I believe that God himself gave us the choice, the freedom of choice, for a reason. He wants people to come to him because they have chosen to and because they love him. Would you want someone to come and be with you and love you because you forced them? Or would you rather have them come to you because they chose to out of respect and love for you? You'd want them to come on their own accord. It would mean so much more. I want to be clear about this point.

There is a scripture in the Bible that states, "Therefore there is now no condemnation for those who are in Christ Jesus," Romans 8:1. I have met so many Christians in my day that tried to place guilt on me in so many ways, causing me to feel unnecessary shame, and I hated it. If I had not known about God myself and understood his love and what that means, I'm not sure I would've stayed at some churches. In fact, there were times when I didn't. Why would I want to be around a bunch of people who judge me and make me feel bad about myself? Through the years in my walk with the Lord, I had to learn that church and people are not always an example of who God is. And while I had many wonderful mentors and was quite blessed, you know, people are people and are not perfect, and there were some that set a terrible example of control and abuse. We come to God not because we think we are perfect but because we need him to help us be better people. In every walk of life, there are always those who will make the denomination, or the culture look bad because of the bad behavior. Unfortunately, it's all too common. But there are those who set good examples, aren't there?

Mother Teresa was one of my role models, and a good one, she walked what she talked. The reason was because she really loved God and she showed that to the people. She accepted people for who they were the way they were, and she just wanted to help; there was a sincerity in her ministry of helps to others and she was very humble, exemplifying God. She wanted to help ease their pain, their suffering, to build them up through encouragement, and so much more. More people came to know God through her example, not because she made them by insistence but out of love and letting them make the choice. It was what she did, not always what she said. She was a role model and a good one. She was highly respected because she didn't push, she was all about helps in love. She was a sincere woman who knew her God and loved mankind, and through her, people could see who God was because she reflected a good, loving, caring Father of the fatherless. Her example helped me to understand how to be the hands and feet of Christ to a hurting people in a difficult world.

I can tell you from experience with her as my role model, I have had more success in ministry by just loving people for who they were the way they were. The rest was up to them and God. People do have to feel it in the heart, and if they don't, as I said before, it is their choice. Don't people want to be loved and accepted for who they are? After all, it will never happen through judgment. If you have not love, you have nothing. In 1 Corinthians 13:2, "If I have the gift of prophecy and can fathom all mysteries and all knowledge, and I have faith that can move mountains, but do not have love I am nothing" (NIV). I personally could never be drawn to a religion with people who make you feel bad for any reason. I don't know why some religions are like that. When people are hurting and afraid, all I need to do is hold out my hand, and say, "It will be all right, and you are not alone." If you're nice to people, they will, nine times out of ten, respond positively. I have learned throughout my life and the good role models God put before me, that it is my responsibility to ease people's pain and encourage them in that pain, that's all! And then maybe they will find their way. And I do believe, that with God, you are never alone.

While camp Wampatuck required us to go to church when we attended the camp, they never pushed anybody in their beliefs either, and that really impressed me. They accepted everyone for who they were the way they were. They offered Christianity as an opportunity, not as a demand. Some came away inspired and went on to Christianity, some came away with a beautiful experience directed by beautiful people. But we all have the same thing in common whether we received Christ, or we didn't, we all agree that we had a beautiful experience with treasured memories and lasting bonding friendships that have lasted and will continue to last a lifetime.

I'm still in touch with some of those girls today and we all have the same thing in common: sensitive hearts and a love for each other and our fellow man. Camp Wampatuck molded us into the very loving and sensitive women we are today, no matter what walk each girl has chosen, I see this commonality in every single woman I talk to today who went there.

The bottom line is we all learned how to work together, accept one another, and not only learned to love each other as sisters but to love others as well. And isn't that something? No matter whether we were Jewish, Christian, Buddhists, etc., we learned to respect one another and not judge.

I'll say it again, I do believe in Christ, I believe he died and rose for my sins, I believe in sharing that with my friends and other people when asked and when the opportunity arises. But I do not believe in forcing anyone to believe the way that I believe. It's just not right. A true follower of God, and I can't say it enough, will be an example and then pray they find their way. Love always wins!

I think of camp Wampatuck often, especially during the summer months. I was one blessed kid, and I'm grateful for the love they showed us, it taught us to love. At this camp, I did develop my first spiritual roots and grew as a person. And as time went on, those roots grew deeper and deeper as I experienced life. It did help to mold me into the woman I am today and I'm thankful for it. I now live in Washington state, and sometimes when we go to the state parks here, I recall my camp experience as I walk the trails, soaking in the pine fragrance and the smoky smell of the campfires, and it brings me back to a place that I will always remember. A camp that left so many with such sweet memories. It saddens us because the camp is no longer there. I was told it was torn down in the 1980s and replaced with condos. But we have photos and our memories. Memories we will treasure all our lives.

And what happened to Alan? Well unfortunately, he didn't stay at an overnight boy's camp more than a week, he remained the gum shoe kid, and returned home crying because he missed all of us. Alan has been and is still today that sweet, sensitive, family-oriented person, one we all appreciate and love. He just couldn't stay away from family too long.

Chapter 10

The 70's and the Vietnam War

By the '70s, our country found itself in the middle of a war in Vietnam, and it seemed nobody understood why it was even happening. We heard the song "War" asking, "What is it good for?" The singer, Edwin Starr, declared "Absolutely nothing." And we would hear evidence of it in songs and on television at the time. The song "War" was calling for the end to war during a very turbulent time in history and for peace with all men.

As a friend and I celebrated the new year of 1970 together, this was one of the songs I remember hearing on the radio. We spent the evening until midnight ringing in the new year with a feeling of independence and enjoying ourselves. We weren't totally aware of the world around us and what was really going on, but, of course, at the young age of 11, we didn't understand, how could we?

And with the shelter of our parents, we were encouraged to enjoy life and not to worry about world events, even though the times around us were spinning with songs like "The times, they are a Changing," by Bob Dylan. His song, while still played in the '70s, was originally released in 1964. Our decade was going through a major shift in society, and the beginning of the '70s was another time in history that would exemplify some significant changes. And rock and roll music, as many of you know, reflected social and cultural change.

The decade would begin to lean more toward self-rights and less about the needs of others. We were hard-pressed to understand the Vietnam war and so much protest in 1970. What was really going on? What was the opposition really about? Were young men going into combat and being killed for no apparent reason? My understanding from what little my parents shared with us was that many Americans opposed the war on moral grounds and were appalled by its devastation and violence. Others claimed the conflict was a war against Vietnamese independence or an intervention in a foreign Civil War; others opposed it because they felt it lacked clear objectives and appeared to be unwinnable. Either way, I remember so many people talking about what a waste the war was.

We had young men going off to fight for our country, only to come back to opposition to them, as if they had done something wrong. I remember how awful it was for them when they returned home, only to be ridiculed and blasted by people who really didn't understand. It was sad because what they really needed was to be embraced with praise and honor, which they deserved. They should have been appreciated for their service. As I recall from news stories and people that I knew who were experiencing it firsthand, it was shameful the way they were treated. One of my friends recently commented on this. When I shared with her that I was mentioning the Vietnam war in this story, she told me that she remembered young men returning from Vietnam.

She said she was a teenager then. "As they got off the plane, people greeted them by throwing fruit and rotten produce at them."

I thought, how awful! Talk about disrespect! While Washington state is known for its nice produce, that's no way to use it and appreciate it. Better they should've greeted them with baskets of produce, so they could eat and feel the warmth of home again after being gone so long and the suffering they endured. But that's people for you, always wanting to make a statement, no filter, and without all the facts. And that to me is one reason why we have wars. It's people jumping to conclusions, making assumptions and acting upon what they believe is truth without knowing all the facts. I also feel its people wanting their own way and wanting to be noticed at others expense. Selfish behavior at best.

That's why the Bible tells us in Matthew 18:15, "If your brother sins against you, go and tell him his fault, between you and him alone. If he listens to you, you have gained a brother." Communication! It's vital if you want to have peace with people. If you have a problem with someone, go right to the person, give them a chance to explain what they really mean. Get the facts, don't hear it from a third person. Otherwise you get the wrong information and you act on that wrong circumstance, hence an argument or a war breaks out over something that wasn't even said or done. We need to give each other grace. That's why proper face-to-face communication is so important. It leaves no room for misunderstanding and gives an opportunity to shake hands and forgive one another rather than ending up enemies.

During the war, I remember many of us purchasing bracelets with a name of one of the soldiers that were missing in action engraved on it. They were called POW bracelets. The bracelets were first created in May 1970 by a California student group called Voices in Vital America (VIVA), with the intention that American prisoners of war in Vietnam not be forgotten. The POW bracelets were made of nickel or copper and were sold for $2.50 to $3 apiece. I remember those who wore the bracelets, including myself at the time, vowed to leave them on until the soldiers named on the bracelet were either found or their remains returned to our homeland. Between 1970 and 1976, approximately 5 million bracelets were distributed. I was so proud to wear one; as I wore it, it reminded me to think about him and pray for his safe return. I remember this like it was yesterday, although I don't recall his name. It's hard for me to believe that it was that long ago.

I prayed hard for God to answer my prayers for this man's safe return and protection. But I never did ever find out if he ever did return safely. I always wondered about that. But what I also don't know is how God may have used those prayers on behalf of him and his family. I still wonder if my prayers kept him protected and safe. Was I interceding to keep him warm and dry when it rained? Were my prayers dispersing angels to comfort him when he was afraid or overwhelmed? While I may never know how my prayers for him were used, I now understand that when we pray for others, we have no idea how our prayers will manifest in their life. Or what they were shielded from. My hope was that in some way they did help him, and I believe they did. Prayer is very powerful, and I believe it can move mountains in ways we may never know. I just knew at the time I was supposed to pray, and the answers were up to God.

I have often thought of U.S. Sen. John McCain who was one of those prisoners of war in Vietnam, and I'll bet someone had his name on a bracelet they wore on his behalf. I'm sure there were many praying for him. How else could he have endured such hardship? While he went through so much on behalf of our country, he did come back safely and recovered from incredible torture during his captivity. This war hero turned senator was in captivity for more than five years as a POW and decorated and described as a true war hero.

I never did hear the details of my father's captivity, and it was just as well. I'm not sure I could have handled hearing what he truly went through, and I believe it was the prayers of others that helped him too. I have great respect for Meagan McCain and John's other children for their courage to be able to hear of their father's story. They must have felt a mix of emotions, proud, honored, and saddened but grateful they had him as long as they did.

My brother Alan recently shared with me, "The reason he endured so much hardship during the Vietnam war, was because, the Vietnamese were mad at our country for dropping so many bombs on them during that time. By the end of the war, seven million tons of bombs had been dropped on Vietnam, Laos, and Cambodia, more than twice the number of bombs dropped on Europe and Asia combined during WWII." The Vietnamese wanted a confession for crimes committed against the North Vietnamese. They were determined. Unfortunately, John McCain and men like him suffered in the crossfire. Much like my father did during the Korean war.

I believe someone had McCain's name on a bracelet and had been praying for him. I'm sure several someone's were praying for him. And not only did he survive all this, but we all know that he went on to make a difference for this country in politics. He became a husband and father and had a special calling on his life for many reasons. God clearly had a plan for this special man.

His continued destiny began in 1982 when he was elected as a Republican to the U.S. House of Representatives from Arizona and later as a senator, because he was all about moving on. My mother was that way, too, and it's what I modeled after. I love role models like this. Any other attitude can leave you stuck and unproductive.

In my eyes, McCain was a true American war hero who endured hardship for his country. His focus was on hope and restoration. He recently passed away and will always be remembered as someone who cared, and the world is a lonelier place without him. As was said at his funeral, "He made this country better, and we should follow his example in making a difference. Sacrifice for others!"

Prayer moved mountains for John McCain, he was a role model to me personally of how to endure suffering and work it for good. In my lifetime, I have endured a lot of suffering, but it was people like John McCain who inspired me to press on toward hope and a future.

Jeremiah 29:11, "For I know the plans I have for you, declares the Lord, plans to prosper you and not to harm you to give you hope and a future. Then you will call upon me and come and pray to me and I will listen to you" (NIV).

No matter what he had been through, he remained optimistic. These are the true role models I look to. Not someone who stands up in front of a camera looking pretty and it's all about them. They have no story of hardship to inspire the suffering of others, no message of hope, just self-promotion. I have never found strength or comfort in those stories. I saw arrogance and a pride and self-love that would lead people astray, into thinking only of themselves, and not minding the people who have less than they do. Suffering brings strength and comfort to others as we share our stories.

It says in the word of God, and this is not a direct quote, but it's what I understand from what it says, that we go through things, so we can be there for others. II Corinthians 1:4, says, "who comforts us in our troubles, so that we can comfort those in any trouble with the comfort we ourselves have received from God" (NIV). Who hasn't received comfort and inspiration from McCain's and other POW's journey? If they haven't, they need to read his story. Vietnam veterans were prayed for and saw hope as a result. When all hope was gone, through prayer, God made a way for many of them. John McCain went before us but so did Christ. I believe He died on the cross for us. Christ went before us to provide eternal life and forgiveness of our sins. John McCain went before us to bring us hope and inspiration, and it gave me personal courage to press on through some very rough times in the torture I endured physically. Not to compare because as I was never in the service; I wanted to be, I was just too weak and frail from illness, but many of my family members were, and I have a heart for those who serve our country. It's a sacrifice for others that deserves honor.

The other side of the war brought another perspective. While John McCain was enduring his captivity and the country was divided over the conflict, another story was unfolding. It was a question of "What are we doing for our country?" And some couldn't answer that question. In addition to the bracelets we wore, I remember families being so afraid that their sons and brothers and husbands would be sent off to fight and possibly die. It was a common feeling, as I said, that the war was for absolutely no reason. Remember the song, "War." "What is it good for? Absolutely nothing!" I never cared for the melody, but the words were meaningful, and it got you to really think. What was war good for anyway? I had no idea, I just knew it involved a lot of suffering, and a lot of people were hurt and destroyed by it.

An example we experienced personally was with one of my mother's close friends from childhood. She had an older son who was drafted during the Vietnam era. From what I was told, he was so frightened of going to war that he fled to Canada to escape the draft. Canada, at the time, welcomed young men like him as immigrants. They felt it would boost the economy because many of them were educated, skilled workers. My mother's friend's son was what was known as a draft dodger at the time. He was afraid he wouldn't come back, afraid of suffering at any cost. No one wants to suffer, but there is this thing called suffering and sacrificing for the sake of others. Not everyone was or is quite as strong and determined as John McCain was. He was unusual and came from several generations of servicemen; he was taught this and had the faith to carry him. It was engrained in him.

Without faith it is impossible to please God. And without it, we are subject to fear and giving up too easily. Those who dodged the draft feared being wounded, maimed, captured, and tortured, which you can see from John McCain's story and my fathers, was a reality. But it was a sacrifice, laying down one's own life to help someone else and trusting for the results. In McCain's wildest dreams, I bet he never imagined he could live through all that to tell the story. But he did, and he is a role model we should all be proud to follow. If we all did, what a better country this would be.

While for some it was considered an honor to serve their country, some gave in to fear, and fled to Canada. Because they were not formally classified as refugees, but were admitted as immigrants, there is no official estimate of how many draft dodgers and deserters were admitted during the war. So, the majority came to Canada legally.

Draft dodgers refused to be inducted and often fought their cases in federal courts. They were not exactly praised, and they were thought of as cowardly. But not everyone had the chemical makeup to endure such a challenge. Everyone is different. There was conflict about why the war was even happening, and the country was so divided. It was a confusing and turbulent time. It wasn't easy to know what to do. Has fear ever gripped you? It has me. Yet it seems, and we learn from history that every generation has trouble of its own and the Vietnam war had plenty of it.

So, what is the definition of draft evasion? It is basically known as willfully refusing to present yourself for and submit to registration ordered by the government that was punishable by a maximum penalty of up to five years in federal prison. It also had a fine of up to $250,000. There have been no prosecutions of draft registration registers since 1986 (Wikipedia, draft evasion). President Jimmy Carter pardoned the draft dodgers in 1977.

I can't remember how my mother's friend's son got out of all of this. If he had to serve jail time or if he had to pay a fine, did he fight it in the federal court? That piece of history I may never know. All I know is after it was all said and done, he did get married and have a family, so I guess he came out Okay. I remember how upsetting it was to Mom's friend and her husband. They had no control over the situation, he wasn't listening to them, and this frustrated them terribly. While they weren't happy about the draft either and feared for his safety, they still felt it was an honor to serve. But he was 18 and considered a man, and it was his choice. For whatever reason, he chose to not go. I often wondered to myself, was he so afraid that he had to flee? No one could have known the mindset and the struggles they faced, and none of us understood this at the time, although people tried.

My mother's friend and her family often visited us because she was so close with Mom. One weekend in particular she and her husband came with their two daughters for the weekend. I thought it was so cool that she slept in my room. She was someone I looked up to, one of my many mentors and role models growing up. Because her daughter and I were the same age, she spent a lot of time with us, and I enjoyed every moment of that time. While she was my mother's best friend, she was like an aunt to me and my siblings. My whole family loved her. We have home movies of her and Mom traveling together with my father and her husband and other friends from the early '60s. She was one of those people that you laughed with, someone who was there in the good times, and when times were tough, a very faithful friend, especially to my mother! She was funny, uplifting, an attractive woman, and someone I could model after.

The weekend she spent with us was special. My sister had a picture of the '70s rock singer, Lee Michaels, famous for the song, "Do You Know What I Mean?" It was hanging on my sister's dresser mirror, the room we shared at the time. I remember Mom's friend sitting on one of our twin beds, talking to me and my sister. Our bedroom was something like what you would have seen on a *Brady Bunch* episode, decorated in '70s style décor—pink and colorful with off-white bureaus with brass handles on the dresser drawers. My mother loved the best styles for me and my sister.

So, as Mom's friend sat on the bed, we observed her glancing over at the photo of Lee Michaels. Finally, she got up, went over to the bureau, turned the picture around, and chuckled. She didn't want to look at it because it reminded her of her son. It was clear she was disappointed in him.

She then said to us, "I want a divorce from my son," but true to who she was, giggled as she said it. No matter how serious she was trying to be, she had an unusual humor that brought joy and made you smile. We were so blessed to know so many funny people, and she was one. That humor helped in tough times. Sometimes it helps to laugh at things, it lightens situations. Sometimes when she was sad, she would often chuckle to sort of shrug something off; my mother did that, too, and. I find myself doing it. But it was clear she was pretty disappointed in her son. I knew it was hurting her inside. In fact, I can remember her talking to my mother about how angry she was with him and ashamed; out of her anger, she even referred to him as "a self-centered big baby."

"I didn't raise him this way. Maybe I spoiled him too much," I heard her say. It was so sad, and it was one of the few times I saw my mother's friend so serious and angry, as most of the time she was quite jovial.

She was all about fun, and her husband, while he worked as a TV repair man in his own shop during the day, part timed as a magician for special shows and events, at hotels, and vacation resorts on the weekends. Oftentimes they would invite us when he was appearing as a magician somewhere; it was so much fun! One of the places we frequented was the Kennebunk Inn in Maine. It was right on the ocean and so much fun with lots of activities. Her daughter and I really enjoyed our times together there on weekends.

But that was my parents who really loved to have fun, and they had so many friends to have fun with. People were drawn to them and I could see why. My father, coming from a large family and with Italian descent, was quite social. You know how those Italians are jovial and expressive, a little angry at times, but they loved to have fun and *vino* (wine in Italian). I still have trouble understanding how the mob in my father's family background fit into the picture, but I never had the whole story. The bits and pieces I heard while growing up didn't seem very happy or feel-good to me, so I shrugged it off. Growing up, I didn't hear much about it, I was shielded from it, and understandably so. It would have made us fearful. And most families that were in the mob didn't tell the children until everyone was gone, which was true in our case. We weren't told about it until we were much older. During my impressionable years, thanks to my parents, my life was full, and I was sheltered from behind-the-scenes goings-on. At least for a time.

So, every weekend it seemed there was something to do. They kept us active, social, bonding, and very busy. We were taught to be goal-oriented and to think of others. And this is what my mother's friend taught her son, but when fear takes over, no matter how we were raised our children, it can send them to a place that we never thought they would go, and for him, it was to Canada. I can't even pretend to understand what was going on in his head at the time, only he would have known, but I'll bet he had a good reason. And as I said, it was his choice. Eventually, his parents reconciled with him and they were able to reunite as a family.

Mom and Dad together enjoying a night out.

A Special New Year's Eve

It was almost 1970, and we were living in Sharon, Massachusetts. I was 11 going on 12. It was New Year's Eve, and I was spending the night at my friend Diane's home. She was one of many young, close friends I had the privilege of knowing back then.

I was always drawn to compassionate, caring, and loyal-real people even as a youngster. I think it was because I was unsure of myself at times due to the trauma, I had suffered that left me feeling limited and different myself. Diane was all of that and fun, too. She was trustworthy, and I never felt she was judging me. She just liked to be with me in a sincere way, and when we were together, it showed. She came from a nice family, and while she could be quiet and shy at times, she was fun to spend the night with on such a special occasion. I remember how grown-up we felt being able to spend the night, just the two of us with no babysitter. In fact, it was many New Year's eves later that she and I had our chance to be babysitters. But this one we got to spend together, just the two of us, while her parents went out. It was a big deal to us!

I remember we made snacks and played games together, finding things to do together that we liked the most. Diane's uncle was a disc jockey at the time, so we spent the evening tuning in to what he was playing, which included The Carpenters. I loved Karen Carpenter, and most of the girls I was friendly with loved her, too. She had such a beautiful alto voice. I can still hear her singing one of her famous songs, "Close to You." Her songs were so mellow and soothing, and she was a good role model for young girls to look up to. At least from appearances. Back then we didn't know her struggles behind the scenes. Just listening to her music and being inspired by them was all we needed to know.

I took a personal interest in her career and I wanted to model after her, which later led me to a career of my own in music. As an adult, I sang in and produced a CD.

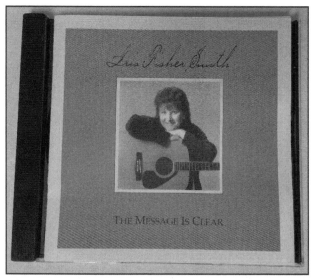

My first C.D. that I sang in and wrote many of the songs, it was a fun experience, I'll never forget.

It was something I dreamed of during my childhood. Early on, when I went to school for music, I took courses in music theory, percussion, classical guitar, voice, and song writing. It took me longer than most, as I had to be specially tutored, but although I learned at a much slower pace, I still excelled. My mother and other family members were proud of me, as they knew it wasn't easy for me. I specialized mainly in voice but also had a knack for rhythm and percussion (drumming). While I had to be tutored due to the brain injury I suffered during my appendix episode, I still managed to push through a lot of frustration with learning and my ability to grasp the music theory especially, which was much like learning a new language and very challenging for me. I was a fighter and probably partly why I survived the appendix episode. Determination was instilled in me by my mother and grandparents. I learned that you excel by not giving up. Much Like Karen Carpenter. She had her challenges, but for a time, had determination, which brought her to a successful career.

Her challenges led her to an eating disorder called anorexia nervosa. And unfortunately, little was known about it at the time. She struggled with it mainly in the 1970s, which led to her untimely death in February 1983. She died at just 32 of heart failure caused by complications related to her illness. I was 24 when she died and just beginning to explore a music career. When I heard of her death, I was so saddened, as it struck a chord in me, no pun intended! It was hard to understand why someone who was so attractive and so successful could struggle with such a deadly condition. But my thoughts quickly turned toward the legacy and the beautiful music she left behind. And her legacy was this; in addition to her music, her untimely death would turn circumstances for good.

Since little was known at that time about anorexia, this was a big deal. Her death did lead to increased visibility and awareness of eating disorders. Her work continues to attract praise today and she has been included in Rolling Stone magazine as one of the 100 greatest singers of all time. So, she left a legacy, one that would make a difference in countless lives through her music, example, and her struggle with the disease. Even after her death, she was able to affect other people in a positive way. Her music and story still inspire my heart and the hearts of many others. Her will and determination made it possible for me to push through my struggles and watch good come out of them. One life can inspire another; our suffering doesn't have to go unnoticed or without purpose. Stories like hers and my faith in God inspired me to want to help other people.

1970 was a milestone for me and my young friends in music. As young teens, we were drawn to the messages in song and emulating them. Our young minds were being molded by the messages we meditated on as we related to them, and we dreamt about what our futures would be like. We enjoyed listening to singers/songwriters, like Simon and Garfunkel, best known for their song, "Bridge Over Troubled Water," a meaningful song about not being alone and how a friend would lay down his life for another. This was something I was beginning to ponder as a young adult and what my purpose in life might be. While my mother had instilled some of these values in me, this song in particular was encouraging sacrificing for others. What better message—something my mother was modeling for me. She lived the example she wanted me to follow, teaching me to do what she felt was right. She was always thinking of others. Had she not lived what she was telling me to do, I'm not sure I would have gotten the message of right from wrong.

The difference between then and now were the messages broadcasted in the media and in song. While some messages today are uplifting and life inspiring, so many aren't, and it's causing today's children to grow up with way too many conflicting messages, leaving them wondering about their identity and what their purpose is. While there are many who are quite grounded, there is an alarming rate of those who are lost and turning to unhealthy, life limiting choices, stunting their potential. My concern is our country has become too divided.

As President Lincoln said, "A nation divided against itself cannot stand." I believe this is a true statement. While tolerance and acceptance of each other's differences is very important, finding commonality within the cultural differences is also crucial. It can bring good change and a more unified society. There is no easy answer, only integrity, faith in our creator, and love can lead us in the right direction.

Another strong, inspiring message we enjoyed listening to was sung by the group The Supremes: "Aint No Mountain High Enough," which was about pressing on and not giving up. Another good message in moving in a good direction and not caving in the moment life becomes difficult.

In Diane's home that New Year's Eve, I remember it as being such a fun sleepover, and yet a time of such transition for our country. My parents had gone out for the evening, as well as her parents, but they kept checking in on us during the night by telephone. My mother must have called me seven times that night.

I eventually said to her, "Why are you bugging me? I'm okay, I'm having fun, I'm not a baby you know!" No, I was a big girl at 11, a real woman of the world.

Mom said, "I trust you; I just want to make sure you're okay."

I remember Diane and I looking at the clock and seeing that it was 11:50 PM.

"Mom, the new year is about to begin, I got to go." With that, we hung up with only ten more minutes left of 1969.

Our thoughts turned toward what 1970 would be like. 1969 would be forever gone. What did that mean? For the first time in my life, I remember feeling what it was like to grow older and to move on to a place where we could never look back, moving into a future of "what will be?" It was an eerie feeling in some ways and exciting in others!

"Diane, what do you think 1970 will be like?" I asked.

"How do I know, I just hope it's fun," she answered. A profound and thought-provoking answer from such a young girl. I don't know what kind of an answer I expected from an 11-year-old, but it was simple and honest. I was like a little sponge at the time, absorbing the world around me, and I was always looking for answers, but maybe another 11-year-old was not the place to start looking. We naturally felt we had things to look forward to, as most children do; we were young and ambitious. But as life would have it, there would be some good and some bad life events to look forward to, as there are in everyone's life. What we choose to do with those ups and downs, however, can make all the difference in our own destiny.

So, as the clock turned toward 1970, it brought with it some interesting changes into the world. I remember in the news there was talk of The Concorde's first supersonic flight, then the jumbo jet went into service, we heard of the Isle of Wight Festival taking place, and we also heard about the Chicago Seven being found guilty, to name a few events. For those of you who aren't familiar with the Chicago Seven, there were seven defendants: Abbie Hoffman, Jerry Rubin, David Dellinger, Tom Hayden, Rennie Davis, John Froines, and Lee Weiner. They were charged by the federal government with conspiracy, inciting to riot, and other charges related to anti-Vietnam War and counter-cultural protests that took place in Chicago, Illinois.

The Aswan high dam was completed that year, and U.S. and the UK lowered the voting age to 18. I can still hear the voices of my parents and their friends echoing in my mind talking about that. In 1970, there were a 100,000 people that demonstrated in Washington DC against the Vietnam War, and the first Earth Day was established as people were becoming more aware of the environmental issues. During the '60s, as we drove down the highways, the medians were lined with trash, and it wasn't uncommon to see people tossing trash out the window of their cars while driving. No one gave it a second thought, but it was one of the issues that prompted the Earth Day to be established. After that, you were fined if you were caught tossing trash out of your car windows.

In the news also that year was the famous and popular group, The Beatles, disbanded. That was sad news for all the teenagers that idolized them and for the adults who had grown up listening to their music. It was kind of the end of an era in a way. It was a new decade, it was the end of times we knew, times of familiarity. Moving on to new things, new times, and new events. A new year, especially at that age, can seem so exciting, and we looked forward to some newness, for sure.

One of the popular television shows during that year we used to love to watch was *The Mary Tyler Moore Show*. What young girl didn't want to look like her? We watched shows like *Adam 12* a popular police show. I enjoyed *Marcus Welby, M.D.*, and who doesn't remember *The Carol Burnett Show*, a popular variety show back then? My parents loved *The Odd Couple*, which first aired in 1970. As an 11-year-old, I enjoyed *Walt Disney's Wonderful World of Color*. This show aired theatrical live-action features and other material from Walt Disney's studio library. And the heartwarming theme song to that show was, and this is for you, Disney fans, "When You Wish Upon A Star." That song inspired me as a youngster to dream and that dreams can really come true. The song spoke of wishing upon a star and that dreams really could come true.

I like to sometimes relate it to scriptures I find in the Bible, in Matthew 7:7, "Ask and it will be given to you; seek and you will find; knock and the door will be opened to you" (NIV). Wishing, to me, is praying, trusting, believing, and receiving, along with a little hard work and determination. Television was becoming our role model, and we looked forward to and related to so much as we watched and learned and laughed.

Also, in 1970, *The Brady Bunch* was airing in its second season, depicting two widowers combining their children from former marriages to make a complete family. The show did have some really good life lessons and examples of combined family life. I liked that show, but my younger brother Lance liked it more than I did. I just remember so many television shows that were healthy to watch, giving life lessons and inspiring messages we could really apply to our own challenges. I loved them then and I still do now.

Another favorite of mine was *My Three Sons* that starred three boys and their widower father. I noticed, as the seasons progressed, the boys who starred on the show turned into very, very good-looking young men. Even at 11, I had an eye for the boys. My favorite in the show was Don Grady (real name Don Louis Agrati), who was a former Mouseketeer from the original Mickey Mouse show in the 1950s. He was also a composer and musician. Boy, was he handsome! I loved watching him each week. The show had life lessons that I could learn from, and it was family oriented, which was something I was always drawn to.

Which brings to mind a question. I ask, what are we teaching our children on television now? The uplifting entertainment of long ago inspired us to be positive, to think of others, to make right choices, and to pursue goals and dreams. There were some exceptions; you had television entertainment, like *All in the Family*, which was quite controversial back then, but they got away with it because it was considered humorous and funny. And our parents, the adults of that generation, loved it. It was different and upcoming and considered modern philosophy. I remember when the show *Maude* came on the scene, depicting a very liberal woman who didn't respect her husband at all. My mother didn't think too much of that show. I remember her and her friends talking about how obnoxious it was. But it was still humorous. And guess what? I love to watch the reruns late at night when I want to laugh before settling down for the night. It's a good way to end the day.

How many shows on television today inspire us? I guess I shouldn't generalize. I'm sure there are some, but it's hard to find them. Occasionally, I tune in to the long-running soap opera *General Hospital*, which I have watched off and on for decades, but I wouldn't consider that one of the shows on television that teaches good values. Oh, goodness, no! It's just entertaining to see what happens next. There is plenty of drama, breaking up, having affairs, etc., yet we still enjoy it, but I wouldn't recommend taking many life lessons from it! The show *The Walton's* is really more my speed and something we can learn from. There are plenty of good, warm, life lessons from that one. I've been accused of being a little prudish (a little?). I'm the one who thought of becoming a nun. Boy, that made my Jewish mother's eyebrows raise while my Catholic-oriented father actually liked the idea! I think he thought it would keep me safe. But I appreciate the woman that I have become. And I pray that I can inspire some of the younger ones with some of the positive messages I received when I was growing up. I had some incredible women role models, whom I learned a lot from.

I spend a lot of time praying for our nation and today's culture. I often pray that things will turn around for the sake of our children and future. When I was growing up, there was so much hope for a bright future, and we received messages like, "You can do anything you put your mind to." Don't we want our children to have the same bright future?

1970 was the beginning of adolescence for me. I was going through a lot of changes physically but also emotionally. I was on the verge of becoming a young woman. I spoke of Camp Wampatuck and the major influence it was in my life every summer for several years and some of the special friendships I was starting to experience. So, that year brought a lot of good, inspiring, fun things to look forward to for me personally. Being there each summer taught me some great values and gave me direction. I loved that camp and the friendships I made, it taught me discipline, challenged me, and helped me to grow. Since we were required to go to church each Sunday, that also had a big impact on me.

What were my adolescent years like? I had lots of family time, as I have said, and there was always something to do on the weekends with family, friends, or both. Although I was challenged by disabilities, nothing seemed to slow me down. I pushed ahead as best I could and focused, not on my disabilities and what I couldn't do, but on my abilities and what I could do. I began babysitting and even did some overnights. I was making good money, and over time, building a good reputation. This really helped my self-esteem, which was challenged at times due to my impaired learning. My mother would not settle for anything less than to push forward. She insisted I have a full life regardless of my limited ability to learn and physical limitations. She never thought disability, although sometimes I wish she had given in a little; there were times when she would push too hard and it would frustrate me, feeling like she was pushing me beyond what I could do. Sometimes, it made me feel like there was something wrong with me that I couldn't do what she asked of me, as if I couldn't do anything right. There were times when I felt she was too demanding and didn't understand.

One particular time I was babysitting in a really nice home in a woodsy section of Sharon. It was one of my first times babysitting at night. I had been there for quite a while and the kids were asleep, when suddenly, I heard rocks being thrown at one of the windows. It happened several times, and I became frightened, so I called my friend Debbie, and she being sensible and mature, said, "Iris, I think you need to call your mother; that doesn't sound right to me." And that being said, I now was even more frightened. If my friend was concerned, what did that mean? So, I called my mother and she came right over, what a good mom, but wait! I was hoping my mother would come and be a little discreet, right? That would have been too good to be true, however.

Upon her arrival, she got out of the car and hadn't even reached the door yet when I hear, loud and clear, "Iris, where are you? Open the door," in her Fran the Nanny Russian/Jewish accent. I was torn in my thoughts and now wondered if whoever was out there was going to kill us both or run for their lives. Hopefully the second choice. My mother was a little threatening, but even so, my heart sank, not only was she announcing herself, but she was also announcing my name.

"Mom," I said, "get in here and be quiet; whoever it was will know who I am now."

"I'm sorry, I just wanted to know where you were," she said.

"What do you mean?" I yelped, "Where the heck did you think I was? Can you come in here and stop yelling my name. Gee, Mom." Now I was sounding like the Beaver on the show, *Leave it to Beaver*, with the "Gee, Mom."

So, she came in and stayed with me until the parents of the children I was babysitting came home, and of course, we explained what happened and they totally understood why my mother was there. While she could be demanding in one sense, she was a good, loyal mother in another. I was a little embarrassed with her arrival tone that evening, but she made me feel safe and secure that I was not alone, and I didn't have to be afraid. As I look back on this experience, just who was it I embarrassed for? Robbers? She did the right thing, and I'm grateful for a mother who always came running. In light of the way she was, she was trying to make me strong in other ways.

She once said to me, "If I give in and don't push you along, I'm afraid I'll cripple you in another way, and I don't want to do that to you." What she meant was if she babied me too much, she felt I would be too weak and dependent, and she wanted me to be independent, at least as best I could. And you know, as hard as it was, I have her to thank for how strong I am today. Because of her drive and determination with me, I have a can-do spirit that has seen me through many struggles that could have crushed me and caused me to give up. Instead I became stronger. I learned to be very determined and to never give up. My two brothers and sister were determined, too, and I was encouraged to think of them, not just myself. My mother wanted us to be strong emotionally, so she didn't give in much. How about ever! She came from strong Russian roots. Putin had nothing on her. As a young person challenged by some of these limitations, I often thought my mother was uncaring and harsh at times.

Now I thank God every day that she pushed me along and encouraged me to be the best I could be while always in the background, she wasn't going anywhere. The world can be a hard place at times, and she knew that and was preparing me! I didn't understand it then, but I do now. I thank God for her and her tenacity.

On to Junior High

So, as I progressed through junior high and I discovered make-up and boys, I was insecure, and at times I struggled with a poor self-image. I walked with a limp and had a lot of visible scarring on my abdomen. Although I was petite and could have worn a bikini, and people did mention I had a cute figure, I usually didn't because I was concerned about the scars being too noticeable. I wore a bikini once on a summer afternoon while at our town lake with friends; with that I got a lot of stares and whispers, so I was reluctant to do it again for fear of judgement and embarrassment. I didn't like to talk about what had happened to me. I just wanted to be viewed like everyone else, whole and normal, when in fact, I felt quite awkward. I would look at myself in the mirror and think of how pretty my much older sister was, and I felt like I didn't quite measure up. Although people thought I was pixie cute, I still wanted to be like my sister and seen as pretty. While my sister had nice, thick, wavy, beautiful hair, mine was very thin and wouldn't grow right because of a malabsorption issue I had due to the trauma of the burst appendix.

Those scars where I had tubes in my stomach bothered me. Today, I realize those tubes kept me alive while they continued to drain the poison from my body and lymph nodes. The abdominal scars were something I liked to hide in my clothing, although it made me feel like a freak at times. But as I look back, I must be thankful because the doctors were trying to save my life; they didn't have time to think about the scars and how they would look. It was an emergency and I was dying, there was no time to think about cosmetics, and the medical practice was different back then.

I also had no idea I had celiac disease, which was not discovered until much later, partly because there was little known about it then. At the time, it was thought of as a pediatric diagnosis. Nobody thought to look at that with me because they assumed everything that was wrong with me had to do with the burst appendix, which later made sense to me. So, while my sister had a beautiful shape and meat on her bones, I was thin and frail and had fragile bone issues. I had to navigate into becoming happy with who I was, and my sister was who she was. I didn't need to be her, I needed to be me. And it would take me decades to discover just who I was after such trauma to my body. I was also plagued with a lot of psoriasis, which I found out later was related to the celiac disease.

I have learned that celiac disease is hereditary, and we believe my father's mother (Grandma Leah Jean) had it, as she had was plagued with a lot of the same symptoms and health issues I had. Her story made sense to me. Yes, she had polio and I had the appendicitis, but I believe we both had the celiac disease, which brought a commonality in our health challenges. We often shared together about what it was like, and she was an encouragement to me while growing up, feeling slighted by health issues. She knew what it was like, she had gone before me, and I knew she could comfort me and help me to see things differently, particularly about myself.

At that age, I envied the fact that my sister was so healthy and wondered why I was plagued with so many health issues. I was beginning to envy her. What I didn't realize, however, as with most people, she had her own struggles that challenged her just like anyone else. All I saw was her beauty and felt she was just perfect and could do no wrong. I can remember thinking, she doesn't struggle, she's strong and invincible. That's the way I saw her!

As a kid, I never connected the appendix episode with all my health issues, and of course, that incident had an awful lot to do with what was going on with me. In my teen years and early adulthood, I blocked it out, dismissing what had happened, not realizing it was traumatic for me and had affected me so. I just wanted to put it out of my mind and be like others and live as normal a life as I could. After all, I had been in a coma for about a month when the incident happened. While my sister was leading a normal life and loved to dress well and look nice, I had to fight my way back to some level of normalcy. I wanted to be like her, which I viewed as carefree and whole.

Can you believe I was told that she was jealous of all the attention I received during that time? That surprised me, but I guess it goes to show that we never really understand what others are dealing with. She saw it differently, too; she felt slighted and not as loved as I did, she felt a lot of responsibility was put on her to pitch in and help my mother while I recovered, which was also eye-opening. I did feel loved and supported, probably more than most, and it saddened me when I learned that she didn't. But she was loved the same as I was, but why couldn't she see it? What was she going through at the time? My mother and father made it clear that they loved us all the same, but she just couldn't see it. I wish she had.

While I envied my sister, I always loved her and wanted the best for her. I was sad when she was sad but didn't always understand why she might feel that way since it appeared, she had everything. But I would've given my eye teeth to have been as healthy and beautiful as she was and still is. Not that I blamed her at all, she wasn't doing anything wrong and didn't flaunt it in my face, it was my perception of it. It often puzzled me that she couldn't see how beautiful she was, no matter how many people told her so. And I'm not sure why, I guess she struggled with a poor self-image much like I did but for different reasons. We were two different people but both feeling inadequate for different reasons, not understanding, but I had hoped we could both overcome them, and I think she did, as she raised two very good children, my niece and nephew. And over time and with age, I did, too.

So, who was I? When you are impaired by trauma, it's difficult to know who you are. I know my grandmother went through that, too, in trying to find who she was in the midst of physical issues. It really takes its toll on you emotionally.

My mother encouraged me to be myself and have confidence in my abilities, but that was easier said than done. As I remember, I liked dressing more plainly and I didn't want to wear a lot of make-up. It was clear my sister and I were very different! I was plainer but a bit more happy-go-lucky, in spite of all I had gone through. I still am today. But deep down inside, I knew that's who I was. I was just very simple. I was more outdoorsy, loved to go to camp every summer, and enjoyed riding minibikes with my brother Alan. I was more of a tomboy, whereas my older sister was more feminine, quieter, and more serious. It was who she was, and as I got older, I came to understand that it was Okay to be different. I was who I was, who else could I be? I am all I have, I can't be anything else and I didn't realize that at the time, but I wish I had. Since life is a process, it was something I had to learn over time and as I got older.

I had a best friend, Marcy, at the time when I was around 13. Once again, I found myself with a friend who loved me for who I was, as those were the people, I was most drawn to. I never did well with surface people who were not who they appeared to be and went behind your back the first chance they had. I had a knack for being able to tell who they were. I had them as acquaintances but didn't go very deep with them; it was a lesson learned as a teen that "you can't trust everyone." I found out mainly because of personality differences and not everyone can handle what you're telling them. That was a strength I always had, I could always tell how people were, and over time, I learned to meet them where they were and not expect much from them. Anything else wasn't realistic or even fair.

In the spring of 1972, Marcy and I were riding minibikes, horses, and hanging out with our brothers. We liked to wear dungarees and flannel shirts. Since I had trouble walking distance due to damage to my left leg, I was drawn to riding things and found lots of creative and fun ways to be active. Bicycles were a different story. While I could ride some, I found it difficult to pedal for long periods of time due to pain and limited mobility, so I often shied away from that activity. And Marcy was very willing to do whatever it was I was able to do. We had great times together, and I have fond memories of our young friendship.

Charm School

I can remember our mothers becoming concerned because we were too tomboyish. They wanted us to act like young ladies and be more feminine. So, they got together and decided to send us to charm school, thinking this would do the trick. I must tell you; it didn't go over too well because it wasn't who we were. We tried very hard and we did what we were told, but it didn't change us. We were two tomboys, enjoying a close, fun friendship in the outdoors. Camp Wampatuck was a part of that for both of us. We were little buddies, best friends. The charm school we attended tried to get us to walk a certain way, exercise etiquette, dress more feminine, choose more feminine activities to do such things, such as sewing and quilting. But Marcy and I could not see ourselves sewing and quilting when all we could talk about was the next time, we could take the mini bikes out into the woods and how much fun that would be. It wasn't long after this that our mothers gave up on us and let us be who we were with the hopes that over time we would come around to their way of thinking. I can remember a conversation they had about it.

"Charlotte," Marcy's mother said, "I think this is who they are, and I think we need to let it go for now, what do you think? I actually think it's kind of cute."

"I guess so," my mother answered with a laugh. "I think it's kind of cute, too, so let's see what happens, I just don't want them to get hurt in the process."

"I think it will be Okay," her mother said, "after all, remember Bruce and Alan are good older brothers, and I know they are looking out for them."

"That's true," my mother answered, and at the same time, I could see her relax knowing that Alan was looking out for me, making sure the minibike was in good working order and being in the background watching. And he was. We eventually did come around to their way of thinking, at least a modified version of it. It wasn't long before we both discovered boys and school dances and social events involving both boys and girls. It caused us to use some of the things that we learned in charm school, but we never gave up those outdoor activities. In fact, Marcy does horse shows today and has really excelled in it. I still ride horses when I'm able and ATVs with my husband. Our husbands now have buddies to ride and camp with.

At 13, I was starting to develop crushes on different boys. I remember how much fun and how exciting that was. I needed affirmation about my looks, and this began to happen more for me. It was simple back then; I remember having crushes but more in terms of friendship and simply dreaming about one day of being married with children. We weren't thinking of sex because we were too young to understand it; when I had a crush on a boy, I was thinking more relationship and just being together. I feel at that age, you're just too young to be thinking along the lines of any kind of a sexual relationship, and it was what I was being taught and examples I was following. I tried to make right choices; after all, I had Debbie, Alan, and several other friends and family members looking over my shoulder. I got away with nothing.

The abdominal scaring was also a deterrent. I think God had that in mind, and that was His way of protecting me as I grew older. I wish more kids could think that way today.

One of the reasons I believe my husband and I have remained married for 38 years is because we were friends first, then we became romantically involved and got married. By being friends first, we discovered we liked each other, we had common interests, and of course, we were attracted to each other. I believe if you can start a relationship this way, it's more likely to last, and enjoy being in each other's company. I wish today's generation would take things slow as our generation did. I feel it would be more rewarding and longer lasting for them with more assurance and stability. And they'd feel better about themselves in the long run. Hey, I was one of those kids who listened to reason, resulting in right choices. Not all the time, but mostly. I was afraid of doing the wrong thing, and consequences from my mother. To me, viewing sex as a recreational activity was just too much to think about.

I had several close girlfriends that really stuck close to me and were dedicated, loyal friends. We looked out for each other. Having close friends made me feel so secure and complete, I never felt alone. And when I had questions about anything, like boys for example, I always had friends to go to and encourage me. That's why connecting face-to-face in friendship is so important. As I remember, I think my friends were aware that I struggled and really looked out for me and stayed close, they seem to understand the meaning of the term "coming alongside of someone else." A real friend doesn't leave another friend when they are having a hard time. A real friend is loyal and will love you for who you are, regardless of your shortcomings. They don't leave you in your toughest moments. I always had friends who hovered over me, knowing I needed them. And I understood it, too, and I was there for them as well.

Was this another provision from God for me? I remember being aware that God knew I was weak, and he never left me alone and he always made sure there was someone to come alongside me to help me along. Someone or someone's that I could always count on and bond with like sisters. But it didn't just happen, I had to put it out there and first be a friend and care for them, too. A lesson I carried with me throughout my life.

While I was 13, I made another significant choice. I began attending a youth group with my friend Karen, who was my younger neighbor. I would go to church occasionally with her mother Carol and her family. Karen invited me to youth group at a Baptist church she attended, and I wasn't quite sure I wanted to keep going because I was concerned about my mother wanting me to be more involved in a Jewish youth group. And I did some of that, but my heart was more in Catholicism at the time. My father and his family's influence were more profound.

I didn't quite understand what Baptist was. This was a new term of denomination for me. But I accepted the invitation partly because I liked to be with her and her family and partly because I was curious. Curious about what she liked about it so much, curious about who the kids were that attended. What was this all about? So, one Wednesday evening, I went with her. We arrived early, and the youth group hadn't gotten started yet, as the kids our age were having choir practice. Karen and I sat and waited, listening to the practice as the director instructed them in song and teaching them how to sing as a group with different harmonies.

As I was sitting in the pew in front of the choir, my eyes were drawn to one of the teen members as he sang. He looked to be around my age, and his name was Ricky. I don't even know how being attracted to someone could happen that fast, but it did. My heart beat faster and faster as I sat there. I couldn't believe it or understand it. Holy crap, was this my first crush? Was this even what a crush feels like? It hit me hard. Talk about Cupid shooting an arrow at your heart, was Cupid in the choir? This literally felt like it went through my heart, like nothing I had ever felt before. I couldn't wait to meet him. I knew Karen was well acquainted with him and his family. And as I looked at him, guess what? He looked back at me, and before I knew it, it was a mutual crush. So, from then on, every time there was something going on with the youth group, I was there. With bells on! Wild horses weren't going to keep me away. I was there for all the church functions, every single one of them. Especially events that were held in Ricky's home. I was attracted to everything about him, his looks, his family life, everything about him imaginable.

However, at 13, there wasn't much we could do together, especially alone, and the way our parents were back then, being alone was not an option. So, everything we did together was always with a group of other kids and supervised by adults. We were learning accountability and it was good for us; it taught us respect and to be better people. I always wanted to be around Ricky, puberty hitting with a vengeance. He was my first crush, which was then referred to as puppy love. It felt like a puppy all right! Every time I heard his name, it was a big deal and I loved everything about him. I was even dreaming of marriage at 13, if you can believe it. But eventually, he lost interest in me, which was hurtful, and I remember being so crushed by his loss of interest in me; at 13, he wasn't interested in commitment, no kidding. What did I expect—his hand in marriage? Actually, I think I did. He ruined everything by moving on, it just seemed to happen. He became interested in other activities that separated us and moved on. But as we grew older, and eventually I grew past this experience, at least on the surface, I seemed to move on, too.

For a time, I dated one of his friends and Karen ended up dating Ricky. While I was happy for Karen, I remember being a bit jealous. After all, he was my first crush and it took me a long time after that to find someone else to fill those shoes. Since I am now married for 38 years, you know I did find that special one, the one God had for me. We all have a destiny, I believe, and Ricky clearly was not a part of that. God had other plans for him, too, and it didn't include us being together. Darn it, he was so cute! My first cupid story, and I'm not sure I ever really got over him until I met my husband Cy. And, of course, when I met him, the heart fluttering thing happened all over again and the rest you'll read about. Not to be mushy or melodramatic, but to this day, my husband still makes my heart melt until he gets on my nerves. While we have a great marriage, it's not realistic to think you won't have those moments, and we do, but we are both loyal and we are there for each other. So, those hard moments are just that, moments!

After Ricky

Lance, Mom, and me in the front. We were at my cousin Jay's Bar mitzvah. Pictured left to right in the back are my cousin Elise, Dad's brother and our Uncle Martin, cousin Jay, and My Aunt Elaine.

217

After Ricky and before Cy, I did date quite a few nice boys during my high school years. As I grew a little older, my shape and my looks improved and I began to be more confident in myself as my body was healing. One young man I dated, for several years actually, even wanted to marry me when I was 17. Of course, I said no. Not only was he not the right one, but I was too young to go there, gosh, I was still riding minibikes. There was another guy from Boston I dated in my junior year of high school. I really liked him as well. He was a few years older and such a gentleman. He would always call me and politely asked me for a date, usually picking a nice place to go. He really had a knack for knowing how to treat women. My mother even loved him! He would pick me up for a date, take me to nice restaurants, nice theater plays and movies, and brought me flowers. He was it, again! I really liked him; I was falling for him for sure. I don't think I loved him, but I sure did like him.

There was something that puzzled me though, I never could figure out why he would never kiss me. I wondered if he just thought of me as a friend, was there something about me he didn't like?

Well, I found out much later after we broke up what the issue was. One of my aunt's knew him well and told me that he was gay. I can't tell you how disappointed I was. Okay, he was gay, that was his choice, and I respected him for it, but in the course of our dating, I was beginning to picture myself with him. I remember how disappointed I was again. He was so good look-ing and so nice, and he had a bright future as a lawyer. But again, this rela-tionship was not to be permanent, so we moved on and I never saw him again. I was crushed again for a while. But I had hoped he was happy. I hear about him from time to time today, mainly through my aunt who still lives in the same town near him in Boston. I understand he never married but that he's happy and has a full life; I'm happy for him. I hear he still is others-oriented and has a positive impact on his community. Oh, well, I had to move on again. And move on I did. I was learning to deal with disappoint-ment, its not easy, but it helps us grow.

In addition to Ricky and the future lawyer, there was one other guy I dated through another aunt. He, too, wanted to marry me, but I was the one who broke it off; we were too different, and I knew I needed someone with more common interests, so that relationship didn't last more than a year. These were learning curves I'll never forget. As I look back, I was taking my time, using wisdom, and I'm glad I did.

Chapter 11

A Special Event and Turning of Events

This is me, my mother and Lance in Disney world.

In 1971 my family took part in a special and exciting event I'll never forget. Disneyland, which first opened its doors on July 17th, 1955, made its day in history once again on October 1st, 1971, when Walt Disney World resort officially opened in Orlando, Florida. It originally included the Magic Kingdom Park, Disney's contemporary resort hotel, Disney's Polynesian resort, and Disney's Fort Wilderness resort and campground, and on that particular day, William Windsor Junior was recorded as the first guest.

I remember being disappointed because I wanted to be the very first guest there, but it wasn't possible. My parents, upon hearing of the opening, made plans for us to take the trip. It took time for my father to plan to take time off work when he could get a vacation. We had to make reservations, plan how we get there, and all of the things that are involved in planning a vacation with a family. Things had to fall into place just right. It was a big deal to go to Disney World at the time; it was considered the trip of a lifetime. You were privileged if you could go. It wasn't as commonplace as today. There was talk of this in our family a couple of years prior to the opening, as we knew it was coming, and it was exciting to think about. It was all my siblings and I and then my friends could talk about. My friend Debbie in particular was very excited for us and wanted to hear all about it when we returned.

Our Dad's Cadillac that we traveled in on our way to Disney World when it first opened in Orlando.

Living in a world today where everything is so instantaneous and we can have things so quickly, it's hard to imagine having to wait so long for something, but it taught us patience and it taught us to appreciate things and gave us something to dream toward. Waiting for things never hurt us, it caused us to be patient and dream big. The trip was planned, and I can remember how excited my friends were for me at the time. I was the envy of many, and it made me feel proud and respected by my peers. I remember the days of peer pressure and how everybody was talking about how they wanted to see my tan when I got back and souvenir of Donald Duck or Mickey Mouse as proof I actually went. As if I was taking Donald Duck hostage as proof. This was the day before Facebook; we couldn't show off everything we did, our sharing remained geographically limited to friends and family locally, which made the world seem bigger as our ability to reach out was limited to the places where we lived. And that seemed enough for us, and I think it was as I look back on this. Little did my friends know that due to the appendicitis episode I was already starting with autoimmune problems, which made it hard for me to tan no matter how long I sat in the sun. I didn't realize I was developing photosensitivity (sensitive to the sun). I knew I was sensitive, but of course, no one knew why.

So tan or no tan, in late October 1971, we headed off to Disney World. My parents booked us at the contemporary resort hotel, which was huge and expensive, a real experience of the future, very exciting. For the first time in our lives, we rode on new technology known as a monorail back and forth between the hotel and the theme parks. We had two glorious weeks of so much fun and magical adventure in this world of fantasy and future of technology. My brother Alan took so many pictures and so many home movies of us there, and the memories of that time were etched in our hearts and mind. I love to look back at those home movies and watch my mother and father together with us again. It was a magical time for us, one I will always cherish. And I know my brothers and my sister will, too.

When we came back from Disney World, I remember my friend Debbie saying to me, "You don't even have a tan, how did that happen? You couldn't have sat out in the sun!"

"I have no idea, I did sit out in the sun," I answered, and she peered at me with a bit of a puzzled look, trying to understand. She was intelligent and often looked for ways of resolving things. It didn't make sense to her because she had no trouble tanning. As an adolescent, she couldn't figure it out, and I think she was disappointed because she cared for me

Debbie was one of my best friends who always looked out for me. Even as a young teen, she was loyal to those she was closest to. Especially her family, and I was blessed to have had her as a young friend and be included in her special bonding circle. She was wise beyond her years and her maturity was evident. She didn't mess around; she was goal oriented and knew what she wanted out of life even then. She was one who remained very focused, and it has paid off for her in the choices she made that have affected her family life today. Debbie is someone I would consider quite a success. Even though we were the same age, still, she was a role model for me. My mother liked the idea of me hanging out with Debbie because she knew that if I was with her, I wasn't getting in trouble; that's how accountable she was. I learned a lot from her. I was not a leader by any means, I was more of a follower, and I had an eagerness to want to learn and make right choices. Debbie was one who kept me on track. I was told I was teachable. Debbie loved to lead, and I loved to learn, and we were a perfect match.

There were times when I felt like my mother trusted Debbie more than me, and perhaps there was a reason for that. While I was a bit all over the place at times due to my attention span, I still felt that drive to do right. But there were times I would waver a little bit and had a hard time knowing what that meant. So, Debbie was one that would reel me in and keep me centered on making right choices. She was so mature, it was like having another older sister, sometimes a second mother (I'm smiling as I say this), but she loved us as a family that much and it was evident. And I have to confess, I have always appreciated her for that. We double dated off and on throughout high school, and then when we went our separate ways off to college, still stayed in touch and have remained close friends to this day; we are family and I'm grateful for her. Throughout our life, we shared in our weddings together, the birth of our firstborn sons, to the marriage of our children, up to the birth of our first grandsons.

I seemed to have a knack for drawing friends who looked out for me. What a blessing. While she was a prevalent one, I was elated to have had many. Throughout the ups and downs of my life, I always had someone to share in the good times and grieve with me in the hard places I found myself. I learned this bonding from my own family and perhaps the time we were living in. I often wondered why I bonded so well and had such close friends! Maybe it was because they sensed I needed extra encouragement due to my limitations, maybe it was because I reached out to them too, maybe a little of both. I'm not sure, but I'm grateful. Debbie was special to me. Perhaps she was practicing on me, who knows! Either way, it brings joy to me to think about it. I also like to think, due to examples I had that I became one of those good mothers, too. And based on my son and his accomplishments, both career wise and in family loyalty, I must have done something right, too. Being around some of these motherly friends, it felt like growing up around a bunch of June Cleavers. It was amazing! My mother couldn't say I was around bad influence, at least not most of the time, and it brought her a level of peace. I could see a look of approval from her, and it felt good.

Throughout junior high and high school, I had several best friends who looked out for me. If I got in with the wrong group or even looked like I was going to take a drink of beer or anything like that, several of them would lecture me and tell me it wasn't good for me—just what you want to hear from your best friends. I swear they had a secret pact with my mother. Could she have been paying them? No, she didn't have that kind of money. I didn't get offended because I knew where they were coming from. I knew they were good, caring friends.

My history with Debbie was different as to why we became friends. She and I became close because our parents were close friends. They were high school friends from Chelsea, Massachusetts. Her father and my mother went to Chelsea High School together. So, we would get together as families, and Debbie and I soon continued the trend in our family.

In a recent conversation with her, she recalled how much fun our families had together. She said, "Iris, do you remember us going to that restaurant called Cristo's?"

The memory clicked in. "Oh, yeah, I had forgotten about that."

She continued, "We all loved that restaurant, and the Greek food was incredible, remember?"

"Yes, for sure," I answered, thinking of the mouth-watering Boneless breast of chicken dipped in a sweet batter. I remember it was served with a delicious Greek Salad, topped with amazing feta cheese and olives. It was an excellent restaurant with mouthwatering food.

"That was when your family was together and things were so good, you had a beautiful home, great parents. Your father was so handsome." She went on and on, and I was reminded once again through a loving friend just how nice things were, and she was there to share the memory with me. Debbie and I did have a lot of fun together. In the course of this book, you'll come to understand that true friends and loyalty meant the world to me, and I looked for it in all the friendships I encountered throughout my life. My mother was that way, too, something she not only spoke about but modeled as well.

As we were entering adolescence and were discovering boys, there were times when Debbie and I went on double dates. I remember we attended a showing of *Gone with the Wind*, the famous movie from the 1930s. Here we were, in the movie theater on a double date when we were about 14. It was so much fun, and I remember how grown up I felt, as I was beginning to gain confidence. And after all, my second mother was with me (teasing again, I can't help it), so what could go wrong? We dated nice boys that our mothers approved of, and we felt good about that. I can't emphasize that enough, my son and husband will be reading this book, you know, and Debbie, of course, so I want to be careful.

We went roller skating together with other girls and sometimes boys, went to bowling alleys, and we enjoyed going to this excellent pizza place called Town Spa Pizza in the next town of Stoughton, Massachusetts.

I believe it was God's love and provision for me to have friends to enjoy like this. Proverbs 17:17 says, "A friend loves at all times" (NIV). In other words, a real friend loves you no matter what; they're not going anywhere. I did learn the importance of social relationships and family from my mother and my father both. Because I would be facing challenges later, God knew I would need that love and loyalty to get through hard times as a young adolescent. After all, they say the adolescent years are the hardest times because you're trying to find yourself and your body is changing hormonally. You're literally growing up, the hormones begin to rage (first noticing it with Ricky), and the question of "who am I" really begins to hit hard at that age. It felt like my destiny was being formed by God himself. I knew he was watching over me by sending me loving, caring people, and he was teaching me to do the same. This is the theme you'll see repeated throughout my life as I continue to share my story: God's continued provision for me. He used people to show his love and faithfulness to me.

So, while things had been so much fun for us and had gone so well for quite a while, something was about to take place that would rock my world and that of my siblings. Especially earthshattering for My brother Lance, because he was so young.

Let me give an example of the true friends I had and what a difference it made. Remember Ecclesiastes 4:10-12? "Two are better than one because they have a good return for their work; if one falls down, his friend can help him up. But pity the man who falls and has no one to help him up! Also, if two lie down together, they will keep warm. But how can one keep warm alone? Though one may be overpowered, two can defend themselves. A cord of three strands is not quickly broken." Notice it says pity the man who is alone, who has no one to help him up. God put that in his word for us for a reason, he never intended for us to do this life alone; he knew there were going to be hard times. He recognized it with Adam and created Eve, so that Adam would not be alone in the book of Genesis.

This was a common theme of God's provision in my life that I should never be alone. It was a gift I never took for granted. Today, texting has become so common, and communication is less face-to-face and more on the computer and phones. My goodness, what is that doing to our society? As I said before, and I'll say it again, it's caused people to feel isolated and alone, and it's caused very young people to consider or commit suicide. In their times of confusion and turmoil, they had no one to turn to. They felt isolated and alone and afraid, needing affirmation. Not being able to see the person's face or feel the warmth of their touch made them feel depressed and without hope. There wasn't someone there to hold their hand and say, "It will be all right, I'm here for you, you're not alone." With texting, they can't hear a voice, they can't feel the touch to comfort them. I'm sorry, but it's not only not good, but it's terribly destructive, especially to young people who are trying to find their way. God gave us each other as a gift, one I will never take for granted. Should you do the same? Think about this!

As I continue to share my story, I can't emphasize enough how having God in my life and the people he provided, the older mentors who taught me, how important it was and how it made a difference in the choices I made. I would've lost hope, I wouldn't have known what to do. I always had a best friend or a group of best friends to come alongside of me during life's most difficult challenges. I learned what bonding and giving to others also was all about. I learned that relationship should never be about one person, it should always be about both. Friendship is a gift, not to be taken lightly.

I mentioned the appendicitis episode, and that was quite traumatic with years of recuperation, and left me with lifelong challenges. I suffered a brain injury with an incredible amount of internal damage. It was a miracle of God, and the people who prayed, that got me to where I am today. Thanks be to God for his love for me!

A Change Coming

By now, it was 1974, and things began to take a different turn with my mother and father. While for years they were fun-loving, jovial, and good consistent parents, there was a strange distance gradually taking place between them, although I was not always aware of it. They suddenly found themselves in a place where they didn't have as much in common anymore, and the closeness was gradually fading. What was happening? What was going on with them? My secure home was now being threatened. I could feel it and so could my brothers. My sister by this time was in college and on her way to her future. So, I'm not sure she noticed as much as we did, but I know it affected her. I'm not totally sure what was happening, but religious differences were coming up a lot. At least I believe that's where it started.

My mother of Jewish of Russian descent insisted my father be Jewish, too, and that we as children follow after that. For years my father wanted to go to church and celebrate Christmas, like his mother, as this is how he was brought up. At first, in the early years of their marriage, the religious differences didn't seem to cause too many problems; they seemed to work it out. My father would give in and go to religious services with my mother in the Temple. But when he was with his family, his one brother, one of his sisters, and of course, his mother, he would go to Catholic church. In the beginning of their marriage, I think they were excited about being together, raising a family, and enjoying life together and were able to overlook that difference. You know how it is, the newness of a relationship and looking toward a bright future—the white picket fence, the children, all the things a couple dreams of. At least back then that was what it was like. Especially having such difficulties of their own, they wanted a better life for each other and their children. But unfortunately, even as hard as we try with best intentions, things don't always go the way we expect. But we have to make the best of things and go on. And go on they did but not together forever.

When we were young, I can remember celebrating both holidays, Hanukkah and Christmas. But as my father grew older, he wanted to revisit his spiritual roots. After all, he was of Catholic-Italian descent, and it wasn't much talked about. Back then a lot of women thought they could change the way their husbands were, but I think today's society has evolved from that, and I believe it's a good thing. I noticed the religious differences between them when I was at Camp Wampatuck. During the closing ceremonies, as I have mentioned, my father really resonated with the songs and the spirit behind the ceremony. While we as a group of campers, marched down an aisle toward a campfire of awards for good conduct, best archer, best swimmer, etc., we sang, "Onward Christian soldiers." My father, touched by the event, went into prayer mode and was quite blessed by it. But my mother was disappointed to think that I would remain with the Catholic faith. Her mouth literally dropped open when she realized the spiritual impact this was having on me. But she was right! Because that's who I was becoming as I grew older, I even toyed with the thought of becoming a nun. Very early on like my father, I discovered I loved God and knew I wanted to spend my life serving him this way. I guess everybody has a calling, and as my mother would've said, "Right, wrong, or indifferent, this is the way it is."

So, this became a big wedge between my mother and father and later with me. And the wedge over time became broader and broader. So, in 1974, when I was 15 years old and my younger brother Lance just eight, Alan, 16, and my older sister, 21 and making wedding plans, my father found another woman whom he called a Christian. He felt he had found his soulmate, but behind my mother's back was not a good choice and way of handling things. It had a disastrous impact on our family. And by this time, there was talk of divorce. It was very tough because we literally went from having everything to having nothing suddenly. I wish my father could've handled things differently. But I think he was extremely unhappy and anxious to find contentment again. So, his decision-making became quite inward. And I doubt he realized the impact it would have on all of us as a family, because I know he loved us. He was going through a life change and he was becoming ill, with what, we didn't know the cause yet. He was making his decisions based on fear rather than common sense and the welfare of his family.

We went from a fairly stable and happy family life to a separation of family and having to give up our home and the things we loved. It was anything but a peaceful divorce. You can only imagine how my mother must have felt and what that did to her emotionally. It broke my heart to think that because my father introduced another woman in the mix of this and called her Christian, that this was my mother's first real example of someone who called themselves a Christian. Being introduced to Christianity this way made her angry and bitter, understandably so. My father and this other woman began to spend evenings together, and my father wouldn't come home until very late. It set a bad example to Mom, hurt her deeply, and who could blame her? She was having to separate from the man she loved and had counted on for 24 years or so by now. And her thoughts were probably like this, "If this is who Christ is and Christianity, I don't want anything to do with it. It's hypocrisy!" Because of the way my father handled it, she felt he was a phony and hiding behind a false cult-like religion.

From my perspective, a true, mature Christian would not have done that. It's not who God is, and people in their weakened states can set a bad example of what Christ really represents. That's because people are people. People don't come to Christ because they're perfect, they come to Him because they're not, and they need direction and protection, if from nothing else but themselves. People come into churches wounded and in a need of a savior, not because they have it all together but because they are broken. And this is something I wish my mother could have understood. I wish Dad could have prayed and asked God for wisdom, waited, and did things differently; it would have made such a difference. But my father was looking for happiness. I'm not excusing his actions because he really hurt my mother, and without realizing it, hurt us too. But he was probably going through things I'll never even know about. All I knew is he wanted to have a relationship with God but didn't seem to quite understand how to go about it. Over time he did grow to understand the consequences of his choices. He didn't abandon us, we still saw him regularly, but it was never the same.

At this time, my sister was planning to get married, and right in the middle of the divorce, she had the wedding anyway. I remember it went well, we all had fun, and it was a beautiful wedding. It seemed my sister had the best of everything, and of course, she was a beautiful bride. But in the background, there was a lot of tension between my parents and we could feel it. The wedding was in August, of 1974, and just weeks after that my father moved out of the house.

And here is where I found solace in friendships again, when I needed it the most. I wasn't alone. God blessed me with the best of them, and I was learning, once again, what loyalty and the love of friendship was all about.

The night that my father was supposed to move out, my parents sent me to a friend's house, so it wouldn't be quite as upsetting. For some reason, my mother didn't want me in particular to see him packing his clothes and moving out. She knew I had a special connection with him, and she didn't want me to be in the middle of it. One of the things my mother did, which probably was not the best choice, was to keep Lance there with her. But as I look back on it, he was her baby and she wanted him by her side, but he was too young to handle such responsibility. But she was hurting, and when someone hurts, they don't always make the right choices, acting on emotion and neediness rather than common sense. And I have to say, we all do it. After all, who could think clearly amid so much turmoil.

While he was quite young then, if you talk to Lance today, he declares that it made him stronger, and I think it did. My younger brother is resilient, as he's come through his own challenges quite victoriously while always remaining loyal to his family.

During this event, my brother Alan, went to a friend's house, and at the age of 16 was thinking of dropping out of school and joining the service; he was going through his own challenges with the goings on. But I think Alan was trying to find his way and had learning disabilities of his own to deal with. My mother convinced him to wait until he was 17. And I'm glad he waited, with all this change happening and upheavals going on. I was glad I had a chance to spend a lot of time with him and his buddies in high school. He dated one or two of my friends, and I dated one of his. We had a nice time together sharing each other's friends in high school for a while. It kept us close. He later told me he was going to join the Navy because he wanted to help the family. I was proud of both my brothers because they both were very others-oriented and cared for their family.

So, there was Lance, just a little guy kept there for security to comfort my mother. It was from that day forth that my mother held very tightly to Lance. He was her youngest child and she loved him dearly and she held him so close, probably too close from my perspective. But he was her little man. It broke my heart to see him become responsible for her, and even back then, I remember feeling he was too young. He was loyal to her till the day she died; we were all loyal to her and each other. Family was important to us and we made it because we stuck together. But it would never be the same, there was a split, and we certainly could feel it. It gave me a feeling of uneasiness, and during the adolescent years, I remember feeling quite insecure at times, but instinctively I knew to turn to others for support. It caused me to think about God again and look to him. It caused me to want to go to church more, not less. I understood it was God I needed and not perfection in people, especially in church, which did not always go over well with my Jewish mother, as I've mentioned.

The Night my Father Left

The day my father left, I spent the night with another very close friend and her family. Beverly was again, like a sister. Of course, Debbie and others were supportive, too, but this was Beverly's opportunity to come alongside, and she took my situation seriously for someone so young. She was a compassionate young friend, quite concerned about me, and it showed. Back then I had a hard time understanding why people were so drawn to me. Was I like a poor little puppy with no home and appearing needy? As I've aged and matured, I came realize that wasn't the case. I didn't need to be so hard on myself. But my poor self-image, often dictated those thoughts to me.

What was surprising to me but very comforting was when I received feedback from the people who knew me best. They said I was always laughing and smiling. That's what they observed and were surprised to later hear of my struggles. When I was told it was my fun-loving joviality that was contagious, like my father, it brought a little confidence to me and I realized it was Okay. Okay to be me! During this very hard time, I remember looking for the positive and wanting to make things better, like I was taught. I looked for people like Beverly and Debbie and others to go through those hard places with that were a more positive influence on my outlook. Today, when people say that to me, which sometimes I still have a hard time receiving, I think it's God's love they see in me. At least I hope so.

My friend Beverly circa 1973.

Anyway, Beverly and her family went out of their way to comfort me and support me through this difficult transition. I remember spending that evening with them, and I remember how compassionate my friend was. If I cried, she cried with me, if I wanted to do something fun, she did it with me, too. I learned a lot from that friendship and I, of course, wanted to reciprocate. While I was there, her parents talked with me to make sure things were Okay. They were modeling for their daughter how to respond to a friend who was hurting. I had the support and comfort I needed. I was not alone. Was this God's provision once again? I believe so, because this is God's promise to us as we go through those deep dark places called trials.

In Hebrews 13:5, it says, "Never will I leave you; never will I forsake you" (NIV). And as I continue my story, you will see and come to understand just how faithful God was to me personally. And because he is no respecter of persons (is not influenced by social status or prestige), he is fair and just what he does for one person to do for another. I'm not unique, I just trusted him. I believe he will do that for you, too, you just have to ask. He is there every minute of every day, and he loves all of us dearly. In Romans 2:11, it says, "For God does not show favoritism."

Compassion Beyond Measure

Bev's parents as I remember them.

I was being comforted by my friend and her family; they entertained me, trying to soften the blow of my father leaving. However, my worried thoughts couldn't help but turn toward how my brother Lance was. But during the night, my friend and her family diverted my attention to some of the good things that were happening, a great diversionary tactic. At least they were trying. Her father in particular mentioned some of the good things that could come out of my situation. Like how strong this would make me, and what a good helper I could be to my mother and be able to encourage her, how it could give me opportunities to focus on what I like to do best, how was school going, etc. They talked about events around the world that were interesting to focus on as her dad read the paper. They showed me all the happenings in the news, and had me watch favorite sitcoms on TV, etc. It was a full evening for sure. They went out of their way to keep me busy and focused.

I'd like to share with you some of what I remember was happening in the world around us in 1974. What was in the newspaper back then? What was lifelike for other people in the world? After all, it wasn't all about me, or was it? I learned at an early age it wasn't. This is where I believe our trials work for good. They cause us to be that much stronger, more others-oriented, and better people in general. Can hard times work for good? I think so; in fact, I've lived it. And I'm a stronger person today as a result. While it's not easy while you're going through it, the end result can be quite rewarding when you can see the good that came from all you experienced. I did!

There were a lot of interesting events happening at that time. I remember the struggles of world events our parents had to deal with. I have heard that every generation has trouble of its own, and it certainly does.

So, in 1974, while we were dealing with our own personal struggles, I recall some of the events of the country. For example, inflation was beginning to really spiral out of control around the world, reaching 11.3 percent in the U.S. and 17.2 percent in the UK and caused the global recession to deepen. I remember gasoline shortages, and we had to deal with long lines at the gas pumps. During two separate oil crises in the 1970s, Americans all around the country faced persistent gas shortages as the organization of petroleum exporting countries, commonly known as OPEC, flexed its muscles and disrupted oil supplies. And there was an energy crisis to deal with to boot.

Of course, this wasn't what Beverly's parents were trying to get me to focus on, but nevertheless, it was in the news. And I was told these temporary problems didn't need to frighten us, they were just that, temporary, and over time, as things often do, would work themselves out. The events of that time period were worrisome and sometimes scary because nobody knew how long it was going to last or where it would lead. These were trying times once again, but like other times in history, would eventually get resolved. I can remember some of the energy crises happening during the winter where every household was forced to turn down their thermostats to conserve on energy. I remember being a little concerned and didn't like being cold.

And then I remember being in the home of one of my wealthier friends, and her mother saying as she held the younger one wrapped in a blanket, "The hell with the energy crisis, my baby is cold." And she instructed my friend to turn up the heat. I can remember wondering if this woman was at all concerned about others and our country, why was she doing that? To me it seemed most families I knew were trying to do the right thing, even if it meant being a little cold during the winter, most seemed they were trying to do their part. But this woman didn't seem to care, and in fact, was a little arrogant, and I always wondered about her after that. But this friendship was short-lived, so I didn't see her very much after that, and I was learning another lesson in this, that not all people are going to be kind. Not everyone was going to like me, people are all different, and it was Okay. I had to learn yet another lesson, that it wasn't all about me. But a hard one in adolescence.

Nothing New Under the Sun, more Interesting Facts

There is nothing new under the sun. On a more interesting note, in the news during that time, we were hearing about a famous skeleton they named Lucy, which was discovered in Ethiopia and was said to have lived between 3.9 to 4 million years ago. As a young teen, I thought that was amazing and quite interesting, and I followed the story for a while.

I remember there was more and more talk about digital-based consumer products that would appear in shops, along with the earliest forms of word processors, which at that time resembled a typewriter more than a computer. Kind of funny to think about now. The strides we have made with computers since then is amazing. It's hard to imagine, but we had no computers back then, no cell phones, and we relied on just answering a telephone when it rang without even a message machine. We depended on going to the library to look up important information, where we could see other people and be social.

Whether we were doing research or in school working on a history project, the library was the place to go, and we would often run into people we knew.

While the computers, answering machines, and cell phones of today seem to make life a bit easier, I feel it's made people busier and more stressed and isolated than ever. While we didn't have access to instant information all the time, we sure had a lot more peace. And while everyone was busy, we weren't crazy busy like it is today. We were busy accomplishing things, not just busy running everywhere, exhausting ourselves, which I feel is destructive to a person's peaceful existence. It's so important to take down-time and not to be busy every moment. God never intended that for us. He told us to go in peace, not in stress. That in quietness and confidence would be our strength. Not craziness!

Another important story I remember from this time in history was the findings of the Watergate scandal with Richard Nixon, which began in 1972 and ended with his resignation. I remember so many of us watching this on television together. Some were viewing this on black and white televisions, as television was considered still new and progressing in technology. So many of us were limited to this; if you had a lot of money, you could purchase a color television, but it wasn't common at the time. They were quite expensive, and very few people had more than one, unless you were wealthy. It was considered a luxury for sure. This was so different from today, where everybody seems to have large, flat-screen televisions as they become more affordable. It's not uncommon to see two or three in an average household.

My mother's friend's husband, who was a TV repairman, was beginning to slowly go out of business over time because television had changed so much. We were entering the throwaway television age, I'm not sure when, maybe it started in the 1990s. However, in 1974, there were still television repairmen because we still had these things called picture tubes that had to be replaced and also the wiring within the television. But even then, television was changing, and the repairman would soon be a thing of the past.

The Divorce

After my parents' divorce, we moved into a small apartment on the second floor of an older home rented to us by an older gentleman. It was across from an intermediate school, grades sixth through eighth, that I once attended. We began a new life together, me, my mother, Lance, and Alan for a little while until Alan joined the service. During that transition, my mother struggled to go back to work after being a stay-at-home mom for 23 years. It wasn't easy. While it was challenging at best, she still encouraged us to do fun things on the weekends and remain focused and determined. I was proud of how she handled things. And in the midst of this, she wasn't alone. She had lots of support. She had her mother, her sister, her friends from high school who would come at the drop of a hat if she needed them, and Debbie's mother and father were there for support. These were relationships she had cultivated for years; longtime friends and family members were there to lighten the load of a very tough situation. She was first a friend to them, and their loyalty was returned to her in her time of need.

This was a hard time, but we had each other! And we still found joy in spending time with friends and family on the weekends. We tried to keep up the same momentum as best we could. As a teen back then, I did struggle with the divorce and was sad at times, but I followed my mother's lead, tried to remain positive, and focused on hanging out with friends and enjoying the new movies that were coming out. One of the movies I enjoyed in 1974 was *The Sting* that starred Paul Newman and Robert Redford who were quite popular back then as very attractive actors. In fact, just before my parents' divorce, we had purchased a player piano that my mother restored. A player piano is one that can be played automatically when the keys are actuated electronically or by a pneumatic device controlled by a piano roll. It could also be played manually, and my mother knew that. The player piano's heyday lasted from 1900 to the depression in the 1930s. Affordable radios started becoming commonplace in 1927. My mother got a very good deal from an antique dealer; this piano still had the old scrolls of the music we could play. It was the type of thing we really didn't even have to know how to play, just had to have really strong legs, which was tough for me. On the top of the piano, we would put a scroll in of our favorite song. We didn't have to do anything with our hands; we just pumped the pedals while the piano played the song with the keys. It was quite something. So, my mother took this old beat up naturally wood-finished piano, and she restored it herself by painting it in antique blue, and if I say so myself, she did a beautiful job. It looked like a brand-new piano.

She purchased a nice piano bench to go with it, topped it with some nice artificial flowers, and away she went to have me take piano lessons. I knew she had a plan. There was always a method to her madness. But she wanted me to excel and have the best opportunities. Which brings me to my point, after quite a while of arduous lessons, I learned to play the song, "The Sting," from that movie. I remember taking those lessons from an older woman, Mrs. Rosen, from Canton, the next town over. She was quite a strict teacher and couldn't understand why I had such difficulty learning. And because I was still recovering from that burst appendix episode, I had a lot of fatigue, and I would literally fall asleep at the piano while playing. She thought I just wasn't paying attention and was just lazy, which was not the case, but as I would fall asleep at the piano, she would slap my fingers with a ruler to wake me up.

"Very nice," as my mother would have said. My mother, being the determined woman, she was, insisted I keep practicing and try not to fall asleep. Easier said than done, I got to hear my mother say, "Debbie takes lessons and she doesn't fall asleep."

"But, Mom, Debbie is healthy and doesn't have the problems I have."

She just shook her head. "It doesn't matter, I know you can do it, push yourself and don't give up. I'd really like to see you excel in this." She never gave in, oy!

And I half-heartedly answered, "Okay, but it's hard, I don't know if I can do it."

"You have to apply yourself, have a little confidence, I want to see some effort," she insisted.

What she didn't realize is that I was doing my best. I was 13 at the time and I struggled terribly with exceling at most things. I was still dealing with the ramifications of the appendix episode, my doctors felt my struggles would be life-long, and they certainly have been. But not everything was hard, some things came more easily to me, like horseback riding.

So, I kept playing and eventually I learned to play more music and began to like it and not feel so frustrated with the learning. I was determined to press through hard times and not give in so easily, and I'm so grateful my mother pushed me. Had I not learned that hard lesson, I would've never succeeded or excelled in anything. It goes to show you, it never pays to give up. My mother was right, even if I didn't understand her methods at the time.

During that year, I also learned a lesson in what not to expose my mind to. One of the movies I regretted seeing was *The Exorcist*. It was the first and last horror movie I ever saw. You see, I was quite the sensitive viewer and was highly suggestible to what I let my eyes view! I was better off focusing on funny, uplifting, and even humorous movies. After I saw *The Exorcist*, which depicted a young girl possessed by the devil, I had to sleep with the light on for three months. It was quite scary and spiritually upsetting to me, and I found myself feeling sorry for the girl and wondered why a movie would depict the enemy being stronger than the Lord. Which I believe is not true!

The Bible states in I John 4:4, "You, dear children, are from God and have overcome them, because the one who is in you is greater than the one who's in the world" (NIV). So, even though the movie depicted the opposite, I knew better because I was leaning upon the truth found in the word of God, and it brought me peace and eventually I didn't need the light on when I went to sleep at night. Movies, like *Herbie Rides Again*, a Disney flick starring Dean Jones, was more my speed, no pun intended.

When I told my father about the movie, he encouraged me to stick to Disney, it was safer for me and wouldn't upset me. After the divorce, he used to come and pick up my brothers to take them out for a day of recreation on his Saturday visiting day and would take them to movies that were funny or more suitable for children most of the time. A favorite of my father and brother Lance was *The Towering Inferno*. Disaster movies like that were popular back then. Dad also liked *Blazing Saddles, Young Frankenstein, Benji*, and *Earthquake*. Lance thought Benji was fun to watch because he liked dogs, but the disaster movies really caught his attention. They were exciting for a little boy, and his special time with his father.

I remember my mother going with some of her friends to see a movie entitled *The Great Gatsby*, another movie starring Robert Redford but with more romantic quality; my mother liked that stuff. A second *Godfather* movie was coming out that year, *The Godfather Part II*. I remember my father enjoying movies like that, especially with his background and some of his family involved with the mob back in the 1930s, '40s, and '50s.

Then there was a Saturday when my mother wanted to take me to the movies, and we went to see *Billy Jack*. If I remember correctly, the movie was about violent motorcycle gangs causing havoc in an Indian community. My mother had no idea what the movie was really about, and neither did I, but I remember there was a sex scene. I was a young teen and remember being embarrassed that my mother was with me to see that scene. I glanced over at her to see what her reaction was and saw that she was asleep and snoring. Boy, did I breathe a sigh of relief. However, the snoring in itself was a little embarrassing. I looked around to see if anyone was looking, but it was dark, and I couldn't tell. Whatever, I couldn't seem to win, but I was still was glad to be with my mother. It was special that she and I had that time together while my dad took my brothers; our parents were still trying to entertain us. She loved to do things with me; it meant the world to her. I was so grateful that she took me out and spent special time with me the way she did, just she and I. I miss those times. I miss her.

There was another embarrassing moment that happened while out with my mother in the 1970s. I was probably about 13 or 14, I'm thinking. We were out as a group to eat to a restaurant known as Howard Johnsons. My friend Debbie and her mother and several other mothers with their daughters met us. I loved those mother and daughter events, and there were lots of them. This was during the streaking era, where people thought it was funny to run through a building completely naked just to make a statement, I guess. It's kind of stupid to think about now. Ray Stevens even wrote a song about it called "The Streak."

So here we were, sitting in a group of about 20at a long table. We were eating dinner, having conversation, and a good time. I was sitting next to my friend Debbie, chatting about something, when all of a sudden, this man appeared at the front door of the restaurant completely naked. When he got our attention, he instructed everybody to be quiet as he was going to run through the restaurant with not a stitch of clothing on. Since I had never seen anybody naked before, especially men, I was intrigued. Debbie was giggling, and at the same time, I thought to myself, *this should be good.*

At that moment, Debbie said, "Look, Iris, he's naked," and she laughed; we both tried to stand up and look because we were curious, no kidding, and before we knew it, our mothers grabbed us, covered our eyes, and told us to sit down. They were appalled and upset that their daughters would be exposed to such indecency.

"What the heck are things coming to, I don't believe this," my mother sputtered.

"I don't know, but Debbie, sit down and quit trying to look." Her mother kept pushing her back in her chair.

The streaker ran through quite fast and was gone in the blink of an eye, and since our eyes were covered, we saw nothing. While I was disappointed, I remember I felt secure knowing our mothers were protecting us. We laughed that one off for quite a while. And as I look back on that today, it was our experience with something that was history-making, and we got to be a part of it, as silly and ridiculous as it was. What a crazy time with some crazy people, but it was our time and our memories just the same.

Debbie and I and some of my other friends also enjoyed singing groups, like Abba, who were coming on the scene and becoming more popular. I loved their song, "Dancing Queen." It resonated with me because when the song came out, it talked about how the Dancing Queen in the song, "was young and sweet and only 17," as the lyrics stated. And I was 17 when that song came out. So, it became a little personal for me, a song I could relate to, and encouraged imagination as I danced to it with friends at high school dances.

I also enjoyed listening to The Carpenters, Paul McCartney and Wings, which Paul McCartney established as his own band after breaking up with The Beatles. I love the song "San Francisco." The Beach Boys were still popular, they had a long run of popularity. From what I understand, they still have concerts today, not with all the original people, but with the same songs. Some of my friends and I enjoyed listening to Stevie Wonder, popular at the time. I really enjoyed Van Morrison and his song, "Wild Night is Calling." I loved music that was uplifting and fun with positive messages. I guess that was the nun wannabe in me from Catholicism back then.

I remember watching the *Six Million Dollar Man* on television and wanted to be as strong as he was since I had a somewhat weak body. And you'll be interested to know that on November 11th, 1974, the actor Leonardo DiCaprio was born. Also, Jimmy Fallon was born that year; it's hard to think of them that way as I watch them on TV today occasionally. Yes, they were once babies, too. We all were.

I was always drawn to family-oriented television shows. That year *The Walton's* began airing. This was an American television series created by Earl Hamner Junior, based on his book, *Spencer's Mountain*, a 1963 film of the same name, about a family in rural Virginia during the Great Depression and World War II. There were 221 episodes in nine seasons, and it originally aired on CBS. I loved the story because it was all about family and family sticking together with God in the midst.

It reminded me so much of what my mother used to say: "The way that people made it during the Great Depression back in the 1930s is they had each other, they stuck together with God in the center. They were not alone." And this particular show on television, for me, was a beautiful reminder of the gift that God gave us in family and friends. And it became my dream that one day I would have a beautiful family of my own with God at the center once again. These are some of the things I focused on during the course of my parents splitting up. I did grieve that my parents were no longer together. It was hard, but as I focused on what I did have and not what I didn't when my life began to turn a corner, a different corner, but nevertheless, a good one. I would discover that perspective was half the battle, and I had many mentors along the way, to encourage this attitude in me.

Beverly's Family's Influence

My time with Beverly and her family still brings me some life-changing memories of the kind of friends they were. In Beverly's home, the night I spent there while my father packed to leave, I had spent a really nice evening with her and her parents. The next morning, my parents' separation was on my mind. I hated to go home and experience the finality of my father's time with us. I felt like an orphan or like someone had died. We would never be the same family. And it was hard for me. I wondered how Lance and my mother were doing. Lance and his welfare during this time weighed heavily on me.

Bev's parents in their elder years.

But as a nice diversion, Beverly's mother had prepared a substantial breakfast of bagels and cream cheese, eggs, juice, and bacon, for us. Around the table were me, Beverly, her dad, and mom. I loved her parents; they were so sweet and kind. Their attitude was reflected in my friend because that's how she was. She, too, had a mature attitude and maternal instincts at such a young age. And I was blessed to be a part of their family, even if it was just for a season. Beverly had an older sister my sister's age and they were friends, too. By this time though, her sister was married and living in New Jersey, and mine was attending college. She had an older brother, too, but he also was grown and out on his own, having graduated in 1969 and then married. Bev was the baby of the family, much younger than her siblings, and I could see she was special to them due to her much younger age.

As we ate, they spoke of the day and also spoke to me words of encouragement of how I would get through this and how hard they knew it was. I still remember her mother's words that helped so much. "If you ever need anything, know we are just a phone call away, we are always here for you, remember, just a phone call away." And at that, she winked and gave me this beautiful smile that is hard to forget. Her mother not only had a physical beauty, but her inner beauty also spoke to me as a role model. And of course, Beverly smiled at her mother's comment as if she was proud. I'll bet she was. These were examples of real people I was blessed enough to have in my life to love and support me. Even if it was just for a season.

After breakfast, I packed up my belongings, and my friend and her family drove me back to my home. My father also had filed bankruptcy, so not only were we losing my father, we were also losing the home we loved. A home that was now being foreclosed upon. The place of comfort, the place of shelter from life's challenges outside in the world around us. The place where we felt warm and safe was disappearing before my very eyes. My security was literally being torn out from under me.

As we drove up to the house and I stepped out, I recall Beverly's mom winking at me from the passenger's side of the car, and, once again, she said to me, "Remember what I said. We are here." I got to tell you, I had a knack for knowing the kindest people, it had to have been God's love for me that I should be so blessed to have people love me enough to take me in as their own. I think God knew I was all about love and needed much assurance and affirmation. So, he kept providing and still does, even to this day.

I would often look up to the sky and speak to God myself and say, "Thanks, I needed that." But not only during this time was I receiving love, I was also learning to give it as well. My destiny was beginning to unfold. A destiny where I would be called "To comfort the broken hearted and bind up their wounds." It was a scripture given to me at a very young age, and my new role model would become Mother Teresa. Isaiah 61:1 says, "The Spirit of the Lord God is on me, because the Lord has anointed me to preach good news to the poor. He sent me to bind up the brokenhearted, to proclaim freedom for the captives and release from darkness for the prisoners" (NIV). I was experiencing things, so I could be there for others later, it was hard to grasp at such a young age, but in my own way, I already understood that God had a plan. And his plan would be less about me and more about him. But I had to experience pain, so I could understand others' pain. Beverly and her family were just one of many examples of people who reached out to me during one of the toughest times in my life. But I made it because I wasn't alone. And caring for others was what my destiny was calling me to.

Beverly Haffey with her husband today.

Back at my House

When I came in the house, I remember looking in my father's closet to find all his clothes gone. I almost didn't look in there because I knew how painful it would be. But I needed to see, and I remember how sad that made me feel. And I recalled, once again, several older mentors explaining to me that a divorce is like a living death where you grieve. Just as if the person had died, because it is suffering a loss. And that brought me a measure of comfort.

After that I remember going into the kitchen, seeing my mother's face, looking so sad and defeated, it killed me to see her that way. I could feel her sense of abandonment once again, just like when her father died when she was ten years old, holding her hand. And I'm sure she felt it all over again. She was literally going from a happy household as a stay-at-home mom to a single mother that had to work and care for three children. What a sense of heaviness and stress she must've felt. It broke my heart to see her this way. I can still see with my mind's eye, her sitting at the kitchen table with her head in her hands, crying, with my brother Lance by her side. He was such a little man, just sitting with her so patiently, not understanding but wanting to help his mama. When he saw me come into the kitchen, he ran to me and hugged me. He was such a strong little boy but needed to be comforted, too, he was so young, as he was only seven. I comforted him as best I could because I was still quite young myself. But I was very aware that he needed me at that moment, and it helped me to feel stronger as an individual and kind of mother-like; being responsible for someone else took my mind away from my own pain.

They say when you focus on others, it takes your mind off yourself and your own problems and gives you a strength you didn't know you had. I have always found that to be true. As you can imagine, we were always very close after that. I remember feeling a little helpless, as I was still trying to find my way. Who am I? is a common question in adolescence, and I found myself asking that question often.

So, upon my arrival into the kitchen, as my brother ran to hug me, my mother arose from the table and came toward me, gave me a hug, and asked, "Did you have a nice time?"

"I did, I always like to be with Beverly and her family," I hugged her back, "but it was hard because I was worried about you and Lance."

My mother gasped and looked into my eyes. "We will be okay, we will do what have to do, we'll move on. We have lots of support in your grandparents, other family members, and friends. You know, Iris, we are never alone. I know leaving this house will be hard on you and Lance and Alan, but we will find another place. Life doesn't stop here; this can be a new beginning for us if we can see it that way. And yes, it will be tough for a while, but we can do this, we have each other. We have your sister, too. Lance needs you; I need you, Alan needs us, too, we all need each other. We have to be strong, and in time, you'll see how it will work out, we'll make it, we are survivors." I could see the apprehension in her face as she said this to me, like she was trying to convince herself, and I know she was trying not to frighten us.

I remember her words of comfort to me, felt re-assured, and yet still worried. I could see how hard it really was for her. The road ahead would be very tough for her, but she, too, believed in God through her Jewish faith, and I believe that's where she found a lot of her strength, through her faith in God and through prayer. I would often hear her talking to Him and asking him for strength and wisdom as she cried to Him. She was afraid and overwhelmed, and I felt it. And it scared me to see my very strong mother beginning to fall apart. She spoke strength, but her actions and emotions said otherwise. My security was being challenged, and as I look back on this moment, I leaned on what my mother taught me, determination and strength, and that giving up was not an option. And even though she was wavering a bit, I knew somehow with God's help, we would be alright.

She once said to me, "Once you give up, then there is no chance of moving ahead and being successful. There is no chance of fulfilling your destiny." She and I both believed that. I thank God every day that my mother never let us give up. Had she and I done so at that moment because it was so tough, we would have missed out a lot of blessings in life and so would my brothers. Lance, being the youngest, would experience the challenge of pressing through to his destiny, and because he was so young, I believe it was hardest on him. But he never wanted to disappoint us, and he never let the hurts show, he was and still is his mother's son, kind, caring, compassionate, and he shows it in the way he cares for others. This was especially true with our mom.

Moving Out

While we had about a month to go before moving out of our home, we would experience another little tragedy in the midst. During the divorce, my mother decided to get Lance and me a new dog to comfort us. So, she brought us to an animal shelter, Angel Memorial Animal Shelter, located in nearby town. So, Lance and I had the privilege of picking out a new dog. Alan had taken a job at the Bradlees department store after school, so he was quite busy and not able to be there. He was busy trying to help with finances, another amazing brother.

The dog was a two-year-old German shepherd who came with the name Sheppie. That dog was such a comfort to us, and we loved him so much. Well, one fall afternoon while my mother was out shopping, I was babysitting Lance and the dog. Alan was at work, and Lance was out in the front yard playing with a neighbor friend. I opened the door to call Lance inside because it was getting dark and cold. Just as I opened the door, our dear dog Sheppie ran out as fast as he could before I could stop him. He saw a squirrel and ran after him right past Lance and into the street. This is something most dogs would do. Before we knew it, we heard the screeching of tires. Sheppie had been hit by a car. Lance and I saw him flying literally through the air. Sheppie was gone.

Lance came running to me, and I held him close to me as the woman who hit the dog came to us. She was a woman in her 40s, as I remember, and she felt awful. She was thoughtful and kind and stayed with us because we had told her our mother was not at home. She came in the house and called the police to let them know what happened and waited till Mom got there, to make sure we were okay. Once again, we were not alone. It didn't make it any easier, but nevertheless, we were comforted. When Mom came home, Lance and I ran and clung to her as the woman was so apologetic. My mother, being the woman, she was, also comforted the woman and thanked her for staying with us.

I remember her saying, "Please don't blame yourself; it was an accident, these things happen, you did the right thing, and I want to thank you for staying with my children because they loved that dog."

"I'm so sorry," the woman kept saying. My mother kept comforting her and us, and even though my mother was going through so much, she still found the strength to comfort us and think of others. I think it gave her strength and took her mind away from her own feelings. My mother was such a strong example for me. It was her example that got me through some very, very tough times in the future. And she always found strength in caring for others and not thinking about herself. She never wavered from this, even until her death later in my life.

Beverly's Comfort to Me

I called my friend Beverly. I was so upset; I was crying about the dog.

"Another loss." I talked to her about how I felt like I was losing everything, and I kind of was. I also told her I wasn't feeling very loved, which makes no sense to me now with all the support I had. But we see things differently when we are young, what can I say. My friend cried with me, once again. This showed me how sensitive she was.

And I'll never forget what she said to me, "I love you, you're my friend, you're like a sister and you mean so much to me, please know you are loved, like my mother said, we are here and you're not alone, it will be all right." I believe if she could have hugged me through the phone, she would have.

As if I was surprised, I said, "You do?" But I needed to hear that, and it brought me great comfort and assurance.

She then said, "Yes, I do, and you need to know that."

And I thanked her. That reassurance did a world of good for me and gave me the confidence to move on. At that moment, I realized just how lucky I was to have a friend say that to me, and it really helped to comfort me during so much turmoil and transition going on. It gave me a sense of belonging still and a bit of security with an anchor out there, for when I felt like I was sinking. I also had my friend Linda and her mother I could go to, and they were always there, too. Another caring friend that I spent some really nice times in high school with.

Therefore, this is why we should never be alone, there is strength in not only others but numbers as well. There would be fewer suicides if everyone had a sense of belonging and being loved and cared about. Someone to lean on during times of feeling so lost without a clear perspective on how to take the next step. Someone to help them figure out just who they are.

But it wasn't just a chance thing, I believe this was another one of God's provisions to hold me up through a very arduous and difficult time. He never left me alone, and He would continue to send his angels to watch over me in the form of people and in angelic form. Throughout my life and circumstances to come, He never left me and proved it to me time and time again. Arms that I couldn't see that would hold me in those lonely places in some very hard times to come. And it would take me years of maturing to realize the impact of this. As time went on, this theme kept repeating through my own history. I would go through a heavy trial, and He would provide that someone or someone's to hold me up, so I wouldn't fall. Sincere and loyal people who truly loved me. I would pray and either provision would come, or circumstances would change, or I was given the grace to get through whatever it was I was facing. And over time, as things progressed, I came to realize it was God's provision for me.

It was as simple as Mathew 7:7 says, "Ask and it will be given to you; seek and you will find; knock and the door will be open to you" (NIV). And He-brews 13:5 (NIV), "Keep your lives free from the love of money and be content with what you have, because God has said, never will I leave you; never will I forsake you." And leaving me was something I never experienced if I asked. God was faithful. He answered.

Chapter 12

The Wonder Years

Me, Alan, and Lance in our home in Sharon. Circa 1972.

I entitled this chapter, "The Wonder Years" because it was a wonder I had so many who cared for me, and it was funny, I couldn't always see it. I had Karen and her mother Carol, my friend Linda and her mother, my friend Sharon and her mother, and more. Still, I found myself asking the question, who am I? It didn't seem enough that God's provision of support and guidance would be enough to bring me a confidence and peace that would sustain me. No matter how many people He sent me at the time to love and support me, I couldn't see that I was worthy of it all, that there were reasons he blessed me so. Because of all the medical issues, I had a poor self-image and often found myself comparing my looks to my older sister. It would take decades of love and affirmation to finally accept myself for who I was and that it was Okay. It didn't seem possible; was I worthy of all that love?

My father leaving had something to do with those feelings of insecurity and abandonment, but even he showed he loved me and said it often. Would all the joy disappear with my father leaving? No, I would find that I had to choose joy, even when others would disappoint me. I also would have to learn what loneliness was all about. But God promised to hold me, and He did, and many times it was his hand alone. In Proverbs 4:11-12, it says, "I guide you in the way of wisdom and lead you along straight paths. When you walk, your steps will not be hampered; when you run, you will not stumble" (NIV). I was learning to trust, and throughout this book, I will quote Mother Theresa, saying things like, "I'm a little pencil in the hand of a writing God, who is sending a love letter to the world. I was learning to love and be loved.

My health issues were often at the forefront of my focus because I was dealing with multiple symptoms. Symptoms of weakness, digestive issues, as well as psoriasis, and I lacked stamina. I had trouble walking, and I was always wondering what was coming next. I often didn't know what to expect from my body, and I didn't realize the impact the burst appendix episode had left on my body. Could that be why God gave me so much love and provision? Would the love and provision always be there?

There is a scripture in Philippians 4:12, "I know what it is to be in need, and I know what it is to have plenty. I have learned the secret of being content in any and every situation, whether well fed or hungry, whether living in plenty or in want" (NIV). I was just beginning to understand what this meant. I had to learn throughout my life the meaning of being content no matter what my circumstances, whether I had a lot or a little and I was just beginning this journey called life to move me toward my destiny.

I was starting to experience life and its challenges in a big way but certainly not alone. In the midst of this, I found the support and closeness of others to help me discover who I was and where I was going. I was never alone, not at this point!

Someone once said to me, "I have never seen so much provision for one person. You have more than most." And she wondered why. At the time, I didn't know how to answer her. I just listened and tried to process what she said. However, as I grew older, I began to understand why. It was my constant acknowledgement of my dependence on God, and I began to walk so closely with Him that I was constantly asking Him to provide for me, to help me, and guide me. I was always wondering about the future. What would it be like? Who will I become? What will become of my health? The wonder years of wondering how it will be. They also said I'd never have any children, and the thought of that saddened me. And because I didn't always understand, I was asking God to show me his way.

James 4:2, "You desire but do not have, so you kill. You covet but you cannot get what you want, you quarrel and fight. You do not have because you do not ask God" (NIV). So, I was asking, but not for myself but for the plans He had for me and with the right motives. I saw others around me making wrong choices and suffering consequences as a result, and I was learning what not to do through them. I wanted to avoid unnecessary conflict as much as I could. And I think that was the key. Because God does desire to give us good things, all of us, it's important to recognize that we need to follow his lead where he knows best. And that's not an easy thing to do. I have come to understand that the easy thing to do is not always the right thing to do. It requires spending time with him in prayer and hearing his voice through reading his word, as that is how I believe God speaks to us. Since God is a spirit and we don't see him, he connects with our spirit as we pray and read his word. He doesn't promise we won't go through difficulty in the process, but he does promise to provide and be there for us as we navigate through events. This is the benefit I have found in leaning on my creator, and I have never felt alone in the process. Even during times when no one else was around, I was always aware of his presence, and those times alone were short lived, but necessary, so I would learn to lean on him.

Mathew 7: 7-8 (NIV) bears repeating, "Ask and it shall be given you; seek and you will find; knock and the door will be opened to you. for everyone who asks receives; he who seeks finds; and to him who knocks the door will be opened." In verse 12, it says, "So in everything, do to others what you would have them do to you, for this sums up the law and the prophets." In my wildest dreams, I could never have imagined what God was going to do with me next. But not just for me but for the sake of others as well. Doing unto others what I would want others to do unto me. What did that mean? It meant being people-oriented and having compassion for them, and this is not something teenagers usually focus on. But while some of my other friends were enjoying life for themselves, I was now in a place where I was beginning to understand

and experience what suffering and being cared for was all about. And caring for my friends who were going through things, too, caring and being cared for. I never imagined He could use me as his instrument to help and encourage in a positive way.

As a youth, I loved people but didn't always understand what to do with that or how to show it. And everyone around me was so different and trying to find their own way. I didn't recognize this at the time, but that's exactly what was going on. And as I listen to my grade school friends today, I'm not surprised to hear what they were dealing with, but at the time, I did think I was the only one. No one is exempt, we all have something in our lives to challenge us, make us better people, and help us mature if we let those challenges do so. I wanted to make things better for my friends who were going through heavy trials, I didn't know why, but I wanted to lighten their loads. If I couldn't do much, at least I was learning to listen and pray for them.

A good example of this was my friend Mary. She and I and several others used to hang out together in high school. After school Mary and I would walk home together and just talk. This was after my parents' divorce and I was struggling to find meaning in it all and understand. I didn't realize she was struggling with home life, too. We didn't share a lot personally, just talked about how we were feeling. Mary was very sensitive to people's feelings and had a lot of compassion.

She would say to me, "Iris, you seem a little down today, what's wrong? How can I help?"

I would respond, "I'm just feeling a little lost since my parents split up, I'm not sure what to do sometimes, and it's hard to watch my mother struggle. I do find a lot of comfort in going to church though, but what does that mean? Mary, have you ever thought about God?"

She would answer, "I think about God all the time, I actually find a lot of peace and comfort in just sitting in the church by myself. I often go there just to sit and pray after school when no one else is there, just me and God, have you ever done that? It's a great comfort to me. Peaceful. You should try it."

"Maybe I will," I said. It sure sounded like a good idea. Not necessarily fun but like destiny calling. I'm not sure how else to explain it. The peace and serenity that she was expressing resonated with me, and I wanted what she was describing. But how could I attain it, and what would a future of Catholicism look like for me? At the time, I wasn't able to talk to my father about it, he was distracted with other things. And I couldn't talk to my Jewish mother, forget that! I started thinking about being a nun. Mary was another friend that seemed to know when I was struggling and took the time, even though she had struggles of her own. So, it wasn't a surprise to me that years later when we connected on Facebook that she revealed to me that she became a strong Christian woman and was serving others in need, like a nun would.

Now as older women, we can share all that God has done for us and how far we both have come. But as youths, I always wondered how I could help someone else. What did that mean? And was this my calling in life? Was I being groomed through life's challenges to be able to understand what others might feel like and would this journey of circumstances beyond my control give me the wisdom and compassion I needed to extend a hand of mercy? My journey to learn this was not easy and just beginning. I was learning the secret of being content in good times and bad times. And this journey is called life, and for anyone of us, it's not without its challenges, and challenges leading to purpose if we let them. I feel we all have a destiny, and part of that destiny comes out of suffering, bringing us to a greater place.

Anyone who tries to tell you their life has always been good and without hardship can't be completely honest because if you live here, and long enough, you're going to experience something. At some point, even if life seems to be good and unusually blessed, there does come a time in everyone's life where trials will come, and sorrow will face you at a time when you least expect it. If it's not through the death of a loved one, it may be sickness or financial, or someone leaving you. Whatever it is, we all face it. But the good news is during those turbulent moments, we have God to give us the strength to continue and friends to support us. We are never alone, even when no else is around, God is always there. No one gets out of this world without something to challenge them in some way. We live in this world, and we are subject to its problems. The rain falls on the just and unjust alike.

"He causes his sun to rise on the evil and the good and sends rain on the righteous and the unrighteous" Mathew 5: 45 (NIV). What this means is no one is exempt. We all have lessons to learn, what we do with those lessons is up to us. It's in seeking the truth that we find it. It's in giving that we get, it's in listening that we are listened to. Luke 6:38 (NIV) says, "Give and it will be given to you. A good measure, pressed down, shaken together, and running over will be poured into your lap. For with the measure you use, it will be measured to you." This helped me understand just how we receive what God and life has for us and do it gracefully. It's by putting others before ourselves. Extending a hand of mercy to those in need, the misunderstood. God's grace extended to me would put many mentors in my path in the days to come to confirm this. Mentors both Jew and Gentile and from other walks of life. While I believe in Christianity, I had mentors in friends and family that taught me the same thing, how to be a person of integrity and be a good person in general, how to bless others, it's called being a good human being. This is my conviction, and my hope is that it encourages you to think of your brother in need.

My Parents' Divorce

While my parents were divorcing, I had friends that were so kind, and their parents took a special interest in me. I was intuitive enough to recognize mentoring, even if I didn't know what it was called back then. I really enjoyed the people that were taking an interest in me, and I was learning from them. My younger brother Lance and I had this in common, we always wanted to learn the right ways of doing things. And we were both quite teachable. A good quality to have if you want to grow and make right choices. So, as my brothers and I were navigating through a very difficult time, we kept asking questions and leaning on those who would support us. I found that people would take the time with us, because we were a captive audience, trying to do the right thing. I have found out myself that it's hard to come alongside people who don't want to make things better for themselves and take responsibility. They remain stuck, and it makes you stuck right alongside of them. Through others, I was learning the difference, and it would bring me a lot of clarity in boundary setting in days to come. Help the helper is what I was learning, don't make it hard for someone to help you. I was a work in progress, and all these messages I was receiving would help me later on and understanding others.

By now it was 1974 and I was 15 and learning a lot and maturing fast as a result. What an interesting era it was. While things were hard at times, there were plenty of good things to focus on. It was the fun era of bellbottoms, pooka beads, hip hugger jeans, tie-dyed T-shirts, Mexican peasant blouses, folk imported Hungarian blouses, ponchos, capes, and military surplus clothing. In addition, we had gauchos, frayed jeans, miniskirts, and ankle-length maxi dresses. I remember several friends of mine and their parents driving around in cars like Ford Pintos and Pontiac Firebirds and anything with a vinyl roof.

The disco era was born on Valentine's Day 1970 when David Manusco opened the Loft in New York City; it was a fun time for a while but peaked in 1978 to '79 and faded in 1980. It was the era of The Bee Gees, a popular English singing group and their disco songs. In 1977, the year that I graduated, the big disco movie *Saturday Night Fever* came out, starring John Travolta. During the '70s, he also starred in a show on television, *Welcome Back Kotter*. As young girls, of course, we all thought he was incredibly good-looking, and he was one of our teen idols at the time.

I did the remainder of my growing up years in Sharon, Massachusetts on the east coast. Sharon was different from living in North Boston. It was the suburbs, not the city. Before my parent's divorce, they liked the idea of having us live more suburban. We would have a safe, freer, more open haven to play and grow up in with a better school system. There was more space between homes in nicer neighborhoods and even some farms. There were playgrounds and a town lake called Massapoag, where we could swim and hang out with our friends and family all summer long. At the lake, every Fourth of July, there were barbecues, fireworks, and fun events where families and friends gathered to enjoy together. We had bonfires there, Fourth of July parades, all kinds of fun. It was a great place to grow up, and all my classmates agree and reminisce how blessed we were to grow up in such a nice town. That's what my parents wanted and that's what it was.

In Sharon, like a lot of places back then, we still had penny candy stores. Our local store, Bendinelli's, was in the center of town where it seemed just about everybody went. It had aisles and aisles of penny candy that really cost only a penny.

Bendinelli's, was the store we all went to for penny candy as kids.

When I would go there with my friends, if I had fifty cents to spend, it seemed I had a million dollars as it bought me a lot of candy. There was so much to choose from: banana split candy chews, bb bats taffy suckers, black cow candies, and who doesn't remember candy cigarettes? Button candies that were little candies on a white sheet of paper that you would bite off one at a time. I remember so well wearing candy necklaces—literally a necklace you would put around your neck and pull out one candy at a time. There were jaw busters, mint julep candy chews, Mary Jane peanut butter candy, water taffy, smarties, sugar daddy pops, tootsie rolls. There was wax candy in the shape of little Coke bottles with different flavors in each bottle. There was saltwater taffy, candy rolls, fizzies, and so much more. And of course, plenty of chocolate. It's amazing we have teeth today! But we didn't think too much back then about eating too much sugar or how it would affect our teeth, we just enjoyed the moment. We didn't worry so much about every little thing.

It's no wonder society today is so anxiety ridden, there's too much advertisement on what is wrong and how bad it is and not enough emphasis on what is right, or lovely. If we can go back to focusing on what is right, maybe we'd have a more relaxed society. But perhaps a society with no teeth! We knew about nutrition but not like today. Our nutrition back then was Kentucky Fried Chicken, Chinese food, pizza, ice cream, etc. The best food one could ask for but maybe not necessarily for our future health.

Speaking of ice cream, we also had a place called Crescent Ridge Dairy Farm that made homemade ice cream to die for. It was the creamiest ice cream you've ever tasted with so many flavors and sizes to choose from, so how is it I was so thin? I didn't know I had celiac disease. I'm thankful in a way I didn't know, because I would have missed a lot of fun food. The problem was I did have a lot of symptoms to deal with. I remember Crescent Ridge Dairy well, as back in the day, they used to home deliver milk, eggs, chocolate milk, butter, etc. to our homes. Those were the days when you knew your mailman and milkman and even trash man and gave them Christmas gifts to show your appreciation. We were thinking of others. Putting a smile on someone's face and showing them what they did was important and significant. That you appreciated them. How hard is it to tell someone you're thankful for them and that the hard work they do matters? It's true what it says in Ecclesiastes, "Pity the man who is alone." Even in the midst of my parents' divorce, I never felt alone. Because I never was, not back then.

My father and mother, while together, were good about taking us to these places with other family members; we always had such a good time. A lot of our friends and relatives from out of town used to visit us in Sharon because it was a nice place to be and it had a great reputation. Growing up, my friends and I did things like roller-skating as groups. We would go to the movies and bowling together. In our teens, there were school dances held on Saturday nights at the recreation center. I remember how exciting it was to see all our friends and hear our favorite music. The dances were chaperoned to ensure things remained calm and uneventful. However, there were some of us who would sneak outside for various reasons, like smoking cigarettes or pot, some had alcohol, some to just be together, if you know what I mean. So, behind the scenes, it wasn't always so uneventful. It never is! Still, Sharon was a nice town with nice people, but it wasn't Pleasantville. I'll just say it was just a nice safe haven to grow up in because, while it didn't have a lot of crime, you did hear of occasional issues. No place is perfect!

Speaking of crime, an event stands out in my mind when I was at my friend Tracy's home. She and I did a lot of overnights together; I loved this friend and her family. Her grandmother made the best fried chicken I've ever tasted. Kentucky Fried Chicken had nothing on her grandmother's southern fried cooking. I remember Tracy's family as being very fun-loving, positive people. Tracy and I had a lot of fun together, again, you never forget the young friendships and the lasting impact certain ones had on you. Because there was a low crime rate, no one thought it was dangerous to walk the streets as young girls; certainly, Tracy and I had no idea about the dangers.

So, one afternoon, she and I walked from her house to a nearby store, just the two of us. I think we were around 12, just enjoying a beautiful spring afternoon together. As we were nearing her house, a scruffy older man pulled up near us in an old beat up car and tried to flag us down by waving money at us. As I think about this now, I realize how stupid this guy was. We both immediately sensed something wasn't right, and we were scared. But we recognized the danger and Tracy began to scream and grabbed my hand, yelling, "Run, Iris," and we did, holding on to each other very tightly. I remember how frightened Tracy was, and I wanted her to be Okay, too. As we ran, the car chased us, but we held on to each other and wouldn't let go and ran as fast as we could. He followed us until we made it safely to her home, where her grandmother was waiting for us. When we arrived, we told her grandmother about the incident and she immediately called the police and reported the man.

Tracy and I were scared enough that we never walked alone again after that. When I think about what could have happened to us, it gives me the creeps. But we were spared. Was someone praying for us? I think so! All I know is we had each other to hold on to, and that was probably what saved us. When I spoke with Tracy recently about this, what she recalled most is how we held on to each other and thought of one another and the concern we had for one another. It caused us to run even faster for fear of what would happen to one or both of us. Talk about dodging a bullet. And we are both thankful today that we were both Okay. We were able to report what we saw, and while we never knew the outcome of this man's fate, our hope was that perhaps we were able to stop one pedophile from harming another child. I pray so.

But that was the only crime I ever knew of personally. Of course, a lot was hidden back then, so I'm sure there were things going on, we were not aware of. It made life more peaceful and less anxiety-provoking not hearing so much. We were spared knowing about so much, and I thank God for that, it made childhood more pleasant for us.

There were tragedies that took place in Sharon, no town is without some because life happens. This incident affected both Tracy and me, and we then witnessed yet another event, or at least heard about it. It was something that happened to a mutual friend of ours. We were so young, and life was beginning to make itself known to us. The reality of dangers were coming into play.

It was one summer afternoon and a friend's younger sister was swimming in their home pool. Her parents were away for the day and they had the family maid watching her. She took her eyes off of her for just a moment to go do something. When she returned, she found her at the bottom of the pool. She had drowned. What a horrific tragedy, enough said. It was one of my first experiences with a death, and it was very hard for all of us to endure, all who knew the family at least. And we supported our friend during that very difficult time for her and her family.

I remember her mother well. She had a lot of faith and family and friends to lean on, and it got her through. I remember seeing her in church a few months after the incident. She was inspiring others and teaching them what she knew about the Bible. She was eager to make a difference and allow her circumstances to be used for good. It was that attitude of being others-oriented that really spoke to me. She was a role model I'll never forget. Since I was gravitating toward Christianity, role models like her caught my attention, and I wanted to emulate that. Here was a woman who suffered such a tragic loss, thinking of others. I was beginning to understand through her, that God can use us, even in our darkest moment. Especially something so painful. She was reaching out to others, and I watched the difference in them. Their burdens lifted, and I wanted to do the same. She took time with me personally, trying to help me put things in perspective, and I adored her and the time we spent together.

As I was gravitating toward the church, I was remembering my mentors and what they taught me, so I never smoked or did much that would get me in trouble, but I did drink beer on occasion with my friends but never felt good about it or felt well physically. I didn't tolerate it well and I'm grateful. Beer has grains, and I had celiac disease, but I didn't know what was wrong. Hey, I had to fit in and push those boundaries somehow, even if it gave me diarrhea and terrible stomach aches. I guess I thought I would get used to it, but of course, I never did, so church was always something I went back to and those mentors God had put there to teach me.

I had a close group of friends but tended to float to other groups as well because I was very social. I loved all my friends, no matter where they came from. The close friends I had were great and very loyal, they had their own issues they were dealing with from home life as I was, but we didn't let it stop us from being together, supporting one another, and enjoying each other. We didn't let the challenges we were facing bother us much; we just did the next thing next.

As older teens, we would travel to other towns, like Stoughton, Massachusetts, which was the next adjoining town, we enjoyed the Town Spa Pizza, which I hear is still there today, and it was the best pizza ever. I was into the gluten for sure. I was so underweight back then. I could eat like a horse and never gain a pound. I wish I still had that problem today. But on Saturdays, we would go out for lunch either there or a place called Papa Genos Pizza Place, mainly known for its pizza but other Italian food specials as well. Sometimes we would have luncheon specials at the local Chinese restaurant. We loved Chinese food; I still do today. I was relieved after finding out I had celiac disease that they came up with gluten free Chinese restaurants. Thank God, PF Chang's caught on to this, I hated being without Chinese food, it's the best. Everything was about food, wasn't it? It was Okay, as long as you're young and active.

Back then, most of us would take our allowance and go out together. And it was affordable! Those luncheon specials back then were $2.95. Can you imagine? What are they today? $22.00 a special if you're lucky. There were so many good restaurants to go to, and yes, eating became a hobby. Not a healthy hobby but social and fun. I have the cholesterol today to prove it. Before my parents' divorce, my father would often bring home take-out chicken from this place in a nearby town called Fontaine's Fried Chicken. What restaurant wasn't nearby? As I'm writing this, I can understand why so many of us ended up with so many health issues. Oh, what the heck, we loved it. Fontaine's Fried Chicken was delicious but a killer on the fat content.

My brother Alan and I often joke about why we ended up with such high cholesterol, but no one knew back then the consequences of eating such high fat meals. It was the best fried chicken, served with garlic rolls, that we had ever had, dripping with butter and fat, I think even lard. As I look back on our diet back then, while my European grandparents were eating so healthy and preparing homemade food, my parents felt deprived growing up and thought it was fun to take us out to eat so often. Yikes! But a lot of that changed after the divorce. My grandmothers got a hold of me and taught me to go back to the way they showed me, and I agreed. I could see I felt better. I guess my parents had forgotten the benefits of healthy eating.

The American diet was heading south, and no one realized it. Eating white flour, the wrong kinds of fats, too much sugar, etc. Do you ever wonder why we see so many autoimmune disorders today? We weren't eating real food.

Both my grandmothers were instrumental in helping me make right choices in foods as they recognized some of my health issues were food related. Grandmas know best. So, while we were torn between our parents bad but fun choices in eating out, we were very active, which I feel offset a lot of the calories. We were running around outside, riding our bikes everywhere, playing baseball, kickball, or swimming. We weren't sitting behind computers and with our cell phones all the time, like many of the children today. Unfortunately, they don't have the blessing of the freedoms we had, especially with being outdoors. We had more sports activities at school, we weren't wondering about budget cuts and cutting school programs. And if we weren't involved in school sports, we were active in other ways, as I mentioned. As much as my family loved television, we still took time to be active.

I loved where I grew up. It's a place I'll never forget. Even when my parents got divorced, I still enjoyed this great Town. My mother loved it there, too. She encouraged us to stay focused on playing and being social and being goal oriented, to think about making a nice future for ourselves, to be productive and make a difference. She worked hard, helping family, and recreating in between. I don't know how she did it, but she showed us how strong one could be. The hard times that we faced due to the divorce would cause me to have a different perspective. I went from feeling secure to feeling like my life had been ripped out from under me in some ways. The large, fun family was now separated and struggling. My mother, who had stayed at home raising her children, was now forced economically to go from a nice home, a boat, a Cadillac (considered a very expensive car back then), and all these nice material things to losing our home, and all that was in it. Working full-time left her feeling frightened and overwhelmed at times. Her fears caused me to be fearful and unsure.

When he left, my father filed bankruptcy, so we lost the house and were forced to move into a small older apartment. He became ill with bone cancer and liver problems, which I believe were attributed to his time spent in captivity in the service. I don't believe for one moment that he wanted to take all those things away from us and put us in such a compromising place. He was ill and could no longer work, so in the process made some unwise choices but did the best he could. He began to gravitate toward the Lord and church. In fact, in doing so, he began to gain perspective. I remember one time shortly after my parents separated, he took me out for dinner, just he and I. I was 15, and I remember how special that made me feel that my father would take the time just for me. And it was shortly after I had started attending church. I remember the conversation we had. It went something like this as we had dinner together.

"Iris, I have something to tell you."

While I had no idea what he was going to tell me, my ears sure perked up. "What is it?"

He said, "I decided to go back to church, and while I've been struggling, I have found a lot of hope and peace."

I smiled and said, "I did the same thing. It's something I've always wanted to do."

As I look back on our conversation, I can't help but wonder what a miracle it was that we both made this decision at the same time, but neither one of us knew it. It was clearly God's plan, and it drew a deeper bond between the two of us because we had that in common. Catholicism was in his heart, and so it was in mine. And in the days to come, we would be able to share in that special bond of praying for each other and encouraging each other.

My mother would continue to go her way and go to synagogue as a Jewish woman. But she, too, loved God and I often would hear her praying in Hebrew. She had her Jewish Bible, which was called a Haggadah. They both loved God, but in different ways. They just were very divided on this, and it made it difficult for us. It was hard because I had to deal with my mother always thinking that I was siding with my father, but eventually she understood that it wasn't a reflection on her, that it was just who I was.

Alan and I remained close during this time, and we supported each other. We were pretty good about helping our mother and especially helping out with our younger brother Lance. When my mother started working, I would come home after school sometimes with friends to help in the house by making dinner. It wasn't a bad thing, and although I didn't see it that way at the time, I was learning to be a homemaker at a young age. This was reinforced by my grandmothers; they were behind the scenes encouraging me to help my mother and be strong. No one realized the learning disabilities and limitations I had, but it did teach me to be strong and think of my mother, in spite of the fact that it was so hard. There was homework to be done and chores to do, so life kept me busy. There was little time to wallow in my limitations. Learning to be a homemaker was a destiny I did long for, so I didn't mind.

Alan worked as a bus boy after school and would ponder his future and how to go about it. Religion was not something he was thinking about. He dreamed of what was to come in a different way. While I did dream of the day I could have my own family, be married and have children, Alan had bigger dreams, seeing the world through the Navy. We were both learning what hard work was but still having fun outings with friends and family. It was a good thing. This season was a growing time for me that caused me to be less self-focused and more mature, thinking more of my family and less of my own needs. This was real life and it would prepare me for the huge challenges I would face when one day I would be out on my own. I had God to lean on, and it brought me great comfort. I was more drawn to Him than ever believing for that happy family life I would one day experience again. I needed strength, provision, and wisdom, and I knew where to look. I can't emphasize enough how important it was to me to have people around me. While it would be a tough road ahead, I trusted God was providing everything I needed, not necessarily what I wanted but certainly what I need.

I had another special mentor during this time. She came alongside me and helped me to grow. I remember fondly my friend Sharon Sandman's mother. Sharon was someone who was very close to me during my high school years.

Me and my friend Sharon when we were in high school.

While I had many friends, she was another one of the ones who stuck. by me and loved me deeply. She and my friend Linda were also like sisters to me. My friend Mary had moved away to Connecticut, several other friends were off doing other things, and we went our separate ways. I could see where Sharon got her kindness from. It was from her mother!

Gertrude Sandman was amazing. She recognized early on that I needed another mother role model while my mom had to work to make ends meet. Gert (as we called her) was a heavy-set woman with blond frosted hair and glasses. She always dressed well, always smiled, had so much integrity, and loved people. She was from Canada and her family was Jewish. She was the most generous person I knew. She treated me as her own. During my high school years, I spent a lot of time with Gert. While she told me she didn't want to take the place of my mother, she wanted to be there for me. She was a very giving woman. As I remember Gert, she always had kind things to say, she worked in a hardware store, and took her daughter Sharon with her and they worked together. She loved her children, Sharon and her brother, and it showed.

Me, Sharon, her mother Gert and my son Paul enjoying a visit together. She loved Paul as her own.

But it was some evenings during the week and sometimes on the weekends that I got really close to her. Sometimes Sharon, Linda, and I would go out on the weekends together; as by this time, we had our licenses. We would take turns driving each other around town, we adored our time together. We would frequent parties, sometimes dances, sometimes concerts, there was plenty going on. But it was after we were out for the evening that I would come back to Sharon's house and sit and talk with her mother. I loved our talks, I learned so much from her. I felt supported by her. She was a true friend, that took me under her wing.

On a Saturday evening, for example, I would come to her house from being out with Sharon and our friends, and she would just be coming in from being out to dinner with her friends and her husband Kenny. She would say to me, "Come and sit and talk for a while, I want to hear how you're doing. How is your mother?" She always asked about my mother and my younger brother Lance. She loved my bubbly personality and our time together was precious. Sometimes we would sit until the wee hours of the morning talking, and she encouraged me with the things that I struggled with and we would laugh at the funny things I was experiencing.

And it was interesting, my friend Sharon, being as sensitive as she was, understood that I needed that time with her mother and she would go in another room and just let us talk together, but that's how Sharon was, very others-oriented. Other times Sharon would be in on the conversation. But they both would encourage me that my mother was having a hard time and to be as supportive as I could be. And like my friend Beverly's parents, and my friend Karen's mother, Carol, said they would be there for me when I needed it. And they were for a while, but I got closest to Gert and our relationship would last a long, long time. While the others were still there, it was different with Gert; we had a special bond. My grandmothers were still available too, along with several of my aunts, but they were a distance away. My grandparents were still on the northside of Boston, while I was now on the south shore. Gert lived near me at the time.

Either way, I was never alone, and it brought me great comfort. What all this provision was teaching me was not only that I was not alone, but I also needed to extend the same compassion and time to others along the way. My destiny was being formed by God himself and I could feel it. All this love and all these examples would train me for my future with others in need.

Gert would remain a mentor for me for many years to come. While we were getting close, my mother was understandably getting a little jealous, so on the weekends, I would spread my time and go out with her as well. I felt honored that people wanted to be with me. "You only have one mother," Gert would remind me, "and she loves you dearly." I knew she was right.

I still wanted to attend the youth group on Wednesday night with Karen and her mother Carol, and I did when I could. It was amazing I had any time to myself. During the course of my high school years, I also wanted to be dating and I did, and I had a lot of fun. And then there was my father, who wanted to spend time with us on the weekends. But due to the fact I was in such demand, my time with him was limited to going to church with him sometimes on Sundays, visiting his home with my brothers, and eating out, of course. Who could forget eating out? I was feeling torn at times, but it was a good problem to have. My younger brother Lance spent time at my fathers on the weekends and I did on occasion, too. I always kept my eye on Lance because he was so much younger, and I felt he was vulnerable. The time I was spending with him was precious. My father on the other hand, was like a chameleon, he went from Catholicism in his growing up years, to trying to appease my mother by following some Jewish customs while they were together, right into the Pentecostal faith with the Assemblies of God. I think this was a bit confusing to Lance when he was with him, but he still seemed to enjoy his time with his dad.

Back then I didn't understand The Assemblies of God denomination, and what it was all about. It seemed a little extreme to me at the time. But as an adult with my husband, we were drawn to it and remain there till this day. The Assemblies of God to me has a good balance—a balance of believing God for miracles while acknowledging that there is suffering with real challenges in life but knowing that God is there in the midst to help us. In most of the churches I have attended with the Assemblies of God, it seemed they always supported each other, and I liked that. They are people-oriented! I found that not all churches were like that, in fact I found some churches over the years were quite judgmental and self-focused, not really reaching out to people the way I was taught. I have not found that to be the case with this denomination. They provide a lot of good teaching on how to reach out to others and help the poor, which is very important to me, and learn to hear from God through prayer. Because that was the family that I came from. As my grandmothers and my mother helped others in need, so did my church family. And since

266

Mother Teresa was one of my role models, I always looked for that in any church that I attended.

High School and Church

While still in high school, like my friend Mary, I continued to be drawn to the church for comfort and out of curiosity. I felt at home there. I began to explore becoming a nun. Gert, being Jewish, didn't quite understand what in the world I was doing but supported me anyway. My mother, coming from a Russian Jewish background, saw this as a sort of siding with my father and rejected it. No, it didn't go over well with her, and as I look back now, I can understand why. She didn't want to lose me. She didn't understand why my father went to church, because of his actions and the way he left us; she saw him as a hypocrite and felt he had abandoned us. She didn't understand everything he was going through, and she was irate with him.

She eventually forbade me to go to church with my friends, Karen and Carol and others much of the time. Instead, she insisted I go to synagogue with my Jewish friends, like my friends Debbie, Beverly, Diane, Linda, and Sharon. Which was fine because I enjoyed them as well, but church and the Italian culture was already engrained in me, like my father's mother., It was what was in my heart, and I had to follow that voice calling me to a destiny I would later enjoy. I hated the thought that I was hurting my mother, but felt I wasn't rejecting her, and I wished she could have seen it that way. I had hoped she could understand that I loved my father, too, that I also had a relationship with him. My mother and I loved each other and over time came to terms with our differences, but it would take time and grace for each other, with decades of patience and hard work for both of us.

While religion was causing a gap between us, we were still able to spend some precious time as mother and daughter. And because she loved her children so much, she always remained with me and never abandoned me. She was one of the most loyal, loving mothers I knew. And her children and her family were everything to her. But there was one thing she said to me that convinced me not to join the convent. As I did ponder this, she said, "Look, if you don't want to practice Judaism, that's one thing, but if you become a nun and join a convent, you will miss out on having a family and children, and I think you'll regret it. You can still worship God as a married woman, you don't have to give up on being married to serve God. While I don't understand why you're drawn to this way of worshiping, I hope that one day you'll come around to my way of thinking."

And as she said this to me, it made sense, as I did long for marriage and family. So, I did listen to her advice. I also was way too interested in dating to give that up, so it didn't take much convincing. My mother knew how to reach me. She knew just which button to push. But per her advice and the lessons learned in church, from mentors, etc. I did pursue marriage and family and felt I had made right choices. The choices I made felt right but didn't always lead to easy situations. I did my best to listen to sound advice while growing up, and because I listened, I believe I avoided a lot of obstacles that would have led to unnecessary consequences. I was teachable, and it led me in a healthy direction. But not without its challenges.

I mentioned before about how my mother was a little jealous when I would spend time with my friends' mothers, so I began to take a little more time for her. As tired as she was, she loved to spend time going out to eat with me, going to visit my Bobe, taking me shopping, and to special mother and daughter events at the Temple with my friend Debbie and her mother.

One example was each year she would help to raise money with a Bazaar at the Temple. This was an event where people would set up booths at the local high school gymnasium and sell a craft or baked goods. The purpose was to sell whatever you could to raise money for the Temple and for those in need. In my mother's case, she made homemade baked goods: brownies, chocolate chip cookies and homemade fudge, as I remember. She was very good with homemade fudge. Her specialty was penuche and chocolate marshmallow. It was so good, incredible fudge, and as good a cook as I am, I'm not sure I could ever make it the same way she did. My brothers can attest to how incredible it was. All Sugar and so sweet!

So, we set out to put up a booth where the Bazaar was taking place. My Russian grandmother (Bobe), was unable to go due to her age and various health issues. She had a rheumatoid arthritis issue, along with Meniere's disease, an inner ear disease, causing dizziness and various other age-related health issues. Being the caring mother, she was, Bobe helped behind-the-scenes by baking things for my mother to sell. Mom picked up the baked goods from my grandmother, an assortment of jelly rolls and butter cookies with fruit spread in the middle and her famous Russian sponge cake, which was amazing. Her Russian cooking was the best, too. She made Borscht, a beet soup, to die for.

The fundraiser Bazaar took place on a Saturday in the fall. We were excited as we headed for the high school to set up my mother's booth with the baked goods. These events were fun, and it was another chance to socialize and have a good time.

As we pulled up to the high school, my mother said, "Iris, wait in the car for a minute while I check my place for the booth." So, with the table and baked goods in the back seat of the car, I sat and waited for her. I could only see a glimpse of her but could tell she found her spot to set up. I remember it was a cold fall, rainy, very damp day. No wonder my grandmother with her arthritis couldn't go. That's the worst kind of weather for arthritic conditions, causing terrible inflammation with debilitating pain. I even thought it was cold and raw outside the school. Shortly, my mother came back to the car and told me she found the spot where she was supposed to be. So, we gathered up everything, our folding chairs and card table, along with the baked goods and headed into the gym.

As we began to set up, a woman came over to my mother and said, "That's my spot, you'll have to go somewhere else."

My mother said, "Oh, no, I reserved this spot a month ago and there are no other spots to go to, so you'll have to go somewhere else yourself, don't start with me." *Oh-oh, a fight is coming*, I thought. Yikes! What was going to happen next? Well, I was about to find out. At that point, the woman refused to move.

Oh, no, lady, I said to myself, *you don't know my mother, quit while you're ahead*. Fortunately, she couldn't hear my thoughts. My mother handed me some change. "Iris, go get yourself a hot dog and a Coke, give me about 15 minutes and then come back."

I was puzzled. "Why?"

"Never mind, just do what I tell you." She spoke with a firm tone.

"Okay, but I wonder what you're up to." I looked at her with a smirk on my face and then concern. I knew darn well what she was up to, keeping in mind my mother was from Russian background and wasn't easily walked on. So, I did as she said, and I went away for about 15 minutes, thinking to myself, *Gosh, I hope we don't end up getting thrown out, how embarrassing would that be?*

As I walked away, I overheard the woman saying there were no other spots, except outside in the rain and that my mother would have to be the one to go out there. I thought again, *this woman has no idea what she's up against.* But I hoped for the best and that none of my friends I ran into noticed what was going on. I wondered aloud, "Oh, God, should I go back?" Well, 15 minutes had passed, I had my hot dog and my Coke, saw some friends, and I figured by now I could go back and see what my mother was up to. I felt it was safe because I didn't see any police. Lo and behold, when I arrived back at my mother's spot in the gym, there she was, all set up, looking all happy and even whistling while she continued to carefully place all the baked goods in separate plates. The other woman was nowhere to be seen.

Oh-oh, where was she?

"Okay, what happened to the woman?" I asked. With a smug, cocky look, Mom pointed outdoors. I glanced out to the spot where that lady had wanted my mother to be, and there she was, sitting in the rain with her arms folded, looking quite defeated and very wet. I didn't want to think of how Mom got her out there, but I don't think that woman ever messed with my mother again after that. God only knows what my mother did. I didn't dare press her for answers. But as I think back on that time when she did that, it makes me laugh, and it makes me realize just how strong my mother was. And how thankful I am we weren't arrested.

On a serious note, it was her example that taught me to be strong and survive. In life there is no other choice. My mother was not a force that could be reckoned with. While I knew her tactics were not quite "kosher," no pun intended, I was still proud of her because I knew no one would ever take advantage of her ever. She had this way of dealing with people without hurting them (physically anyway), thank God, but making her point and getting the job done. My mother, the Russian Rambo! I don't mind saying, I have a little of that in me, too, but I do it with a little more integrity and compassion than she did and thank God I have that Italian joviality to balance me out. I use the encouraging approach, and if that doesn't work, I just move on. I'm not sure physically removing someone and threatening them is the way to go. I have discovered through many other mentors that a kind word turns away wrath, and even demanding, difficult people need understanding. Still, to this day, I'm proud of my little Russian Rambo, standing just under five-feet tall. She was short in stature but tall in my eyes. People loved and respected her, a little woman with a lot of spunk.

My Mother at a 60th Birthday party we had for her.

People often said my mother was so funny, and most of the time she wasn't trying to be, but she was just a delight that way, like a little caricature. People respected her, and every now and then, felt a little threatened. But still, she had a lot of friends and loved her family. Later, as I grew older, into the '90s, people often compared her with Fran the nanny on the show *The Nanny*. A silly woman with a silly accent who took no prisoners. Because of her, we all have a wonderful sense of humor and are quite resilient. My father had a wonderful sense of humor as well, and I miss them every day. They were characters, that's for sure. Even during the divorce, I remained quite close with both of them and learned to enjoy them as individuals and so did my brothers, and life, while challenging, was still enjoyable because we chose joy and we had each other.

Chapter 13

Transition to College

My high school graduation photo.

It was my senior year in high school, and I was still struggling with learning disabilities and physical problems, but I did the best I could. Even though I was frustrated at times, I remained focused and determined to enjoy my last year. Alan and I had spent our junior and senior years in many of the same classes and enjoyed spending time with each other and the friends we had in common. Alan was easy going, and fun to be with, and we were always together. This time, we were also thinking of our adult future, and what it would mean knowing we would have to be apart. While he and I weren't twins, we were so close in age, it was very much like being twins. In fact, people in school often thought we were.

I was now thinking of college, and Alan was thinking of going into the military. While learning was a challenge, we were often told that we were smart, and that helped us to have the confidence we needed to move forward and fulfill the goals we had in mind and give it our best. *What could I even major in?* I thought! *What could I do? What do I like that I can do?* I began to explore my options and prepare for what would come next.

One of the things that was necessary for applying to college was taking the SATs, (Scholastic Achievement Tests). That was interesting to say the least! I literally could not get the correct answers on the tests. The teachers couldn't understand what had happened because my scores were so low, and it didn't fit with my test scores in my classes. They didn't know what was wrong. I think they thought I was either developmentally impaired and hid it quite well, or just wasn't trying. I think it was a little of both, can you imagine? This made me feel bad; to put it mildly, I felt like I was stupid, but I would later learn that not only was I far from stupid but quite intelligent. What they didn't know about me was that while I was in my classes, mainly math, I was cheating from other students to get by. I couldn't understand why it was so hard for me and I didn't want to tell anyone. But it sure showed on my SAT scores. I was nervous and afraid of my mother's reaction—no kidding, look what she did with the lady at the bazaar, crap, was I next? *No, that can't be,* I thought.

A woman from my school phoned my mother at her workplace about this and said, "Mrs. Fisher, we need to discuss your daughter Iris's test scores from her SATs, do you have a moment?"

"Yes, I do," she answered, "what's this about?"

My mother at work in her job with the state. Circa 1976.

"Well, her scores were alarmingly low. Can you help us to find out why; it doesn't fit with her schoolwork test scores."

"You're kidding," she said. "I don't understand, but I'll get to the bottom of this. She may not have been trying, how low were they?"

"Quite low," the woman answered.

"That's not possible," my mother said, "she could not have been trying." She then urged the woman to let me take the test again, insisting I could do better. So, before I knew it, I was set up for a retake. What none of us realized is that during the appendix episode, I had suffered a brain injury from being septic because the peritonitis was so far reaching. It caused an injury to the left side of my brain, which affected my ability to learn and also my balance, but no one understood this back then. So, I continued to struggle, but being related to my mother, I had plenty of determination, which helped me in the long run.

My mother left work early that day and waited for me to come home from school. As I walked in the door, she was sitting at the kitchen table reading the newspaper, probably the obituaries to see who had passed away that she might know. That always lightened things up for us. Not!

She then looked up at me and said, "I guess you're wondering why I'm home early today, right?"

"Yes." I flinched inwardly. *Busted! What could she have possibly found out?* I wondered to myself. *Could it be, she knows I skipped a class with my friends Linda and Sharon? No, that's not it, she knows I went to the church youth group, no, couldn't be, she looks more compassionate than that, does she know I know Alan's been smoking pot?*

I finally caved. "Okay, what is it already? What are you looking at me like that for?"

"Sit down right here next to me, I want to tell you," she replied.

At that point, I was afraid to sit too close because sometimes when she was upset with me, I got pinched on my arm. I hated that, ouch! It was worse than getting a shot. But that was as abusive as she ever got, because this was my mother and she loved me, remember? This was her way of making a point. Needless to say, she had a conversation with me about how I needed to try harder, she couldn't believe I couldn't pass the tests.

She said to me in her Jewish/Russian twang accent," Iris, you've done it before, I've been very proud of you, you can do it again, now cut it out and buckle down; let me help you try to study ahead of time." While I didn't understand what was wrong because I thought I had tried, I did understand I had a hard time focusing; the struggle was familiar and had happened far too often. But what could I do? I didn't understand the connection between what had happened to me when I was young and the events of today. When I was later tested for the brain injury, they found I was very intelligent but impaired and had a hard time with learning. I'm not sure my mother understood the connection of the coma and illness causing a mild brain injury leading to problems learning either; maybe she did, but she never said. Probably because she wanted me to focus on what I could do and not limitations that would hinder me. In some ways, this was helpful, in others, not so much.

But she worked with me and got me a private tutor, and it took some time, but eventually I was ready. Well, at least as ready as I could be. So, I took the test again, and this time I passed, but barely. Several of my friends just assumed I wasn't trying hard enough. Oh, sure, easy for them to say. But this was 1977, and not a lot was understood about these things back then. At that time, there was not a lot of attention given to learning disabilities, especially hidden ones that would affect learning. Sometimes classes were so difficult for me, I had other students helping me to pass exams. I was so embarrassed, I would resort to cheating on tests, as I said. In my wildest dreams, I never thought I would graduate, never mind attend college, but I had other students and friends helping me get through. Again, I wasn't alone. It was hard for me to understand, I was smart but had trouble articulating and retaining information. It was frustrating to say the least.

I remember during this time, I also spent a lot of time in detention, probably because I had trouble staying on track in class, and I was much too focused on my friends and having a good time, laughing and joking, but hey, at least I was enjoying myself. I can blame the wanting to have a good time on my parents, you got to blame someone. Their fun can-do spirit rubbed off on me and I focused on that. I didn't mind detention because my closest fun friends were there right alongside of me. My friends, Karen Gaeta and Sue Flaherty, two friends that had a lackadaisical fun-loving spirit as well, resorted to fun rather than schoolwork right along with me. They could be a little goof-off as I was, but at the same time they both were very compassionate and nice to be around. I really enjoyed them. They had their own challenges, but they were a blast. We laughed together a lot, maybe too much. But I will always remember my time with these two girls. It was supposed to be a punishment, but they made it fun.

Karen Gaeta Pace   *Sue Flaherty Sweeney*

Today I still hear from both of them, and we still reminisce and laugh together about our times in detention. They remember me, as fun loving, and saw me as jovial and easy going. But I saw myself in a differently. I often felt misunderstood and awkward, and I lacked self-esteem. I could remember feeling like I couldn't do anything right, and it was surprising to me that others didn't see me that way. During all of this, I still managed to maintain some solid relationships that would last me a lifetime, while continuing to develop new ones. Perhaps it was because I was others-oriented and thought more about my friends and family than myself. This attitude was instrumental in staying positive. I have discovered that being others-oriented is always the key to finding oneself and true happiness. Because if we become too inward, it can lead to feelings of depression, inadequacy, and can leave us stuck and not able to experience life to its fullest. Self-absorption, I feel while fulfilling momentarily, can lead to a life of loneliness and separatism, and it's hard to maintain relationships long term that way. No one likes self-centeredness. I have found by reaching out to others, it took my mind off myself. It caused me to be less depressed and not easily discouraged. By helping others, making someone else feel better gave me purpose, I for them, it gave them the support they needed and another friend, so they weren't alone. And as I reached out, I wasn't alone either.

I have a fun memory from my senior year, a day I will always remember.

We had two feet of snow that day, and school was cancelled, my favorite of days. We would experience snow days like this often, too often sometimes. On that day, Alan, Lance, and I were stuck at home without a lot to do. Back then we didn't have computers to occupy our time, we had each other, and it was amazing. I began to get creative to pass the time. I may have been impaired, but I sure had an imagination. And heaven forbid Alan and I should do homework! It was not in the forefront of our minds. Because we had a sense of humor, and an interesting one, we decided to take a boring day and make it funny.

Not too long before this incident, my mother had adopted a dog named Fritz, a miniature Doberman pinscher. He was so cute, and we loved him. But we thought it be fun to pretend we were in a bar mitzvah with him as the "barmitvee." We set up a stage and used Alan's camera to photograph all this. We dressed the little dog up in what we could be creative enough to make for a bar mitzvah outfit, using Alan's old underwear. The underwear with the top band was used as a shawl. We cut it off to make it look like it was a talus, which was kind of like a scarf that went around the dog's neck. We took another portion of the underwear to make a little round yarmulke for the dog's head. It looked like a little beany on top of his head, and we used adhesive tape, as I remember, to make it stay on.

How this dog cooperated with us, I'll never understand, but he was so good about it. Of course, I'm sure he was wondering when my mother would be home to rescue him. And I think he took his rebellion out on us at times by marking his territory around the bottom of my mother's couch to be sure we knew he could be spiteful. While this bothered my mother, she couldn't punish him because she really loved him, and he was adorable, but he was spiteful at times, especially if we left him alone.

Fritz the Dog's bar mitzvah, he was so cute, and we had so much fun doing it.

If we went out, we would come home to know his territory and what he thought of us, maybe the bar mitzvah was a little revenge on our part, but it was so funny. You know, because he was bad, make him recite the Torah dressed in underwear, that will fix him.

We set the stage with a mini Torah and our mother's statute of Moses. And we set the stage to make it look like the dog was reading from the Torah. We have really interesting photos to show this. So, we replicated a bar mitzvah for the dog. Sound crazy? Okay, it was. We were really enjoying this, and we were laughing so hard and the dog was so cute, we couldn't contain ourselves. I remember Alan and I in tears. I have no idea what the dog thought, except probably, "Where the hell is my mother?" But we kept petting him and laughing.

Lance, in the background, just went along with it, just kind of tolerating us, not quite understanding what we were doing and why. I think he thought we were a little out there, but he went along with it just the same. Being much younger than us, he often looked up to us, which was scary, and that day I think he had some questions; he was a smart little guy. But while my mother worked, we took care of him, another scary thought. I'm not sure our silliness was always a good role model for behavior for him, but we did Okay. While he wasn't quite understanding what we were doing that day, he got the message that we were having fun, and that joviality was rubbing off on him, probably the craziness as well. While home and supposedly doing chores and homework during the storm, my mother called us from work to check on things, wondering what we were up to. I think she was concerned; I wonder why? Hey, we were her kids, what did she expect?

On one of her phone calls with us, we were laughing so hard, she said to us, "What are you kids up to? Are you doing your homework? And where's Lance and how is he doing?"

And we said something like this, "We are doing okay, we are just having a good time."

"What else is new?" She kept at us. "What's so funny, and why are you laughing so hard? Are you taking care of Lance? Let me talk to him. While I'm at work, I'm trusting you to take care of him, I need this like a hole in my head. You kids are fooling around too much."

I said, "We are taking care of him. Alan and I just couldn't resist having fun. Lance is okay, and we are doing some homework." Sure, we were. But it was harmless fun. However, my mother did wonder if Alan was smoking pot, as he was inclined to do on occasion, and she wasn't happy we were fooling around so much. I didn't need pot to make me laugh, it was something I did naturally. Maybe the brain injury was a natural high; they say it can be!

I have to tell you, Alan and I sure knew how entertain ourselves, we had good imaginations, and it was a simplistic fun. Laughter was our medicine and we knew how to use it.

But after all was said and done, we made dinner and tried to have things in order for when Mom came home. We still had that sense of responsibility that she instilled in us; we just often laughed our way through it. We were learning the balance between entertainment and being responsible. And when all was said and done, I think our mother was pleased with the way we handled things. While Alan and I were quite silly, we also knew the importance of lightening her load, as she was under quite a bit of stress trying to work and support us. Alan was my best friend then, and still is today. Times were hard, but because we had each other and the laughter to get us through, things were easier for us. While I was in high school, I can remember so many times when my friends, my brother Alan, and my mother were such an intricate part of getting through rough moments, having each other to lean on and laugh with made some very dark days extremely tolerable. As we struggled at times to view the glass as half full, my mother would remind us to stay focused. She had her hands full but still found time for her children.

One snowy afternoon turned into a memorable moment. My brother Alan and I, with Lance in the background, found joy and solace and something to occupy ourselves in a day we will never forget. We were not alone!

Moving on to Graduation

In the spring of that year, we were preparing for graduation, and I was excited about going off on my own, as most teens are. Our senior prom was coming up, and I was preparing and excited for it. All my friends and I were thinking about who we would go with. At the time, I wasn't dating anyone seriously, so I asked this guy I worked with to go with me and he surprisingly said yes. I remember the excitement I felt and the anticipation. That year, my mother got me a job at Marshall's clothing store in Canton, the town next to Sharon. I worked folding clothes or in the fitting room checking people in; I couldn't work the registers due to my trouble with numbers. I was earning money, and it felt good. I met this guy named Danny there, and we became good friends, so he accompanied me to the prom. It was a beautiful evening, and he was a gentleman. There was dinner and dancing, and I felt quite grown up.

My Senior Prom photo. Circa May 1977.

At the end of the evening, he brought me home, gave me a kiss on the cheek, and said, "This was fun, I'm glad we could go together. Thanks for such a nice time."

I answered, "Thank you, I guess I'll see you in Marshall's, ha."

"Yes, for sure," he said, and that ended a very nice memory, for it was clear to me we were just friends.

My mother was waiting for me inside the door and smiled at me. She knew I was a good kid and that I would just have a nice time, and she knew of Danny and trusted him. it comforted me to know she waited for me. While I was out making memories, if something should happen, I knew she was there. After that, there were class parties, graduation, etc. I have some great memories to lean on. Memories that I will never forget. At my graduation, my grandmother, Aunt Ruthie, my mother, and brothers, Lance and Alan, were all in attendance; there were a limited amount of tickets available, so that was who attended with me and cheered me on in graduating. My dad wasn't able to attend my graduation, he had health issues and was beginning to miss things, but not by choice. While this saddened me, I understood.

During that summer, I worked at a camp on Cape Cod as a counselor. I remember my friend Debbie did, too. That was the beginning of Debbie and I parting geographically but pursuing similar interests while being apart. We would never lose touch, and we remain close friends to this day.

As the summer ended, and after applying to colleges, I was accepted into the recreational leadership program at Greenfield Community college., Greenfield was about two hours out of Boston, and in the western part of the state. My mother thought that would be something I could excel at and enjoy and still be challenged. Debbie went on to a college in Florida to study to be a dietician. We were beginning our new lives and our future was before us, as well as for our other friends and classmates. Our destinies were beginning to unfold, and it was exciting. I wanted to live away from home but not too far, and my mother felt the same way; she wanted me fairly nearby, so she could be there if I needed her, she was that loyal, she never wanted to be apart from her children, they were everything to her.

College on the Horizon

So, in the fall of that year, I went off to college but not alone. I had applied with another good friend, Linda, and we went together. She was accepted into the early childhood program there, as she wanted to work with children. We became roommates in a boarding house near the college. Linda and I were close in high school and did a lot together, so going away together seemed so exciting, and we could look out for one another. My mother liked the idea that I was off to college with a close friend, another one she trusted; she also knew Linda's mother and her family and that brought her some peace. Linda was levelheaded and made good choices, so I felt comfortable with her. Throughout my life, I began to feel like a puppy on a leash, where someone was always with me, no wonder I never got in trouble. I would come to understand that it wasn't that I was a puppy. I had a lot of friends and bonded so well because often times I was first a friend. I liked being with Linda, and I looked out for her, too. In college, we were both social butterflies.

So, Linda and I were in college now, two hours away from the home we were used to. And boy, did we like the independence, but we kept a close eye on each other. We had a lot of fun, and I enjoyed the program I was in and did quite well. The classes were easy and enjoyable. There were a lot of outdoor activities and adventures, camping and nature hikes, etc., and we had the choice to minor in something. I chose nutrition because it was something I knew well and could grasp. I had to have tutoring in some classes because of my struggle with learning but excelled anyway, I began to feel confident in my future with this in mind.

Changes Taking Place

In the fall of 1977, the world was really changing. I was becoming an adult and looking forward to more independence and what the future might bring. While in college, however, my health was showing more signs of something being wrong. In spite of it, I attended classes, dated a few different guys, made lots of new friends, and some of these friends Linda and I shared together.

One of my fondest memories of dating my first year in college was with Jack. He was a dead ringer for Dustin Hoffman. I really liked Jack, he was a bit older and sold insurance. I loved how distinguished he looked in his overcoat when he came to pick me up. He would often take me and Linda to a college disco to spend the evening dancing. One particular evening, when Jack had to leave early from this place, known as The Pub, he asked one of his friends to take me and Linda home when we were ready. And his friend, along with another friend, spent the rest of the evening with us. And since I had never met them before and they seemed fun-loving, I decided to play a little joke on them. I did so, by pretending I was from England. Why I didn't say I was from Italy, I'll never know since I knew the language, but it was a fun time just the same.

We must have connected with them, I'm thinking around 9 o'clock or so, and stayed with them probably till about three in the morning doing various activities that most college students did. We started out by going to a party at a nearby college in Amherst, where so many of our classmates from high school went. It was a fun evening. All the while I was pretending I was from England to these two guys that were with us. I acted as if I didn't know much about the states, so they would explain things to me. Linda, after many hours of this, began to roll her eyes, but I continued and was quite convincing. As I would run into friends from high school though, I found myself speaking my Bostonian accent as usual, while trying not to let the guys that were with us hear my real accent and learn where I was really from. It helped that it was crowded and noisy in there. After a time, the two guys took us out to breakfast at an I-Hop where I continued my charade. I even had the waitress convinced I was from England. Until she asked me where in England I was from, and being only 18 and not having visited England, I didn't have a clue.

So, in an English accent, I said, "Why, London, of course," until she said she had been there and loved it and even knew streets and districts. Now I was in trouble but still managed to pull it off for the sake of these guys. I was determined to fool them. And they fell for it, hook, line, and sinker. After the restaurant, they brought me and Linda back to the boarding house, where we played cards for several more hours.

But by 3:00 a.m., I stood up, thanked them, and announced in my usual accent, "Well, I gotta go to bed." They were shocked and said I deserved an academy award for the performance. They were nice guys. They couldn't believe I wasn't from England. I was proud I pulled it off but always had every intention of letting them know who I really was. One of my many pranks I loved to play on people. Linda just kept shaking her head but laughed it off, and later when Jack got wind of it, he thought it was very funny, as he loved my sense of humor. I only saw Jack a few more times after that, because he moved out of the area due to employment. I really missed him for a while, but being young, I moved on pretty quickly.

Linda and I, along with a number of friends, remained regulars at The Pub on the weekends, and it wasn't long after that I ran into my destiny. I know, now I sound like something from the movie *Back to the Future*. But it was true, and my destiny was there waiting for me.

My Destiny Awaits

While I was at school this first year, things were quite busy for me, but I was beginning to experience some weird symptoms. I had numbness and tingling in my hands and feet, I was experiencing episodic periods of weakness and fatigue, and I'm not sure I realized it at the time, but it seemed to revolve around what I ate. I was quite thin and had always had trouble gaining weight, no matter how much I was eating. After all, eating was a big deal culturally to my family on both sides, as it was for many families back then. The weakness I was experiencing was severe at times, where I was too weak to stand and function, and it would literally send me to the floor. I let my mother know, and of course, she was quite concerned.

In one phone conversation with her, she said, "Iris, during your semester break, I want you to come home and work with me in my office. I think I can get you a job for that time as a filing clerk, and I will talk to your aunt Ann about why you're not feeling well, and we'll see if we can get you an appointment, how does that sound?"

I then answered, "Okay, semester break is still a month away, hopefully I'll feel better."

"Stay in touch with me, and please let me know how you are. I'm worried, but hopefully it's something that will pass."

I hung up then a pay phone where I called her collect as I needed to but not too often, as it was expensive. There were still no cell phones in 1977 and 1978, so that's how we kept in contact. And she wanted to speak to Aunt Ann, who if you remember, was my father's aunt and my great aunt. She was not only the matriarch of this continuing growing family, but she also worked at one of the major hospitals in Boston for one of the top neurologists. So, we all consulted her on advice when it came to medical issues.

My mother was nervous enough with a lot on her mind, with Alan being in the Navy and being out of touch until he had leave. In addition to that, my sister was now married, living about an hour and a half from her, and pregnant with her first child, and Lance, the youngest, was still at home. She was experiencing empty nest for sure but excited about my sister's baby coming, after all, this was her first grandchild. We were all very excited.

In the meantime, while still at school, I went on with my schoolwork and activities and weekend fun with friends. One particular Saturday night, Linda and I went back to The Pub to hang out. We got a ride with some other girls we roomed with at the boarding house. I remember I paid $75 a month to rent the room, and at that time, we thought that was expensive; today, I understand it can be $900-$1,000 a month just to rent a room, depending on where you live. Goodness, times have changed.

So, that evening, we got to the pub, I'm thinking maybe around 7 p.m., and had planned to stay till closing, which as I remember was around 2:00 am. Gosh, I can't relate to staying up that late at this stage in my life, no matter how much fun I think I'm having. But back then, even though I lacked stamina, I still was able to stay up with the best of them. So, as we arrived, Linda and I first looked around for people we knew, and then when we would hear a song we liked, also looked around for someone to dance with, maybe someone new.

As Linda was asked to dance, I sat at the table drinking a beer, which I rarely tolerated but forced at least one down anyway. I sat there doing my usual thing, smiling at everyone, which made it easy to make friends; my father, if you re-member, was like that. I liked most people until they proved to me otherwise, so I was excited to see what was next.

At that moment, I glanced across a very crowded, noisy room and a young man caught my eye.

Me and Cy when we were dating. Circa 1978.

He was blond, about medium height, wearing a red and black striped shirt, standing with some friends with a beer in his hand and just looking around. He looked so much like the character Almanzo, played by Dean Butler, on the then show "Little House on the Prairie." He was cute. He eventually caught a glimpse of me looking at him. And I can't tell you just what it was, but there was something about him that made me inch my way toward him. When I fi-nally reached him, I stood next to him, hoping he would say something. But he just kept glancing at me, while acting interested, but I could tell he was shy and wasn't going to speak first, so I leaned into him and said, "It's crowded in here, isn't it?" Not very subtle, I know, but I didn't know what else to say, so I just said the first thing that came to mind. Talk about a come-on. Since I was religious and thought of becoming a nun, I wasn't good at this.

He answered, "Yeah, it is."

And then I said something original, like, "Do you come here often?"

"Occasionally, with my friends I do. How about you?" He noticed I had an accent, asked where I was from, and then conversation began between the two of us. He then asked me if he could buy me a drink, like I needed another one to make me more nauseous. But I accepted and then several other people came over, and I somehow got distracted. He kept trailing behind me though, and I thought that was weird, so I lost a little interest.

I mentioned it to Linda, and she said, "If you're not interested, just move away from him, he'll get the message." But I wasn't sure if that was what it was. So, I began to play hard to get, and by the end of the evening at closing, Linda and I found ourselves without a ride home, so as I began to look around for someone familiar, I turned around, and there he was.

He said, "I've been waiting for you, do you need a ride home?"

First, I said, "No, me and my friend are Okay."

He said, "I can give you a ride."

I was skeptical at first, but because Linda was with me, I took him up on it, thinking that would be the end of it. He was a perfect gentleman, drove us home, saw us both in, and said, "I'd like to see you again. I'll be by tomorrow night, if it's Okay with you?"

I said, "Let me think about it," and since I didn't have a phone, he gave me his number and asked me to call and let him know. I said I would but never called him. So, the next evening, which was now a Sunday, as I was doing homework in my room, there was a knock at the door and one of the other girls answered it.

She came and got me. "You have a visitor, and he's kind of cute, where did you meet him?"

I shrugged and made my way to the door to see the young blond guy from The Pub, smiling at me. I was taken aback by his persistence.

He said, "You never called, so I thought I'd come to see if you were Okay."

I said, "Well, I got busy, I'm sorry." I let him in, and we talked for quite a while. After he left, wanting to call on me again, I knew there was something about him, but I was still skeptical at that point. Mainly because he was from a totally different culture than I was used to. He was from a rural area, liking country music, his mother drank beer, while mine drank tea and coffee, and I was from the Italian/Russian/Jewish city culture with European background. We were very different, but I was intrigued. I wondered, who is this guy, and what is it about him that is drawing me?

So, after that, we dated here and there until semester break when he actually drove me back to Boston and met my mother, and later, my father. My mother wasn't impressed at first because he wasn't in college pursuing a career; he seemed like he was struggling with what to do for his future employment. But as time went on, the more she saw him with me and the way he treated me, she fell in love with him as I did.

This was Cy, short for Cyrus, which by the way rhymed with Iris, and this was my destiny, as here we are today, married 38 years, and he's still as dedicated and loyal as he started out to be. Over time he made his own way to success in business with very hard work, and I couldn't be prouder of the man he's become.

I felt this was one of many of God's provisions for me, as I would face many health challenges in the days and years to come. This man, while it was tough at times and in spite of the fact that we were so different, never left me or my mother because he was, and still is, the most loyal man I ever met. Our son Paul and his wife Samantha can declare the same thing. He's our rock, easy going, but still our rock. And my mother, my father, grandparents, aunts, and whole family adored him. And they knew, as I did, he was family-oriented and would never leave me. I would never be alone. There was a time when we went to see my grandmother Bobe together, so she could meet him. And while she wanted him to be different, I'll never forget what she said to him as we were leaving her home one afternoon.

She said in her Russian broken English, "Take care of my Iris'l, she means the world to me," and he smiled and said, "I intend to."

And he did keep that promise. He wasn't always perfect but definitely loyal and loving. And since that day, and especially after the passing of my grandmother, which was very difficult, he continued to call me my Iris'l in loving memory of her and his love for me. I'm very blessed. God was showing me his love and care for me through others and that I was never intended to be alone, as I believe we all shouldn't be.

My Health Challenges

It seemed everywhere I went after that, and throughout my life, I experienced this common theme while I was disabled. I had a need, and God would provide what I needed.

My health was continuing to gradually decline, and so as I continued college for another two semesters, it became harder and harder for me to attend school. During this time, I continued to date Cy, and he was always there it seemed, no matter how difficult my health became. He had talked of marriage, so I was upfront about my health challenges. The doctors I continued to see felt that due to all the pelvic scarring from the appendicitis episode and all the tubes I had to live with to drain the poison, it was unlikely I would be able to have any children. But that didn't seem to bother Cy either. He was quite dedicated and loved me so much, it seemed no matter how difficult my health was, he was all in. And the longer I knew him, I came to the realization that he needed me, too, and I grew to really love him over time. So, we were committed, for better for worse, and we both meant it. And over time, we would come to understand what "for better, for worse," really meant.

So, when it came time to see the neurologist my aunt worked for at Massachusetts General Hospital, Cy drove me in with my mother. Over a period of weeks, the doctor ran a battery of tests, everything from MRI's of the brain and spine to blood work and spinals and many others. But when we met back with him with all the results, they were inconclusive, as they say. Which meant it could be a disease of the nervous system in the early stages. He was thinking Multiple Sclerosis, and this horrified me and my mother. Cy felt confident, for a reason I'm not sure of, that it wasn't that disease. At least he hoped not. The doctor felt that the symptoms needed to be monitored, and I would come back from time to time if my symptoms worsened. And this is where life was about to become very challenging. Because there's nothing funny about chronic illness, and a debilitating one at that, I would learn what trials were all about.

In the meantime, monitoring my health and dealing with the ups and downs of it, I went on with life as best I could and with a lot of support. Knowing I was not alone made it tolerable. And when there were times when people couldn't physically be there, I knew I had God. He became my rock, and my faith grew. I depended on Him more and more for what was wrong. Because no conclusions were drawn for quite a while after that, it became frightening.

In the midst of this, our first niece was born. Erin Nichole came into the world on January 16th, 1978. In the midst of having a hard time with my health, having a new baby for us all to focus on was just what we needed. I remember going to the hospital when she was born and how beautiful she was. No wonder she was so pretty, she looked just like my sister. This was a nice distraction from what I was dealing with. And I had the privilege of spending a lot of time with my niece as a toddler, visiting my sister's home with Cy, my mother, and other family members as we were able.

The birth of my niece was the beginning of a new generation for our family. My mother was the proud grandmother. My father, too, but he was out of the picture for a while, which saddened me because he was ill with bone cancer and hepatitis. But he came around when he was able; he still loved us; he was still there.

I was too sick to finish school and sadly had to drop out before I could graduate. Cy, being compassionate, wanted me near him, so we began to plan for a future together and talked about marriage and a wedding. With my mother's help and my friends and other family members, we began to plan. If we didn't get married, I would have had to live with my mother, and Cy and I would be two hours away from each other—he in Western, Massachusetts with me in Boston. My mother was willing to help me because she loved me, but since she was still caring for Lance while continuing to work, we all agreed it was too much on her. So, Cy suggested we live together till the wedding, so he could be with me. He felt, along with Aunt Ann, that if he was going to be my husband that it was now his responsibility. I remember her saying that very thing to me, along with how much it would be for my mother.

The idea of living together went against my Catholic faith beliefs, and even my mother was not in favor of it. Things were different back then, it was frowned upon to live together because it was not only not right in the eyes of God, but it was a sign of not taking commitment seriously. Living together gave too easy an opportunity to back out when things became tough. And since Cy and I were very committed to each other, we thought initially, in the eyes of God, we would already be married. I had a hard time with living together at first, but I really wanted it to work, and I was becoming too weak to run back and forth, so we did it. We got an apartment together out in Western and lived together for about ten months or so while the wedding plans were in place.

By now it was January of 1980, my little niece Erin was just turning two, and wedding plans were underway with thoughts that Erin would be my flower girl, although my sister wondered if she was too young to handle it. But because I thought she was so cute, I really wanted to give it a try. I had asked my sister to be the matron of honor. It was fun planning the wedding with my mother, my sister, friends, and other family members. It was in the back of peoples' minds how I would do physically as we were planning a large wedding of about 200 people. But I was determined as I have always been to have fun, even feeling like crap. Many people have said to me, "If you can have fun with limitations, what would life be like if you were totally healthy?" I probably couldn't be stopped. People still say that about me now.

I want to take a break here and look back in time for a moment and review what history was like back in 1980. Since we were beginning a new decade with much change on the horizon, and I was now 21 and growing into adulthood, I want to look back at what that was like, for me and the world, as I was looking to the future with Cy.

A New Decade

It was a new decade starting, and 1980 started off with a bang in the form of both natural and man-made disasters, including the eruption of Mount St. Helens in Washington state. And I have a personal story with Mount Saint Helens, which I will share later. 1980 also saw the assassination of former Beatle John Lennon. I was driving back to college from visiting my sister and niece on the evening of December 9th, 1980 when I heard it on the radio. He had been shot and killed the evening before. It was sad news to hear because who in our generation wasn't impacted by the Beatles and wouldn't be impacted by it. I was driving Cy's Chevy blazer home that evening while he had to work. I remember how I would have liked to call someone to talk about it, but it wasn't possible, as there were no cell phones at the time. You only had a phone in the car if you were quite wealthy or a business executive of some sort. When I called my sister to tell her I arrived home safely, it was both shocking and upsetting to both of us, but we had each other and it brough us a level of comfort to know this.

Also, that year, Ronald Reagan was elected as President. This was the beginning of his almost decade-long reign as leader of the free world. I personally liked him. He was uplifting and inspiring, something our country needed at the time and something we could use today. Our country needs encouragement and good news, probably more than any time in history than I can recall, at least in my lifetime. I pray that someday we will get a leader in that will bring back those old fireside chats that presidents of old shared with the American people. Those chats brought so much comfort to people as they watched and waited for the world to settle down with wars and rumors of wars. We all have a need to know that everything will be all right. Prayer and trusting in God is very important. I feel it brings a certain level of trust and peace in circumstances I can't control.

Back to history, in 1980, music was getting a shake-up and changing as well, with a move away from the disco and singer-songwriter sounds of the '70s. I'd had a feeling disco wouldn't be around that long. But it was nice, it was a part of our generation's music special genre that we will remember as a special time that was our time in history. New sounds began to hit the airwaves in the form of Blondie, Devo, and the Sugar Hill Gang for something new.

Millions of TV viewers wanted the answer to one question, who shot JR? from the show Dallas, which I liked and watched regularly. Television was changing. I was now watching shows like *Bosom Buddies*, still watching *Mash*, which was very popular back then, and *Three's Company*. I loved and always looked forward to the show *Soap*, which started in 1977 and aired until 1981. All sitcoms that were very entertaining. Television was hosting new crime shows, like *Hart to Hart, Remington Steele, Magnum P.I.* Cy and I were still watching Kojak reruns as they stopped airing in 1978. I was still watching the long-running daytime soap opera *General Hospital*, which I started watching in the '70s, and I have to confess, I still watch it today.

That year I turned 21 and was just beginning life as an adult. While it can be an exciting transition going from teen to adult it can also be challenging at the same time.

I mentioned that I wanted to talk about the Mt. St. Helens eruption that took place that year. Well, as we started our wedding plans, the date we picked was May 18th, 1980. Sound familiar? I had a knack for making a mark in history. And yes, that is the day it erupted.

I went along with the plans, picking colors, my dress, and bridesmaids; Cy picking groomsmen; we ordered a nice Italian meal and the cake. Well, you know. We had a band and a list of 200 from both sides. This was a fun time, even though I wasn't feeling well. Still, I was determined to enjoy the people and events around me. So, what's a little volcanic eruption in the middle of your wedding? The wedding was set for 1:00 p.m. that day, and I was a disappointed that my father couldn't be there because he had just been diagnosed with bone cancer and was too sick to attend. He was just as disappointed. So, I picked the next best favorite person in my life to give me away—my brother Alan. He was a perfect choice because he and I we were so close. Erin, my niece, was the flower girl, my sister matron of honor, and several best friends as bridesmaids.

It was now 11:30 a.m. EST, the time the volcano erupted because it erupted at 8:32 am PST and there was a three-hour difference in time zones from where we were. We were at the hall preparing for the wedding; things were going well, and everyone was there getting ready. The weather had predicted a sunny day, so that's what we were expecting. But because the volcano erupted, several hours later, we had rain. I can't explain this, but here we were, 3,000 miles from where it erupted, and it affected our weather. It was hard to understand how it could, but it did. Cy and his family arrived around noon, and before long, guests were arriving. But were they talking about the wedding? No, of course not. Everyone that was coming in was talking about, "Hey, did you hear that Mount Saint Helens erupted?" It was not only all over the news but all over my wedding.

Still, the wedding went on and we had a great time; my mother so enjoyed it, and we have photos to prove how excited she was. Mom and other family members thought it was funny and made reference to the fact that we had Cy's family and friends from country-rural Western, Massachusetts on one side, and my family from Europe to the city of Boston on the other side. On one side of the room, you had beer drinkers, chanting and singing, "In heaven, there ain't no beer, that's why we drink it here." I'm not kidding, it was a real song, and the other side tea and coffee drinkers with a little wine, singing "Volare." It was quite a contrast but worked out just fine. Our loved ones were there, and that's all that mattered.

Uncle Martin, his wife, my Auntie Elaine, and my Dad's Auntie Ann) Circa 1980.

As I look back, it reminds me so much an episode of *Everybody Loves Raymond* sitcom, when Raymond had his wedding. My mother reminded me a little of his Mother Marie. Okay, a lot! And to prove my point, Mom at that point rolled her eyes, and said "Oh, shit, what are we in for?" And do you suppose she said it under her breath? Not a chance, she said it where everyone could hear it. As unsettling as it was, we all did what we often did with my mother—we laughed it off. I think my mother-in law may have been slightly offended, but still everyone enjoyed our wedding, and it was evident in photos. We even have photos of my mother trying to catch the bouquet, and in the photos, her being single, you could see she was really going for it.

The wedding was like a scene out of something like *The Country Mouse and the City Mouse*. It was kind of funny. And of course, most thought how our names rhymed was funny, too. So, when the justice of the peace, which is who we chose to marry us, said, "Do you, Iris, take thee, Cyrus," I heard a lot of giggles in the room since they thought it was so ironic that two uncommon names with such a common last name would come together. Cy and I had a beautiful wedding that day but not without that history-making event. And we knew because of it, we were in for an interesting life together, although we weren't quite sure what a volcanic eruption on the day of our wedding meant in terms of the days, weeks, months, and years to come. But we were believing for it to be a good sign.

Chapter 14

Our Life Together Begins

Our wedding, the first dance May 18, 1980. Mr. Mrs. Cyrus Smith

So, Cy and I were now married, and we went on a nice honeymoon to Hampton Beach, New Hampshire and had a lot of fun together. I think I was a little attached to my mother though. Now being married, I had a hard time letting go of her. This was the first night of our honeymoon, and I called her to tell her we got there safely, which she was glad to hear, but she said to me, "Why are you calling me on your wedding night? You're not supposed to do that, you should be enjoying your first night together as a married couple."

"Mom, I just wanted to hear your voice and thank you, I miss you!"

"Oh, alright," she said, "but let's hang up now, you're married, we can talk when you get back, thanks for letting me know you got there ok."

I laughed. "I love you, Mom," and she replied, "I love you, too, now cut it out and hang up already." And with that, we did hang up.

We had a great honeymoon, in spite of the fact that I wasn't feeling well much of the time, which was becoming all too common. It was tough to try to do things, but we still had a good time. You find a way. I loved being with Cy, and having his support brought me a lot of joy and comfort once again.

It was interesting I never put it together back then, but as I look back at the pattern, it was always after eating I felt so sick. It took me years to equate the two as it wasn't always obvious what was causing so many symptoms. Sometimes they were very vague and sporadic. Again, symptoms of nausea, stomach pain, back pain, weakness, numbness in my feet and hands, blurred vision, headaches to name a few. I was also very thin and had trouble gaining weight. I would go from feeling like I was starving one moment and then throwing up the next. Back then little was known about celiac disease. It wasn't considered common, especially in adults. And they thought a lot of my trouble was popping up due to the appendix episode, which made sense to me. Because I didn't understand the importance of being totally gluten free over the years, I became sicker, with more autoimmune problems due to the constant gluten exposure. But what can I say, I did my best and functioned as well as I could.

Having the support I needed, when I needed it really helped. Through this journey, I was learning something about God: that he will never ask you to go through things without making provision for you. I learned we will go through things, but not without help, so we are not alone. Where God guides, he provides. And the more I share my story, the more you will see just how faithful God was to me, as he was to my mother and grandmothers before me.

Life Together in Western, Massachusetts

So, Cy and I began our life together in Western, he as an autobody man starting his own business, and me searching for what I could do. Well, I had some schooling in nutrition and fitness, but I wasn't strong enough to work full-time.

So, I prayed and asked for guidance. I started attending church, which gave me a way to make new friends and have a grounding, so I could not feel alone in a new area. And at this church, I did make some new friends, but through this experience, I had to learn that just because someone said they were a Christian, it didn't mean they were going to be exemplify this. Let's just say this first church I tried didn't always have compassion for sick people. They felt I should be healed, which left a bad taste in my mouth. It felt at times kind of like abuse. I was experiencing something new. I was two hours away from everyone and everything familiar—my mother, close friends, and the support of family members. But God was trying to strengthen me, and I knew it. This was a new kind of people I wasn't used to. He was taking me out of my comfort zone, it was hard, and I was learning people aren't perfect. I learned through this time that it was God I had to lean on, and even in those lonely times, still, I was not alone; I could feel his presence. When no one was around, I would discover it was God himself who would never leave me. The more I trusted him, the more confidence I had.

In spite of the fact that I was dealing with a lot of health issues, I began to train in sports massage with a friend. We drove back and forth to Boston each week to a tutorial program, so I could learn anatomy and physiology and then get certified. It was tough, but the class was small, and I had the extra help I needed to complete it. After finishing the program, I worked in sports massage part-time for about a year and found my stamina was low, so I couldn't continue as I would have liked. It required strength, something I had little of. So, I waited to see what was next.

By now we were a year into our marriage, and I began to feel funny. Something was different. Pregnancy hadn't occurred to me, as I was told by most doctors it would be very hard to get pregnant due to all the scaring pelvically from the appendix episode. In fact, they told me not to even bother using birth control because it would be something that would never be. And of course, that bothered me terribly as I wanted children, and so did Cy, but our attitude was if I couldn't have them naturally, we would adopt.

As I talked with my mother and Aunt Ann about it, they suggested I see a gynecologist, so I did. And he reluctantly did a pregnancy test because he felt it wasn't possible, but sure enough, to the doctor's surprise, I was pregnant. I was shocked, but so excited! Cy, my mother, Alan, Lance, my grandmothers, my father, friends, everyone was so excited for us. I can't remember being so excited. This was a miracle no less, and the doctors were amazed. I believe that God gives us the desire of our hearts, and he knew that being a mother was important to me and he came through. While I was pregnant, my younger brother Lance was attending college nearby, and I had the privilege of seeing him often and supporting him in plays he did and other activities. While he had friends there, he says, "There was nothing like having your big sister nearby to help me feel at home." And he got to watch me grow.

Lance, High school Graduation.

I recall one semester as Lance was starting school. My mother came out to the college, and I went with her to help set up his room and support him. Well, as we were making our way from the parking lot to the dorm Lance was staying in, he took my bag for me to carry it, as it was heavy and because I was pregnant. As he was carrying it and talking to my mother about his plans, he began waving his arms around, swatting a few bees and hornets, not realizing I had a half-eaten banana in the bag.

It took a while of swatting when he said, "What the heck, where are all these damn bees coming from?" And as he continued to swat, I began laughing really hard, realizing what was going on but saying nothing. What a stinker I could be.

He was getting annoyed at me laughing when my mother said, "Lance, it's coming from Iris's bag. What's in there, Iris, for God's sake, your brother could get stung to death and you think it's funny. Cut it out."

When Lance realized he was carrying a bag with half eaten fruit in it, he said, "Here, you carry the bag if you think it's so funny." So, I did, and before long, he agreed it was very funny to watch, and we went on to have a good day together. Due to my mother's example, we got past things very quickly. My mother closed out with something like, "You're unbelievable, you're like your father." And I said, "Thank you." She gave me a funny look of disapproval, since she was divorced from him. I often wondered if his sense of humor, while fun in their early years, became an annoyance to her.

In the midst of settling Lance in and keeping tabs on him, I continued at the same church for a while until the birth of my child, and I got sick of the hypocrisy.

And it was interesting because during my pregnancy, I seemed to feel better. I had never felt that good. I was glowing and almost like I had gone into a remission. I also discovered that Cy's older sister was pregnant at the same time I was. This was nice as we got to share in it together. There were several people we knew that were expecting at the same time, so we joined a pregnancy group, which made it fun for us as couples. In the meantime, I wanted to find a nice church to attend to raise my child in. Eventually, I did find one that was grounded with nice people. Because the church I had attended previously was more cult-like, I knew what to look out for in a church.

In this new church, I gained a number of close friendships, one being my friend Chris Szulborski, whom I met shortly after the birth of my son. The other was Rita Deyo. Both were loyal, loving friends who were there if I needed them. I learned a lot through them, especially about prayer. Their example of kindness spoke volumes to me. They loved me and helped me when I was sick and had trouble. Much like Karen, Beverly, Andrea, Debbie, Sharon, and Gert and Angela in my early years. God kept providing what and who I needed when I needed them. These were examples of true friends! But again, I had to be there for them too. It seldom works one way. I'm a firm believer it should be about both people in any relationship. That's what makes relationships successful. This is true in Marriage, friendships and family.

On occasion, while I was living out there, Beverly would come out to visit or Debbie and Karen, or I would meet them in Boston. I kept those close relationships. Angela was someone I had prayed I would someday see again and still believed I would. It would be by faith that I would see her again and in God's timing. I'm not sure how I knew that, but I did. Andrea was someone I saw from time to time as I would visit Boston.

During the time I was pregnant, my good friend Debbie was also pregnant, and we had a ball with our mothers sharing in that season of life together. Debbie would remain a constant in my life, as we went through seasons together like sisters would.

Paul's Birth

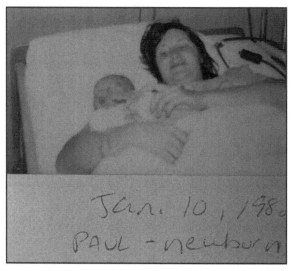

Jan. 10, 198[...]
PAUL - newborn

Paul Raymond Smith, Came into the world on January 10, 1982.
The greatest day in History

On January 10th, 1982, my pride and joy came into this world, a baby boy we named Paul Raymond Smith. Paul, after Cy's dad, and Raymond, for Cy's middle name. He was adorable, and I couldn't get enough of him. I had him delivered by C-section as I had a hard time delivering on my own. Big surprise there! And what a joyous time though. Everyone came to see him—my family, my in-laws, my friend Sharon and her mother Gert, and several friends from Boston. I had a lot of visitors.

But shortly after the birth, I began to have problems. It started with the peritonitis that had been lying dormant in my system since the episode at age eight. Due to being opened up again with the C-section, it seemed to spread again. This was a concern, I was put on heavy IV antibiotics, and I had to stay in the hospital with baby Paul for two weeks. This until I was strong enough and out of danger. Paul would remain in the nursery, and because he was an older baby and so adorable, he caught a lot of attention. I was constantly hearing comments like, "What a beautiful baby, he looks like a Gerber baby on the baby food jars." Boy, I liked hearing that. During my stay in the hospital, as I was watching the news one evening, on January 13th, just three days after his birth, the news flashed on the television screen about a terrible plane crash.

Washington Post article about the plane crash on the Potomac. January 1982.

The report said, "Air flight 90, a domestic passenger flight, a Boeing 737 has just crashed into the 14th street bridge over the Potomac River, just two miles from the White House. It crashed shortly after taking off due to icing. There were 78 fatalities with nine injuries. The aircraft struck the 14th Street Bridge, which carries Interstate 395 in Washington DC and Arlington County, Virginia. It struck seven occupied vehicles on the bridge and destroyed 97 feet of guardrail before it plunged through the ice into the Potomac River."

This was unsettling to see, I remember, as I watched the news, thinking how cold the people who were being rescued out of the icy waters must have been. I remember saying a prayer for them.. It had been snowing that day and I read that the snow ended around 3 p.m. Air Florida flight 90 was the first flight to be cleared for takeoff at the national airport. The decision to fly was left to the pilot, who chose to take off, even though a considerable amount of time had elapsed since the planes last de-icing. At 3:45 pm EST, the Boeing 737 jet taxied the airport's longest runway, which was 7,000 feet. As the plane headed down the runway for takeoff, it struggled to gain proper speed and altitude for safe takeoff. To complicate matters, planes take off to the north, which requires a hard-left turn over the 14th Street Bridge to follow the course of the Potomac River. The jet flew about one mile before it stalled. At 4:01 p.m. it slammed into the top of the 14th Street Bridge, crushing and scattering several vehicles. The 737-jet plunged over the bridge and into the ice-covered Potomac River. The jet broke into multiple pieces as it shattered into the ice and quickly disappeared into the icy water. About a dozen surviving passages bobbed helplessly in the frigid water. Sounds like something out of the Titanic, doesn't it? One passenger, a man about 50 years old, was in the water passing the helicopter's lifeline several times to others, saving their lives. When the helicopter went back to get him, he had already gone under. How sad and heroic, I thought as I watched, holding my newborn son. Four commuters on the 14th Street Bridge were also killed. The total death toll was 78. Only five of the 79 on board flight 90 survived the ordeal. It was ice on the wings of the Air Florida jet that was blamed as a cause of the crash.

As I held my son watching this news cast, I did not know that someday he would grow up to be an aerospace engineer working for Boeing and designing planes. Boeing was also where he would meet his future wife, who also worked there as an analysis engineer.

How ironic as I held him that day, hearing this news cast, that his future would parallel with this report and that he would be someday working to prevent catastrophes like this.

When the infections were under control, I could go home. My mother agreed to take two weeks off work to help us acclimate to new life with a baby. After all, this was her second grandchild, and she was so happy to be with us and help. I didn't have to twist her arm. I don't think she minded taking the time off work either. My mother was amazing, she did whatever needed to be done, rarely thinking of herself, and what a comfort it was to have her there while I recovered. I think this is where she and Cy bonded for the first time, as she spent so much time with him.

Samantha and Paul on their honeymoon in Paris. August 2018.

Paul age 3, one of my favorite photos of our son. Circa 1985.

We were renting a mobile home in Western, as we applied for new home ownership. While exciting changes were taking place, I wasn't well. The infections I was dealing with were relentless, and it would take a long time to get them under control. My mother understood this and was very concerned, and she didn't say anything, but I knew it was becoming a constant reminder to her about what had happened to me at such a young age. I didn't know at the time, but she blamed herself for waiting so long to take me to the hospital. I could see it in her eyes, and it saddened me because I knew she had done the best she could.

She spent two weeks with us. While I was bedridden much of the time, I was able to get up for short periods to hold my son and love on him. I would sit with Cy, Paul, and my mother and just have some nice family bonding time. Cy and my mother limited other visitors because I was so sick. My mother was getting exhausted, and there was one night in particular I heard her on the couch, feeding Paul and cooing at him. She adored her grandson. It was a very cold January winter night, and I could see frost on the window beside my bed. I remember being concerned if Paul was Okay! Was my new little guy was warm enough? But he was. Cy and my mother saw to it. While my mother cooed at her grandson and fed him, the long hours were taking their toll on her, and this was the result. It went quickly from quiet, contented bottle feeding to the baby crying suddenly like something was wrong. It was the middle of the night, I was in bed with Cy, who was trying to get some rest, as he too was exhausted.

I heard the baby cry, Cy jumped up, and I yelled from the bedroom, "Mom, what's wrong? What happened? Is the baby alright?" Cy dashed to see what was wrong. I heard talking, and I could tell my mother had handed the baby to Cy to take a break.

Then I heard them whispering a little, not to alarm me, and before I knew it, my mother yelled back, "Everything is fine, go back to sleep." I was concerned and needed to see what was up, so I crawled out of bed as best I could and came into the living room to see my mother in her nightgown, getting ready to go to sleep on the couch while Cy was now feeding the baby.

I said, "Okay what really happened?"

Cy looked up and smiled at me. "Well, your mother fell asleep while feeding Paul and accidently dropped the bottle on his head. He's fine, no harm done, I think he was just startled."

And my mother, looking a little embarrassed, giggled. "What can I say, I'm exhausted, the baby's fine. I'm so sorry though."

I then said, "As long as he's all right. Thanks, Mom, I'm so sorry you're so tired."

She simply shook her head. "He's worth it, and between the two of us, we can handle it."

And with that, we both went to bed, and just as Cy got the baby down, we suddenly felt a rumble. The whole mobile home shook, I mean really shook, for about a minute. At first, we thought the heater was acting up. But then things began to fall, and it became clear it wasn't the heater. At that moment, Cy grabbed Paul and held him. He then said it felt like an earthquake. My mother jumped up to turn on the television to see if there was any news, and sure enough an earthquake had hit in our area. It was a magnitude of 5.9 centered in New Brunswick, Maine. And we sure felt it. Everything was alright though, and Paul was fine, we all survived the night, but the events are ones I'll never forget.

Two days later, I began to feel stronger, and it was time for my mother to leave. I hated to see her go, and she hated to leave me.

As she prepared to leave, I looked into her eyes and said, "Mom, your eyes are all red, you look exhausted, are you going to be Okay to drive home?" I was very concerned.

She said, "Are you kidding, this is like a full-time job, I can't wait to go back to work, so I can relax. I can't remember being this tired, how the hell did I do this when you kids were little? Come to think of it, I'm not sure how I did it. I can't remember anything sometimes. Shit, and I have to drive two hours." My mother could be so blunt at times. But the way she spoke in her Yiddish/ Russian Bostonian twang made me laugh as it often did. "What's so funny, what are you laughing at? I can stop at the halfway mark at your sisters on the way home."

I said, "I'm not laughing at you, Mom, I'm laughing at the hilarious way you said it."

She answered with, "Oh, Okay, now cut it out." My sister had a little one, too, and I knew her stop there wasn't going to be relaxing either. But she did it, and she called me to tell me she was fine. I always thought my mother was invincible back then. I'm not sure she would have agreed, but she was an amazingly strong woman. I'll always admire her for that. So, time went on, Paul grew, and we had many, many wonderful family visits to look forward to. He was fast becoming the apple of many people's eyes, my mother was one, my mother-in-law, and later Gert Sandman would "adopt" him as her own first grandchild.

About six months after his birth, we were able to buy a new home and we were getting established. But unfortunately, my health issues were just beginning again, as the peritonitis was relentless, and often returned with a vengeance.

I started to attend mother and child groups with a few close friends, and church was something I was trying to find my way in, although it was difficult at times, being in a new area and all.

I had to see the doctors often as they were monitoring the abscesses I was battling in my pelvic area. But when Paul was two, I was strong enough to go back to work part-time in social work with the Association for Retarded Citizens. I planned activities for them and could take them on field trips with volunteers, assisting and encouraging them in their lives.

Paul as a toddler.

I loved that job. It gave me an awesome opportunity to serve others and make a difference, and the co-workers I had, as you can imagine, were very compassionate people. It was a perfect place for me to work with the disabilities I was dealing with. And I believe God knew this was the perfect setting for me.

One of my many volunteers in that position was a personal friend, Rita Deyo. She offered to babysit for Paul while I worked, and it was good. I trusted her and didn't want to leave Paul with just anyone. And while things can happen, I trusted her judgment and care for him. I had met Rita at church a few months before. She became a very close friend, and because I was so far away from home, she lovingly took care of Paul whenever I needed her to. She babysat for others in addition to having her own children, so she was a good choice. She was a bit strict, which I thought was good, as I felt children needed discipline, and I was in agreement with her. Rita, was also a true friend, offering help when needed. She also had a good listening ear, offering encouragement while I was trying to work and maintain my health. She became like a sister to me, we shared everything and prayed together often. She was another one of God's provisions, so I would have the love and support I needed to get through those very hard places I would find myself as my health became more challenging. We laughed, we cried together, etc., everything real friends do.

And then Chris Szulborski became very instrumental in my life. She, too, was very faithful and loyal in helping me find my way both physically and spiritually. She was always there for me, and I for her. Chris and I shared so much. She had a son, Po, and he had a lot of health issues similar to mine that as we look back, we felt it could have been celiac disease. He had numerous food sensitivities and suffered from severe eczema over most of his body. I loved Po, and he and I shared a lot about how to find our way around all of the eating challenges. At the time, I had no idea why we were both like that, and neither did Chris. Because of Chris and Rita, Po and I were both never alone. We didn't have to go through this valley of physical pain with numerous symptoms by ourselves. We had each other and others to help soften the suffering. Unfortunately, Po passed away from the health issues he suffered. It was a sad time for all of us. He had been on a snowmobile outing with a friend and had an accident where he crashed. The crash shattered his spine that was already fragile and weakened from malabsorption. He was in the hospital recovering when suddenly he died of what they said was a stomach aneurism. The stomach aneurism we thought, could have been related to undiagnosed Celiac Disease.

So much of the disease was not recognized at the time, and yet it is so damaging if not being treated, as you can see in his story, and you will continue to see in mine.

I ended up hospitalized on numerous occasions for the stomach and abdominal abscesses that finally resulted in a hysterectomy at age 27 in 1986. After being hospitalized so many times to save my tubes and ovaries, the infections and endometriosis were so severe, there was no choice but to remove everything little by little, one surgery at a time to save my life as the doctors put it. When they went to do the final hysterectomy, they first went in with a laparoscope to explore the pelvis and be sure this needed to be done. When the doctor went in, he said things were such a mess from the appendix episode that it looked like I had laid on a hand grenade.

"Things were a mess," as he put it. And he felt terrible because I was so young. He was surprised I was able to get pregnant at all. So, the hysterectomy was inevitable. It was such an emotional time for both me and Cy and other family members. Our son Paul was too young to understand.

But the night before I went into the hospital, I had a nightmare about a daughter I would never have. I walked in my sleep that night, and while still asleep, I saw a little girl sitting on my couch, probably around seven or eight, laughing at me, saying, "You'll never have me." Talk about a nightmare from the devil himself. I awoke and was shaking and started to cry, realizing the finality of it all, this was it, I'd never have any more children. Cy, realizing what was going on, came out to comfort me, and prayed with me. I believe I had had that nightmare because I had had two other miscarriages. One we knew was a girl, and I wanted a daughter so much, it was no wonder I had such an extreme nightmare. This was a loss and grieving I had to experience, and I did it by the grace of God and others supporting me and praying. During this time, I was gaining wisdom and a strength unknown to us in the natural sense. When I was admitted the night before the surgery, I remember lying in the hospital bed, feeling very ill from all the infections, when the phone beside my bed rang, and it was Cy. He was crying, and I was surprised to hear him cry, as I rarely saw him cry.

When I asked him what was wrong, he said, "It's you. I'm worried about you; I don't want to lose you."

And I said, in a confident voice, "It's alright, I'll be Okay, God's not going to let anything happen to me." And somehow, I knew in my spirit, that was true. I had a peace I couldn't explain. I knew people were praying and that things would turn out all right. What I didn't realize was that my family, along with Cy, didn't think I was going to make it. And while the recovery was hard and long, still I was not alone. I had friends and family that helped nurse me back to health while caring for Paul and Cy.

I had God's presence and assurance to see me through. I don't know how I knew it, but I knew God was training me for a greater purpose. One where I would understand the pain and suffering of others. So much so that I would be able to be there for them as well. Later, Cy and I did consider adoption, but I had an underlying disease that was yet to be discovered that kept me very sick for a long time to come. My mother did her best to comfort us but was so sad that I had a hysterectomy at such a young age. At that time, the doctors still assumed my issues had to do with the appendix episode, which made sense, but they also thought I had M.S. in the early stages. This was because I had so many neurological symptoms and some brain lesions showing on MRI's. And the thought of that disease was very frightening to me. During this time, I held Paul very close to me, and it brought me great joy and comfort. I was so thankful I was blessed with one child, and he would go on to be our pride and joy and one we could be very proud of.

My Brother Alan and a New Wedding

It was now 1987 and I still saw my family as often as I could. And we were hearing of a new wedding that would soon take place. My brother Alan. I was proud of him and so happy that he had found someone he could spend the rest of his life with. While I would miss him and the time we had had together and the attention he gave me, his attention would now be on a new woman. He still remained there for me though, and I was grateful. It seemed nothing could break the bond we developed so early in life.

The date they chose for the wedding was November 15th, and it would take place in Oak Park, Michigan, near Detroit. This was where his bride-to-be came from. Alan met her in California while stationed there at Moffett Field in the Navy. I remember how proud he was the day he brought her to meet me. I knew how important it was to him that I approve, and I did. I liked her very much. Upon arriving at my home while I was still recovering in Western Massachusetts, he and his fiancé pulled up to my driveway, and I stood with my young son, who was now five, to greet them. Paul was as excited as I was, as I had told him what was happening. His uncle was bringing his girl-friend to meet us. They got out of the car all smiles.

Alan introduced her. "Iris," he said, "this is Bunny." At first, I thought he was joking about her name, or perhaps it was a nickname.

I said, "Is that her real name?"

He nodded. "Yes."

She laughed and said, "I get a lot of funny looks when I tell people my name, you aren't the first."

All I could think of was cocktail waitress. But she was a medical technol-ogist and that was her name. So, we hugged, had a beautiful time together for two days, and the rest is history. I was getting a new sister-in law and I was ex-cited. Bunny had been married before, but he had passed away. She had one son, Christopher, who at the time was eight. I had an opportunity before the wedding to have Christopher and Bunny stay with us while Alan was called away for duty. He asked me to take care of them, and we did. Paul and Chris-topher were three years apart in age, but they did well as new cousins-to-be. It's funny because when people see both Paul and Chris together today, they look so much alike, people think they are blood related. Truly, to this day, It's hard to believe they aren't.

So, they stayed with us for two weeks, and we enjoyed every moment of it. While Alan was away, Chris and Bunny were not alone; they had the support they needed in meeting their new family.

A few weeks after Alan came home, Bunny and Chris went back home to Detroit to plan the wedding with family. Since most of us were to go by plane, we had to make plans where we would stay. My mother and Lance would stay in a hotel, while room was made for me, Cy, and Paul to stay at Bunny's mother's home. I have always assumed this was because they knew I was ill. It was nice of them to do that, not even knowing who we were. But I guess Bunny wanted to reciprocate after staying with me, so her mother agreed. She had her aunt Diana stay with us, too. And that was a blessing, I really got to know her, and loved it.

It was a cold, unusually snowy November day when we arrived in Oak Park, Michigan. But we were excited just the same. The first day we arrived at Bunny's mother's home, they planned a big turkey dinner for us. We had only been there about an hour, and dinner was ready. We all sat down at the table—Cy, me, Alan, Bunny, Lance, Chris, Bunny's mother Irene, her husband Morley, her Aunt Diana, and Paul. And there we sat, no one knew what to say. Everyone was a little uncomfortable as this was our first meeting with the in-laws. But my mother knew how to break the ice, as she often did. Leave it to Charlotte! So, while we waited for Morley, Bunny's dad, to start to carve the turkey, my mother, wearing a black and gold tiger sweater, reached forward and grabbed the turkey leg, literally pulling it off the carcass and put in on her plate for a moment, then picked it up and starting gnawing at it, looking a little like a cave woman.

At that point, the ice was broken; we all burst into laughter, and from then on, all we did was laugh. We had a great time that night all because my mother let go of all composure, declared she was hungry, and away she went. I'm not sure Bunny's family knew what to do when she did that, but it didn't matter, they thought my mother was hilarious. And she was, mostly because she didn't mean to be, and that's what made my mother so funny. Laughter and family were, and still is, such great medicine for me. I'm so grateful for a funny family, I believe that is what has kept me alive through all the health issues I dealt with.

The Bible tells me that "a cheerful heart is good medicine, but a crushed spirit dries up the bones" Proverbs 17:22 (NIV). God knew what I needed, and it was his joy that carried me through a very long and challenging illness. I actually died twice in my lifetime. However, it was Aunt Diana's comment to me that helped me realize just how blessed I was with the right perspective. She said, "this is for you Iris, He who laughs in the face of adversity will always overcome". It was her feeling that the humor I grew up with and learned so well, was amazing and fun and so healing. She thought I was the most fun sick person she ever met.

Bunny's Family and the Wedding

During that evening, I had a chance to get to know Bunny's aunt Diana, and we connected and became great friends and are still to this day. Even during my stay in Detroit, I was able to make a new friend. I could never have enough friends, and I loved it. And laugh, boy, we did! It was more laughter all at once than I can remember. Even while I was there, my abdominal abscess was flaring up and we had to put a call into my doctor, but it didn't stop the laughter and the great time we had. I was determined not to let my health ruin a good memorable time.

The next day, we got ready for the wedding. It was the most hilarious wedding I've ever attended. It was amazing how well the families got along for just having met. We were at the hall, waiting for the bride and groom to arrive. Alan had stayed at the hotel with Lance and my mother while the rest of us were at Bunny's mother's home. Cy, being in charge of picking up Alan, was late getting him because he got lost. Cy was kind of laid back about it all and wanted to take things in stride, so he took his time trying to find his way while poor Alan, in his white tux, was seen pacing back and forth at the hotel wondering where Cy was. Well, finally, Cy arrived and brought Alan to his wedding where we were all waiting. Bunny looked a little concerned, but after all was said and done, it was a beautiful ceremony. It was now time to go to the reception.

Alan had hired a DJ long distance and put him in charge of the songs. None of us realized what the night would bring. It started off with the bride and groom's dance. So, we were all expecting a beautiful love song, and we were all waiting in awe. When the song started, the first thing we heard was the lyrics of Elvis Presley's song, "And Now the End is Near, and So I Face My Final Curtain," wait, no, really? We all looked at each other in disbelief.

"What does he mean the end is near?" declared Bunny's father, and we all laughed, it was so ridiculous. And as the night went on, the DJ kept playing all this really drab music, so Bunny's best friend Karen went up to the band stand to talk to the DJ about being so morbid on such a happy occasion.

And she said, "Can you get less mellow please?"

He said, "Sure, I can do that." And the next thing we hear over the loud-speaker was, "Les Mellow, come to the band stand, Les Mellow, your family is looking for you."

We all looked at each other confused, thinking, who the hell was Les Mellow, and why was he being beckoned to the band stand? We all thought it was the janitor. When we later found out the truth of what had happened, we laughed again. There was so much more to the wedding and our time together, all I can say is it was so much fun, we all hated to leave. But leave we all did. I stayed in touch with Diana and we visited often, her in Colorado, and me still in Western, Massachusetts until circumstances changed in our geographical location later on.

So, Bunny and Alan went on with their lives, living now in California. Two years later in 1989, my nephew was born. Bryan Robert Fisher came into the world during something so significant, it was amazing everything was Okay.

It was October 16th, 1989. Bryan was delivered by C-section, and just hours after he was born, the big earthquake that rocked the San Francisco and Monterey Bay regions of California occurred. Older brother Christopher was at school for the day, and he was in good hands, from what I understand.

When I later asked him about what it was like for him, he said, "Aunt Iris, I literally thought we were going to die. It was so scary; we were at a gas station coming back from a school field trip ice skating. But the teachers held it together and things obviously were Okay." I asked him if he was afraid, and he said, "Yes, I thought it was over." Thank God it wasn't, as I had many years to look forward to spending time with Chris, his wife, and new baby boy they are expecting as I'm writing this.

So, Just after Bryan's birth, before the quake hit, my brother Alan stepped out to get a burrito at a nearby restaurant. After sitting down, suddenly the earth began to shake. The movie *Earthquake* had nothing on this real-life catastrophic event. Alan, jumping up, tried to run out the door of the restaurant; as he did, he could hardly keep his balance. As he looked out at the parking area, "The streetlamps were waving back and forth like crazy," he said. "People were screaming and trying to run for cover." Alan tried to make it to his car, trying to get to his wife and newborn as he feared the worse.

On the other side of the city, the world series game was just about to start between the San Francisco Giants and Oakland A's. The game was interrupted by the earthquake, causing a massive evacuation and panic. The stadium was evacuated fairly quickly from what I understand, and some of the structures collapsed, but there were very few reported injuries. What was interesting to me was that the quake only lasted 15 seconds, with a magnitude of 6.9. that seemed like a lifetime, and the damage that was done in those few seconds was phenomenal. A section of the bay bridge collapsed, and 63 people were killed. There was panic and chaos everywhere.

But then, after the quake was over, Alan drove as fast as he could to the hospital. It was only a couple of miles, but it took him an hour and a half because, as he said, "Traffic lights weren't working, and cars were all over the place." There was a lot of mayhem to say the least. Horrified of what might have happened to his wife and the baby, he was determined to get to the hospital. With Chris in the back of his mind, he was certain he would be in good hands at the school, so his focus was his wife and newborn. It was an arduous trip to get to the hospital and very upsetting. When he finally got there, he said, "It was dark and there was drywall all over the place, and cracked walls."

When he reached the maternity ward two floors up, he yelled for Bunny, and he breathed a sigh of relief when he heard her voice answer, "Al, I'm over here." He turned and there she was. He relaxed a bit to see that Bunny and Baby Bryan were safe. A good thing that happened was since Bunny was holding Bryan when the quake hit, he wasn't in the basinet. I felt it was God's intervention that she was holding him, because the basinet flew across the room and toppled over. What were the odds he wasn't in it at that moment? Back home we were praying for the safe delivery of Bryan and it seemed God's hand was on him. The TV in her room, which was very heavy, was bouncing and dangling above her head but didn't fall completely off. If it had, it certainly could have killed her because those 20-inch TVs weighed about 100 pounds. I could see God's protection again on my sister-in-law's life and the baby. When things settled down, Alan was able to get to Christopher at the school and he found that he was a bit shaken but Okay.

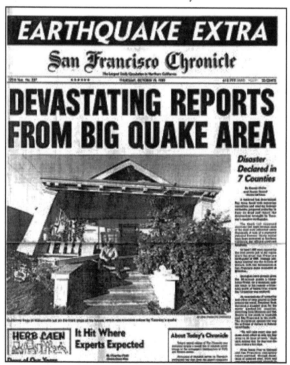

Newspaper article about California earthquake in 1989.

So, this was how we welcomed baby Bryan into the world that day. Wow talk about coming into the world with a bang, yikes! I have to say, he grew up to be a fine young man, joined the service like his dad, and started a family of his own. Christopher married a nice girl from England, and I want to proudly say Bunny and Alan raised two great boys.

Alan and His wife Bunny, Older brother Chris and the baby Bryan, who survived the earthquake.

Nephew Chris and his wife Tash with me, on a visit with us to Seattle. 2016.

My mother, upon hearing of this news, was overwhelmed with fear of what might have happened to her son and his family. What didn't help was there were no cell phones back then and she couldn't speak to Alan until the next day. She was quite frantic until she knew all was Okay. As she spoke with me, my sister and various other friends and relatives, she felt comforted by the fact that she didn't have to go through this alone. But what a frightening experience for us and so many others. We were far away, which made it tougher. When I spoke with Alan, he said people wondered why there was so much devastation in such a short amount of time. He felt it was because San Francisco is a man-made peninsula with the homes and buildings built on soft landfill, which was man-made, not solid rock. It wasn't so much the actual shaking from the quake itself that caused all the damage, the buildings collapsed, because it was the ground sinking.

He said, "We weren't home at the time, so I didn't know what to expect, I expected to see the house flattened, but instead I found it didn't have a scratch on it.

Going in, I noticed a lamp did fall over and break, but that was all. I attributed this to the house being built with more cement on more solid ground. Plus, the house was jacked up underneath on, like stilts. Also, the house was in San Jose, about 60 miles from San Francisco near where the quake was centered. But when we went out to the back of the house, we initially thought the pool was half empty because of the shaking of the quake and it had leaked. What had actually happened, after speaking with my neighbor, is he saw a wall of water coming over the fence. It was a 22,000-gallon pool and it was half full, so I determined about 10,000 gallons of water went over the fence because of the shaking. My neighbor thought it was a tsunami at first." My goodness, I could see why!

As I listened to Alan share the experience, I couldn't believe how powerful the quake was, and the fact that it could move water in a pool like that. Amazing.

He went on, "I was in even bigger earthquakes than that and didn't see nearly the damage. I think it was because where I was in the other earthquakes, the buildings weren't built in a metropolitan area where there were so many people and so many buildings and the sinking that occurred. I thought for sure after the quake hit, I had lost my family. I was so afraid, but I knew what I had to do, and I had the faith to trust that everything was Okay. I knew I would not be left alone without my family."

Alan was and still is family oriented, and I'm so grateful that I can be a recipient of his love and dedication. He has become our family patriarch, and through his son Bryan (the baby who survived the earthquake), he now has a new grandson who adores him, too. Little Wren Morley, is the apple of Alan's eye. He loves his grandson.

In closing this chapter, there is another cute story I'd like to share about Bunny and Alan. Long after the earthquake, around the time Bryan was two, Alan was taking a run through a park in California on Easter Sunday. He lost his glasses and was waiting for Bunny to pick him up, and he couldn't see a darn thing, so began calling for his wife so she could find him. So, picture this, it's Easter Sunday and my brother is running through the park, yelling, "Bunny, Bunny." This, "for about ten minutes," he said. It was cold and he was in shorts and a t-shirt. Needless to say, he said he got some funny looks as people were wondering why a grown man might be looking for a bunny in the park on Easter Sunday.

My mother's response in hearing this: "What a shmuck, he could have been arrested, who the heck raised him to do that? Did I tell him to do that? I didn't raise him that way." Our mother could be encouraging and sarcastic at the same time. It was one of those times she meant that comment with love and an iron fist, meaning, "Don't do that again." She was funny, protective in one sense, and would kick you in the butt when you weren't looking.

Son Paul, Nephew Chris, Nephew Bryan and My Brother Alan, together having a great time at my 60th Birthday Celebration. Snohomish, Washington, May 2019.

Chapter 15

Painful Changes Come, but We are Never Alone

In 1988, we were about to experience a traumatic event as a family that happens to nearly all of us.

Paul was now six and growing like a weed, our pride and joy. While he was an active child, he was jovial and good natured, smart as a whip, and I could see, even at an early age, he cared about people. This was something we had hoped we had passed on to him, and we were beginning to see evidence of this. He was a lot of fun; I could see many of my family traits in him. I kept him at my side and hardly took my eyes off of him, because he had an accident when he was just two in 1984 when he broke his femur. I was so traumatized by his injury, more so than he was, that I wanted to be sure it never happened again.

He was with my friend Rita, grocery shopping while I worked that day. She was babysitting for him and loved doing so. And she was very good with him. The plan was to pick them up when I got off work and when she finished the shopping. She had other children with her, including her own, and somehow while she was shopping, the shopping cart got toppled over with Paul in the seat. I guess they were playing, I never really knew what happened. When I arrived at the store, I heard Paul crying, and it wasn't his usual cry, so I knew something was wrong. I ran to where I heard him, in the meat section of the grocery store. There, I found Rita, the other kids, and Paul in pain with his leg. As I carefully picked him up and held him straight, I sensed his leg was broken. I rushed him to the car as fast as I could, carefully placing him in the seat with his leg straight to try to prevent further injury.

I must have gone through every red light on my way to the hospital, all the while speaking to him in a soft voice to comfort him that he would be all right, that Mama would take care of him. I prayed hard out loud with him all the way there. The ride, which seemed like forever, was about 15 minutes. I know God gave me the strength that day. When I got him to the hospital, they immediately got him into emergency, called a pediatric orthopedist who acted very quickly.

My mother-in-law, father in-law, and Cy met there to support me. My mother couldn't come until later because she was two hours away. What I'm thinking of is, *how much more painful would it have been if I hadn't had the support*. It would have been unbearable, but God in his mercy saw to it that once again, I was not alone. And most importantly, Paul was now safely in traction and being cared for by an excellent doctor. Many relatives and friends were there to support during a very long month for him in traction. To add more fuel to the fire, during that month, I hadn't slept well and became quite ill myself, and not long after he got out, I ended up hospitalized, which eventually led to my hysterectomy.

But on a positive note, during Paul's stay in the hospital, he was such a good boy; what an attitude he had. He expressed that joviality in spite of his limitations. And during that time, it was his birthday. So, his Grandma Gert, along with my mother and Cy's mother, planned a big birthday bash for him and even ordered a clown to come and entertain. He had three grandmothers and his Mom orchestrating this for him. What a blessed little boy! We had quite a crowd, and he was showered with gifts and hugs and fun even while he was in traction. My conclusion, he made it and so did I because we were never alone, and I knew it was all God's provision. And I thanked God for turning a very painful and arduous situation into something good.

Rita, in the meantime, felt terrible, but I assured her that because she was my friend, I understood, and we were grateful he was Okay. Much like my mother and father felt when we had to let go of the Doctor's mistake with me during my ordeal. My bond with Rita as a result grew stronger, and we have been friends ever since. We started out as prayer partners, developed into friendships, and ended in a bond nothing could break. "Two are better than one, when one falls, the other one picks the other up and pity the man who is alone." That scripture from Ecclesiastes is true, and after Rita and Chris, God would constantly bless me with loyal, loving sisters that no crisis on earth could ever break. In spite of the accident, God took care of all of us. Rita's friendship, because I knew she loved us, was more important than any blame, and if I had been angry with her that would have wounded a friend who was already hurting. I often wondered afterward if this was a test God allowed to see how I would handle it. I chose love over blame and learned a valuable lesson in that choice. Rita remains a loyal friend, what better result could I ask for.

She, Chris, and several friends helped me through a rough time. And thank God, my little boy, was Okay. As I think back on this experience, because it was my son, it was more painful for me than any surgery, any coma I could have endured. Why? Because he was my child, and nothing hurts worse than watching your child go through pain. But that experience, along with many others, molded him into the beautiful man he is today. Today, he treats his mother like gold, and I couldn't ask for a more loving, supportive man to some-day care for me in my old age.

Me and my son Paul on Mother's Day having a blast. May 2018.

As my husband Cy has joked, "There is a better nursing home in our fu-ture." Joking aside, he, too, trusts our son will be there if we need him. After all, children learn what they live, and since he's about to become a father him-self, I can see he will be there for his wife and children.

Paul and Samantha at a wedding, she was glowing in her early pregnancy, and so were we. Her due date with Baby boy Smith was due March 7th, 2020.

A Legacy about to Pass

My grandmother was now aging, this was now 1988. While Paul was my priority, still I was concerned for my grandmother. She adored him and his blond hair. It was special to her because we were all darker-complected and brunette. She got a kick out of him being blond like his dad.

In Russian, she would say, "Look at the little *madelech*," as she gave him a great big hug. What it meant was, "Look at my beautiful baby." Or something like that. I was better with the Italian interpretation, either way, we knew it was something really nice because of the incredible smile and look of adoration that went with it. Her great-grandchildren, as with her grandchildren, brought her a lot of joy.

But in the midst of raising my own, I was sadly aware my mother and I had to think about putting her in a care facility, a nursing home, and it brought us great pain to do so, taking her out of her own secure place she knew for 30 years. For us, it was bringing a close to that era and generation that brought us so much warmth and comfort and joy as we were raised. It was heart breaking to think my grandmother, being all about home and family, would have to now be taken out of the comfort of her home and family. The place she found peace and security, the place where she found care and solace away from the memories of the Russian/Bolshevik revolution, where she was separated from her first love and lost much of her family. A place where she established her own home again after being reunited with her Morris, was now all coming to a close.

My Bobe and her Morris in their elder years.

Auntie Elaine and Uncle Martin with Mom in Western Mass, this was brother Lances Graduation party in my home. May 1989.

We agonized over it to say the least. But there was no choice, she needed more care, and my Aunt Ruthie was no longer up to helping her because she needed so much guidance due to her disabilities. My mother was going to have her hands full for sure, but as she was there for us, we had to be there for her. We couldn't let my mother feel alone in this, she was still trying to care for them while holding down two jobs. My family was seeing each other through some very difficult moments. When one was suffering, the other one was there to help lighten the load.

It's my belief when families are in need, it never comes when it's convenient, it requires sacrifice. I've experienced it involves dropping what is important to you and coming to their aid, so they are not burdened to fend for themselves.

Mother Teresa once said, "Spread love everywhere you go. Let no one ever come to you without leaving happier." She also said, "Let peace begin with a smile." And, "It's not how much we give, but how much love we put into giving." And that was many of my family members, my grandmother included. They gave because they loved. Shouldn't we do the same?

With Alan far away and in the service during this time and Lance in college, it was up to me and Cy to help. And it wasn't easy, being ill myself, two hours away with a little guy. I was still dealing with abdominal abscesses and numerous health challenges, and it wouldn't be easy to support my mother during this very hard and emotionally draining transition. But I wasn't to face this alone. Uncle Martin (my dad's younger brother), who rarely thought of himself, along with his wife, Auntie Elaine, offered support. My father couldn't be there because of his health challenges, and it was touchy since he and my mom were now divorced. Even though my parents were divorced, my mother stayed in contact with some of his siblings and family members, as she was close with them and loved them. And they loved her. Aunt Ann and Uncle Martin were the primary ones, and what a comfort it brought to us that they were there to help, even if it was just to listen. They were loyal and sacrificial in the truest sense of the word.

So, as it came time to pack up my grandmother's home, Cy, Uncle Martin, my mother, brother Lance, and I worked together. We went through everything and packed things and prepared her as best we could for the new place where she would spend her final days. As we packed, we could see the pain in her facial expressions, and while my mother picked one of the best Jewish nursing homes in the Boston area, and her Morris would be there with her, still, it was the end to what she had called home for around 30 years or so. As everyone packed, I took my grandmother into her bedroom, and talked with her and listened intently to how hard this was.

One of the things she asked me in her broken English that broke my heart was, "Iris'l, what will happen to Ruthie? She has always depended on me, who will take care of her?"

I answered, "We will. You know my mother will see to it, and we will be behind her helping as best we can."

She breathed a sigh of relief, but I could see she was concerned about all the pressure put on my mother. While I often saw my mother as a rock, I knew she could only handle so much, and I was concerned, too. I wasn't strong either physically, and my grandmother knew it. But as I began to walk out of the room, expecting her to follow me, I turned to her and watched my grandmother pray in Russian to "the God of Abraham, Isaac, and Jacob," the God she always trusted in. The God she knew brought her through the Bolshevik Revolution, across the Atlantic by herself, and right back to Morris 30 years later. She knew He would see her through this season. And then as she finished, I watched relief come over her face and a look of peace that brought me peace. I knew she had met with her God and was comforted. Her faith spoke volumes to me.

Bobe in her home in Chelsea, Ma. Circa 1946.

My Grandmother's Final Home

Before we knew it, we had Bobe tucked in with her husband in a Jewish environment with lots of Europeans who spoke their language. At least culturally, she was at home. Not that they could hear each other, but they still felt a commonality. While it wasn't her own home, my grandmother tried to settle in. It was heartbreaking because suddenly, all her independence was forever gone, and it took its toll on her. I didn't know what to do. I had been told by other believers that unless she knew Jesus as her messiah, she would not go to heaven. This bothered me, no kidding! I was in a vulnerable state and not thinking clearly, so I felt it was my mission as a fairly new Christian to tell her who I thought the Jewish Messiah was.

My Dear Friend Chris Szulborski and I in my Home in New Hampshire. Circa 2012.

Every week, I drove two hours with my friend Chris to see her, as I knew time was short. Chris and I were great friends by now and very close, so we did a lot together. And she was supporting me in this as she loved my grandmother, too. So, after a month of visiting her, one particular Saturday I allowed this friend to talk me into trying to convert my grandmother. Not realizing it wasn't my job but God's, especially since she couldn't hear me. So, when I arrived, I gave her a big hug and she knew me, which was good, and she was glad to see me until I started, as she described, as acting like a *"meshooganah."* Which in Russian/Yiddish meant crazy person. I sat down with her on a couch to talk with her. The main room to the nursing home was full of people visiting relatives. All Jewish and all seemingly hard of hearing, until I started to speak to my grandmother.

I started with, "Bobe, I know who the Jewish Messiah is."

"What?" She waved her hand at me as if to say knock it off.

I tried again, "Bobe, I know who the Jewish Messiah is."

"What? Where's the fire? There's no fire, you're a *meshooganah*!"

After repeating a few more times, I was starting to get some funny looks in the room, no kidding!

Chris, squirming in her seat and fearing we would be thrown out for yelling Jesus in a Jewish nursing home, said to me, "Iris, I think we better call it quits, look around the room."

People were wondering what I was doing; of course, they were. Keep in mind, this was me being young and vulnerable and wanting to ensure my grandmother's place in heaven. Like I had control over this, right! All I can say is it was a good thing my mother wasn't there. Although she would have blamed my father and his Catholic background, that would have started another revolution. All I can say is, when we are in pain and feel desperate, we don't always think rationally. I didn't want to lose my grandma, my Bobe.

Anyway, I finally got frustrated, hoping for one last chance for her to hear me, and I literally, blurted out, "Bobe, I know who the Jewish Messiah is, it's Jesus." At that point, the whole nursing home heard me just fine, every hearing aid was tuned in. Of course, they were. Even the professed hard of hearing ones heard me loud and clear. Sheesh! But not Bobe, she still thought I was yelling fire.

Chris, feeling uneasy, then said, "Do you think maybe it's time to go, we are getting a lot of glares, what do you think?"

I nodded. "Let's see if we can slip out without getting killed."

"Good idea," Chris answered.

So, I said my goodbyes to Bobe, with her still thinking I'm a *meshooganah*, and I felt just a tad bit defeated. The glares I got on the way out didn't help.

What I didn't realize was that my grandmother's salvation was not my job or responsibility, it was God's. All I had to do was pray for her, she couldn't understand me, so it was between her and her creator. If she couldn't hear me and Jesus wanted to get her attention, he was more than capable of doing it himself. The choice was hers, not mine. While it wasn't fair of me to do that, I was young and loved her and wanted to ensure her place in heaven, but again, that was between her and the Lord. My responsibility was to pray and let go, let go of my grandmother who was always there for me and loved me unconditionally. Something I could only do with God's help.

As I look back on this, I realized I loved her so much, I couldn't bear the thought of losing her, never to see her again was just too overwhelming. I wanted an assurance I would see her again, if not here, then in eternity. But that is done by faith, trusting that God would take care of her, and make himself known to her in his way and in his timing.

I knew, as a Russian/Jewish woman, she loved God with all her heart, soul, and mind. She was an incredible role model of a Godly woman. I was very young and impressionable at the time, and if I hadn't learned anything else through this experience, it was to let go and let God. And how to meet people where they are at. Needless to say, Chris and I laugh about that experience today as we reminisce, but we also realize that time and maturity take care of a whole host of situations that are beyond our control. People can hear the word of God, but it's up to them, it's a choice, a choice between them and God. We cannot make people believe a certain way, and why would we? It's the Holy Spirit's job to draw them, not ours. Anything else is dictatorship, isn't it? I would later learn that just because we didn't hear someone say they accepted Christ as their savior does not mean they didn't acknowledge him. Someday when we get to heaven, we are going to have some surprises. People we thought would be there, may not be, and ones we thought wouldn't be, God himself may have revealed himself to them, and they will be there to greet us. I believe my grandmother is one, because I didn't do it, He did.

So, a few months later, on a cold December night at 2:00 a.m., Cy and I were awakened by a frantic call from my mother. She was so upset; I'll never forget her words to me as I struggled to awaken.

She said, "Iris, I've just called your sister, your brothers, and some friends. Bobe passed away a few hours ago."

My heart sank. I began to shake and tremble in disbelief. "How did she die? I mean, I know she was old, but what happened?"

My mother's voice was shaky. "She had a massive stroke, they said, and she went quickly."

This was my first experience with someone so close to me passing away, I didn't know how to respond. I was in shock, Cy held me, and he felt terrible, but he was very supportive, as he loved my grandmother, too. I felt as if a piece of me had been ripped out and thrown away. And this would be the beginning of a downward spiral of many relatives who had always been there for us, beginning to pass away one by one on both sides of the family. I didn't realize this would be a constant for the rest of my life. Coming from such a large family and having so many friends, it was inevitable, and the downside of bonding with so many. I would lean on God's grace being very sufficient from here on.

While it's wonderful to have had so many, what do you do when they leave? It leaves a void that only one person can fill who never dies or moves away and that person, for me, is the person of Jesus.

What I would find is that each time someone passed, and while there would always be others to take their place, it was only God who could truly give me that peace, confidence, and comfort in the midst of such great loss. I would learn while I mourned the dying, I could still care for the living. I would never be alone because even when no one else was around, I had the company of God and his assurance to be there. This was a choice I made, and I have never regretted it. As a song said, "To see with my heart, to hear with my soul, to be guided by a hand I cannot hold, to trust in a way that I cannot see, that's what faith must be."

Again, we don't see God because He's a spirit. Our spirit communes with his spirit, and we feel him as we pray. It is like nothing I've ever experienced. And we don't come into God's presence because we are perfect; it's quite the opposite, we come as we are. He doesn't expect anything else but you. In life there will always be ones in need to reach out to and extend that hand of love. Even with my precious grandmother now gone, someone would always need me. As my mother's daughter with God's help, what a gift I was given to help and love those who need it most. And for all of us, I believe that in this world, there is no shortage of needy, hungry people. You don't have to look far to find them. I believe God placed us all here to love people. To feed the hungry, whether its spiritual or physical.

Another quote from dear Mother Teresa, "If you can't feed 100 people, then feed just one." Start where you live and bloom where you are planted is the place to start.

Letting Go of My Grandmother

Letting go of my grandmother and my security showed me I was now transitioning from being mentored to be a mentor. And it would take years of painful experiences to master this reaching out to those in need thing. But I still had my mother and others like her to exemplify that for me. My role model, Mother Teresa, also said, "I know God won't give me anything I can't handle.

I just wish he didn't trust me so much." I would hear those words echo in my mind as I faced challenges time and again. And I thought I'd never be able to live through some of the experiences I faced.

A few days later after her death, my mother called me, still with a shaky voice. "Iris, someone needs to go to the nursing home to clean out your grandmother's room, I can't bring myself to do it, it's too painful."

I said I would do it. I put a call into Auntie Elaine and Uncle Martin, and my uncle agreed to go with me. It was the saddest thing I've ever done. I cried my way through as I cleaned out her drawers, one by one. Since Cy was there with Uncle Martin, they comforted me and talked to me, so I didn't feel alone. I can't tell you how much that meant during such an arduous time.

When that was done, I said goodbye to one of the nurses, who also comforted me by saying, "She had a hard adjustment, but she was a good woman. I can see she was a good grandmother, and I'm so sorry." I thanked her as I choked back more tears.

My grandmother died on December 5th, 1988. It was estimated that she was born in 1896. We weren't sure of her exact age because in Russia, they didn't keep track of birth records back then. So we guessed she was around 92 years old. She lived a full life, that's for sure. She saw good times and hard times, and just like my father's mother, she was my grandmother and she could do no wrong in my eyes. Several days later, we had her funeral; the service was beautiful. I don't know who had a harder time, my mother or Aunt Ruthie. I sensed that Aunt Ruthie felt lost, and I held her as she cried. While she felt alone and lost without her mother, we assured her she was not alone, that we would be there as much as we could, when she needed us. At the close of the service when everybody left for the cemetery, I waited and watched my mother privately say her goodbyes to the woman she called her best friend. I was in the back waiting for her, and I saw something I'll never forget. I observed my strong mother leaning over her mother's casket, crying her heart out for what seemed like three minutes. Something I rarely saw my mother do.

When I approached her, and she realized I was watching, she stood up, brushed the tears from her face, and said, "Okay, let's go, I'm done."

And I then said, "Mom, don't you want another minute? Please take your time, it's Okay to cry."

She said, "No, I'm done, let's go out to the cemetery and then we'll all have a nice time together."

I'm not sure if she was in denial or if she had mastered the ability to express her emotions quickly and efficiently and then move on. She knew she had responsibilities with her sister and family, and I guess wanted to grieve but move on. Whatever she was doing, even to this day, I find myself doing same thing. I guess it's either learned or genetic. Either way, I'm grateful that I can scream my heart out for five minutes and then go watch a nice movie. Hey, it works, and what a time saver! Why waste time grieving when you can relax and enjoy yourself? Crazy, I know. But it's what she taught me, and I find it does work. I acknowledge how I feel with great emotion and then I'm done. It comes quite naturally, as it did for my mother. She taught me to deal with what bothers me and then move on quickly and not stay stuck in it. It was who my mother was. I thank God every day she taught me that. What a gift. My husband is grateful for that, he thanks my mother every day, too, I'll bet he does!

My son thinks it's a riot! I remember a day when we first came out to live near him in Washington state. He had moved in with us to help us get acclimated to the new area. I was making him dinner and sharing how upset I was about something that was on my mind. And with great emotion. While he was expecting me to go on and on for quite a while venting, he was surprised to see after just a moment of blurting out, "I hate my body and look what I have to live with," and sarcastically declaring I wanted to kill myself, the next thing he heard from me was, "So, do you want broccoli with your meatloaf?"

With that, he burst into laughter. "Mom, how do you switch so fast from I hate my body to what do you want for dinner?"

This photo was taken of me at my Brother Alan's wedding Circa 1987.

I said, "I don't know, I guess I'm done venting." I had to think about it for a moment because I hadn't realized I had done that. But I guess I was switching from feeling sorry for myself to meeting my son's needs. And that is key to not staying stuck, to think about others instead. Just like my mother did at my grandmother's funeral, she was able to find strength from her grief by shifting her focus to thinking of others in need around her. I laughed with him when I realized what I had said. I felt heard, and I guess that was enough. As I'm aging, I'm becoming more and more like my mother, and that's just fine with me. Tough and to the point.

"I am not sure exactly what heaven will be like, but I know that when we die and it comes time for God to judge us, he will not ask how many good things you have done in your life?" Mother Teresa

And I would like to add to that I believe he will ask if we cared and then what did we do about it.

Moving On

After my grandmother's passing, Mom became focused on setting up Aunt Ruthie in an apartment. She found a facility where Ruthie could be fairly independent but not totally alone. Today, they call it assisted living. It was a complex where there were other elderly people with developmental disabilities. She acclimated well and made a few friends, and guess what? Now she was not alone. My mother, in the background, remained faithful in helping her sister, just as she promised her mother. And that's how my mother was so successful in being strong, her focus was not on herself, her attention was often diverted to others.

As I said, it was so hard because one by one, we began to experience more deaths. Next was the death of my other grandmother, Leah Jean. That was just as hard, another blanket of security gone. My loving grandmother, Nonna, who was always there and taught me so much about cooking and bonding, would no longer be there to greet me with those sweet kisses. The assurance that I was loved by her, was now passing away.

In the wake of my grandmother Leah Jean's passing, we had the help of my brothers and my dad's second wife to support my father, and he had the assurance he was not alone. In addition to us, he had all his siblings and his aunt Ann to help console him. We made it through because we had each other. We then heard of Morris passing in the nursing home, an era truly now gone.   Then Cy's father suddenly found he had brain cancer and passed within six weeks of his diagnosis, just one year before he retired. He was 59 years old. This was particularly hard on Cy. He had a very hard adjustment. He loved his dad and couldn't imagine life without him either. I remember Cy sitting Paul on his lap and trying to explain to him at six years old how his grandpa was now in heaven, and he wouldn't see him here anymore, but assured him we would one day see him in heaven again. I remember how Paul cried while Cy held him, but they both had me and other family members to support them. Letting go of what once was and moving toward what was to be. In the midst of this, my health was becoming more difficult and seemed to progress in a bad direction, and we still weren't sure what was happening, although the doctors felt a climate change might help since I seemed to have a lot of arthritic symptoms in addition to the neurological and digestive. As I look back, with all the symptoms I had, I still don't know how I was functioning, but by the grace of God, I did. This was around the time my focus began to shift to learning more about prayer and praying for others. I was amazed to learn how powerful it was, and I've never stopped learning.

So now, with so much change taking place, maybe it was time for a new start, perhaps in a new state. Our thoughts turned toward Florida, where it was warmer, and we had family and my friend Debbie living there. Seemed like a good idea, so, we began to pray and to explore how to proceed. With a home to sell and a business for Cy to let go of, there was much to do. It was a hard decision because we would be far from family, especially my mother and brother Lance. We would be leaving behind both our families and what was familiar, but because I had two aunts and several cousins and a number of friends from high school down there, it seemed doable and exciting as a new adventure. My mother felt comforted by the fact that we would not be by ourselves and she would have a new place to visit. So, we sold everything and moved to Boca Raton, Florida where my two aunts and cousins were. Something that was nice for us is that my father also lived down there, and we would be able to see him more. Which was exciting to Paul as a little boy, and after losing one grandfather, he had my dad to support him.

Here we were, on vacation with my dad in St. Augustine, Florida. Paul was enjoying his time with his Grandfather. Circa 1990.

It was now 1990 and the beginning of a new decade. Again, things were changing. I was watching things on TV like the show *Friends*, *Saved by the Bell*, *Quantum Leap* with Scott Bakula, which Cy and I loved. We still do today. We loved *Murder She Wrote* with Angela Lansbury. Since I was starting to write, I enjoyed watching a show about a murder mystery writer. Paul, at his age, liked *Alf*, and we liked the show *Cheers*. And so much more.

Even though I was struggling with my health, I still managed to have good times in Florida during the three years we were there. It was new, and while challenging due to my energy level, still it was an exciting adventure. I had been to Florida only once while I was at home with my family. It was our Disney vacation, if you remember, and I loved the idea of living there. It was also exceptionally nice to be near family and have Lance, my friend Chris, and Alan visit, too. Paul was bonding with my father on trips to St. Augustine and Disney. We were at Disney so often; I was actually feeling like I had had enough. Hard to imagine, isn't it.

I was also spending time with my friend from high school, Debbie, and her family. I loved seeing her again. Since Debbie and I had sons close in age, we had commonalty in spending time together.

My Good friend from Childhood, Debbie and I on an evening cruising the Florida Coast. We were having a blast. I remember how excited my mother was that I was with her. She loved Debbie.

The world was changing once again. In the three years we were there, a number of significant things took place. The three of us, Paul, Cy, and I were active in an Assembly of God Church, where Cy and Paul did Royal Rangers together (like Boy Scouts), went on many overnights together, and had some really nice father and son bonding time. We went on dinner cruises with our church and friends, spent a lot of time at Disney World, which was my favorite, and holidays with family were so much fun. My aunt Diane and I had a chance to reconnect and spend a lot of time together. I also became a part of a prayer group with older women that mentored me in the power of prayer. I began to realize that this was how I would get through some really rough times with my health, by others praying for me, having shoulders to lean on, and learning to lean on God and trust in him to help me, especially when it seemed I was getting worse.

I was very sick with abscesses in my abdomen that were out of control, and the support I had through these women in prayer was priceless and I grew spiritually as a result. During the time I was so sick and needing to be hospitalized often, this prayer group would come and help us in the house and with whatever we needed. These were true examples of Christian women who really cared, they wanted to mentor me. They were like my mother, thinking of others. In those three years, as I attended their prayer group, I learned from them about intercession and praying for others. I learned how to commune with God, and being chronically ill, I found being in God's presence with so much support, comforting, and it grounded me during a very rough time. My focus was not on suffering, but on what I could do with this and where God was taking me in the process of being so challenged by infirmity.

Chapter 16

My Spiritual Awareness is Awakened Through Miracles I Could Not Explain

A number of significant things took place while living in Florida which caused me to become more spiritually aware. Things began to happen to me personally that you don't often understand through the natural eye and mind. I had suffered a brain injury when I was young, from sepsis and a lack of oxygen, and neurologists did tell me that often times when people experience brain trauma, they begin to have telepathic abilities, like a sixth sense as they say. They have no idea why, but it's common. I have spoken to others with brain injuries that have experienced this, too. There's no natural explanation for it. People have reported being able to see things in dreams and visions before they happen. They have reported being able to see things in people with a discernment that others couldn't. This was happening to me, and I didn't understand it.

Biblically, it says this about it, Acts 2:17, "In the last days, God says, I will pour out my spirit on all people, Your sons and daughters will prophesy, your young men will see visions, and your old men will dream dreams" (NIV). If this was happening to me, and it seemed it was, it had to be that God was giving me this ability and for a good purpose. Because of my religious background, this was my conviction. And if he was, what did he want me to do with it? Was this a prophetic gift I was experiencing?

While enjoying time connecting with family and making new friends, I was learning about God and prayer, how to trust him, and that miracles really do happen. In the three years we were there, while I was enjoying much of it, there was time spent in the hospital trying to get the abscesses I was dealing with under control and discovering I had at least two autoimmune diseases. It was a painful and debilitating ordeal to say the least and very worrisome to my family. The abscesses were quite dangerous and made me very ill when they would flare up, requiring antibiotics and surgery. I can't even begin to describe what this was doing to my digestion and body as a whole. And while there was always the question of why I was forming them, it wasn't always obvious to the doctors. As they read my history, again, they assumed they were from the appendix episode and the unresolved peritonitis that was lying dormant in various parts of my body, especially the lymph nodes. Which made sense, since when they had done one surgery, they discovered my insides looked like I had laid on a hand grenade, as I had said. It was that bad, and no one had any explanation as to why I was able to even conceive a child. A true Miracle of God's love for me. I knew my faith and God's blessings had everything to do with it.

God was allowing this time, so I would be able to be set apart to hear from him. If I was busy running around and working, etc., would I be praying and sitting and listening? Probably not! No one would, he wanted my attention, and he had it. I was developing a strong, close relationship with him, and I was enjoying getting to know my creator. My role model, Mother Teresa, had a relationship like that with the Lord, and this was something I, too, longed for. I really admired her strength and attitude and wanted to emulate this. Through her example, I learned that regardless of what things looked like in the natural, I knew his plans for me would take center stage.

Unfortunately, I could only have so much surgery, but I believe God knew it. He knew I wasn't born with an abdominal zipper. Surgery could not be a long-term solution for healing for me without terrible consequences to my health. It seemed my life was always on the line with this, and it would continue for decades.

This is an example of what I believe God was beginning to show me as to who does the work. In other words, when man does not have the answers, we believe by faith who does. Once again, I was in a place of crisis, where my life was on the line, and God was about to let me know I was not alone.

Before long, there was one mass that grew to the size of a football and did require surgery. Because of this, it was the second time in my life I would come to the place where I would experience near death. Only this time, it was different, and a life changing event would take place, helping me to understand more and more that there is an after-life.

Visions Begin to Manifest

I had a vision I had not seen before while under anesthesia. It's amazing I had any brain cells left. They told me while undergoing this particular operation, my heart had stopped for what they said was only a few minutes. While they were trying to revive me, like I said, I had an experience like I had never had before, something I have no explanation for. I had heard others speak of similar experiences in near-death experiences, but I was skeptical until this. What comes to mind for me is that the brain, as I've been told, does funny things when you are literally experiencing a near death. For one thing, I was lacking oxygen to the brain, and what does that tell you? It's amazing I didn't end up developmentally disabled, although at times my mobility and communication became very difficult. I had even experienced a mini stroke, which they could see on an MRI.

So, I can't tell you for sure where I was during the heart stopping moments, but it sure seemed like I had seen what the Bible describes as Heaven. John 14:2-4, "My Father's house has many rooms; if that were not so, would I have told you that I am going there to prepare a place for you? And if I go and prepare a place for you, I will come back and take you to be with me that you also may be where I am. You know the way to the place where I am going." For me personally, it answered questions and gave me a peace about where I would be spending my time after this life, since we had no idea how long I could live with so much trauma. Of course, I would be exploring all of this. I was only in my 30s at the time, and my doctors that were treating me when I was young had doubts about how long I would live or even if I would reach the age of 20. My life has been one miracle after the other. Talk about God constantly revealing himself to someone.

John 15:16-17: "You did not choose me, but I chose you, and appointed you to go and bear fruit – fruit that will last. Then the father will give you whatever you ask in my name. This is my command, love each other." How else can I explain any of this? It was clear he chose me, and it was for the sake of others. He was building in me a compassion and love for others that not many can understand, unless you experience pain yourself. I want to share this near-death experience with you, and you decide what happened. I told you, I thought I saw heaven. What are your thoughts as you read this?

While under anesthesia, I was in a state where it felt like I had just fallen asleep and a kind of euphoria took me over, which was quite pleasant. There was no bright light, no tunnel. I was just awake one moment, and as I fell asleep under the anesthesia, I woke up to what seemed like somewhere else. The transition was very uneventful, in other words, it was quite peaceful with no trauma. The next thing I knew, I was in a place that was so peaceful and light, I felt no weight or heaviness in my body, no pain, no sadness, and it seemed I just floated from place to place, not experiencing the pressure and effort of having to walk, which has been difficult for me during the course of my life. It was a place of beauty, so serene, that I have trouble putting into words. I saw animals with almost golden-glowing fur, they were just gorgeous. Picture a dog that is so pretty, and just groomed, looking so perfect, and then multiply that ten times over, that's how beautiful the animals were. I wondered if this is the way God originally intended animals to look. Hey, I know mine do. Just kidding!

The animals were also not at odds with one another either, they were kind to one another and seemed to enjoy frolicking together. I then saw streams of water with colors I've not seen here on this planet, a very extraordinarily deep blue, like turquoise. I saw a ladder, which I assumed was Jacob's ladder, that had this unusual green color with bright glowing lights, the rungs had no beginning and no end, it just was there. There were people who greeted me when I arrived, and they were people I knew who had passed. As I moved toward a gate, I was amazed at its beauty.

In the Bible, Revelation 21:21 speaks of this: "The 12 gates were 12 pearls, each gate made of a single Pearl. The great street of the city was of pure gold, like transparent glass. I did not see a temple in the city because the Lord God Almighty and the lamb are in its temple. The city does not need the sun or the moon to shine on it, for the glory of God gives it light, and the lamb is its lamp. The nations will walk by its light, and the kings of the earth will bring their splendor into it. On no day will its gates ever be shut, for there will be no night there" (NIV). Much of what I saw matched this scripture. Is this what I have to look forward to after death? Talk about hope and a future! Jeremiah 29:11, "For I know the plans I have for you. Declares the Lord, plans to prosper you and not to harm you, plans to give you hope and a future."

The first person to greet me was a cousin of my mother's, whom she was very close to. She had died of a heart aneurism at age 65. Before she died, since she was quite ill and we knew time was short, I tried to tell her about Jesus and her eternity, too, once again, thinking it was my responsibility to get her there. She never responded to me with that, so I assumed she never knew who God even was. I have learned since never to judge a man's heart. We shouldn't judge as to who will be in heaven and who won't because no one knows where they stand with God. But God obviously spoke to her and received her because she was there, looking so young and free and happy. This was the opposite of her life here on earth as we knew her to be. What impressed me most about her was that in life, she was so unhappy and bogged down with so many painful things in her life. I can't remember an unhappier person, to tell you the truth. But when I saw her, she greeted me with a beautifully glowing smile. She reached out her arms to me, with a love that is indescribable, I then followed her. I had never seen her like this in my life. And I remember how happy it made me to see her happy, as I had been concerned about her. I was amazed at how perfect she looked. Her teeth were bright, and she looked young and healthy, and she kept motioning to me to look around and observe what was there. She didn't say anything, but it was like I could feel what she was saying in my spirit; it's hard to put into words. As I glanced where she was motioning me to be, I looked toward the gate made out of gold and pearls. I never entered the gate but only peeked in.

What the apostle Paul says in the Bible, "that to be absent from the body is to be present with the Lord," rang true for me. As that is exactly what it felt like I had experienced. I felt like I was out of my body and in the spirit. Having a Catholic background, it all makes sense to me. That's my own take on it, I felt I was there, it was what I experienced, and as my mother would have said, right, wrong, or indifferent, it happened to me, what else can you say. Now, could my brain have been having hallucinations while losing oxygen? Perhaps! But it was an amazing one if it was and so detailed. It brought me hope for life after I die that this is not the end here but the beginning. This vision showed me that, especially in death, not only is it not the end, but I'm certainly not alone. Not here, nor in Heaven! That's what I believe!

So, while still under anesthesia, I found myself turning away from the gate, and it was clear I was being sent back. I heard a voice say to me (and I only heard a voice), it seemed like it was a soft spoken male voice calling me by name, and I heard him say, "Iris, I want you to go back, but let go of burdens, you have been too worried. They are weighing you down, you're taking on too much." With all I was dealing with, who wouldn't worry, my thought was, are you kidding, God. But I didn't want to ask God if he was kidding, it's not nice to do that. Lol!

I then heard him say, "When you feel those burdens, pray and let go, give them to me, let me carry them for you. Worry is exhausting you, pray and let go." While I was listening to his voice, I was aware of how light I was, and I realized I was so light because the burdens I had been carrying were lifted while I was there. I didn't realize how weighted down with worry I had become. Life can do that to us. But it doesn't have to. There is a place we can go to experience a peace that passes all understanding, and I would continue throughout my life this practice of letting go of the things that concerned me the most.

The next thing I knew, I was in the recovery room and not liking the pain I was in after the surgery. I remember being so uncomfortable and trying to understand where the heck I just was, was it a dream or someplace else I had gone, and I was cold and in pain. I was like a baby coming out of the womb for the first time, trying to adjust to a new environment, as if I was feeling cold and pain for the first time. It gave me a sense of what a newborn must feel like. But this vison I had, or whatever it was, changed the way I thought. It caused me to pray instead of worry and let go and let God instead of trying to control situations and fearing their outcome. I had no control. To rest before running, to trust instead of trying so hard. And what I learned has brought me a peace and assurance, for such a time as this, that I cannot explain in human terms.

But I recovered from that surgery, still having a hard time healing. The incision wouldn't close on its own and had to be packed and cleaned as I recovered at home. Because I had limited medical insurance, I couldn't afford a visiting nurse at the time but needed one. But I prayed instead of worried, which wasn't easy; it involved sitting and meditating. But as I did this, it was as if God took care of it for me. I had prayed and let go, then to my surprise, a woman I knew from the church who happened to be a surgical nurse offered to come and pack it and clean it for me; she did this voluntarily and daily until the incision finally closed. She volunteered after I prayed. Coincidence? What do you think? I believe it was another provision where I was not by myself trying to figure it out. I believe it was just one of those times where God was letting me know he loved me enough to send me the help I needed. I learned through that experience that God would never take me to a place where he wouldn't provide for me. I was learning to trust that things would somehow work out and work out well according to his plan. He knew what I needed and he didn't disappoint.

After I healed up from that episode, another football size mass developed. It was unsettling and scary. But it seemed God was continuing to make himself known to me. *Was he testing me on this worry thing?* I wondered. The doctors didn't think I would make it, as doing another surgery, especially so soon, was not a good idea. It was dangerous and putting me at risk where I had such a hard time healing. I had a number of physicians working on my case and were all in agreement that this was life threatening again. Talk about feeling like a cat with nine lives. One of my doctors was a praying woman of faith, however, and she asked if she could pray for me. She did and then my prayer group prayed for me also. I prayed so often that I started to wonder if God was sick of hearing from me, but hey, He had told me not to worry. He was in for it with me. I learned and believe he never tires of hearing from us though. He loves it when we come to him, there's no such thing as praying too much. During this time, I was learning to talk to him like a friend. There were a lot of people praying for me, and I felt it was powerful and that I would be Okay. And I knew something was about to take place that could not be explained in the natural, once again.

Are Miracles Real, is God Real?

It was the day before they reluctantly scheduled another surgery for me. I went in to have an ultrasound to see how big the mass was and monitor the progress of it. At that point, I told the surgeon that I felt different, I didn't feel as sick, and I wasn't in as much pain abdominally where the mass was located. Upon examination, my abdomen was not as distended as it had been.

The surgeon's reply to me was, "Oh, you're just apprehensive about the surgery, and understandably so, you just don't want to have the operation. I understand, but let's see what the ultrasound shows once more because yesterday it was quite large. I want one more look before we go in again." Well, to make a long story short, the surgeon's mouth dropped when she compared the two ultrasounds just one day apart, where it went from a football size mass to the size of a walnut literally overnight. She kept shaking her head, showed it to my rheumatologist, who was the woman of faith, who had prayed for me, too.

The rheumatologist was amazed, and when she met with me, she said, "Can I show this to the other doctors as a testimony of a miracle? We have no explanation for this, except that you were prayed for. A football size mass just doesn't disappear overnight by itself," And of course, I said yes with a huge smile and sigh of relief because I had dodged another bullet. At that point, the surgery was cancelled, and I could not have been more relieved, and so were my family and friends when they heard this.

The long and short of it is, as time went on, while I was challenged with small abscesses forming occasionally, I never had to have another surgery. There is no other explanation; to me it was God allowing this situation that seemed so impossible to prove his love, not only to me, but to others as well. It wasn't man, it was a miraculous answer to prayer. I was quite encouraged to see that it caused others around me to have more faith for the things they were facing. It wasn't just about me. Knowing this, that the God of miracles is no respecter of persons (status), what he does for one, he will do for another. I know he's thinking of you, too. Nothing is impossible, nothing. But we do have to believe beyond what we see. I was living by faith, not by what I was seeing. Believing for things that are not, as though they are.

And this is the scripture that carried me through so many other tests and trials that would come my way. Joshua 1:5-9. 5: "No one will be able to stand up against you all the days of your life. As I was with Moses, so I will be with you, I will never leave you nor forsake you. Be strong and courageous, because you will lead these people to inherit the land I swore there for fathers to give them. Be strong and very courageous. Be careful to obey all the law my servant Moses gave you, do not turn from it to the right or to the left, that you may be successful wherever you go. Do not let this book of the law depart from your mouth, meditate on it day and night, so you may be careful to do every-thing written in it. Then you will be prosperous and successful. Have I not commanded you? Be strong and courageous. Do not be terrified, do not be discouraged, for the Lord your God will be with you wherever you go" (NIV).

My life was on the line so often, I learned to lean on God and the unseen, and on His every written word with the intent that I trust him and his plans for me. That I was not going to leave this earth one moment before it was my time. That his plans would be to prosper my life and not to harm it. To un-derstand his undying love for me, as if I were the only one. He wanted a bright future for me, and I knew it and I knew it well, in spite of all the health chal-lenges. No matter what things looked like, I could trust him to lead me down a path of hope and a future, leading me to help others in the process. I had the Catholic background that taught me much of this, but I was still learning and growing through this experience. I learned of Mother Teresa at an early age and emulated her teachings. She impressed me with her love for the poor and needy, the outcasts, the lowly. Her quotes about thinking of others, along with the Bible, were like a compass to help me along this journey I was on.

"Go out into the world today and love the people you meet. Let your presence light new light in the hearts of people."- Mother Teresa

Another Miracle from a Prayer Prayed Long Ago

During the course of my life, I have experienced many miraculous answers to prayer. Situations with results I could often not explain, I felt the Lord was revealing himself to me in ways only I could understand, he was meeting me where I was at.

This was a time of transition for me with significant things happening. It seemed I would ask and then receive the answer.

So, here we were, now three years in Florida, and our thoughts were turning to another move to help my health. The doctors felt the humid climate was compromising to me. They spoke to me about moving to a drier climate. So, my husband and I began to think about this, and we began to talk with other family members and friends about this with my mother at the forefront. Even though she liked visiting us and other family while in Florida, she just wanted us to come back to Boston. She was very worried about my health but often tried to hide it.

Here's an example of what I mean!

In the course of one of the surgeries, she visited me while I was in ICU. When she did, as I was coming out of surgery, I could hear her, and I felt her holding my hand and kissing it, but I couldn't respond. As I felt her holding my hand, I could hear her crying and saying, "My poor baby." She was so upset, I wanted to sit up and encourage her to tell her things would be okay, but I couldn't speak yet. Later, when I could respond and she came in on another visit, I asked her about this.

I said, "Mom, I heard you crying and saying, 'my poor baby.' I'm so sorry, are you Okay? I didn't mean to upset you."

And her answer was in her Russian/Yiddish twang, "I did not! I didn't do that." I was a little puzzled at her response, but I remembered she didn't like to show weakness and was not going to admit she was falling apart and so worried. She didn't realize I could hear her, and she was taken aback by this, and probably feeling exposed and a little embarrassed. It was true, she was busted, and I witnessed once again how sensitive she was. As I thought about it, this must have reminded her of the appendix episode and how she almost lost me once before. I'm certain it was so painful for her, and this was another reminder to her of what had happened and the long-term impact it had on me.

This was something I hated to see her carry, and for so long. She felt responsible for what had happened and how it affected my health long-term. I tried to tell her so many times it wasn't her fault, others did, too, but still, she carried guilt over this, she loved me that much. My father carried this burden as well. I wondered if they ever came to terms with the fact that they listened to the doctor and trusted he was right, what else could they have done, especially during an era where the doctor was always right and had a God mentality. People back then felt the doctors were kind of God-like and could never be wrong. A bit of arrogance that I think has been softened with doctors today.

So, anyway, I knew she was worried about Cy and Paul, too, and who would take care of them if I had passed.

So, I asked her again, "Mom, it's Okay to admit you were upset," and she said, "Cut it out, I didn't do that." She immediately changed the subject. "Let's see what's on TV. Did you hear how the weather is going to be?"

"I can guess," I said, "we do live in Florida. How about sunny with a little rain and humid?" No kidding. Talk about moving on quickly though. I guess I was alive and talking and that was good enough for her, she wasn't going there. What can I say? I loved my mother who didn't always make sense. So, moving on like she would, with my story.

Angela- A Prayer Answered

This was a significant answer to a prayer prayed long ago. It concerns my young friend, Angela from Canton.

After I recovered from my last episode, now it was our last few weeks in Florida, and one Sunday we were at church. Cy was serving as head usher and getting ready to close up the church. While he was doing this, I was sitting and waiting in the office, just reading an article in a magazine. The next thing I knew, a missionary walked in carrying books to place back in the church library, which was adjacent to the office where I was sitting. I had just met her briefly a few hours before through the prayer group I had been praying with.

She said, "Hello, how are you?" I greeted her back, we exchanged a few more words, and then I said, "Your accent sounds familiar, where are you from?"

She answered, "I'm from Canton, Massachusetts."

I perked up. "Oh, I lived in Canton once a long time ago with my family when I was around eight; it was only for a year, but I remember it." I then asked her name, as I didn't remember hearing it.

She said, "My name is Angela." While talking with me, she began packing papers for a project of some sort.

I then said, "Where in Canton did you live?"

She said, "I lived on Washington Street, my mother was a realtor back then, and we lived next to the cemetery."

Excited now, I said, "Wait, I lived on Washington Street also across from a cemetery and a realtor, Forte Real Estate, I believe it was." Now picture this, Washington Street was this very long road that extended between two towns with only one cemetery about in the middle. Interesting, ha!

She turned to me in amazement. "Iris, wait, it's you! We had no idea what happened to you."

At that point, my mouth dropped. "Angela, I can't believe this."

We spent the next few moments hugging and reminiscing, confirming. Here was my good friend who I thought I would never see again, 26 years and 1,500 miles later. I got to see her again. How can this happen? And not only her, but back when I was eight, I prayed and asked God to make it possible to see the people that had prayed for me to live through the appendix episode, as I wanted to thank them for praying me through such an ordeal. I was aware, even so young, that this was significant and caused me to explore who God was. Not only was Angela there, but also the prayer group I had been praying with over the last three years in that church in Florida was the same group of people that prayed for me to live 26 years earlier. A few days later, Angela brought me to them and reminded them of who I was, and they were amazed, they had remembered the incident and me as a little girl. Because my family had moved shortly after the episode, they didn't know if I had lived or not; we never connected again. Until now! But not only had they discovered I had lived, but I also became very close to God, which they had prayed for, too. Prayer is powerful, and I was just beginning to realize just how powerful it was.

God answers prayer is what I've discovered, but it's not always right away or in ways we expect. Incidents like these caused me to have an unusual understanding of who God is. One where I would walk very closely with him. Answers can take a while, as you can see, but they do come. He does it in his timing and his way for reasons we don't always understand. It's been my experience and it's biblical that he expects us to live by faith.

So, you tell me, was this coincidence that I happened to meet Angela in the office that day? Remember as a youngster, I had missed her for quite a while; she was a loyal friend I wanted to remain with. What impressed me, even at such a young age, was that for such a young person, she stuck by me and was very kind, and that's what I liked about her so much. She was someone who I could call friend and rely on. We all need them, and sometimes they are hard to find. It was because of this, I asked God to bring her and that prayer group back into my life, so I could thank them and let them know I was Okay.

Was it coincidence that the same group of prayer people that prayed so long ago in Canton, Massachusetts was now there and had been teaching me all about prayer and praying for me once again? No, I believe it was divine intervention because I had asked. And it happened in a way that it was once again clear that this was a miraculous answer to a prayer. It would be hard to convince me that it just happened. But what do you think? Do you think God is real? And what causes some to believe in him, and why don't some acknowledge him? It's complicated, I know. But I can't help but wonder if you were to ask him, what you may find?

A Prophetic Dream? Or Just a Dream After Eating Too Late!

Then another thing happened, about a week before I left for Colorado. It seemed my time in Florida was a time of awakening for me spiritually. Before I went to sleep, I prayed as I always did, and then as I slept, I had a significant dream.

As I drifted off into a deep sleep, I dreamed I was seeing New York. Okay, I'm from Boston and once lived in New York, not so unusual right? But in the dream, I saw very tall office buildings and other smaller ones. I saw planes flying overhead and even the colors on the planes as they were flying. Before I knew it, I observed them crashing into the buildings. I remember feeling a sense of alarm as to what was happening. I saw smoke and fire and people running and screaming. I saw people with severe burns on various parts of their bodies; it was such a detailed dream; I couldn't help wondering if it was really going to happen sometime in New York. Now this was about 1990 that I had this dream, around ten or 11 years before 9/11 happened. The dream was so startling and so real and so incredibly detailed that I woke up in a sweat, wondering how I could have had a dream like this that was so upsetting. I convinced myself it was just a dream and not real, and eventually I relaxed and went back to sleep.

But it was so incredibly detailed and visual that it prompted me to call my pastor the next day to ask him about it. I guess I was looking for comfort and perhaps some answers.

His response was not as encouraging as I had hoped. He said to me, "It was probably just a dream." So, I went on to try to dismiss it as just that. As time went on though, I would think of it from time to time. I wondered, did I really have the ability to see something happen in the future, and if so, why was I having this dream or vision? Why me? I tried to conclude that maybe it was the Lord prompting me to pray. But it was one of those things that happens that you just don't always have all the answers for. So, I prayed and tried to let go and let God be God and put New York's future in his hands. But it was hard, as I was concerned about a catastrophic event. The dream was so vivid, I couldn't help but wonder if I was seeing something before it happened. Did I? And for what purpose? By the time ten years had passed, and while it was in the back of my mind from time to time, I was able to put it to rest.

But just when I had put it to rest, many years later while living in Vermont, the attacks of 9/11/2001 occurred. I couldn't believe it and it was horrifying to me that I had seen this in detail in a dream so long ago. I again called my Pastor in Florida and asked him if he remembered me having this dream. Of course, he did, but he didn't say much about it, he just said he remembered, and of course, sounded a little taken aback. This was an event that was upsetting to everyone. I also asked a question, if I saw this in a dream and I prayed, then why did it happen to begin with? It was hard to justify so much suffering and needless death. Could it be it was because man has choices and God doesn't always interfere with those choices? Or was it because so much evil exists in this world and people make awful choices that affect the lives of others? I wondered was the dream even about 9/11, or was it as my Pastor said, "just a dream" and a coincidence. I just know what I saw in my sleep and the detail and correlation to 9/11 was astounding. Whether it even had anything to do with 9/11, who knows. But it sure seemed like it, the detail in the dream and what really happened was just too much to deny the similarities.

So what was the significance of this dream? I resigned myself to trusting that someone's life may have been spared or changed because I had a dream that prompted me to pray. In this and other circumstances, I have learned how powerful prayer is and that it does change things. I don't have all the answers, I can only trust. And when I don't know what to do, I pray and wait, and the answers always come. So, I'll ask you, was this just a dream ten years before 9/11, or was it a prophetic word prompting me to pray to prevent further destruction? This really bothered me, as it would anyone. Although I can't imagine it being much worse, could things actually have been worse, if I and others weren't praying? I had so many questions, all I knew was that there was a lot of suffering, and it was hard to take when 9/11 occurred. Many of you know the story and some of the miracles that took place. I believe they were a result of prayers prayed. You heard accounts of people that were supposed to work that day and couldn't go in for whatever reason and their life was spared. There were a lot of stories and a lot of miraculous things that took place. But I wondered about the people that either died or had lasting impairments. I had a hard time wrapping my mind around the ones that didn't make it.

Life is interesting, isn't it? And as I said, we may never know why things happen the way they do, all I know is when events like this happen, while prayer is good, helping those suffering is good, too. And maybe events like this cause us to be less self-reflective and more others oriented. For that we can be sure.

Colorado on the Horizon, Experiences Shape Us

So, I did eventually put the dream behind me as we moved on to Colorado. I was hoping the climate would help me, and in a way, it did for a while. I found though that the altitude with my breathing problems became an issue.

When considering such a long move, there are many important details to work out, not the least of which is money! I had asked our church and friends to pray that God would provide the funds necessary to make such a big move and that we could sell enough things to not only move but to support us until Cy started working. I was pretty sure we should go, but Cy wasn't quite there yet. One morning while lying on the couch, he was praying and asking God to show him in a way he would understand, that Cy would understand that moving to Colorado was something He really wanted us to do. That it was right for us.

About ten minutes later, the phone rang. I answered it, and it was my friend Yvonne. She was another one of those sweet friends who loved me dearly and hated to see me go.

She said, "You know, Iris, I've been praying, and I wondered, how much money are you short to go to Colorado?"

I said, "I'm not sure, let me ask Cy," which I did and replied, "he said we still need about $2,000 more."

To which Yvonne responded, "I can give that to you, I want to see you succeed."

Now that was certainly an answer to Cy's prayer in a way he could understand. While taking gifts like that was not something we wanted to do. I'm not sure how clearer the message we were to go could have been.

Yvonne continued, "I believe you are supposed to go, and I want you to get there safely." I have to tell you, I was amazed, and I cried that a friend could love me so much that she would just hand me that kind of money. But God had his ways, and they were different from mine. I felt we were always supposed to work and make our own way. In the midst of this, we were both also learning to let others help us, so we could help others, too. It was becoming clearer that God had plans for us in Colorado. Maybe there were relationships out there yet to be had. Maybe a need to meet, maybe some experiences yet to be experienced all in his plans for us. So, while I hated to take the money from her, I was also learning that when we deny someone else's help, it actually robs them of a blessing coming to them. So, with that in mind and a promise from her that she would visit, off we went.

In the back of my mind, I had another concern; it was for my son, because we were moving again. I hated uprooting him, and I know it was hard on him, but my doctors warned the Florida climate was really compromising my health in a serious way. While traveling could be fun and the adventure seemed exciting, Paul was on my mind. Before long I was comforted by his pediatrician's comment that "he was quite an adaptable young man" and knowing he was, brought me an assurance that he would be Okay. I also knew as he was growing, he would have his own journey of growth, and of course, as a mother, I wanted to shield him from harm as best I could. But given the circumstances, it was very difficult. During this whole process of transition, I was always praying and trying to make the right choices with him in mind. While he was a bit torn about leaving friends behind, I could also see an excitement in him about a new adventure, especially to out west.

And our family would often visit us out there. He had his cousins on Cy's side of the family he was close with. No matter where we went, they always took the time to come see us. My niece Emily, Cy's sister Vonnie's daughter, carries on that tradition today from Boston to Washington where we now live. I so, appreciate her. My nephews, Christopher and Bryan, Alan's sons and their wives do the same. This is a blessing with the next generation, which I'm enjoying. My point being, Paul was never alone either, as his cousin Emily is more like a sister to him.

Me and My Niece Emily at my home In Washington State. She was visiting us at Thanksgiving with her husband. Circa 2017.

On Our Way to Colorado

When we got to Colorado, it was an interesting time. It seemed God had us on a three-year adventure in each place we lived, and Colorado was no different.

I always stayed in touch with Mother during our journey, and her response was always the same, "Maybe you should come back home near family, I miss you and Paul and Cy." It was a thought I had in the back of mind for quite a while after we spoke, as I really missed her and the familiarity of New England where I was raised, and all my friends, too. But when you are young like that, traveling, whether you're sick or not, is quite appealing. The new adventures were fun and enticing, and my hope was always that a new climate would bring hope of feeling better. So, my mother resigned herself to the fact that she liked the idea of seeing another new place, and she would come out to see us from time to time. Colorado had such beauty with the gorgeous mountains and the western style of culture. It was quite transient and hard to settle into, but it was fun seeing the sights and new surroundings.

We drove towing a camper, and as we climbed such a steep mountain up to Glenwood Springs. We had to unload the car we were also towing, as it was too heavy to tow up such a steep mountain. I had to drive separately up the mountain, and while it was overwhelming, it was exciting too. As I drove, I was alone in the car with just Paul's hamster, Porkchop. He was in a cage in the passenger's seat, propped up where he could see what I was seeing. Paul and Cy were in the truck pulling the camper in front of me. Meanwhile, I was looking at the incredible beauty of the very large mountains, I was in awe at what I was seeing. And we had no cell phones back then, so the only one I could talk to about what I was seeing was Porkchop.

I kept saying, "Look, Porkchop, have you ever seen anything so beautiful." I swear that hamster was just as impressed. I could almost hear him saying, "If you think those mountains look big to you, imagine how I feel?" Hey, I had no one to talk to, and I did have a good imagination.

Another thing that was going on was my brother Lance in transition. Upon hearing of our exodus to Colorado, he decided he would move from Boston to Colorado Springs to be near us. A new adventure was exciting to him also, and we were close, so we wanted to be together. While in Colorado, so much took place, some of it with spiritual overtones we had never seen before and some major blessings I didn't expect that would have lasting positive consequences.

A Cute Story

Sometimes I think God has a sense of humor. Heck, he allowed me to be raised with very funny parents and *The Three Stooges*. I think that was his plan, too. He knew I'd need an imagination and humor to boot.

So, my brother Lance arrived shortly after I came. We spent time together, meeting for breakfast and touring the Colorado sights We were enjoying our time together but were finding it hard at times, due to such a different transitional culture. This was very different from Boston; we weren't feeling like it was home. We were from the east coast, and it was not always what we expected. But we had each other and our humor in those hard places we found ourselves. I thank God every day for the humor my family often brought especially during hard times. Lance and I had heard of all kinds of ghost and spiritual activity in Colorado. And we were about to witness something Lance and I didn't expect.

This photo was taken in our first home together in Washington State. This is the home we shared with our son Paul. Brother Lance came for a visit, and we had some nice bonding time, and made new memories together. Circa 2015.

While visiting him in his apartment one evening with a friend of mine, Paul and Cy back home, something happened we didn't expect. The trip was only a half an hour drive. So, Lance said something to me that was out of the ordinary. Since he was following the Jewish faith for a while back then, like my mother, he was still trying to figure out his spiritual calling. He knew I was a Christian and prayed about most things. So, he felt I could pray for what he was about to tell me.

He started by saying, "Iris, there's been some weird things taking place in this apartment."

"What do you mean?" I asked.

"Well, do you know those Russian dolls I bought a while ago that are on my bathroom medicine chest?"

I nodded. "Yes."

"Well, this is going to sound really weird, but each night, I see that they are all facing forward in a nice neat row, and the next morning, I wake up and they have all been turned toward the window, as if they decided they liked the view better."

I laughed. "Really, you're kidding, right?"

He shook his head. "No, really, I'm being serious, and no earthquake would cause them to move every single night so neatly in a row like that; can you pray over them, so they'll stop moving and changing positions?"

"Yes, I guess so," I said, "I've never done this before, but sure, if you think it will help." I wondered about this, I wanted to believe Lance, as he never lied to me before, but I still couldn't believe this. My thoughts turned back toward the exorcist movie from the 1970s. Could this stuff be real, is there really a dark side to our existence? What I don't understand, I was taught to pray about, so, I did.

My friend, rolling her eyes, wondering what was next, said, "Don't forget to pray in Jesus' name." And I did just that. This was an example of my brother and I sticking together, a little out of the ordinary, but nevertheless sticking together. I love both my brothers, they are definitely unique.

A short time later, I left, and just as I got home, the phone rang, it was Lance.

In a horrified voice, he said, "Iris, the darn dolls have not only moved again, but their facial expressions look pissed and things are beginning to move around the room, and my cat is horrified. I think you made them mad, what do I do?"

I laughed, only half believing what he was saying. "Just do as I did, pray in Jesus' name and it will stop."

His response to me was very funny. "I can't, Mummy won't let me, I'm Jewish." He was quite dedicated to my mother to say the least. Like she could hear him, oh the guilt!

So, I said, "Listen, you have three choices then, live with the Russian dolls and their antics, or pray over them, or you could throw them in the dumpster, you know."

His reply: "I can't, the Jewish guilt."

All of a sudden, I had this vision of the cowardly lion on *The Wizard of Oz*, and Lance being that cowardly lion, so I laughed. "Hey, show them who's king of the forest, knock 'em from top to bottomus."

He said, "Iris, stop joking, this isn't funny."

"Then throw them out in the dumpster tomorrow and that should end it."

So, he did, and when all was said and done, my very brave younger brother soon after moved from that apartment. I thought that was a good choice.

And my mother's response after hearing of this, "The two of you are *mashuganas*, I raised two *mashuganas*." In Russian Yiddish it meant, "Two crazy people. Where did I go wrong, what are you two doing out there?"

Soon after that she, Alan, Bunny and Chris and little Bryan came out for a visit. I think they thought Lance and I couldn't be trusted on our own. But we weren't alone! And my husband Cy, well, sometimes he would just shake his head at us and laugh, no kidding, right? I think he had his own thoughts, but I didn't always ask, as I was rather afraid of his response. I often wondered if he thought we were *mashuganas*, too. But he loved our humor and he loved us. There was never a dull moment in our family, and Cy loved it since his family tended to be more serious. I think his English background accounted for this.

We had some good times while my mother visited us in Colorado. She could be such a delight and so much fun, and her humor was incredible, especially when she didn't mean to be. She came to have a nice visit with her daughter, grandson, her son-in-law, and son Lance, whom she missed very much. On occasion, however, she was reminded through our actions and reactions that Lance and I were still young. We were still learning and growing up as they say, so in her visits with us, the term "mashugana" would occasionally echo in the background under my mother's breath. So, what can I say, we were still growing up, we had plenty of antics while she was with us, but they were great times. I cherished the times she visited us out there, and when Alan and Bunny would come, it made it all the richer. I loved having them visit us.

During our time living in Colorado, Lance and I had both interesting and strange times, but no matter how tough things became, we always had each other and humor to fall back on. In the midst of so much, Lance was observing me without me even realizing it. I was just being myself. A woman who depended on God for my every breath. I had a chronic and ongoing condition that caused me a lot of suffering, and he watched how joyful and peaceful I could be, and often wondered why. Maybe it was Curly Jo, Larry or Moe's fault. But as the Bible says, I led Lance gently, he was my younger brother and I wanted the best for him. My reactions to tough situations spoke volumes to him. He felt safe enough and secure enough with me that he opened up and shared his deepest struggles, and this in turn blessed me. In Colorado, he and I had special times with just the two of us, sharing and reflecting.

He once said to me, "I am in awe at how you would quickly resort to prayer instead of worry, where did you learn to let go like that?"

I answered, "When you are as weak as I can be and have a body that doesn't serve you well, where else can you go? It is God's strength that keeps me from day to day, sometimes hour to hour. Looking at the glass full instead of empty helps, and also looking to what I have and not what I don't have helps, too." Lance was like a sponge soaking up my every word, he was so teachable, I love that about him.

Back then there was so much talk about, how long I would live, but I knew I wouldn't leave this earth one moment before God himself said it was time. I was just being myself with my brother, all the while not realizing my life experiences, my daily walk, was having an impression on him. He was intrigued by this. Not because of what I was saying necessarily but by my actions and reactions to my circumstances, that I was like a book he was reading. And he was like a sponge searching for answers himself. We shared a lot together, as he was having his own journey of discovering who he was and how God would fit into his life. He began to share with me of his struggle with being gay.

My answer to him was this, "You come to God just as you are, you don't have to be anything different, come as you are, and He will be the one who will work with you and show you the way." What else could I say, whether or not I agreed with him wasn't the issue. I was not to judge but to love him for who he was and walk with him in his difficult journey of finding who he is and where God fits in to his life. My words seemed to free him up, as he shared with me that so many others, people whom he called friends, were now ostracizing him and rejecting him. He told me that he was dating another man and wanted me to meet him. Without hesitation I agreed to and I welcomed him. Remember, when we were first coming to Colorado, I knew God had plans, I didn't know what they were, but could this be one of them?

When I met his friend, I remember him as being such a sweet, sincere young man in his early 20s. He was laden with terrible guilt, trying to understand why he felt the way he did. I don't recall his name now, but that's not important. When I met him, he shared with me that his parents were Christians, they had rejected him, and this was a struggle for him; he was in pain and I could see it. All I could do is tell him it would be all right and that God loves him for who he is, the way he is. I felt if he prayed, he would feel God's peace, and eventually his parents would come around.

"As I told Lance, and I'm telling you, God loves you for who you are, come just as you are, and God will help you." I told him that the God I know is a God of love, not judgement. I wanted so desperately to let him know that he would be Okay, and he seemed encouraged when I left.

Then just two days later, I got a call from Lance. "This is awful, I don't know what to do. I just found my friend on the floor of the garage; he had drunk some poison. He's gone, he committed suicide." Lance was in tears, and my heart sank when he said this to me. How sad that his friend would end his life because of the judgement and lack of understanding from others. He was struggling with who he was. I didn't understand because I saw him as such a sweet, gentle young man. This was who he was, it was all he had, how come it wasn't enough?

Days later, Lance told me the young man's parents had told him they were horrified at the thought that because he was gay, he wasn't in heaven. My first thought was, wait a minute, how do they know that? We don't know a man's heart; how do they know he didn't receive God's love at the last moment? God's word says, "I will never leave you nor forsake you." Their view of their son's destiny and a loving God didn't fit. I then felt led to write them a letter to encourage them, and it went like this:

> *Dear Mr. Mrs. So, and so,*
>
> *I am Lance's sister, and I had the delightful privilege of meeting your son. I want to tell you, I am so sorry for your loss, and I can't imagine how you feel. But I know this, if you were praying for him, I believe God did answer your prayer, and I believe because God loved him so much, he took him home, and I believe he's in the arms of the Lord now. No one knows a man's heart, but what I saw in him was so much love, that I think he went willingly into the arms of God. I hope this encourages you, and I'm praying for you, Remember, God is a God of Love and Mercy, not condemnation. He would not have left your son. With Great Sympathy. Lance's sister*
>
> *Iris.*

They wrote back, thanked me for my kind words, and said it brought them peace, that it was a perspective they hadn't considered. You see, our words can either wound or heal. Mathew 7:1: "Do not judge, or you, too, will be judged" (NIV). You don't know where someone else has been and the pain they have experienced, so isn't it easier to extend a hand of mercy rather than judgement? To offer grace rather than hate. It says in Proverbs 15:1 "A gentle answer turns away wrath, but a harsh word stirs up anger" (NIV).

I believe the Lord was prompting me to encourage them that day, to lighten their load, to give them a different perspective. They suffered a loss no one can understand, unless you've been there. I allowed God to use me to free them up, and it made all the difference to them. It helped Lance, too, and eventually he became a believer and he is allowing God to walk him through his journey, and he feels more at peace with himself as a result and has a confidence that he didn't have before. This was a sad moment Lance and I shared, but it caused us to cling to each other with God at the center, and knowing we were not alone made all the difference. So, what does a miracle look like? This time in the form of a man who was lost, but through tragic circumstances, was later found. I went on faith on this one, and I know my God would not have left this young man, no matter what his struggle was. I believe in his last moments he cried out to God and God answered him. We are never alone! God's amazing Grace.

While Still in Colorado

As time went on, and I was finding my way there, I had my sister-in-law's aunt Diana with me; she was such a blessing. I also began attending a church where I was making new acquaintances. The trend continued that no matter where I lived, I always found true loyal friends. I had learned that it doesn't just come to any of us. I had to first be a friend and then receive friendships as a result. It was priceless to say the least.

While I had many acquaintances, through a Bible study I attended, I met two friends who would remain with me to this day. Tammy and Brenda really stood out to me. They came along side me originally when I was going through a lot of health struggles in Colorado. While I was comforting Lance, I was being comforted. It seemed to circle back to me and always in a big way. It seemed I gave, and I got. Not that I did it for that reason. I simply loved and it came back to me. You spread hate or bitterness and that comes back to you as well. Some call it Karma, I call it wisdom and right choices. The three of us, Tammy, Brenda, and I, were inseparable. We did lots of things together, and we enjoyed a bonding experience that most long for. When I was sick, they were always there. During the holidays, when we were so far away from family, they always made sure we were included. They were just that loyal, and I love them dearly.

When I eventually moved from Colorado back to Massachusetts, and Brenda back near family in Missouri, leaving behind Tammy, the three of us vowed to remain close and stay in touch, and we have till this day. On occasion one of us would visit the other, and sometimes the three of us would meet, but we vowed to be there for each other, so we were never alone. Loyal friends, anytime I need them, or they need me, are always just a phone call away. I have learned that having friends to talk with saves an astronomical amount of money on counseling bills. Just having a listening ear can bring a comfort and perspective you can't put a price on. The comfort and security of a friend's presence helps so much. True friendship takes time and cultivation, and the rewards are endless. I love my friends, and they love me, what a comfort to know that I have been given such a rich blessing that no material item could ever replace.

During our last few months in Colorado, my mother came for another visit. She finally convinced me to come back to Boston. While Colorado was nice, it just wasn't home to us. She stayed with us for about two weeks. One afternoon, she asked me if we could go sight-seeing, if I felt up to it after Paul got out of school. It happened to be on an afternoon where he had a detention for bad behavior. Since detention was becoming a habit with him, my mother was getting tired of hearing that he was ending up there. She loved him so much and wanted the best for him, and this behavior was not acceptable. I was comforted by her presence during this and felt very supported by her. And it was her longing for her grandson that convinced us to go back to Boston. Family is another blessing, and especially important to children, so Paul was our priority.

My Mother with her Grandson Paul, she loved spending time with him. She loved all of her family. Circa 1998.

So that afternoon, it was time to pick Paul up from detention and then go to dinner, at least we had hoped. My mother was determined to put her foot down. When she did, I would often duck. So before heading out for sight-seeing and dinner, we stopped to get Paul at school in the detention hall.

We pulled up to the school, and my mother said, "You wait here, I'll go get him."

I said, "Okay, but don't you want me to go with you?"

She shook her head, a determined look on her face. "No, I'll cure him of this detention thing."

I cringed. Oh-oh, what is she going to do to Paul? I was concerned but wanted to honor her wishes; besides, I was ducking and feeling compliant at that moment. As I waited in the car, I sat there wondering, what in the heck was taking so long? What was she doing? What was Paul doing? My mind was really spinning since it had been 45 minutes. At that point, I'm picturing the bazaar incident during my youth and what she did to the woman who took her spot, which to this day, I still wonder what happened there, but wait, no, surely she wouldn't embarrass her grandson? Or would she?

At that point, I said to myself, *"I'm going in, I'm not 14, and this is my son, I can't take it anymore."* I was concerned about Paul, and especially my mother at that point. I knew my mother well and knew she wasn't afraid of anything. And needless to say, this concerned me. A flash went through my mind, a frightening thought, I was once again picturing the police! With her behavior, could she end up in detention, too? So, into the school I went, down the hall to the detention classroom, and what did I find? As I peered through the window of the classroom door, I thought, oh, no, say it isn't true. There was my mother, pointing her finger at Paul and literally blasting him on his behavior in front of at least 20 other students, lecturing him on why he shouldn't be misbehaving in school, and what kind of future would he have, and to boot, how she would fix him if he didn't straighten out. I was now picturing *The Wizard of Oz* again, you know, the movie where the wicked witch of the west said, "I'll get you, my pretty, and your little dog, too."

She was such a strong presence that the other students were shuddering in their seats, probably thinking she was a truant officer and that they were next. But when they realized it was his grandmother, I observed pats on the back with expressions of sympathy toward Paul. I heard comments like, "Oh-oh, Paul," and "Poor Paul," and he looked quite defeated, not to mention embarrassed. The result: Paul didn't get another detention again in Colorado ever. Knowing his grandmother my mother wasn't far behind was incentive enough to toe the line. The embarrassment alone was enough to fix his behavior. My mother could threaten a hurricane and it would reverse direction. She was amazing and took no prisoners, but she was the best, and with her in our lives, we were certainly not alone. Poor Paul, but he did learn. I just can't wait for his wife to read this, as she will learn how to deal with him in a Russian way should he get out of line. Now I'm wondering if he's reading this, now at 37. Like his grandmother, he may be putting me in my place in my old age. Could it be, because I see a bit of my mother in him. Awe Oh! Stay tuned!

A Visit to Aspen with My Mother

Then there was the time Cy and I took my mother to Aspen, Colorado to sight-see. Paul stayed with friends for obvious reasons. The trip was interesting, as she was now in her 60s, coming from sea level in Boston to 11,000 feet or so in the Colorado Rockies.

As we headed to Aspen, my mother mentioned she was dizzy and lightheaded due to the high altitude. So, I encouraged her to drink a lot of water, which resulted in a lot of stops, if you know what I mean, but at least it helped her dizziness. She also noticed a difference in her breathing. It was during this trip I found my mother had some noticeable weaknesses, ones she found difficult to hide. Aha! My mother was human after all. First, we were driving around some very high cliffs with no railings at 11,000 to 12,000 feet, where you could clearly see how high up we were. Right smack on the edge with the car.

Gazing at the Colorado beauty, I turned to her in the back seat and said, "Hey, Mom, look at the beautiful scenery, can you see how high up we are?" I think that was the wrong thing to say because clearly, she could. At first glance into the back seat, I couldn't see her. Did she jump out? Where the heck was my mother? I turned to look further, and what did I see, my mother was not on the seat at all. In fact, I had to look down, as she was on the floor, saying, "That's nice, Iris, but are we there yet, I can't take this." She was horrified at the height of the drive around the ledges. Cy laughed as he thought my mother was so funny. Needless to say, I discovered she had a fear of heights. When we eventually came down and arrived in Aspen, my mother sat back up in the seat, relieved and breathing, which I thought was a plus. Although still struggling with the altitude, she did her best to enjoy her time there. She thought it was such a beautiful place with the nice shops and all but couldn't wait to see Boston and sea level again. And she had no trouble telling me so, as she mentioned it numerous times.

"Are we going back yet, Iris?" was what I heard a lot.

Before leaving Aspen, we took her to one of the ghost towns, trying to show her things before she went back. So, thinking she would enjoy that, we parked and began walking toward the ghost town. As we did, I turned and observed my mother looking back and forth, once at the car and then where I was, numerous times. She was trying to decide what would be best, the car where it was safe with no height or stroll with us, dizzy as heck, through the ghost town. Do I need to say it, she chose the car! I actually never saw her move so fast. On the last day of her visit, back at our house, I went into the bedroom where she was supposedly sleeping, just checking on her, and what did I find? My mother with her head out the window, trying to breathe. My poor mother!

I asked her if she was okay, and she said, "What time is my flight tomorrow? I can't take this." And the next day back, she flew to Boston with bells on. As I thought back on this experience, I thought, if she could have flown without the plane, she would have. She later called me to tell me she arrived safely and wondered when I was leaving to come home. Lance eventually followed back, too. It was then my mother felt so much better. We were all at sea level again and together. She was happy!

Chapter 17

Back to Boston and Family

My mother holding me as a baby.

Again, while it was interesting in Colorado, it was very difficult to be without family. I was remembering what it was like with my mother when I was very young, and I knew we belonged together. There were so many events that required us to be around for not only ourselves, but also as our families were aging, they would need us, and it would be important for us to be nearby. We loved our family and friends and wanted to be there for sure. And Paul would do better with the help and support of family as he entered adolescence. I can't emphasize enough how important family and friends are, and how we were never intended to do it alone, especially with a teenager coming up. How dangerous it can be to isolate oneself and the hard consequences isolation can bring. It was always God and his provision, friends, and family that carried me through both rough times and good times as well. Let me elaborate.

Back in New England, around 1997 or 1998, Paul was now 15. My mother breathed a sigh of relief that she could be near us again. Lance was soon to follow, and she felt better about that, too, as all her family would be nearby. My sister and her children also had moved closer, so this was a chance to be there for each other. And I have to tell you, it felt good. During our first few months, since it was summertime and school was not in session, it gave us a chance to stay with my mother and find where we wanted to be. By the fall of that year, we settled on Cape Cod for a while.

There on the Cape, we attended a Baptist church with a family who really ministered to us and helped set us on a course of ministry ourselves. My pastor's wife and her mother were very instrumental in helping me find my way, both physically and spiritually. Her mother, Eunice, would become one of my greatest mentors. She had a condition like mine and knew just what to say to me when I was struggling physically. She helped me find purpose in my suffering, to find understanding that my suffering was not in vain. She helped me find my way in music and the gifts I had been given. It was her encouragement that led me to become a ministry associate with Joni and Friends, a ministry to the disabled, where she knew I would thrive and be instrumental in helping others struggling with disabilities. It seemed wherever I lived, I had the support I needed when I needed it. I would encounter mentors and friends that would help me to grow and find my true destiny. If it were not for those who went before me, teaching me and praying for me, showing me by living, I would have never learned how to do life, and do it well in the midst of so much limitation.

This photo was taken at one of the retreats held by Joni and friends in New Hampshire. Me, with Joni Eareckson-Tada. Circa 2006.

While on the Cape, however, we began sensing that this was not a permanent place for us. The school system wasn't the greatest, and we felt we needed better education for our son. Our concern was he was nearing high school age and wanted to be able to better prepare him for college. We began to explore Christian schools for him with solid curriculum. The closest one we could find at the time was a good one in Vermont. But it was four hours away. We thought of moving back to Boston where there was one, but the housing and tuition for a school for Paul was too much for us, so we looked toward Vermont. Initially, we started him there in their boarding program, where we would visit on the parent visitation days, which worked for a while, but we were missing him. We didn't want to miss out on time with him in his high school years, which would basically be his last years at home. So we relocated again, all the way to the Canadian border, to be near him, where he would eventually attend school in the day program.

Talk about culture shock. And climate shock. The winters were very cold up there, a lot of snow and sometimes reaching 30 below with the wind chill factor. Burr! It reminded me of a Dr. Zhivago movie in Russia. You think me being half Russian, the cold weather wouldn't bother me. Nope! The half Italian in me didn't like it. My body was then longing for southern Italy. But we were there and did okay. It was another new place to explore and visit. The culture was quite different and hard to adjust to at first, but over time, as we got involved in a church, it helped us to acclimate and make new friendships. It was here my spiritual life really began to be tested and where I felt I did a lot of growing as a person. Being so far away from Boston was challenging, but our son's education was important, and it caused a lot of positive changes for not only Paul but me and Cy as well.

We were up there eight years, and in that time, as with all the other places we'd lived, my health was challenged. It was also where I found an old-fashioned country doctor who provided a lot of answers that would change my health situation over time for the good. The other doctors I had seen knew there was an underlying cause for my very challenged health, but couldn't pinpoint the root cause, leaving me to believe all my troubles were caused from the burst appendix I had suffered. This made perfect sense and I'm sure much of it was. But from the moment I walked in his office, he knew what was wrong and he said so. While a number of doctors at that point felt I had M.S. in the early stages, he felt there was a rare condition mimicking it. And it looked like M.S., both symptomatically and on MRI's.

But he said after looking at my ethnic background, realizing I was half Italian, he said to me, "I know what's wrong with you, and I can prove it." So, he ran blood tests, did a spinal, and a whole range of tests.

And his conclusion was, "You have celiac disease." My first thought was, what's that? I had never heard of it. He explained, "It's when the body's immune system overreacts to gluten in food, the reaction damages the tiny, hairlike projections (villi lining in the gut). It's a hereditary autoimmune disease, where you can't ingest gluten." He went on to say, "The unfortunate thing though, is that it has gone undiagnosed so long, you have developed two other autoimmune diseases, Sjogren's disease, a rheumatoid disease that damages the eyes and effects the salivary glands in the mouth, causing major dental issues with dry mouth."

It made sense as my vision was already damaged from the scarring of the corneas. So, it was limited already. The second autoimmune disease he said I had developed was Hashimoto's disease, an autoimmune disease where your body attacks the thyroid, causing it to shrink. That disease alone has a whole host of symptoms involving your digestion, energy, weight, etc. In addition to that, he discovered I had a brain injury that probably had occurred during my lack of oxygen and coma incident when I was young. So, he was able to explain why I had been so sick, and unfortunately, I now had to find a way to balance the three diseases, along with the brain injury, to be able to live and function near normal. You see, all of this combined made it seem like I had M.S. It then made me wonder, how many people were getting misdiagnosed. Probably more than I realized.

With his help, I was able to get proper braces for my arm and leg, therapy again for balance issues and living with the brain injury. It would be long road for me to recover. I was in rough shape, and it was hard. I later learned that both autoimmune diseases are very common, and often occur with undiagnosed Celiac. Celiac disease does so much damage, and yet if caught early, does very little damage. But because I had had the appendix episode, which he said probably caused it to be so extreme, they didn't think to look at Celiac disease with me. He also said in two more months, if he had not found it, I would have died from all the abscesses and pancreatic problems I was having. In addition to that, I was beginning to suffer mini strokes. At that time, Celiac was thought to have been rare, today it's becoming a more common diagnosis. Back in the '60s when I had my appendix episode, they did know about Celiac disease. It was thought of more as a pediatric diagnosis, so as an adult they didn't look at that with me, until now.

My thoughts began to turn toward why God orchestrated all this. I mean, the timing of it all! I had a lot of questions in my mind. What were the odds that Paul would need to go to a good Christian school we could afford, the only choice being on the east coast and affordable for us? And what were the odds that it would be on the Canadian border of Vermont, where I just happened to find an old country doctor that would have all the answers I needed? How did he know about a disease that was considered rare back then? This was the late 1990s. What were the odds of me reaching this doctor just months before it would have been all over? I have discovered that God's timing is right on. He's never late, but he sure ain't early either. But because of prayer and God's timing, this man was used to save my life, once again. My body couldn't take much more, and neither could I at the time. I was tired of being so sick. No, it wasn't coincidence. I had people praying with me on the Canadian border for answers, and friends I had left in other places were praying, too. I want to emphasize again, if we hadn't sent Paul to that school, where by the way he excelled, I would not be here today. I felt that God used Paul and his education to bring us to a place where I could fulfill the destiny God had for me. Nothing is wasted. In everything there is a purpose, we just have to have the right perspective.

After all the diagnoses, this doctor also told me that it could take ten years for me to feel better and for my body to heal. And even then, with all the damage, my life would be very limited, and I would need constant monitoring and care.

He kept shaking his head and saying, "What a shame it took so long." But with diligence and prayer, it seems each year things get a little better. I'm able to exercise now, have dropped the braces, and I'm functioning almost near normal, although I still need a cane. My thoughts turned to "just in time to get old." Great! Have I gotten sick of all the monitoring and flare ups that would send me to the hospital? You bet!

I also was struggling with feeling like I had missed out on life until a woman at Paul's school said to me, "Have you ever considered that this was the way God made you, and this is who you are? Have you ever considered He could use all this to help others?" That one comment changed my whole perspective. She was right, who the heck else could I be? How the heck else could I be? And why couldn't I turn this around to help someone else? But there were times when I wanted to give up, but each time, God's grace would send me a new friend to hold me up. No matter where I lived, this provision was set before me. And not only that, it seemed he hand-picked the right husband for me, who loved me unconditionally. He has walked through this with me. And while he has had his challenges, too, and says he can't imagine life without me, we are a good fit for each other. Neither one of us was expected to do this life alone. God gave us each other.

I came to understand that God would never lead me to a place where he wouldn't provide for me and not without a purpose. He knew friendships and bonding were important to me and that I would need help in my weakened condition if I was going to fulfill the destiny, he had for me. After all, he had spared my life not once, but over and over again. I would have a flare up of something, my life would be on the line, people would pray, help, and support me, and I would recover. This theme became common place. It was God showing himself faithful as he would carry me through every day and every circumstance that were beyond my control. He didn't expect me in such a weakened state, to go it alone. That's what helped me to realize how compassionate God is.

There were times when I encountered Christians who were very human. People who were not perfect and had all kinds of baggage and wounds, hurts etc. who portrayed God to me as condemning and with an iron fist. Demanding I be healed, that I was sick because I had sinned. How incredibly ridiculous and mean, as if I had burst my own appendix. Oh, sure, a coma was an occupation and career I longed for. For goodness sake, things happen to all of us. That's not the God I know. He loves us all the way we are. There's no judgement, no expectation, he just wants all of us to come to him just as we are. He doesn't care where you've been or who you are or what you've done, as long as you love him. Your destiny with him will evolve the way it is supposed to as you follow him. It's not a person's job to tell you how to live, that's called dictatorship and not particularly uplifting or helpful to one's well-being, it wasn't to mine. As a human being, it's better to come alongside someone and let them be who they are. Love always wins! Compassion is always needed.

You can tell I've experienced some real winners in some of the churches I have attended, but as I asked, God always provided the loving real people I was proud to call godly, caring human beings to walk beside me. They loved me for who I was, those were the real representations of God I allowed to help me. They were all about love. The other ones were just people trying to find their way. It doesn't mean that's what a Christian is or looks like, and so many equate meanness with Christianity and don't want anything to do with it because of these misguided attitudes. As in every culture, you have your good ones and your bad ones. I had to learn this, so I wouldn't feel resentful and lose my zeal for loving God and worshipping as a Christian.

So, while in Vermont, He began to provide those loving people, those examples of kindness and love. There, I began finding my purpose. I began writing and producing music and became involved as a ministry associate of Joni and Friends, a worldwide ministry to disabled people. Here was where I found that my suffering could be used for good. Joni's life as a quadriplegic inspired me. She was wheelchair bound at 16, due to a diving accident. She wrote books I read, held retreats around the country I attended, she spoke at Billy Graham crusades, you name it. She was working and inspiring others in her weakness but not without help. She had lots of people come alongside her to make this possible. Her ministry was growing, and my life was becoming a leg of her ministry. While being associated with her, I attended retreats where I was able to host their talent nights during the weeklong retreat each year. I did this for about five years.

I found help in a friend who very graciously attended with me. I met her while attending church one Sunday; I happened to speak to her and her husband, and we agreed to get together later for coffee. At the same time, she did some shopping for me as it was hard for me, and Cy was working long hours. Well, it wasn't long before an incredible bond took place, and a friendship was born. She became interested in what I was doing and offered to help me. Gunilla became a friend who walked beside me in a way that most long for. She attended retreats with me and helped with the talent nights, along with my husband. Each year we would do this together. And did we have a ball! Gunilla was such a gift to me, not just because she helped me physically but also because she and I together laughed so much and so often. She made everything fun and hysterical. To this day, 25 years later, there is never a time when we talk that we don't laugh and laugh hard. Our personalities just seemed to mesh that way.

Gunilla and I at one of the Joni and friends retreats New Hampshire, circa 2006.

I'll give you an example:

Because there was not much known about Celiac disease when I was diagnosed, there wasn't much available in gluten-free products in the stores, and restaurants didn't have a clue. Not like today. It was hard. I had to cook a lot of my own food from scratch, and Gunilla, my friend Chris, and some others were so gracious to help with this. During the retreat, I had to have my own kitchen, so Gunilla and I stayed at a campground close by to the retreat in my camper instead of in one of the dorms. The whole week was amazing. Not only was being there and hosting the talent night and participating in the activities so much fun, I also can't remember laughing so hard with my friend.

At the beginning of the week, Cy set us up in the camper along a beach near where the retreat was held. He left us with a car to use and then went back home for the week because he had to work. So here we were, setting up, Cy had just left, and now what? Well, we had a day to adjust before the retreat started, so that's what we did. We soon realized that we had the beach to ourselves because of the time of year, it wasn't a busy time yet for beachgoers. At first, it seemed nice to have all the quiet and space to ourselves until night came. After the sun went down, we realized it was pitch black outside with no lighting at all. We were quite alone, plus there was no way to lock the camper door, which left us feeling a little vulnerable. A little? Yikes, thanks Cy, I guess you forgot that. Two women alone in the dark woods, I don't know why we were worried. We had a dog, but she was a service dog and quite friendly and mild, and if someone were to come in, she would have licked them to death, I just knew it. Or she would have rolled on her back for a belly rub.

The camper, being a fifth wheel, allowed me to have the bed in the upper loft. Gunilla had the kitchen table that converted into a bed. That right there made me laugh. I did offer to let her sleep in the upper bunk, but she insisted on taking the table since I was wheelchair-bound at the time, and she was concerned about my mobility. At that, my thoughts quickly turned to, oh, my gosh, what if someone comes in during the night, what would we do?

I voiced this to Gunilla, and she said, "Well, you don't have to worry; you're up there with a sliding door for privacy, I'm the one down here sprawled out on the kitchen table ready to be sacrificed. They'll just go right for me and never see you."

I said, "Oh, good," and laughed.

She giggled too. "All that's missing is the apple in my mouth, like a roasted pig waiting to be served." Needless to say, neither one of us slept well that night. But we woke up just the same without harm. No kidding, I am writing this, aren't I? Thank God!

So, the next morning, she went poking around to make breakfast for us, and when she looked in the refrigerator, she noticed about six half-eaten black bananas on the metal shelf. I was eating bananas due to their high potassium content, as mine was low. I have since learned to buy smaller bananas, so I don't end up wasting fruit like that.

Anyway, she said to me, "What's with the banana morg?"

I laughed again. "What do you mean?"

She pointed. "Look at this, there are six half-eaten black bananas that looked like they've died all in a row lined up, side by side, looking like corpses lined up in a morg on a metal rack. Are you saving them for a reason?"

I shrugged. "No, I just didn't want to waste them."

She made a wry face. "Sure, it makes a lot of sense to start a banana morg instead of eating the other half later or buying smaller bananas, so you eat the whole thing. What was I thinking?"

I laughed even harder but knew she was right, so I vowed to stop doing that. What was happening was I would eat a half a banana, forget I put the other half in there, and then felt guilty about throwing them away. After the banana episode, we went on to attend the retreat.

On our first day there, as we began to meet people, some had the impression she was my full-time care giver and upstairs maid, not realizing she was accompanying me just for the week as a friend. But I was saying nothing! Of course, I thought it was funny. I loved to poke fun, and she was such a good sport.

She later said, "Hey, Iris, do you suppose we could tell people I'm not the maid, but I'm actually married with another life?" I laughed again but gave her the impression I was going to continue to let people think that just to tease her. We would tease each other back and forth that way; it was all in fun, and we both got a kick out of it. We laughed together so much! We had such great times together in those five years doing the retreats together. Even after our time doing the retreats ended, our friendship grew and we loved to be together, it was so uplifting and entertaining for both of us.

Her humor reminds me so much of Jackie Gleason from the *Honeymooners*, the sitcom from the 1950s. She's amazing. I have often told her she missed her calling as a stand-up comedian. She didn't agree, as she told me her humor was more behind the scenes and spontaneous. She reminded me I had a brain injury and that her humor was just an illusion. She was again being funny. If you knew her as I did, you may find it hard to believe that others wouldn't think she was funny. My husband and others thought she was hilarious. She has always been so quick with the puns. It's no wonder I eventually healed with all those silly moments with such a loving friend. She made my illness so much more tolerable with the humor and all the fun. What a friend. But that was just one example of our times together, I could tell you more, but Gunilla thinks we'd be the only ones thinking it's funny. You know, the "you'd have to be there" kind of thing. Maybe I need to send a video of her in to *Jimmy Fallon*, he'll tell her.

Moving On

Shortly after the retreats, Gunilla moved to New Hampshire from Vermont, and Paul by then had entered his first year of college in Florida. At this point, Cy and I felt our time so far away from our parents and other family had been long enough. I agreed, there wasn't much keeping us up there since Paul was going to aerospace engineering school. Again, I would be leaving to head back closer to Boston, my home that I loved so much as a child and teen. Once again, I would leave behind a lot of other friends I had bonded so closely with in Vermont. It was tough to leave them, but till this day, I'm still in touch with the ones I was close to.

Right to left: Gunilla, me and Mom in our home in New Hampshire, Gunilla loved my mother, and would visit her often. Circa 2006.

Cy, however, still didn't want to be in the city, so we came up with a compromise, settling in New Hampshire, just two hours from Boston. In New Hampshire, we would be near his family and mine, and he would be more rural as he liked so much. So even though we didn't plan it, Gunilla and I ended up living close to each other again, quite rural in the woods with plenty of snow in the winter. In fact, there was one winter when we had a huge snowstorm, and the electricity was out for four days. We were living like pioneers, and I got such a kick out of Gunilla living 1800s style. Still in her nightgown, and without makeup, she told me she was trying to catch water dripping from her roof, so she would have water to flush the toilets in her large home. Picture this, my Swedish-descent friend, in her 60s by then, resembling Shelley Winters the actress, living like the old west. She said because there was no electricity, she couldn't get her hair done or put make up on; I have to admit, this was hard for any woman. While I was on the phone with her, a knock came on her door. It was a neighbor wondering if everything was okay and d if she needed anything. I heard her neighbor say, "Oh, Gunilla, you look tired."

With that, Gunilla said, "I'm okay, we don't need anything," and slammed the door, a little insulted, and came back to the phone. "That's it, I'm tired of living in the 1800s; when the electricity comes back on, off to the hairdresser I go. I hate looking like Ma Barker."

And guess what I did, you guessed it, I laughed. I had never experienced anything so funny. And her reactions to situations were priceless with the humor. Gunilla, to this day, still visits where I live here in Washington State, and it's great, no matter what we are doing or how many others are around, we laugh and enjoy our friendship.

As Jackie Gleason would have said, "Baby, you're the greatest." Although in Gunilla's case, I would say, "Friend, you're the greatest." Although, It's hard to call your now 74-year-old friend "baby." I'm still laughing!

So, living in New Hampshire also had some great benefits. It was a beautiful state with beautiful mountains, and it wasn't hard to visit with my mother, who was aging and needier. Also, during this time, I began writing newsletters with Joni and Friends, encouraging people who were going through hard times. I did this with my friend Tammy from Colorado, whom I have also stayed in touch and visited with when we can. Tammy and I share everything together, and she is such a blessing. Our friendship, while it also had its funny moments, was a bit more serious, and we were able to articulate this in the newsletters we co-wrote.

During this time in New Hampshire I also began singing more in churches with gospel music. I had started somewhat in Vermont but began to excel more in it while in New Hampshire. While there, I also sang and wrote songs, producing my first CD. That was fun, I had a band that helped me, and my music skills were really coming along. Because I had majored in music in a tutorial program, I also was teaching guitar and voice. I played drums for a while, too, which I loved. The drums were an integral part of helping my coordination issues.

My mother was proud of this, but when she heard my finished CD for the first time, she said, "This is so good, I'm so proud of you, look how well you've done, this is great, but did you have to mention Jesus so much?"

I guess she missed the point that it was gospel music. In gospel music, you do tend to mention Jesus on occasion. I was doing concerts, and while it wasn't easy for me physically, I always had the help I needed; it seemed people came along at the right time. I even had an agent that wanted to send me to Branson, Missouri to showcase my music, talent, and songwriting abilities. I was about to do it, but I wasn't up to it. I was just not strong enough to keep up with the activity of a busy life on the road. Cy would have done it with me, but it was just too much. So, feeling very disappointed, I bowed out reluctantly, realizing this was not the plan God had for me. Otherwise, things might have been different. I really felt he was using my weakness to redirect me to my real purpose and destiny, which was encouraging and loving people whom I would encounter. I loved doing that more than anything, and it came easily to me. Having so many physical challenges of my own helped me to understand others in their struggles. There's nothing like seeing someone's face light up as you take time with them and encourage them.

But during this time my brain injury began to re-surface, making it hard to function. I was losing some of my memories, there was talk of another possible mini stroke. I needed a leg brace again, I was off balance dealing with a foot drop, and my vision and speech were also affected. I was dealing with a lot. Having numerous health challenges, was tough and frustrating. So, I paused to re-group, believing that through prayer, I could rise above this, too, as I had in the past. Doctors and therapists were quite supportive and recommended I exercise my body and my brain. They suggested taking up a language in addition to physical therapy. When I told them, I knew Italian from my grandmother and culture I lived in, they encouraged me to get back into that. While I knew I spoke Italian, I had forgotten a lot of it and had to re-learn some of it that I had learned as a child.

So, I contacted the local college, looking for a tutor; a classroom situation would have been too much to try to focus. Anyway, the college put me in touch with a teacher there who started me out with some books in northern Italian. But he later told me I would benefit from someone who was the real thing from Milan, Italy, given my background. Milan was where my father's family was from, and I found this interesting. He knew of a woman who was from Milan working at the college and felt she could help me. Was this another Co-incidence? If she had been from southern Italy, it would have been tough for me because the dialect is so different from north to south. In fact, when people in the different regions of Italy try to speak to each other, they often find it difficult to understand each other.

Anyway, I called her. Marta ended up tutoring me and helping me live the Italian ways once again, like I did when I was young. This was life-changing for me and so inspiring. Marta became a wonderful *amica* (friend), she was loyal and was there as much as she could be. She was an answer to prayer, and her influence set me on a course of my life being put back into perspective, bringing me back to a place that was familiar. She met with me each week, and she and her boyfriend, a cardiologist from Germany, included us in their social gatherings. It was so much fun, much like being in Europe, as most of her friends were from Germany and Italy. This was a gift that reminded me so much of being with family again. She and I, as I did with so many of my other friends, had some wonderful times together and laughter was also common in our meetings together.

Living in Washington state, I don't see her much anymore, but I will always miss her. I'll never forget how she made me feel when I was leaving to come to Washington. She treated me as family. She had tears in her eyes, and she made it clear we had bonded and that she would miss me. I owe her a lot, and I pray every day God blesses her for her kindness and hospitality. Marta had a special gift of compassion in sharing her culture and friendship with me while allowing me to heal. She extended to me her time and energy while bringing me back my roots. And in the process, she gave me the gift of friendship, which as I have said before, is priceless.

While living in New Hampshire, I had several other friends that were so good and kind. Ones I'll never forget. It seems I had such a gift in so many of them, it's difficult to mention them all. I'm reminded of this every Christmas as I watch the holiday movie I never grow tired of, *It's a Wonderful Life*, starring Jimmy Stewart. It was released originally on January 7th, 1947; it left me with a feeling that if you have friends, you are never poor and certainly not alone. His quote at the end of the movie, after a lot of struggle both financially and emotionally, went like this, as an inscription written in his Tom Sawyer book by given to him Clarence the angel, "No man is a failure who has friends." Frank Capra, after the wrap up of the film, was also quoted as saying to Jimmy Stewart, "No man is poor who has one friend, three friends and you're filthy rich."

I guess that's my story, I never had a lot of money, never had my health, but I'm filthy rich with relationships. And for that, I'm grateful and will always be. Two are better than one, for when one falls, the other one picks the other one up, and pity the man who is alone. Make it a point to reach out, you'll never regret it. I never have!

Chapter 18

Saying Goodbye to My Best Friend

Before I ever came to Washington state to live, I experienced the pain of losing two people so close to me that I didn't think I would recover. My family has and had always been everything to me. The two people I had known my entire life were aging and needing help. They had been my security, my go-to when life became difficult. Losing your parents to me is one of the hardest things to go through, aside from losing a child, which is even worse. I watched several friends I was close to go through that, and it takes your breath away.

While my parents were not perfect, there was no doubt in my mind I was loved by them, and they were always just a phone call away. The time they spent, the stories they told, the laughter we shared, lessons I learned from them were now about to become memories. My times with the two people who raised me were going to soon become distant memories in my mind, memories that would carry me through for the rest of my days. My mother and my father had to leave me because no one lives on this earth forever. I would learn that it was God himself who promised to be there and never leave me, and I would lean on him in a way I had not done before. Let me share how all that came about.

It was February of 2008, and my brothers and I got a call from our step-mother Pat regarding our father, who had been struggling with bone cancer for many years. The time of his passing was near, and it wouldn't be long. His cancer battle was almost over. I was in New Hampshire, Lance and Alan by this time were both living in California. So, we had to make a plan to get to see him for the last time together. Given my physical condition and geographical distance for all of us, it wouldn't be easy. But we all had each other, and together, we could do this. And Cy was always a tremendous support, so he would see to it I could get there. The plan was because our son Paul was living right near my father, we would stay with him, and Alan and Lance at a nearby hotel. Paul had a lot of opportunities to visit with my father while in college in Florida and was glad to have us stay with him. I was so happy my dad was down there while Paul was in college. It gave them a chance to visit more, and I had hoped it would create lasting memories for Paul of his grandfather. I felt better knowing family was nearby. My mother-in-law was also living there at the time, and that was good, too. He also visited her when he could. This was answer to prayer as I felt it was important for Paul to spend as much time as he could with his grandparents while they were still here. To bond with them, learn from them, and share some day with his children where they came from and who his ancestors were.

It wasn't long before this that Paul had graduated from Embry Riddle Aerospace Engineering School, and we were so proud of him. My dad lived long enough to his grandson graduate, which was a blessing to him, as he was proud of him. But now several months later, it was time. Time to say so long to the man who taught us how to laugh and play. But his laughter and humor would live on in us and with each other. And, boy, did it.

Anyway, we went down and spent a week together with our father. And it was amazing, my dad laughed often, and while he wasn't well, he was happy to spend time with us laughing and playing games. One of his favorites was the game Risk. That's how he wanted to spend his last days with his children, laughing, and playing together as we had done when we were young. Paul and Cy were there in the background experiencing this with us.

I love this photo of my Dad with Paul at his graduation from Embry Riddle College in Florida. It was nice, for a while they lived near each other, May 2009.

While there, my friend Yvonne, who had helped me get to Colorado, came to spend time with me. Gunilla and Chris called me often while I was away to see how things were going. My friend Debbie from childhood was living down there, and we met during this time, which helped to take my mind off the sadness I was feeling. Debbie spent time with me laughing, having fun, and taking pictures together for Facebook to show our friends. I felt anything but alone during this time. I had cultivated those friendships over the years, and my true friends were there when I needed them.

There is a scripture in the Bible that I have always taken to heart, Proverbs 18:24 (KJV), "A man that hath friends, must show himself friendly: and there is a friend that sticketh closer than a brother." Throughout my life, I showed myself friendly first, not expecting much. I shared with others and made myself available, and in turn they came along. Solid loyal friendships. I have experienced the most amazing friends. Friends I could count on, friends I can look forward to, friends that make a difference in the world around me, friends that know how to be themselves, friends that love unconditionally, giving of themselves. Friends like nothing in the world we have ever seen before, and I have them in my life. I am rich! And in the wake of my parents passing, I needed them, and they didn't disappoint.

Before my father passed, while the three of us went to see him, my mother remained at home because it was too difficult for her. Knowing the man she loved for so many years was passing away and leaving again, was just too much for her to take. So, we supported her from a distance. Our stepmother, his wife Pat, was an incredible support and took care of him. She was amazing, and I'll always be indebted to her for loving our father and caring for him during this very difficult time. Just two months later, April 25th of that year, he died. I spoke with him just days before, and his last words to me were, "I never found out who my real father was."

I said, "Dad if he's in heaven, you'll soon know." This was hard for me. And I felt I wanted to try to find out who his real father was. It wouldn't be until much later; my son Paul would begin the process to help me find him.

Anyway, the day he died, Pat said one of the last things he did was laugh, and he had all this joy and he called out for my brother Alan, his first-born son. It saddened me and Alan that Alan couldn't be there with him when he passed. It was difficult for all of us. But my dad was a strong Christian, and I know some day I'll see him again.

So, this was the beginning of a spiral downward of losing what we knew as our whole lives. On February 8th of 2011, my mother lost her sister Ruthie, and that was heartbreaking. Born on Saint Patrick's Day, March 17th, 1928, she died at 82. This woman never married and had no children of her own but loved us all unconditionally. In the midst of her own developmental disabilities, we knew we were loved by her. It was particularly heartbreaking for me because I was too ill to go to her funeral. To this day, I feel terrible that the travel was too much. In the interim, my brother Lance was able to step in where Alan and I couldn't and took care of everything with my mother, as I had done for her during my grandmother's passing. It seemed an era and a generation were gone, and a sadness overwhelmed me that I had never felt before. A void was created I didn't know how to fill. The people who loved me and were always there, one by one, going away.

One of the things that stood out most to me when Auntie Ruthie passed was that my brother Lance, just before her funeral, was able to pick up the mantle for our mother, open the casket to view her body one more time, to say goodbye. It was too difficult for our mother, so Lance, in his loving compassion, took that on. I can see him as it was described to me, viewing her body, gently lifting the casket cover and kissing her on the face, he said, "Goodbye, Auntie Ruthie, maybe in heaven together, one day we will have tea for two." And he said that because "Tea for Two" was her favorite song. This was a beautiful example of how close and caring we all were with one another. Lance stood in, and I'll never forget the example he set for all of us. It wasn't easy for him, but he carried us just the same and lifted the burden off of our mother.

Growing old is something I'm starting to experience now. Losing loved ones is one of life's most challenging seasons any of us will ever face. But we all face it, don't we? But if we have friends and family with God at the center during those times, it lightens the blow, giving us the strength to go on. Giving us meaning to such a hard season. Having others to cling to, gives us the strength and will to endure the painful loss. This is the only part I regret in knowing so many people. When you outlive them, it's so hard, and it perpetuates. In the natural course of life, first, it's the grandparents, then your parents, then it goes into extended family, then accidents or illness takes ones you didn't expect and then classmates and on and on. One by one, you say goodbye for one last time.

But for me, there is a scripture that brings me comfort, knowing this life is not the end but it's just the beginning. It says in John 3:16, (NIV), "For God so loved the world, that he gave his only begotten son, that whoever believes in him shall not perish, but have eternal life." I believe that life goes on from here, and of course, I believe that way is through Christ eternal. What do you believe? What brings you hope in times like this? I mean that as a sincere question because I like to hear other people's thoughts and understand where they are coming from. I don't claim to know everything, my life is based more on a sharing with others and not telling them what to do. I enjoy meeting people where they are, anything beyond that, as I have said, is pure dictatorship. I'd like to say, if it weren't for my faith in the eternal God, I would be in a constant state of grieving with all the people I've lost. The bonding and the close ties and then the permanent separation is just too much to bear without a savior to fill that void and bring a new perspective to life.

Since Auntie Ruthie's passing, I have heard of the passing of many classmates and other relatives. But the hardest one to wrap my mind around came next, my mother. Little by little, I watched her decline, especially after Auntie Ruthie's passing. I think she felt life was ending, and she was showing signs of dementia, which was heartbreaking to observe and try to navigate through. Our hard-working mother, who seemed to know no fear, who held our family together for so long, was now fading away herself. She would now need us. My mother came from a well-bonded class from high school that remained close until one by one they passed. During this time, I found solace and comfort in the support of a few of my mother's closest friends who knew her best after a lifetime of relationship with her.

In particular, I had gotten close to her friend Barbara from high school. In their later years, as two single women, they had done everything together. Barbara and my mother visited me in just about every place I lived, while they were able. I loved those times with them. In the process of spending time with them, I had the privilege of meeting and getting to know Barbara's daughter, Amy, and her husband, and because of our mothers, developed our own special bond.

Barbara became a great support and mentor to me during this time, where I would find myself trying to decide how to help my mother and where she would end up in assisted living. I also had the help and support of my aunts, Diane and Elaine, my friends Chris, Tammy, Brenda, Ursula, Gunilla, and on and on. I wasn't alone and found tremendous comfort in this. Alan, Lance and I found ourselves gradually figuring out what to do, as we worked together to find the right situation for her. They would come out from California occasionally to help while the rest of the time Cy and I and her friends and various relatives would visit her and help her. We saw to it she was cared for. This, until it became tough for my mother to live on her own, and it was time.

Through some friends, we found a beautiful assisted living home with just six residents in New Hampshire near where I lived. My brothers and I were in agreement that this would be the place for her. It was a beautiful cottage-type home nestled in the woods of with home cooked meals and activities with much one on one time. She had her own room, where we set up photos of family and we gave her a cell phone, so she could talk to her friends and other family members. She would be close enough to me geographically, so I could visit with her several times a week, and along with Cy, take her on outings. During her first weeks there, Alan and Lance came out and the four of us worked together to pack up her apartment where she had lived for 30 years. Aunt Elaine, Uncle Martin, and Cousin Elise came along with her friend Barbara to support us; we all cried, as it was again the end of an era. And being able to cling to each other and share the load, made it much more bearable.

We cleaned out her home, which took a week. One week was all Alan and Lance had, so we had to work diligently to dispose of things that were heartbreaking to let go of. But we couldn't keep everything, so we kept what we could, and the most important things were put in storage. Because my mother was still with us, we wanted to keep things for her, mementos that meant a lot to her. It was important for dignity's sake that she have her things nearby. We also kept her car for her, as she kept asking for it. I didn't have the heart to tell her she couldn't drive anymore; it would have been too shocking as that was her only form of independence she had left. So, we told her we were holding it for her. And it was true, my aunt Elaine kept an eye on it for us while we left it in the parking lot of her apartment building, where she and Auntie Elaine had lived in Boston.

So, my mother had, by this time, been a resident at the assisted living for about a month. She had a hard adjustment, mainly because it wasn't what she was used to. She was used to the city, but we needed to have her nearby and she liked being close to us. For that reason and easy access to her made it okay. Her friend Barbara and Auntie Elaine and several others talked of visiting her, and she looked forward to that. Unfortunately, they never had the chance. One Thursday she had visited the doctor and she wasn't feeling well at all. After she was home and settled in, I called her, and she said she was going to take a nap. This was about 3:00 pm on Thursday, May 31st.

Before her nap, I told her, "Mom, Cy will pick you up tomorrow to come here to our house to spend the day with us. We can have lunch and hang out, maybe watch a nice movie, whatever you want to do."

And she said, "Okay, that sounds good, I'm very tired, I'm going to take a nap. I'll call you when I get up."

"I love you," I said, and she answered, "I love you, too."

Just two hours later, I got a call from Lance. "Iris, are you sitting down?"

My heart sank because I knew. "Don't tell me, please, I know what you're going to say."

"Yes, it's Mummy. I got a call from the assisted living place. Mom died of a heart attack, she got up from her nap and just dropped. They were there very quickly to try to revive her, but to no avail, she's gone."

I had to hang up, it was too difficult. While I wasn't surprised, I was still shocked my mother, my lifelong loyal friend was now gone. What struck me most is I couldn't call her anymore. I know my siblings felt the same way. Later, what came to mind is that if this had happened just a day later, she would have been at my house with me. We would have been alone, and that's how I would have remembered her. God in his grace had shielded me from having a visual memory like that. And while I was grieving, I was aware it could have been so much worse, if I had seen her for the last time dropping that way. I could not have taken it.

Now came an even more difficult task, calling friends and relatives, and planning her funeral. There was a lot of sadness surrounding my mother's passing. It felt as if Moses had passed. What would life be without her? At her funeral, there were about 200 in attendance, it was said if more people had been alive from her school days and relatives hadn't died, it would have been twice the amount, if not more.

At her funeral, I recall being in a room together as a family. Just before it began, I turned to see where my husband was, and I saw Cy sitting in a corner crying because he was going to miss her so much. He loved my mother that much. He respected her and thought she was an amazing woman. In all the years we were married, they never had one argument. He couldn't do enough for her and vice versa. When we entered the funeral parlor, the plan was that each of us children, my sister included, would speak about our mother. When it came to my turn, I had such a difficult time, that my mother's friend Barbara stood with me as I spoke. I'll never forget the comfort I felt with Mom's friend from childhood standing with me to mourn her loss.

There were people from Revere and the old days; Foomie and Stacy were there; my friend Karen and her mother Carol from the old neighborhood in Sharon were there. We had plenty of support, her friends who were still alive from places we lived were there. I had several friends that came to support me. Lance, Alan, and my sister all had support from friends they grew up with. My son Paul and my sister's children Erin and Charly came. It was bittersweet, as funerals often are. But we were far from alone, and as hard as it was, we had each other, and it made all the difference. My thoughts turned toward the next generation as I watched Paul with his cousins.

Soon another heartbreak came when several weeks after my mother's funeral, her friend Barbara showed signs of declining. As I talked with her daughter Amy, she filled me in, and we would pray. But it wasn't long before Barbara passed. It was hard to believe the woman who stood with me at my mother's funeral was now gone, too. It didn't seem to end. What helped though was in the midst of all this, my son was asking me about where I wanted to be on a more permanent basis. He knew I was hurting and missing family, and he felt he was settled in Washington state with a permanent job, working with Boeing in Seattle. He wondered if we would consider moving out there to be by him. It had been ten years since living near him, and that sounded so nice. I wanted to; we missed living near our son. He shared with me that he had a new girl he was dating. And of course, we wanted to meet her, too. This was a new person to look forward to and it shifted my focus. Since Alan and Lance and nephews Bryan and Chris, also lived out that way, it seemed very enticing.

Paul said, "I can't help you if you live so far away, and really, what is keeping you in Boston anymore? I would love it if you and Dad could be near me again, and I want you to meet Samantha." After talking with him, I sensed he was right, and I was excited at the thought of living near him. Cy was, too. After speaking with several aunts and friends, and having much prayer support, we decided to put our home up for sale and head that way. Paul was very excited when we finally made the decision, which took some time. Another new adventure, only this time, I knew the move would be permanent, so this had to be prayed over and thought through. We sold all our belongings, packed up a brand-new camper and truck, and our dog Abbi and moved to the west coast, a place I'd never seen before.

But just before we did, we met with some friends and relatives. And one of those friends was my first best friend from Revere, Andrea Pivnick, now Andrea Pivnick Malcom. We had an awesome last good-bye with her and my brother Lance's friend, Jennifer. The four of us met at a restaurant that happened to do gluten-free food. During this time, restaurants were just starting to understand the concept of gluten-free. This was in May around our anniversary, and we spent it in Salem, Massachusetts on the ocean. It was lovely. While there, we were able to meet Andrea one last time. I have to tell you, it was special, and I'll always remember that visit.

Several months later, we headed west, and we experienced a great trip, pleasant with good weather. Very uneventful in terms of problems. We took out time and vacationed. We saw sights, like Yellowstone Park and places we had not seen before. It was summertime and the weather was just perfect. We stopped in Colorado and stayed at my friend Tammy's home for about a week, and we had a great time together. My time with Tammy was particularly special as we'd shared so much together. I saw my friend, Aunt Diana, and it was a good old-fashioned vacation. Alan and Lance were excited because I'd be closer. When it was time to leave Tammy's, it was bittersweet, too. Although we knew it could be quite a while before we might see each other again, we knew we could still talk to each other and pray for one another, and we do and it's very special. Tammy and our mutual friend Brenda have become like sisters to me and I to them.

Along the trip, I had connected with several pastors I knew through other mutual friends who were ready to help when we arrived. One of them connected me by phone to my first friend in Washington state who prayed me through the whole trip. Virtually every friend I met throughout the course of my life always had a special place in my heart. Each one came with their own special uniqueness.

Moving to Washington was a whole new adventure, a whole new life experience. We were making a new start, but my son and his girlfriend Samantha would be instrumental in helping us acclimate. What an impression she made on us. Could this be the girl we had prayed for our son? We would find out as we got to know her. My first meeting with Sam was over the phone when Paul had to have jaw surgery months before we would come out. And she was amazing. She would call me and give me updates on how he was doing, and she was there for him and cared about us, too. I enjoyed getting to know her. I could tell she had come from a nice family because she had integrity and thought of others. She was and still is full of joy and enthusiasm. I found her inspiring and fun to be around. Was this the beginning of a new start with family? I would soon find out! I had prayed for a good wife for my son and it seemed there she was.

For the first year and a half, we lived in a large home that we rented with Paul. Soon we were able to meet Sam's mother Cindy, and things were beginning to feel a little like home. I liked her mother very much; she was my age and we had a lot in common.

Before long I began to explore churches in the area. I called my friend Ursula from New Hampshire to pray with me about this, so we did. After we prayed, we headed to a nearby vegetable stand, not far from where we lived. It was a weekday afternoon and a beautiful sunny day. On our way back from the stand, heading back to the house, we stopped at a building that had a large field to walk our dog Abbi. The building looked commercial, but there were no cars and no activity at all. And yet something seemed strangely familiar about it, but there was no sign to tell us what kind of a building it was. We finished walking the dog, headed back toward the house, and something told me to go back there. I wasn't quite sure why, but we did. I got out of the car, walked the dog around a bit, and stood for a moment, pondering why I was there. What had drawn me there? I was about to find out. At that point, something told me to turn around, and I saw this small sign that said Assembly of God church. I couldn't believe it, as that was what my friend and I had prayed about and what I was looking for. And it seemed I was led right to it. That weekend we started attending this church. The message was good, we liked it. People were friendly, and I met two women, Wendy and Linda, the first day. They were lovely and welcoming and instrumental in helping me acclimate. They had no trouble welcoming us and making us feel at home. As time went on, we socialized with them and went on camping trips with them as couples. The three of us became instant buddies, and our husbands became friends, too.

Samantha with Paul, she is a delight. 2019.

I had also become friendly with another young woman I had met at a luncheon. She and I happened to sit together, and in talking, we both discovered we had Celiac disease. Rachel and I became friends and bonded quite closely, and here five years later; we are like family. This was a different friendship for me. She was my son's age, and I wondered what we may have in common in addition to the Celiac disease. I discovered we could pray for one another, and I taught her things I had learned in my life. I was feeling more like a mentor to her. It was nice, the tables were beginning to turn for me. I was now the older one supporting the younger one. No longer was I the younger being taught by the older women I knew. Since I had had so many mentors myself, this was a new opportunity to give back, and it felt good.

Our Dog Abbi.

This was a promise from the Bible, as I was losing the family I had always known, and had come 3,000 miles to a new area, I was discovering God still had family out there for me. Only this time, it would come not only in being related but also through some very solid friends. I was discovering that family didn't always mean blood relation. God was beginning to put a new family in place for me. It began with Paul and Sam. He was providing sisters and other family, so I didn't feel alone. He did say in his word he would never leave me. He was showing himself faithful by providing the desires of my heart. This was an answer to prayer of not being alone in a new place. Wendy, Linda, and I spent a lot of time at church functions and prayer group meetings, and we were really enjoying our time together. When suddenly things changed. I guess I was getting a little comfortable.

The church we were attending decided to divide up its campuses and the one I was attending would be closed for six months. At the same time, the other campus was too far away for us to attend on a regular basis. The three of us were in limbo, not really knowing what to do. In addition to that, the house we were renting with Paul was for sale and we would have to move. So, we began to pray, but it was hard; just as I was feeling like I was settling in, all of a sudden, all these changes were happening. I was being uprooted again. It didn't feel good. In addition to that, I was in crisis once again with my health. I needed answers quickly on what to do and where to live. I had little strength to move again but had to trust my needs would be met. I was beginning to feel like a nomad. Where would I go? What would I do? While Wendy and her husband were setting their sights on a move to Arizona, and Linda and her husband were praying about church attendance, we were scrambling, trying to find another home to rent. We didn't have the time or resources yet to buy a home. We were new to the area and couldn't decide where we belonged, and we felt it was too early to buy.

So, we prayed, and Paul thought it would be best to get his own place again, as he and Sam were getting serious, and there was talk of marriage. So, I began with Wendy and Linda searching around for a place to rent. Cy was working and didn't have as much time to look, although he eventually came across a place in the newspaper. While several women in the church helped us pack up our home, Cy made an appointment to see a home for decent rent on a place we weren't familiar with yet called Camano Island. It was literally the only place for rent at the time, at least in the area we were getting used to. But we prayed and felt this was the provision we had prayed for. So, with the help of Paul, Sam, and our church, we packed up and moved from Stanwood, Washington to Camano Island nearby. And I can't complain. It was gorgeous, and we had nice neighbors. The home was in a golfing community. It was owned by a sweet older woman, who liked to golf and had just bought the house to rent out, so she could golf while she lived in another town. So now we were on Camano Island. I have often thought we were sent there after praying, the reasons at first were not always clear, but over time, they became very clear.

One of the reasons I came to realize is while I was resting and being treated medically again, I knew I was going to be writing a book and needed a quiet place to do so. That and some help. I also didn't realize Cy's job would require more travel, so things were falling into place for us. Here on the island, I could get the rest I needed and more answers on my health because much of the time it was beginning to decline again. My eyesight for one thing was worsening and I could hardly see. I was getting very weak with a lot of muscle weakness and wasn't sure what was happening. What was going on now? My health had always been a constant battle, something new was going on, and it was very debilitating in many ways. But God wasn't going to leave me without answers yet. By faith I knew he would provide the answers I needed, it would just take time.

I was having weakness and it was something that seemed to waver. My left arm would become so weak, I couldn't use it. I was getting muscle twitching, a lot of symptoms of what they were questioning as M.S., so my doctor had me see a neurologist. After a lot of testing and knowing I had Celiac disease, she discovered I had low potassium. The low potassium was from malabsorption due to the Celiac disease, causing what is known as Hypokalemic periodic paralysis. So, I was given a lot of potassium and monitored it regularly because the low potassium was beginning to affect my heart, so now that had to be watched like a hawk. The malabsorption issues were causing a lot of problems for me. In addition, the two other autoimmune diseases, Hashimoto's and Sjogren's, both were playing havoc. So, once again, my life was being challenged, and I was struggling with functioning and needed a lot of help. With Cy traveling more, what was I going to do?

So, since the church we had been attending was closed, we began attending a local church just because it was close by. The denomination was different from what we were used to, but we wanted to give it a try. At the least it would help us adjust to a new community. We thought. So, we went. And we went. I became concerned because we were just weeks away from Cy's first trip. We went again to this church. And on this particular Sunday, I was having a very difficult time seeing. I needed to go to the rest room, and Cy felt funny about taking me there. I literally could not see enough to find my way. It was very unsettling and not really knowing people yet, I was afraid to ask. But a woman came up to me, realizing Cy and I were struggling.

And she said, "Hi, I'm Dana, can I help?"

I sensed a sincerity in her that I had seen many times. I could tell she really wanted to help, so I said, "Yes, my husband would love it if you could help me find my way." So, she took me by the hand and led me and waited with me and then accompanied me back to my seat. She stayed with me and sat nearby. After the service was over, she, with some others, sat near me and I happened to mention to this group of women that my husband would soon be traveling and that I would need some help. Did they know anyone who did that type of work?

Dana spoke up. "I do that type of work, call me and we'll talk about what you need." She said to me later that when she said that to me, I had such a look of surprise that she couldn't believe it. Dana was just what the Lord ordered. In the three years I was on the island, she stuck with me, prayed with me, cried with me, and laughed with me. She was quite dedicated and loyal. But it wasn't just about me, she also was going through some very heavy things in her life and needed a friend, so we were able to be there for each other. A bond was created in a friendship that is not only hard to describe but also to find. This very loving, compassionate woman became like a sister. And to this day, I will always cherish our time together.

While on the island, I also became acquainted with my neighbor Brenda. She, too, became very close to me and I to her. Another great dear friend. Brenda and I spent a lot of time together, as I was more home bound at the time. She, another sweet, giving friend, met me where I was at. We helped her, too, and it was and still is, a beautiful friendship of sharing. My friend Linda would also stay with me when Cy traveled. I was certainly not alone. God's provision for me seemed indescribable and never-ending. He knew I had lost family and was determined to prove himself loving and faithful, and He did, time and time again. It wasn't ending! God's word declares, "God sets the lonely in families, he leads forth the prisoners with singing. He will place the lonely in families. Psalm 68:6.

Dana and I in my home in Washington, 2019.

Later through a Celiac group, I met another dear friend, Norma. I had started a Celiac support group and blog, but the group began to dwindle. Just when I was about to close the doors, a woman showed up. It was Norma and she offered to help keep things going, and we did for a while, but in the process of this, I made another good friend, and we shared, and we prayed. She too has been very loyal. God was showing himself faithful. Over and over again, he was sending me these precious friends. And there was a pattern, it always seemed to come in threes. To this day, I'm not sure what it means, but it didn't stop there. I was literally bombarded with support while I was so sick. Most of them came to my home when I had trouble getting out. It seemed I had a need, and it was met. I prayed and God answered. But it was difficult at times because I was becoming so sick and so weak, and after so many years of dealing with so much, I was getting weary and felt like giving up. It was at that point I mentioned this to my son, who remember was clown-like and jovial-like my dad.

I said, "You know, Paul, there was one day I felt like hanging myself, but I had just been to the chiropractor and he had just adjusted my neck. And I hate pain. I couldn't think of a way out that wouldn't hurt, and I believed wholeheartedly that whatever means I would try, I would probably live through it and be worse off." I was so frustrated. I didn't really want to kill myself, what I really wanted was to be well.

So, my son's reply to me was this, "Well, Mom, do you know what happens to people who hang themselves?"

I answered, "What," and he said, point blank, "They poop in their pants!" I laughed, and it turned my whole attitude around, of course. He then went on, "And knowing how clean you are, I know you wouldn't want to be caught with poop in your pants, dead or alive, right?" I laughed so hard, and he knew he had accomplished his mission by turning me around. He grinned at me. "See, Mom, I know just what to say, don't I?"

And I said, "You certainly do." It was rare after that I ever thought of giving up. When I became discouraged, I thought back to Paul's comment and my thoughts quickly turned back to humor. At that point, my support system began to pray for healing for me, and little by little, I was beginning to get stronger with more answers from the doctors and specialists that were working with me.

By the end of the three years, I was sensing another change coming and felt I wanted to get off the island and be back in Stanwood. We felt conflicted about where to attend church, like we hadn't found our home yet. I felt torn, after all, we had a nice place on the island with nice neighbors. Our landlord had told us we could have it as long as we needed it. So, what was this change I was anticipating?

I was longing for my European culture from Boston. I always wanted to go back to Boston, but clearly it wasn't meant to be. Here, while I had been given so much, I was still feeling out of sync, even in the midst of so much provision.

So, I prayed for direction. "Lord, I know you can hear me, help me to understand where I am, and help me to fill that void of my culture that I love so much, please send me another Italian Christian that I can bond with like family." I prayed, but thought, how in the world is that going to happen?

There are hardly any Italians in the area. I asked several others to pray with me about this.

So, it was a Sunday evening; Cy and I decided to go shopping in Stanwood. First, we went to PetSmart with Abbi our dog, then to Rite Aid pharmacy for a prescription, and then over to the grocery At QFC, we parked and I stayed in the car with Abbi with the windows rolled down while Cy ran into the store to get some things. As I sat there, talking to Abbi because she was so cute, a car pulled up next to me. A man got out of the car while his wife remained in the car.

He noticed Abbi in the back seat, and said to me, "Do you mind if I pet your dog? She's so adorable." I said yes. So, he did and began to talk to me, so I got out. I was talking with him when his wife decided to come out to join in. As the three of us were talking, the conversation somehow came up about his wife, whose name was Jenny, was Italian and she went to a Lutheran church.

I then said, "I'm of Italian descent, and this is going to sound weird, but I just prayed that God would send me an Italian Christian friend."

Jenny and David Brandt.

Jenny's eyes lit up. "I've been praying for that, too. I miss being around family." We then exchanged phone numbers and stayed in touch. We would talk about things and the subject came up that she would soon be looking to rent out her second home next to the house she was now living in. The house used to be her mother's, and the tenant would soon be moving. I asked her about the house, and it sounded nice. It was in Stanwood right up the street from the church I was now attending. I liked Jenny and her husband, and it sounded nice.

I mentioned it to Cy, but he wasn't ready to move and the house we were renting was Okay, too. We didn't need to move out, it seemed there was no rush on this. I asked Cy if he would at least look at it. The rent would be cheaper, and we would be closer to Paul and other things. So, Cy went to see it with me, but he felt it was too small, so we put it on the back burner for a time. I did pray, if we were supposed to do this, that God would show Cy in a way he would understand. So, guess what happened next? Our current land-lord who'd had no intentions of selling her home called us and said we'd have to move. Wow, I sure didn't see that coming. I guess you

have to be careful how you pray. Even though I knew God had a plan, I was still upset. When we went to Paul's home that weekend, I sat in his garage with him and told him how I was feeling. "I have no roots anymore since I left Boston and Nana is gone, I don't belong anywhere, I feel like a nomad with no place to call home."

I just cried and Paul held me and said, "Mom, why do you think I bought such a big home, it's so you have a place to go to. I'm now your roots."

My son's comments once again changed everything. I went from feeling like a nomad to a place of security once again. I really hadn't thought of him that way because a mother is supposed to be there for her son, not vice versa. I wanted to give to him, not take. But I needed to allow him to be there for me, for us, and it was a blessing to him and Sam. And she felt that way about her parents, too. I'm proud to say, we have two great kids.

As my mother would have said, "I must have done something right." I needed to understand, as I was there for my mother as she aged, so my son wants to be there for me. I feel blessed.

Anyway, as we searched for a new home to rent, most of the rentals Cy was checking out were too much rent and too big.

So, I called Jenny. "Do you know what's happening with your rental?"

She said, "We've been waiting on it, I'm not sure."

I told her what had happened, and I cried again. "Jenny, I feel like a nomad with all this moving, I'm not sure what to do, I don't know where I belong."

She immediately said, "Iris, come home, the rental is yours."

I got to tell you, my heart melted, and I felt incredibly loved again at that moment. The last person that had said that to me was my mother to come home. Now Jenny and Paul were affirming me.

Left to right: Jenny, Me, Samantha, Cy and Paul. At a fourth of July celebration! I'm surrounded by joy! 2019.

The long and short of it is we ended up moving quickly. Since it was Christmas time, and Paul and Sam were away, and Dana had hurt her leg and was laid up, I mean on and on, it was hard to find help. But again, I prayed and then my friend Linda, like Superwoman, took a week off of work, swooped in, and helped me pack up the house in record time. I had another friend Debbie who helped also. Little by little, we moved in. And from the moment we arrived, this house that was so special to Jenny because it was her mother's felt like home again to us. Jenny felt like family was back, and we have become like sisters. We share a lot together, including meals, just like family.

I have to ask you, did God answer my prayer that day? Or was it just coincidence that I prayed for an Italian friend, and just hours later, I met her by chance in a parking lot. And incidentally, her dog's name is Chance. LOL! And what if I had decided to go shopping a few minutes later or reversed which stores I went to? I would have missed this precious opportunity, a destiny. I believe this was God's divine appointment for me and for Jenny because he knew we needed each other. He knew better than we did how to meet those desires. Isaiah 65:24 says, "Before they call, I will answer; while they are still speaking, I will hear" (NIV). God knows what we need before we even ask. He just likes us to ask.

So, I ask again, is this coincidence or is there really a God who hears us? Do miracles really happen? And how? You have read my story, and I describe situations where I needed answers, and they came as I asked. You decide, but if you have any doubts, ask Jenny, she's Italian, she'll tell you., No seriously, try asking in prayer and see what happens. God is no respecter of persons, what he does for one he will do for another. Romans 2:11 "For God does not show favoritism". (NIV)

My favorite photo of Jenny. It shows her joviality which I love.

Chapter 19

God's Gift to Me in Family and Some Surprising Conclusions

My Son Paul and I at a Christmas Concert. 2017.

Living in Washington state near my son has been a blessing in so many ways. After growing up on the east coast, moving 3,000 miles to be near our son, while it presented a bit of uncertainty and was a difficult adjustment moving so far away, has turned out better than I expected. I have found so much here. Moving near our son has been such a time of change. Letting go of the past and who I used to be wasn't easy, but because I had prayed and felt this was God's plan, I had faith and a confidence that things would not only be Okay, but fruitful as well in many ways, and it has. Coming here has brought me out of my comfort zone and challenged me to find new things. Who I used to be with and the life I once knew, while it is gone, the newness has brought hope and a future brighter than I could have imagined.

Jeremiah 33:3 says, "Call upon me and I will answer you and tell you great and unsearchable things you did not know" (NIV). His promises are true, and his word does not return void. In other words, God does not go back on his word to us. I never thought that letting go of what once was and moving on to a new beginning could be so freeing. I could have stayed in Boston because it was easier to remain in the past, longing for what once was. Instead I chose to follow God's lead with my son and see things happen I never thought were possible. Experiencing new adventures in a new place with new people has been both exciting and rewarding. I found that sharing my culture with others has been an amazing opportunity and blessing to others. My past experiences are not forgotten. I have learned that the easy thing to do is not always the right thing to do. It's the hard things that make us grow and move on. Let me tell you some of the things that were answered as I remained steadfast into the unknown.

I mentioned my son wanted to help me through Ancestry.com to explore the possibilities of being able to discover who my dad's real father might have been. So, we did, and in doing so, I heard from a number of Italian relatives who were listed as my second cousins from the Boston area.

My Cousin, Carol Miceli Meenan and her father frank Miceli.

They got in touch with me, and we began the journey of putting all the pieces together. One of my cousins, Carol Miceli, had her father tested and discovered he was my father's first cousin. Very close relation. Through her and our search together, we were able to not only discover who my grandfather was, but also, we discovered his name was Leonard. I put the pieces together and found that my grandmother had named my father after his Italian father. Leonard Miceli. Carol was able to provide photos of him, and it was clear to all of us that there was a strong resemblance to my father. She shared photos of other family members, and still strong resemblances. One of my cousins, Mark Miceli, and I discovered we share the same grandfather, my father's real father.

My real grandfather, Leonard Miceli. Now since passed. The photo was provided by another Miceli cousin, Mark, whom I appreciate very much for sharing our Grandfather with me.

Mark Miceli and his family, my cousins from Boston. Pictured from left to right Lenny, Patty, Mark, Linda, Laura. We share the same grandfather.

What saddened me though, was that my dad was not here to see this. He longed for it, and for some reason, it was kept from him. The reasons I may never know. But in heaven, he now knows. And I sometimes wonder if he knows we know. I love to imagine the smile on his face when he entered heaven, maybe his real dad was there to greet him. While I will never know for sure, I can imagine him at peace with this now. At least his children know and that would have made him very happy.

I have several friends who often wondered why my prayers were answered so quickly. My answer was because I asked and then put some work behind the question to find the answer. And I felt I was working with God to find those answers. I asked but expected the answers would be with integrity and according to the destiny he had planned for me. I learned that if my prayers didn't get answered, it was because I didn't ask with the right motives, or it just wasn't meant to be.

In asking, I believe God loves his children and wants to do good things for them. Mathew 7:7-8, "Ask and it will be given to you; seek and you will find; knock and the door will be opened to you. For everyone who asks receives; he who seeks finds; and to him who knocks, the door will be opened." This is a promise in the Bible, its God's word telling me to ask, and he'll give it according to his will and the plans he has for me, so they will come into fruition. This is my conviction, it's what I believe, it has been life to me. As I said, I'm not saying this to convince you, I'm sharing a true account of my experience, and so I'll ask again, what do you think? Is God real? Do miracles really happen? Is there really life after death? And what does that mean? We are living in challenging times that I have never seen before, where do you find hope? Where can you go to find peace in the midst of life's storms? I believe I have found it; you decide. Ponder that and pray and ask God to reveal himself to you and see what happens, perhaps a miracle will take place in your life. It's not just me, God loves you, too, and is waiting for you. He never intended for any of us to be alone.

All my best to you!

Iris.

Epilogue

I have come to discover that prayer can move mountains. During the course of a lifelong challenge of illness, I found I was cared for and kept encouraged, so I could encourage others. I could not have done this alone. Because of the support of friends and family, my health is stable for the first time in my life. I never thought I'd see it. After many years of struggle and hard work to get back after brain trauma and numerous problems, I'm elated. I try not to focus on the time lost over the years but on the time gained and lessons learned through the process. Was the time really lost? Or was this all part of God's plan, so I could understand and be there for others? The glass half full and all his provision in the process of all this is what I have chosen to focus on. Blessed to be a blessing is my conclusion, and I had my family and older mentors that went before that came alongside me to show me the way.

The climate in Washington state alone has been good for me. I'm thankful my son with God's leading brought us here. While I still have a whole host of physical limitations, I'm more mobile with more energy and better able to live my life again. I wanted to live again without so much compromise to my very existence, and I believe God knew this and wanted the best for me. While it hasn't been easy, in fact, quite painful at times, there has been a lot of joy in between those times. Joy has been given to me as a gift from the God I have come to know and trust in. I could not have done it without prayer, family, and the help of friends. I hope you can see, through my story that I was never alone in the challenges I faced, and it made all the difference; it kept me strong and encouraged. God never abandoned me but neither did people. A real friend doesn't leave you when you're hurting.

You can see the miracles that took place, as I asked for them. Especially as I asked with others coming alongside of me. In the midst of this, I had a cheering section in support that most long for. The provision in medical care has been amazing, as that was not always the case. Finding what I could do in the midst of so much disability helped me to live and live well. It seems that God used my son to get us here but had many other reasons in doing so, one I have discovered being this book. And I hope it has blessed you to hear my story and that of my family. My hope is that it brings you hope that we are not alone in this life.

Being near my brother Alan again and starting a new chapter with him, his wife, and sons and their families has brought hope for building the family again. Being near to my brother Lance, my son, and now daughter-in-law Sam, and being a part of their beautiful wedding with family and friends in attendance has brought so much joy back into my life. I love what my family was and is now becoming. Being a part of their future has brought anticipation of joy for the times we'll have together. Feeling loved and supported by them has meant the world to me and brought me to a place as my son described as, "being rooted again in family."

At times I didn't think there was life without my mother. But I know she'd be happy to see I've moved into a place she would have been delighted with. Beginning with new friends that have become like family, combined with my immediate family, has brought new direction and an excitement in moving onto the next generation. It's brought clarity that has caused me to remember the ones who have passed but also to move onto caring for the ones here now. I found that I didn't lose my family, but I was finding them again in the generation coming behind me. Like my mother before me, I am now the older one teaching and caring for the younger ones. A new season in which I feel the best has yet to be discovered, and my life has once again just begun. I'm alive again and there's much to do. The chain of events that have happened in my life are just too amazing for me to not believe in God and his miraculous ways. My family is restored, my health improved, and I look forward to what he has in store for us. My God is faithful!

And, oh, those friends from when I was five in Revere are still a part of my life, too, along with many others. I followed my mother's philosophy and found I was never alone. She said, "When you have a friend, they are your friend for life." I often wondered if she ever realized I'd be exhausted from keeping up with them. But that's a good problem to have, isn't it?

So, what is a friend? She's delightful, and things are always better when she's around, you'll never be alone. And the best friend of all? It is God. He's always there! And Oh! We have a new future blessing on the way. Our son Paul and daughter-in-law Sam are now expecting. Baby boy Smith is due to arrive on March 7th, 2020. My future is arriving soon.

A Final Thought from my Brother and Friend

My first memory of my sister Iris occurred one wintery New England morning when I think I was four. We set out with my brother Alan to toboggan with the neighborhood kids down the massive hills of what was the "sand pits" just in the distance from a field separating the two and a half acres of land where we lived. I remember how excited I was to experience this neighborhood event, even though I didn't really understand what the excitement was about, but I trusted my big sister and tagged along.

That's how Iris impacted my life from that point on and onto this day. She loved animals, most outdoor activities, God, and I found that years later I ended up trying to do what she loved, as she was my ultimate role model. Sitting for hours listening to her 45s–pop music of the early 70s. I still listen to those songs to this day as they bring wonderful nostalgia feelings of life prior to age ten. Songs like, "Half Breed," "Seasons in the Sun," "Afternoon Delight," and so many more while she jogged indoors in the basement of our home. I loved *The Brady Bunch* because of her, too. Whenever there was a fight between Iris and Alan, I always took Iris's side. Although my brother and eldest sister also positively influenced me over the years at different periods of my life, I most looked up to Iris in my formable years. She was the most present in my life, more so than anyone. She understands me better than anyone from our own unique relationship perspective, particularly our journey with God dating back to 1970.

Iris suffered terribly over the years with Celiac disease. Her strength emerged, however, through the years of fighting the battle with her health. It was her strength over the years that inspired me to remain strong and steadfast regarding my own health issues from just a few years ago. Iris talks about this strength in her book, articulating the strong generations of women who made up our history from not only a Jewish perspective but also a nationality perspective since we had both strong Italian and Russian roots. This history of strength is the underpinning of our family's ability to endure life's most difficult moments to this day.

As soon as I ventured off into the real world from college, I found myself checking off the list of things my sister used to do: rollercoasters, swimming,

411

snowmobiling, boating, horseback riding, water skiing, jogging indoors in our basement, playing musical instruments, singing, softball, biking...anything outdoors. However, during all this time, I didn't always know she was struggling with health issues because, like me, she wanted to keep it private for fear of judgement. So, she didn't always let it show until anxiety hit me for the first time, when we traveled to Florida in 1973.

The craze of the early '70s in hotels were high diving boards. I remember we stopped at a Holiday Inn along the way to Florida the year Disney World opened. After seeing Iris jump off the 15-foot, or higher in some cases, I was mesmerized about following her lead. I kept running up the ladder and jumping off with no abandon until one time I belly flopped. It felt like I landed on cement. Practically knocked the wind out of me. I remember trying to pretend it didn't happen, and of course, I was done for the night. No one witnessed this. As a seven-year-old, I remember not wanting to tell Iris because I was ashamed that I messed up. By the time we reached the Thunderbird Hotel in Miami, my next high diving board, I was petrified. Iris jumped off the high diving board and I wanted to so bad, I just couldn't bring myself to do it. No one knew what was going on in my mind at that point because I didn't want to admit I was fearful. I didn't understand why I was fearful, and Iris wasn't.

This unfortunately carried on later in life, hitting me at different milestones. I first recollected that anxiety was genetically somehow predisposed in our family the day I noticed my father stop riding the rollercoaster with me around that same year. He never explained why. I wish he did. I was too young to make the connection. But it plagued my other older sister and me to this day but somehow missed Iris and Alan.

Iris was always doing something creative over the years. She was also a dedicated woman of God since I was a little boy. I remember she would often take me over to our neighbors', a Christian family where we could witness a traditional Christmas. From my perspective, like my mother, I was following Judaism, all the while remembering the warm feeling of Christmas morning as experienced through Iris and our neighbors. She even once took me to church as a child where I first accepted the Lord into my heart. Then my father's salesy influence on Christianity, which was quite strong, steered me back towards Judaism. I chose to be Bar Mitzvah'd but later I accepted the Lord into my heart again with my father and Iris alongside.

I then was off to college and looking forward to Iris's new marriage to Cy. As I remember back, religion took a backstep with me until 2009. It was then I was introduced to a gay church. For five years, I studied the New Testament there. I also was developing my relationship with God through Iris as she prayed for me. She was one of my most ultimate resources on Christianity I knew, and I trusted her to lead me. In 1996, I had a choice to move to either Colorado Springs near Iris, or San Jose near Alan. Colorado Springs was the choice; however, both Iris and I had difficulty there, finding it hard to be away from family, and eventually moved back to Boston. But no matter what challenges we faced, I knew her prayers were powerful, and I learned to pray, too. The long and short of it is never would I have been able to delve into Christianity so deeply and develop such a true bond with God so quickly if it weren't for my sister Iris, and my years of journaling I did. Iris, alongside my personal journey with God through the Bible and my church enabled me to form such a strong relationship with God to this day. My relationship with God is the greatest gift she's given me.

—Lance Fisher

A Special Thanks

When I turned 60 in Washington, my family had a party for me. It was the next best thing to a wedding reception. With 40 in attendance and a beautifully catered gluten-free affair, my son and daughter-in-law reminded me that the next generation of family was here, and I was surrounded by so much love and warmth. I only wish my mother and father could have been there. Thanks, Paul and Sam and Cy for an amazing 60th. I'll never forget it. And for reminding me once again that I'm not alone!

Love, Mom

With a blast of a Celebration on my 60th, The future is yet to be told.

Thoughts From My Friends

What is a Friend?
Someone Who is Nothing Like the World Has Ever seen Before -
M.H. Clark

What is friendship?

Friendships are what sustain us; it is the support that gets us through the tough days, and the light that adds to the best days. The best friend doesn't have to talk often, but when reunited, it is like no time has passed at all. My friends have been with me throughout all the chapters of my life, resulting most recently with them standing by my side at my wedding. Nothing is better than seeing the culmination of years of great experiences, memories, hardships, and laughter supporting me into another chapter. No friend is the same, each one serves their own purpose in your life and it is because of this that you know that your friendship is God driven.

—Samantha Smith

1). I recall a very sweet time of playing on the swing set and walking trips up the street to an old-fashioned mom and pop store called Joe Snow's. I remember my time with my young friend Iris, laughing and enjoying living in the same house together. We were like family. We played together, went to school together, and were in and out of each other's homes during those years. I have some very fond memories of our parents and siblings.

Then I didn't see Iris for many years, until we reconnected a few years ago. It was heartwarming to reminisce about family and fun times when we were young, and we share memories of times past that I'll never forget. She is my friend, and not distance nor time will ever change that. – Andrea Pivnick Malcolm, Massachusetts

2). When I first met Iris, she was being baptized at our local church we attended together. I remember her testimony as incredible and interesting. She spoke about longing for inner peace and healing that she felt only God could provide. As time went on, we became close, dear friends. Although Iris has endured many health challenges, our now 36-year friendship is very strong as a result. I have observed how strong her faith has been and how steadfast in God's holy word she has remained. It's been an inspiration to me, and an example of God's faithfulness. Our unique friendship has been a blessing to me, the mutual sincerity and loyalty has kept my faith strong, and she is someone I look forward to seeing. – Always your friend, Chris Szulborski, Massachusetts

3). About three years ago, God divinely brought Iris and I together. He knew we would need each other, so it truly was a divine appointment. She has become a dear friend and an incredible inspiration and example of what it means to literally live every moment totally reliant upon our heavenly Father.

We bonded through mutual trust, compassion, and understanding, and because of it, have held each other up as we dealt with some extremely intense and difficult circumstances. We held each other up through the gift of intercessory prayer, sharing our deepest concerns and celebrating together as we watched God answer many of those prayers in his time and in his way. Several of those prayers have been manifested for Iris through miraculous physical improvement, and I have been deeply grateful and in awe to have witnessed God's incredible healing touch on her!

God-centered friendship is a gift he lavishly bestows on us because he cares for us so deeply. For that, I will eternally be grateful!

Look around, how has God given you the gift of rich, divine inspired friendship in your life? – Dana Baker, Camano Island, Washington

4). At a chance meeting orchestrated by God, Iris commented she needed a ride to a doctor's appointment, and I said, "I can take you." It was the beginning of a 28-year friendship that is still strong today. Time and space wear on most relationships, but when God is your common denominator, those things don't matter. There are many times the Holy Spirit prompts me to call Iris or she calls me, and whether it is a time of struggle or joy, we share it together. Pain is hard, but when shared by a friendship grounded in Christ, it eases the burden. I am grateful for the laughter, which has been much, for the pain, more than we would have liked, and the sharing of God's word when he has pressed upon us to share scripture with each other. Iris is my sister in Christ and truly a friend deep in my heart, which I thank God for every day. – Brenda Feldsien, St. Louis Mo.

5). The dictionary defines friends as "one attached to each other by affection or esteem." Iris and I shared both. Our friendship grew close at a time in our lives when life is just plain confusing, adolescence! As we all know, this is a time of many physical and emotional challenges and changes. Sharing a friendship with someone as Iris and I did was a gift! We helped each other maneuver our way into adulthood. We shared so many of life's ups and downs and we made each other stronger. We cried together and laughed together over little and big things... We knew without a doubt that we had each other's back as we navigated life. I haven't seen Iris in many years, but our close bond remains. I am very grateful for social media (Facebook) as this has allowed us to be a part of each other's lives even though we live on opposite coasts! – Beverly Haffey

6). Many people feel as though they are walking through life alone without friends or family. This is a tragedy and is not how it is meant to be. We need people around to help us meet life's challenges and share the joys we are blessed with. Family is always family, but there are friends who can be considered in the same category. Some of them will be in our lives for only a season, and others are alongside us for the duration. Iris and I met over 20 years ago at church in the Denver area. We both have had trials to face during those years. The difficulties she's dealt with are different than what I've seen and vice versa. It's interesting to say we've helped each other through some tough situations, considering for most of those 20 plus years we've been lived thousands of miles apart. We pray together over the phone and pray for each other separately. We've vented to each other, sometimes loudly and with intense conversations. Do we always know exactly how the other feels? No, that's impossible. Challenges are different, personalities and how we handle situations are unique, backgrounds and the paths we take in life are not the same. But here's the thing: you can offer support and unconditional love without completely and fully understanding the other person suffering. THAT is how we get through the difficult times together, not alone.

So, that is how I can best describe the relationship Iris and I have formed and built over the many years we have known each other. It is a privilege to pray with and for someone during a crisis, to rejoice with them during the good times, and to give them our shoulder to weep on when they are too distraught to even talk coherently. God has designed us to do life together. We need each other. We need to be involved in "community," whether that is in the same city or thousands of miles apart. Thank you, Iris, for being that kind of friend who doesn't abandon ship when the waters get stormy. – Tammy Maseberg

7). I met Iris long after I had heard about her. Our mothers were good friends, going back to their high school days, but they didn't see each other much during the years they were raising their families, both as single parents. In their later years, however, when they lived near one another again, they became very close. Theirs was a friendship that stood the test of time. Although they had very different personalities, and they didn't always agree on everything, there was an underlying foundation of love, acceptance, and appreciation for one another. They helped each other in many ways, and the many memories they shared built an enduring friendship on that strong foundation.

In 1997, I remember my mother telling me about "Charlotte's daughter Iris and her family" moving back to Massachusetts from Colorado. I was living overseas at the time, but when my husband and I came to Boston for a visit that year, Iris and Cy invited us to their home on Cape Cod, where we finally met. It wasn't until both our moms passed away in 2012-2013, however, that Iris and I would find that we had a lot in common and could help each other process our mothers' deaths. After her mom passed in June 2012, Iris talked often with my mother, who was also grieving the passing of her friend. When my mother died just eight months later, Iris and I started keeping in touch by long phone conversations. Sharing a common grief can help each one on the path toward healing and having the same faith in the one who can truly comfort us in our sorrows is even more helpful. We both missed our moms immensely, as they had been such an important and integral part of our lives, but we both also knew without a doubt that there is a hope beyond death, and that we will see them again when our own race on earth has ended.

About a year after my mom's death, I was diagnosed with breast cancer, and Iris was one of the first ones I reached out to for prayer. She was a great encouragement and comfort to me during that time of uncertainty, tests, surgery, and recovery, and once again, I realized the importance of not "going it alone" but rather having friends and loved ones who are willing to walk through life with you. I am thankful for her friendship, her openness, her honesty, her perseverance through adversity, and her faithfulness in praying for me and speaking the truth in love. – Amy Ryzi

8.) The day I met you, Iris, was a real "God thing." Who knew us two gals from total opposite sides of the USA, with so much in common, would meet in a Stanwood, Washington, QFC grocery store parking lot of all places? AND…. Who knew we same two gals happened to be praying the same prayer? I don't believe in coincidence, so, by the hands of our Father and by His Grace of PERFECT timing, we two gals began a friendship that grows deeper and stronger day by beautiful day. Iris, you fill my heart with such deep love and laughter. You make me laugh deep (that deep in your gut laugh!), you help me to understand patience with grace, and you love me with that BIG beautiful heart of yours! Having you in my life has made me feel that warmhearted love I feel when I'm with my family and that my friend is truly a gift of grace from God. I am so happy you let David pet your dog, Abbi, on that faithful day! *Ti amo mia sorella! Buona fortuna!* – Jenny Brandt

9.) Dear Iris,

Thanks so much for authoring this book. This inspirational family history is a beautiful compilation of true stories of mostly baby boomer, generational anecdotes of us growing up and interacting. You are remembering and putting into words our life our ancestral experiences, saying to all of our coming generations that they have a rich heritage and should be proud of who they are and who they will become. Our parents and ancestors, as we, were not perfect, but they lived and loved as best they could, and our kids, the coming generations, and we are better for it. Pictures are one thing, but without words to describe them, they are just images without reason. This massive effort on your part will go a long way to document the last 100 years of our family and history surrounding us. Others will also benefit from our trials and successes as they will see similarities in their own lives. Great job! – Love, your brother Alan.

10). From the book my friend gave me for my 60th birthday, *What is a Friend*, which has meant so much to me. It said, "a friend is resilient, the challenges she faces only serve to reveal her strength and capability. She's someone you can count on. She's someone you look forward to. She's simply wonderful, but she's brilliantly complex. And she makes a difference in the world around her, every single day. She's always truly, beautifully, utterly herself, and that is a very good thing. From the book by M.H. Clark—Happy birthday to a great friend, always love and live well. Love from your friend – Brenda Miller

11.) I am rarely drawn to people right away, but when I first met Iris at church, I was drawn to her. You are a very kind, understanding, non-judgmental person. Thank you for being such a good friend. Also, thanks for being so real with no shame. You have taught me to relax and be myself. As well as enjoy the small pleasures in life. We lift each other up in times of need. We have laughed and cried together. I look forward to many more years of friendship and laughter. I will always be beside you for prayer or whatever may be needed. Meeting your son Paul and his wife Sam has been something I never expected, inviting me and my husband into their home has been a gift I did not expect. If you ever wonder if you did things right, just look at Paul.

Love you, dear one, – Your friend Linda

A special thank you to my newest friend Cindy Kinney, who loves people, and it shows in everything she does. We have lots of fun together.

But most of all, to the love of my life who is always there, my Husband Cy, I love you dearly.